The New Macedonian Question

Also by James Pettifer

ALBANIA: From Anarchy to a Balkan Identity (*with Miranda Vickers*)
BLUE GUIDE TO ALBANIA
BLUE GUIDE TO BULGARIA
THE GREEKS: Land and People since the War
THE TURKISH LABYRINTH

The New Macedonian Question

Edited by

James Pettifer
Visiting Professor
Institute of Balkan Studies
Thessaloniki

Selection, editorial matter, Introduction and Chapters 2 and 10
© James Pettifer 1999, 2001
Chapters 1, 3–9, 11–18 © Macmillan Press Ltd (now Palgrave) 1999

First published in hardcover 1999

First published with corrections in paperback 2001 by
PALGRAVE
Houndmills, Basingstoke, Hampshire RG21 6XS and
175 Fifth Avenue, New York, N. Y. 10010
Companies and representatives throughout the world

PALGRAVE is the new global academic imprint of
St. Martin's Press LLC Scholarly and Reference Division and
Palgrave Publishers Ltd (formerly Macmillan Press Ltd).

ISBN 0–333–67356–5 hardback (*outside North America*)
ISBN 0–312–22240–8 hardback (*in North America*)
ISBN 0–333–92066–X paperback (*worldwide*)

This book is printed on paper suitable for recycling and
made from fully managed and sustained forest sources.

A catalogue record for this book is available
from the British Library.

The Library of Congress has cataloged the hardcover edition as follows:
The New Macedonian question / edited by James Pettifer.
        p. cm.
    Includes bibliographical references and index.
    ISBN 0–312–22240–8 (cloth)
    1. Macedonia (Republic)—Politics and government—1992–
    2. Macedonian question. 3. Macedonia (Republic)—Ethnic Relations.
    I. Pettifer, James.
    DR2253.N48 1999
    949.5'6076—dc21

                                                98–53724
                                                CIP

Transferred to digital print on demand, 2002

Printed and bound in Great Britain by
Antony Rowe Ltd, Chippenham and Eastbourne

For Nigel and Maria Clive

Contents

List of maps

Preface to the paperback edition

Macedonia, in the present and recent past, has been the focus of momentous political events. In the months since the first edition of this book was published, the southern Balkans has been engulfed in the Kosovo crisis, in which Macedonia, as a geographical region and FYROM as a political entity played a major role. NATO fought its first war in part from Macedonian territory, and a large NATO force continues to be stationed in Macedonia even after the end of this phase of the Kosovo conflict. The most critical element in the humanitarian effort on behalf of the Kosovar refugees was mounted from Macedonia. The port of Thessaloniki has been a key supply and logistics base for the NATO forces. When the last sentences of the original edition of this book were being written, the October 1998 peace agreement between NATO and Slobodan Miloševiç's government in Serbia had recently been concluded, and it appeared a stable peace might emerge from the months of irregular warfare between the Serbian security apparatus and the guerillas of the ethnic Albanian Kosovo Liberation Army. The soldiers and civilians of the Kosovo Verification Mission were installed in the territory to the north of the border with FYROM and a tentative calm prevailed. The United Nations UNPREDEP force was still stationed on the FYROM borders, and appeared to offer a stable and reasonably effective conflict prevention procedure and early warning process for the international community.

In Skopje, as 1998 drew to an end, a new government was taking power, a coalition dominated by the Internal Macedonian Revolutionary Organisation VMRO-DPMNE, but with ethnic Albanian participation. The new administration had been elected in the parliamentary elections of October–November 1999, and represented a major break with the past. The pro-Gligorov Social-Democrats and their allies, with their generally pro-Yugoslav orientation, who had dominated the government for the last five years were replaced by new people, the most prominent of which was Prime Minister Ljupco Georgievski, the founder of the revived Internal Macedonian Revolutionary Organisation party in FYROM (after the end of communism in 1990–91, the VMRO-DPMNE). Georgievski fought the election in alliance with the Democratic Alliance, the party of Vasil Turpurkovski, the last Macedonian member of the rotating presidency of the old Yugoslavia. Turpurkovski is of Greek antecedents, with his father a prominent communist partisan leader in the Greek Civil War, and his party drew much of its support from people in FYROM with Greek family connections. The Albanian minority with its united coalition polled well and took up important positions in the government, in contrast to the largely tokenistic role ethnic Albanians played under previous post-1991 FYROM governments.

Some of the main human rights grievances of the Albanian minority started to be addressed by the new government and a marked improvement in inter-ethnic relations seemed imminent. The political prisoners held by the Social Democrats were released, including prominent figures such as the ethnic Albanian mayors of Gostivar and Tetovo, and the new government allowed a significant increase in the number of senior Albanian appointments in the police and other parts of the state apparatus. With an improving political climate in Skopje and Athens, Greek investors were taking a greater interest in the territory and major funds seemed likely to be made available for commitment to the modernisation of the energy and telecommunications sectors in FYROM. Important foreign policy changes were made, with a much greater orientation towards NATO and its anti-Miloševiç position, and an opening of diplomatic relations with Taiwan. This led to controversy with mainland China, which vetoed the renewal of the mandate of the UNPREDEP border security force in the United Nations Security Council. The UNPREDEP force was subsequently withdrawn.

This period of relative optimism did not last for very long, with an upsurge in the fighting between the two sides in Kosovo during the 1998–99 winter period, and an increasing flow of refugees soon began to appear all over the region. Allegations were made in the Skopje parliament that the ethnic Albanian Kosovo Liberation Army was using FYROM as a base for military activities in Kosovo. A NATO infantry force of over 30 000 soldiers was gradually built up in FYROM and Skopje airport came under military control. The crisis dramatically worsened in the aftermath of the failed Rambouillet peace negotiations in Paris in February–March 1999, and after a period of threats from NATO, bombing of Serbia began in late March. FYROM was at the heart of the crisis. There was an immediate and overwhelming escalation in the flow of refugees from Kosovo to FYROM, which the government attempted to contain at a temporary refugee camp at Blace, on the Kosovo border. Security police attempted to prevent the entry of refugees into the state, and as a result many lived in appalling conditions in 'no man's land' areas between the border fences without water, food or sanitation.

For the first time since the foundation of the state in 1991, Macedonia was at the centre of international attention and in a highly unfavourable light, as forced deportations from FYROM of some large groups of Kosovar Albanian refugees to third countries began. Under international pressure, after an outcry of western public opinion, the government was made to modify its anti-refugee policy, and to allow camps to be built in FYROM to accommodate the refugees. Construction commenced almost immediately and the largest, Cegrane, near Gostivar, eventually housed over 40,000 people. The refugee burden on the FYROM economy increased considerably throughout the spring months of 1999. The financial crisis in Macedonia was eased with international diplomatic help, and promises of massive financial aid for FYROM if assistance with refugee maintenance and then repatriation was given, but not until substantial damage was done to the hitherto generally reasonably positive view of the state among the international community. Within FYROM many Slav-speakers disapproved strongly of the governments pro-NATO stance. Large groups from the Serbian minority community in Kumanovo and elsewhere attacked the American Embassy in Skopje, and US ambassador Christopher Hill, a once-prominent figure who had taken part in the 1995 Dayton Accords peace negotiations, was reduced to life as a near prisoner under heavy armed guard in the building in the centre of the city.

On the positive side, the Skopje governing coalition held together, confounding predictions of the possibility of an imminent break up of FYROM, but the price that has been paid has been very high, particularly in the economy and in tense and deteriorating ethnic relations. Emigration among the Slav-speaking majority increased in 1999, mainly to communities in Australia and Canada, as some see little future for themselves in the FYROM state; a process which is adding to demographic pressures on the 'Macedonian' majority in some parts of the country. The economy has been deeply affected by the NATO bombing campaign and subsequent KFOR occupation of Kosovo as the civil authority. Normal trade patterns with Serbia have broken down completely, along with many transport routes to western Europe for Macedonian exports that ran through Yugoslavia. Much of the remaining manufacturing base of the country has disappeared, with the closure of some enterprises in the textile, shoe manufacturing and other industrial sectors as a result of the war and NATO's bombing campaign.

Unemployment is rising and probably amounts to 40 per cent of the workforce in many places. Wages, pensions and salaries are paid increasingly late in many enterprises and in state sector offices and factories. Many non-Greek foreign investors have withdrawn from Skopje and other parts of the region. The continuing NATO military presence in the country places massive demands on local resources, although the reconstruction process in Kosova, if it takes place as envisaged by NATO, will offer major opportunities for some businesses in areas such as food supply and construction. In the wartime months of spring 1999, the building of refugee camps and reception centres put a heavy strain on the social fabric, with nationalist passions growing on both the ethnic Albanian and Slav-speaking sides of the ethnic divide. It remains to be seen if the international community through the Balkan Stability Pact proposals will actually come forward with the large sums of money needed to compensate FYROM for wartime losses and associated damage to industry and agriculture.

When the NATO bombing campaign ended, and allied troops entered Kosovo from Macedonia on 12 June 1999, one phase of the crisis ended. Although most refugees started to return home to Kosovo quickly, far more quickly than the international community had expected and the immediate crisis in ethnic relations eased, some remained in FYROM awaiting assistance from international organisations. Macedonia remains an essential, perhaps central, element in the future stability – or instability – of the region. In the months after NATO's June 1999 entry to Kosovo, President Kiro Gligorov stood down, the last of the leaders from the old Titoist generation to exercise power in the new Balkans, and was replaced in November 1999 by ex-deputy Foreign Minister Boris Trajkovski, a hitherto little known member of the International Macedonian Revolutionary Organisation (VMRO-DPMNE) party. By the end of of 2000 the vast majority of Kosovo refugees had returned home without difficulty, and much more quickly than had been expected. President Trajkovski's election reinforced the position of the coalition government, and its anti-Milosevic and pro-western orientation. The Opposition leader, Tito Petkovski, leader in the first poll round, claimed Trajkovski's victory was a result of Albanian poll manipulation. The coalition leaders have continued their quest for integration in Euro-Atlantic structures. The main achievement of the government in this recent period has been the passing of long-delayed legislation to privatise the land, and some industrial enterprises, and to dismantle the last vestiges of the old state planning and economic control system. Negative developments include a rise in the inflation rate and the cost of fuel, a rise in organised crime, little progress on the legalisation of the Albanian University in Tetovo, and the appearance of armed ethnic Albanian paramilitary groups allegedly based in FYROM which have made attacks on Kosovo border posts, and within FYROM itself.

An important clash took place in January 2000, with widespread violence in the Arachinovo (*Haracine*, in Albanian) region north east of Skopje, after the murder of policemen on patrol.[1] A few weeks later, about 7000 ethnic Albanian refugees crossed into FYROM in February and March 2000 as a result of the spreading violence in the Presheve valley of south east Serbia (*Kosova Lindore*, eastern Kosova, in Albanian), most of them finding accommodation with ethnic Albanian families in the Kumanovo area of FYROM.[2] The prospect of a major destabilisation of FYROM as a result of internal turmoil and/or spillover from Kosovo remains real, and is likely to be the main preoccupation of the Skopje government in the future. Trade links across the newly opened border between Kosovo and the ethnic Albanian dominated regions of western FYROM are growing fast, and it remains to be seen if the current constitutionalist ethnic Albanian leadership will be able to resist pressures for the political unification of the FYROM and Kosovo Albanians in a new entity that would mean the end of the current FYROM state, or whether more moderate proposals such as the cantonisation of FYROM gain support from the international community. Local elections in September 2000 are likely to be a key test of public opinion.[3]

In this dramatic political context, a creative and openminded study of Macedonia is likely to remain important, and I hope this book may make some contribution towards more rational discussion of the future of the FYROM state and analysis of the historical evolution of the Macedonian Question, in general. I am very grateful to Dragi Ivanovski and Bob Churcher who were kind enough to read and comment on the original manuscript, and to other friends and colleagues who have also been kind enough to comment on what it contains.

All errors are my own responsibility.

James Pettifer

NOTES

1. See report by Amnesty International, London, June 2000, 'Former Yugoslav Macedonia – After the Aracinovo murders: Torture, ill-treatment and possible extrajudicial execution.' on www.amnesty.org

2. See report by the International Crisis Group, 3 March 2000 'What happened to the KLA?' on www.crisis.web.org, also, *Albania Daily News*, Tirana, 2 March 2000 on www.Albanian.News.com
3. For a useful, if somewhat optimistic analysis of the current political forces, see the report of the International Crisis Group, 2 August 2000, 'Macedonia's Ethnic Albanians: Bridging the Gulf'.

Abbreviations

The very complex history of the Macedonian question over the last century embodies a vast proliferation of political and military organisations, which are generally known by acronyms formed from their initials, sometimes in Bulgarian, Greek, Albanian, or Serbian, and sometimes in English. Thus, the Internal Macedonian Revolutionary Organisation is usually known as 'IMRO', but its modern descendant is called 'VMRO-DPMNE' in Skopje, but 'VMRO-UMS' in Sofia. Some of the more important are listed below.

AFOR   NATO forces in Albania, 1998–1999.

ANLA   The National Liberation Army of Albania, a wartime pro-communist Resistance organisation

ASNOM   Anti-fascist Assembly of the People's Liberation of Macedonia, a communist controlled popular assembly in Vardar Macedonia in the Second World War

ARF   The Alliance of Reformist Forces, the party of Ante Marković, in late socialist Yugoslavia. It metamorphosed, in FYROM, into the Liberal Party of Stojan Andov, after 1991.

BCP   Bulgarian Communist Party

BK   Balli Kombetar, militant Albanian nationalist organisation, banned under Communism 1944–1990

BSP   Bulgarian Socialist Party, sucessor to the BCP

BSS   Bulgarian State Security, the communist period secret police

CE   Council of Europe

CEFTA	Central European Free Trade Association
CPA	Albanian Communist Party (also PLA, see below)
CSCE	Conference on Security and Cooperation in Europe (later OSCE, see below)
DA	Democratic Army, communist army in 'Third Round' of Greek civil war
DPA	The majority ethnic Albanian party in FYROM (see PDP (Sh), below)
DPS	The Democratic Party of Serbs, representing FYROM's 40,000 Serb minority after 1991
DPTM	The Democratic Party of Turks in Macedonia, the party representing the Turkish minority in FYROM
EAM	The main Greek resistance organisation in Second World War (political wing)
EBRD	The European Bank for Reconstruction and Development
ELAS	Greek Resistance army in Second World War, military wing of EAM
EU	European Union (previously EC)
FAO	United Nations Food and Agriculture Organisation
FMNU	Front for Macedonian National Unity, nationalist coalition in FYROM post-1991
FRY	Federal Republic of Yugoslavia (the third Yugoslavia)
FYROM	Former Yugoslav Republic of Macedonia
HCNM	OSCE High Commissioner on National Minorities

HDZ	The Croatian Democratic Community, an anti-communist dissident organisation in the second Yugoslavia
IFOR	The first NATO military intervention force in Bosnia (see SFOR, below)
IMARO	IMRO-Adrianople, the first IMRO predecessor in the Ottoman Empire, the Internal Macedonian and Adrianopolitan Revolutionary Organisation
IMF	International Monetary Fund
IMRO	Internal Macedonian Revolutionary Organisation
IMRO-DPMNE	Internal Macedonian Revolutionary Organisation, Democratic Party of National Unity, the main contemporary IMRO-descended party in Republic of Macedonia/FYROM
IMRO-TP	A pro-Bulgarian IMRO grouping in post-1991 FYROM
IMRO-UMS	The IMRO-Union of Macedonian Societies, a Bulgarian branch of IMRO, active in the Mihalovist tradition
IO	Ilinden Organisation, the organisation of veterans of the 1903 Uprising
JNA	Yugoslav People's Army, in the second Yugoslavia
KEF	Kosovo Extraction Force, deployed in FYROM in December 1998
KFOR	NATO force in Kosova, after June 1999
KKE	Greek Communist Party
KLA	Kosova Liberation Army (also known as UCK)
KVM	Kosovo Verification Mission, deployed in November 1998

LCM	League of Macedonian Communists, refounded after 1991
LCY	Yugoslav League of Communists
LEG	Legaliteti, Albanian Royalist organisation
LNC	The National Liberation Movement, Albanian resistance organisation in the Second World War
MAAK	Party for Pan-Macedonian Action, briefly in the FYROM government after 1991, a post-1991 nationalist party
MANAPO	The Macedonian People's Movement, a 1930s pro-communist organisation in Vardar Macedonia
MFEO	Macedonian Federal Emigré Organisation
MPO	The Macedonian Patriotic Organisation, an emigrant Mihalovist organisation, that exists mainly in the USA, Canada and Australia
MPR	People's Republic of Macedonia, the original Titoist state unit after 1944
NATO	North Atlantic Treaty Organisation
NCME	National Committee of the Macedonian Emigration, a Bulgarian front organisation during and before the Second World War
NGO	A non-governmental organisation
ND	New Democracy, a conservative Greek political party
NDP	Ethnic Albanian party based in western FYROM, joined PDP (SH) in 1996.
OSCE	Organisation for Security and Cooperation in Europe (see CSCE, above)
OMO-Ilinden	Pro-Skopje organisation that operates in the Pirin region of Bulgaria, banned by the Sofia government

PASOK	Panhellenic Socialist party, the main Greek centre left party since 1981
PDA	Party of Democratic Action, post-1991 Islamic Party in FYROM
PDP	Party for Democratic Prosperity, one of the two ethnic Albanian parties formed after 1991 in FYROM
PDP (Sh)	The more radical ethnic Albanian party in FYROM, split from PDP in 1994, renamed the Democratic Party of Albanians in 1999
PDT	Party of Democratic Transformation, reformist communist party in FYROM post-1990 (see SKM-PDT, below)
PfP	Partnership for Peace
PLA	Albanian Party of Labour, the Albanian communist party 1943–1990 (also CPA)
PRM	People's Republic of Macedonia, the original Titoist state organisation unit established in 1944.
RAF	Royal Air Force
RF	The Russian Federation
ROM	Republic of Macedonia, name claimed by FYROM leaders after 1991
SDA	Social Democratic Alliance, the governing party in FYROM from 1991 to 1998, controlled by ex-communists
SECI	Southeast Europe Co-operation Initiative
SFOR	The NATO military intervention force in Bosnia, successor to IFOR (see above)
SFRY	The second, socialist, Yugoslav Federation (1944–1991)

SKM-PDT	The League of Communists–Party for Democratic Transformation, a pro-Yugoslav party in early FYROM after 1990 (see also PDT)
SLWP	Socialist League of the Working People, a mass organisation for workers in Titoist Yugoslavia
SOE	Special Operations Executive, a clandestine Second World War British military organisation set up to assist anti-fascist Resistance movements in Occupied Europe
SRF	Neo-fascist Radical Party of Serbia, led by Vojislav Šešelj
SRM	Socialist Republic of Macedonia (within the second Yugoslavia, since the 1960's, previously PRM (see above)
SSZ	*Svetska srpska zajednica*, the World Serb Community, a pro-Serb lobby in FYROM
TAT	Pyramid banking organisation based in Bitola that collapsed in 1997
UDJ	Small ethnic Albanian party in western FYROM
UIMRO	United IMRO, a left wing faction of IMRO absorbed by the Comintern in the 1920s
UMCES	Union of Macedonian Cultural-Education Societies, a communist-controlled Bulgarian organisation
UMNA	United Macedonians of North America, the largest émigré organisation in the USA
UNCRO	The part of UNPROFOR (see below) that operated in Croatia in the first ex-Yugoslav war after 1992
UNDP	United Nations Development Programme
UNESCO	United Nations Organisation for Educational and Scientific Cooperation
UfM	Union for Macedonia, the pro-Gligorov electoral coalition in the 1994 FYROM elections

UNIDO	United Nations International Development Organisation
UNPREDEP	United Nations Preventative Peacekeeping Force, deployed in FYROM after 1995 (see UNPROFOR)
UNPROFOR	United Nations Protection Force, the humanitarian operation in ex-Yugoslavia, 1992–5, in FYROM 1993–5
UNSC	United Nations Security Council
VB	*Vardarska Banovina*, term used for Macedonia within Royalist Yugoslavia, 1918–1941
VJ	Yugoslav army, within FRY, after 1995
VMRO	Internal Macedonian Revolutionary Organisation (see IMRO above)
VMRO–DPMNE	Internal Macedonian Revolutionary Organisation–Democratic party of Macedonian National Unity (see IMRO above)
WEU	Western European Union
WMC	World Macedonian Congress, a pro-Skopje lobby, active after 1990
WTO	World Trade Organisation
YNLA	Yugoslav National Liberation Army in the Second World War
YPA	The Yugoslav People's Assembly
YU	Yugoslavia

A chronology of key events in Macedonian history, 1870–1999

1870	Ottoman Turkey allows the formation of the Bulgarian Exarchate.
1872	The Bulgarian church acquires the eparchies of Skopje and Ochrid, with majority support claimed among local Christians.
1878	Treaty of San Stefano, by which Russia gave Bulgaria nearly all Slav Macedonia
	Treaty of Berlin: the great powers annulled the treaty of San Stefano
1893	Foundation of the Internal Macedonian Revolutionary Organisation (IMRO).
1895	Foundation of the Macedonian Supreme Committee in Sofia. Ex-Bulgarian PM Stambulov assassinated by Macedonians.
1903	Ilinden Rising in August 1903 in Macedonia against Ottoman Turkish rule. The Macedonian uprising is cruelly suppressed by the Turks.
1904–08	Period known by Greeks as that of 'The Macedonian Struggle'
1908	The Young Turk Revolution.
1912–13	The Balkan Wars. Defeat of Turkish forces in the First Balkan War. In the Second Balkan War, Macedonia is contested by the victorious forces of Greece, Serbia and Bulgaria.
1913	By the Treaty of Bucharest, Macedonia is divided between Serbia, Greece and Bulgaria.
1914–18	First World War. Serious fighting on the Macedonian front after Bulgaria occupies much of Macedonia. After the end of hostilities, north Macedonia is awarded to Serbia, and becomes part of south Serbia within the first Yugoslavia, the Kingdom of the Serbs, Croats and Slovenes. Greece retains Aegean Macedonia, much of which is settled with Christian refugees from Asia Minor. Macedonian political organisation is banned by the Serbian monarchist state. IMRO begins terrorist campaign against Yugoslavia.
1923	Coup in Sofia. Assassination of Stambuliski, the Bulgarian PM.
1929	Yugoslavia becomes a dictatorship.
1934	Suppression of IMRO in Bulgaria. Assassination of King Alexander in Marseilles by Chernozemski, a member of IMRO.
1937	Treaty of Perpetual Friendship signed between Yugoslavia and Bulgaria.
1941	German occupation of Yugoslavia. Bulgaria annexes much of Macedonia. Yugoslav Macedonia is divided by the Bulgarians into two provinces, one based on Skopje, the other, Bitola (Monastir).
1943	Anti-Axis Partisan warfare begins in Macedonia, controlled by Tito and 'General Tempo' (Svetozar Vukmanovic).
1944	Proclamation of a Macedonian People's Republic on 2 August.

	Liberation of Greece
1944–8	Discussions between the Yugoslav and Bulgarian communist parties about the possibility of solving the Macedonian problem through a Balkan Federation.
1945	A Macedonian People's Republic is formed within the second, socialist Yugoslavia, with its capital at Skopje.
1946	First Congress of the Macedonian People's Front in Skopje. Removal of the bones of Gotse Delchev, IMRO's most popular leader, from Sofia to Skopje.
1947	The first 'Macedonian national government' is established.
1948	Break between Tito and the Cominform.
1949	Closure of the Greek–Macedonian border. End of the Greek civil war.
1955–75	Gradual industrial and touristic development of Yugoslav Macedonia.
1990	Multi-party elections held.
1991	Kiro Gligorov becomes President in January 1991. In September 1991, the citizens of the ex-Socialist Republic of Macedonia vote for independence as the Republic of Macedonia, and leave the Yugoslav Federation. In November 1991, the new Constitution is approved.
1992	Bulgaria becomes the first country to recognize the 'Republic of Macedonia', (although not its language), followed by Turkey, Russia, and mainland China.
1993	Deployment of UNPROFOR United Nations Preventative Peacekeeping Force in Macedonia, FYROM joins the UN.
1994	October-November: President Gligorov and SDA dominated coalition is confirmed in power in controversial elections.
1995	Assassination attempt on President Gligorov in Skopje. Agreement with Greece over redesign of FYROM flag.
1996	Agreement signed in which Yugoslavia recognizes FYROM's independence, constitutional name and language.
1997	Serious disturbances in western Macedonia in July with four Albanian fatalities. Imprisonment of the ethnic Albanian Mayors of Tetovo and Gostivar for involvement in anti-state activities.
1998	January: Announcement of impending retirement of President Gligorov. October/November: Parliamentary elections, which result in the victory of an Internal Macedonian Revolutionary Organisation-led coalition, and gains for ethnic Albanian parties. December: Deployment of Kosovo Extraction Force in FYROM.
1999	February: NATO reinforces in FYROM, in preparation for military intervention in Kosova. Joint NATO–Greek military exercises in the region. Bulgaria signs military agreement with FYROM leaders, and donates tanks and artillery to the FYROM army. In Sofia the Prime Ministers of FYROM and Bulgaria sign an agreement with a compromise formula on 'the language dispute' between both countries. March: NATO begins military action against FRY. Refugees from Kosova begin to arrive in FYROM.

A chronology of events in Yugoslav–Macedonian relations, 1990–2000*

1990

20–22 January   The 14th Special Congress of the League of Communists of Yugoslavia (LCY) in Belgrade. Bitter antagonism among the leaderships of the different republics culminated in the decision of Slovenian and Croatian delegations to leave the Congress.

30 May   LCY Congress resumed; Croatia, Macedonia and Slovenia did not participate.

11 November   The first ballot of the multi-party elections for the Macedonian Assembly took place; *25 November*: the second ballot was held; the party VMRO-DPMNE won the majority of seats – 37, the League of Communists of Macedonia – 31.

1991

25 January   The Sobranje (the Macedonian Parliament) adopted the Declaration of Independence (declaring right to independence), as well as the Platform for negotiations about the future of Yugoslavia.

27 January   The Sobranje elected Kiro Gligorov President of the Socialist Republic of Macedonia.

30 January   Alija Izetbegović (President of Bosnia-Herzegovina) and Kiro Gligorov held talks in Sarajevo; they declared their intentions to preserve Yugoslavia.

28 March   First meeting of Presidents of Yugoslav republics (so-called 'Summit of Six') was held in Split (Croatia). No agreement was reached.

4 April   Second Summit of Six held in Belgrade; Serbian President Slobodan Milošević proposed a document with regard to the future of a Yugoslav economic community.

11 April   Third Summit of Six held in Brdo (Slovenia); it was decided that by the end of May all republics should hold referendums and see whether YU should be a confederation of sovereign republics (as proposed by Slovenia and Croatia, or a democratic federation (as proposed by Serbia and Montenegro).

---

*   This chronology has been made by Nina Dobrković and James Pettifer on the basis of the book by Brana Marković, *Yugoslav Crisis and the World: A Chronology of Events, January 1990–October 1996* (Institute of International Politics and Economics, Belgrade, 1996), p. 212+Supplement; as well as on the basis of daily and weekly newspapers (*Politika, Borba, Nasa Borba*) and magazines (*NIN, Vreme, Intervju*).

18 April   Fourth Summit of Six held in Ohrid (Macedonia).

29 April   Fifth Summit of Six held in Cetinje (Montenegro).

5 May   Kiro Gligorov gave an interview to *France Press*. He said, if Slovenia and Croatia broke away from Yugoslavia, Macedonia would be constituted as an independent state.

6 May   Violent demonstrations against the Yugoslav Peoples Army took place in Split (Croatia); a shot from the rioting masses killed a soldier in front of a barracks, a Macedonian.

3 June   Kiro Gligorov and Alija Izetbegović announced a joint proposal – Platform on the Future Yugoslav Community – by which Yugoslavia should become a commonwealth of sovereign republics.

6 June   Sixth (and last) Summit at Stojčevac near Sarajevo (Bosnia-Herzegovina). Gligorov-Izetbegović's Platform on the Future Yugoslav Community was not accepted.

8 September   Macedonia organised a referendum on the independence of Macedonia and its possible association with Yugoslavia; 74.4 per cent of those who voted opted in favour. (In Croatia in May 1991, 94.17 per cent voted for independence; in Slovenia in December 1990, 88.5 per cent for independence)

17 September   The Macedonian Sobranje in Skopje confirmed results of the referendum; it adopted a Declaration on strict respect of existing frontiers, rejecting any territorial claims on any neighbouring country.

26 September   Session of the SFRY Presidency with representatives from only Serbia, Vojvodina, Kosovo and Montenegro present. From that time on representatives from Slovenia, Croatia, Macedonia and Bosnia-Herzegovina boycotted it.

17 November   The Macedonian Sobranje proclaimed the new constitution by which Macedonia was defined as a sovereign and independent democratic state.

17 December   The Foreign Ministers of the European Community adopted in Brussels a Declaration on the Guidelines on the Recognition of New States in Eastern Europe and the Soviet Union, and the Declaration on Yugoslavia. All Yugoslav republics wanting to be recognised as independent states should by December 23rd submit their applications and proofs that they met the criteria envisaged in the Declaration on the Guidelines ... . Proofs will be assessed by the Arbitration Committee of the Conference on Yugoslavia (Badinter Commission), and decisions will be made by the EC Ministerial Council after January 15, 1992. Slovenia, Croatia, Macedonia and Bosnia-Herzegovina submitted applications; Serbia and Montenegro did not, saying that they were recognised at the Berlin Congress, 1878.

27 December   Serbian President Slobodan Milošević unexpectedly visited Ohrid and met with Macedonian President Kiro Gligorov (reports speculated that he was trying to persuade him to join the Yugoslav federation); no press conference was held.

1992

11 January   EC Arbitration Commission (Badinter Commission) concluded that Slovenia and Macedonia fulfilled all the necessary requirements for recognition of their independence, while Croatia and Bosnia-Herzegovina should introduce constitutional adjustments, and Bosnia-Herzegovina should first organise a referendum on the issue.

15 January Despite the opinion of the Arbitration Commission the EC recognised Slovenia and Croatia, but postponed recognition of Macedonia due to the opposition of Greece (recognition under the name of the Former Yugoslav Republic of Macedonia was given by the EC much later, during 1993).

17 March Slovenia and Macedonia agreed to establish diplomatic relations.

26 March After signing a document on transfer of facilities and equipment, the Yugoslav People's Army formally left the territory of Macedonia.

25 April The Macedonian Sobranje passed relevant laws granting Macedonia monetary independence; the Yugoslav dinar was replaced by the Macedonian denar.

27 April Serbia and Montenegro adopted the constitution of the new state, the Federal Republic of Yugoslavia.

30 May UN Security Council (resolution 757) imposed sanctions on FR Yugoslavia.

5 August Russia recognises 'Republic of Macedonia'

25 November A Balkan conference on Bosnia-Herzegovina began in Istanbul, attended by Turkey, Croatia, Slovenia, Bosnia-Herzegovina, Macedonia, Hungary, Albania, Romania, Bulgaria and Austria. Italy, Greece and Yugoslavia did not accept the invitation.

11 December UN Security Council (resolution 795), after 'considering the request by the Government in the former Yugoslav Republic of Macedonia', approved the deployment in Macedonia of the United Nations Protection Force (UNPROFOR) consisting of 700 soldiers, 35 military monitors and 26 members of the civil police.

1993

8 April Macedonia was admitted to the UN, under the provisional name of Former Yugoslav Republic of Macedonia.

31 May Serbian president Slobodan Milošević and President of Macedonia Kiro Gligorov met in Ohrid.

11 June Macedonia accepted UN proposal to deploy a contingent of 300 US soldiers within the protection force in Macedonia, the origin of UNPREDEP.

4 September Macedonia decided to strictly apply Security Council resolutions on the blockade imposed against FR Yugoslavia, which caused stricter control of lorries on the frontier with FR Yugoslavia.

23 December The Sobranje decided to apply for the NATO 'Partnership for Peace' programme.

1994

16 February Greece introduced a border blockade against Macedonia.

21 June Population census in Macedonia (finished 5 July); the last census was taken in May 1991, six months before Macedonia proclaimed independence.

16 October The presidential and the first ballot of parliamentary elections held in Macedonia. Out of a total 1,360,729 registered voters, 77.7 per cent went to the polls. Kiro Gligorov won as President with 52.4 per cent of registered voters, i.e. 67.4 per cent of those who cast their votes.

13 November   Macedonia announced results of the population census, which started on June 21: 1,925,000 inhabitants, of which 66.9 per cent identified themselves as Macedonians, 22.5 per cent Albanians, 3.84 per cent Turks, 2.28 per cent Gypsies, 2.04 per cent (39,300) Serbs.

5 December   The Serbian-Macedonian Friendship Society was founded in Belgrade.

1995

16 February   The Macedonian government criticised the attempt (unsuccessful) to open an Albanian university in Tetovo (Western Macedonia), describing it as a violation of the Constitution and Macedonian laws.

17 February   Severe clashes between Albanians and the police near Tetovo; one student died, 18 injured. Demonstrators protested against the decision of the government to prevent the opening of the Albanian university in Tetovo.

31 March   UN decision with regard to Blue Helmets in the former YU; former UNPROFOR will be divided into UNCRO (Croatia), UNPROFOR (Bosnia-Herzegovina) and UNPREDEP in Macedonia (resolution 983).

5 August   Yugoslavia introduced new regulations, according to which citizens of Macedonia and Yugoslavia can cross the common border only with a passport (until then, identification cards were sufficient).

13 September   At the UN Headquarters in New York foreign ministers of Greece and Macedonia signed the Agreement on normalisation of relations between the two states (they undertook to respect mutual sovereignty, territorial integrity and political independence, and accept the present internationally recognised common borders). Macedonia will remove from its state symbols the star of Vergina, and Greece will lift economic blockade of Macedonia within 30 days, introduced in February 1994. Negotiations concerning the name of Macedonia will take place subsequently.

27 September   Macedonia was admitted to the Council of Europe under the provisional name of FYROM.

2 October   Slobodan Milošević and Kiro Gligorov met in Belgrade; both presidents agreed that normalisation of mutual relations was in the best interest of both states.

3 October   Unsuccessful attempt to assassinate Kiro Gligorov in Skopje.

4 October   The Sobranje adopted (by emergency procedures) a new law on the symbols of the Republic of Macedonia.

9 October   The Sobranje ratified the Agreement on normalisation of relations with Greece.

12 October   Macedonia admitted to OSCE, as FYROM.

13 October   After four days of negotiations Greece and Macedonia signed in Skopje the Memorandum on Implementation of the Agreement on Normalisation of Macedonian–Greek Relations which had been signed in New York on 13 September 1995.

14 October   The Greek government issued a statement saying that all restrictions on movement of goods from and to FYROM will be lifted at midnight that day – thus, Greece lifted the blockade it had imposed against Macedonia on 16 February 1994.

11 November   The Permanent Political Committee of NATO unanimously decided in Brussels on the accession of FYROM to the 'Partnership for Peace'.

15 November   Macedonian Prime Minister signed the Partnership for Peace programme. Macedonia is the second country in the territory of the former YU (after Slovenia) which joined the programme.

22 November   UN Security Council (resolution 1022) suspended sanctions against FR Yugoslavia (introduced in May 1992).

30 November   UN Security Council (resolution 1027) extended the mandate of UNPREDEP in FYROM.

4 December   The EU suspended sanctions against FR Yugoslavia.

13 December   Both Macedonia and Yugoslavia participated at a conference on stability and good-neighbourly relations in South-Eastern Europe, held near Paris.

1996

8 April   Macedonia and Yugoslavia signed the Agreement on regulating mutual relations and promoting cooperation between the two countries.

15 May   Flights were re-established between Macedonia and Yugoslavia (between the capitals, Skopje and Belgrade).

7 October   Macedonia and FR Yugoslavia made an agreement with regard to a creation of a zone of special economic and customs relations; Macedonia has reached similar agreements with Slovenia and Bosnia-Herzegovina and the one with Croatia is forthcoming – thus, it will be the only former Yugoslav republic to have such relations established with all other former Yugoslav republics.

1997

2 July   Macedonian Prime Minister visits FRY.

4 November   Agreement at the Inter Balkan Summit on Crete, to promote special cooperation over border issues. Meeting between Slobodan Milošević, and Albanian PM Fatos Nano.

1998

18 January   In response to the Kosovo crisis, the Macedonian Foreign Minister supports a solution within FRY.

8–14 March   Macedonian Albanians demonstrate in supports of Kosovo independence.

12 May   Decision announced that the UNPREDEP mandate will be renewed.

September–October   NATO build up of troops in FYROM accelerates

October-November   Defeat of Social Democrat coalition in parliamentary elections.

24 December   Implementation of the Basic Agreement between Macedonia and NATO pertaining to NATO deployment of the Kosovo Extraction Force (KEF) in Macedonia.

1999

8 February   The government in Skopje establishes diplomatic relations with Taiwan.

9 February   Amnesty signed by President Kiro Gligorov for two imprisoned ethnic Albanian Mayors of Tetovo and Gostivar.

14 February   China severs diplomatic relations with Skopje over government recognition of Taiwan.

22 February   Macedonian–Bulgarian joint declaration signed in Sofia, stating FYROM's equidistance with all its neighbours.

26 February   China vetoes continuation of UNPREDEP border force mandate in UN Security Council. UNPREDEP force begins to leave FYROM.

6 March   Armed clashes between the KLA and Yugoslav army spill across FRY–FYROM border near General Jankovic border post.

14 March   Hundreds of ethnic Albanian refugees from FRY begin to arrive in FYROM.

20 March   Kosovo Verification Mission evacuates to FYROM from FRY.

24 March   Beginning of NATO bombardment of Yugoslavia.

5 April   Mass deportations of ethnic Albanian refugees coming from FRY begin after violence at Blace border crossing. International condemnation of Skopje government, in the following week refugee camp construction begins throughout FYROM.

May   Hundreds of thousands of refugees congregate in FYROM camps.

12 June   NATO takes military control of Kosovo, refugee return begins soon afterwards.

October–November   Presidential election campaign and poll results in victory on 14 November of Boris Trajkovski as successor to Kiro Gligorov after Social Democratic party candidate Tito Petkovski wins on the first round. Allegations of ethnic Albanian ballot rigging made by Petkovski supporters.

19 November   Resignation of Kiro Gligorov.

15 December   Inauguration of President Trajkovski in Skopje.

2000

8 January   Violence in Arachinovo leads to deaths of police and ethnic Albanians held in custody.

February–March   Influx of about 7000 refugees from fighting in the Presheve region of Yugoslavia, mainly to Kumanovo.

Notes on the contributors

The late **Elisabeth Barker**, was a leading British authority on South East Europe for many years. She worked as a Reuters correspondent in the Balkans and as a Diplomatic Correspondent for the BBC. Her publications included *Truce in the Balkans, Austria 1918–1972*, and *British Policy in South East Europe in World War II*.

Gjorgi Caca is Professor in the Faculty of Law, University of Cyril and Methodius, Skopje.

Sophia Clément is a Research Fellow at the WEU Institute for Security Studies in Paris. She has a Master's degree in Political Studies and Soviet and East European Studies at the Institut d'Etudes Politiques, Paris. She wrote a Ph.D thesis on Security Perceptions in the Southern Balkans. She was previously attached to the Centre d'Etudes et de Recherche Internationales (CERI). She has written widely on European security issues and South Eastern Europe. Her more recent publications are 'Conflict Prevention in the Balkans: The Case of Kosovo and the FYR of Macedonia', *Chaillot Paper 30* (WEU Institute for Security Studies, December 1997); editor of 'The Issues Raised by Bosnia, and the Transatlantic Debate', *Chaillot Paper 32* (WEU-ISS, June 1998); chapter on 'Assessing Subregionalism in South East Europe', in Stephen Calleya (ed.), *Regionalism in the Post Cold War World* (Dartmouth, London, January 1999). She is also the European Programme Manager for the Association for the Studies of Nationalities (ASN), Columbia University, NY.

Nina Dobrković graduated at the Faculty of Political Sciences in Belgrade, where she also specialised in the field of international studies. As a Research Fellow at the Institute of International Politics and Economics, in Belgrade, she was mainly dealing with issues of disarmament and security; she is co-author of the book *Disarmament in Europe* (1985), and she has written a number of articles on political aspects of the disarmament problem, as well as a study of local conflicts in the period after the Second World War. More recently, her work has focused on the new situation in the Balkans, and ethnicity problems, including analyses of the relations among the new states, the influence and role of Germany and Austria, as well as of the new security situation in the region and the role of NATO. Among her works there are some background papers (for a SIPRI publication and for a study of the Italian-German Sociological Society in Trento), contributions in English and Serbian in books dealing with contemporary aspects of security in the Balkans in view of the civil war in Yugoslavia and its consequences, and numerous articles in journals.

Kyril Drezov is a Lecturer in the Politics of South East Europe at Keele University. He studied International Relations in Sofia, and was involved in research at the Bulgarian Academy of Sciences before taking up doctoral studies at Oxford. He has published on problems of transition, modernisation and nationalism in Bulgaria and Macedonia, and on the Russian factor in Bulgarian politics. He is also a regular contributor on Balkan, Bulgarian and Macedonian affairs for BBC World Service.

Kiro Gligorov was born in Stip in 1917, and graduated from the Faculty of Law of Belgrade University in 1939. In 1941 he became involved in the Partisan movement against the German occupiers. After the end of the Second World War, he worked in the economic ministry in Belgrade, and subsequently became Assistant Minister of Finance in the Federal government. He was also President of the Belgrade Institute of Social Sciences. In the 1980s he was a member of the Markovic government which sought to introduce market economic reforms to Yugoslavia. He was elected President of the Republic of Macedonia after the first multi-party elections held in January 1991. He was re-elected President in October 1994.

Sir Reginald Hibbert read history at Oxford for two years, joined the army and was commissioned in the IVth Queen's Own Hussars. He joined the Special Operations Executive in 1943 and was parachuted into Albania where he spent a year in the mountains as a British Liaison Officer attached to the Partisans, mostly in the area north of Peshkopia. He returned to his regiment for the last stages of the Italian campaign. After the Second World War, he joined the Diplomatic service and served in Romania, Austria and elsewhere, ending his career as FCO Political Director, and Ambassador in Paris. For five years afterwards he was Director of the Ditchley Foundation. He is an Honorary Fellow of Worcester College, Oxford. He has written extensively on recent

Albanian history, and published his main work on the Second World War period, *Albania's National Liberation – The Bitter Victory*, in 1991.

Naoum Kaytchev was born in 1970 in Sofia. He studied at Sofia University and St Edmund Hall, Oxford. He is working on a PhD thesis on Macedonia in Serbian and Bulgarian consciousness (1878–1972).

Evangelos Kofos is Senior Adviser on Balkan Affairs at the Hellenic Foundation for European and Foreign Policy (ELIAMEP) of Athens, and a Member of the Board at the Institute for Balkan Studies (IBS) of Thessaloniki. He was Visiting Fellow at Brasenose College, Oxford during the academic year 1995–6 and prior to that he served for many years as Special Consultant on Balkan Affairs at the Ministry of Foreign Affairs, Athens. He has contributed essays in various Greek, Balkan and international journals and collective publications dealing with the history and current affairs of the Balkans and Macedonia in particular. Among his English-language publications are: *Nationalism and Communism in Macedonia* (Thessaloniki, IBS, 1964, reissued, with the addition of three new essays on the subject, by Caratzas Publisher, New Rochelle, NY, 1993); *Greece and Eastern Crisis, 1875–1878* (Institute for Balkan Studies, Thessaloniki, 1975); *The Impact of the Macedonian Question on Greek Civil Conflict: 1943–1949* (Athens, ELIAMEP, 1989); *Kosovo: Avoiding Another Balkan War* (Athens, ELIAMEP, 1998) (He co-edited this with Thanos Veremis); *Kosovo and the Albanian Unification: The Burden of the Past, the Anguish of the Future*, which is his most recent book (in Greek), was published in the summer of 1998 (Athens, 'Papazisis').

Dimitar Mirčev was born in 1942, and educated at Belgrade University (degree in Law and Politics), Skopje University, and Ljubljana University (Doctoral thesis in political science). In 1970–2, he studied specialised social science research methods at the University of Bradford, UK. In 1971 he was expelled from the Communist Party ranks because of 'liberalistic deviations'. In the 1980s he lived and worked mainly in Slovenia, and in 1989 returned to Macedonia, took part in 'the Macedonia spring', and was involved in the process of transformation and independence. As a professor of political science and vice-chancellor of the University of Skopje he took part in drafting the new constitution and the basic legal acts of Macedonia. Since the early 1990s he has been an active member of the IPSA Research Committee on Structure and Organisation of Government and served as a regional editorial associate of *Governance* – Oxford. He is currently Republic of Macedonia Ambassador to the Holy See and to Slovenia.

Ivanka Nedeva graduated from the Department of History in Sofia University in 1975, and was awarded a PhD in 1979 on contemporary international relations in the Balkans. After work at the Institute of Balkan Studies in Sofia, she studied at the University of Maryland in the USA, and at Wolfson College, Oxford, where she was a holder of the Charter Fellowship.

James Pettifer is Visiting Professor in the Institute of Balkan Studies, Thessaloniki, and Research Fellow of the European Research Institute, University of Bath, UK. He is a correspondent for the London *Times* in the southern Balkans, and a regular broadcaster on radio and television. He was a Senior Associate Member of St Antony's College, Oxford, from 1993 to 1996. His most recent books include *The Turkish Labyrinth* (Viking, London 1997), the second edition of *Blue Guide Albania* (Norton, New York, 1996), and, with Miranda Vickers, *Albania – from Anarchy to a Balkan Identity* (C. Hurst, London and New York University Press) and the *Blue Guide to Bulgaria*. (A and C Black, London, 1998)

Hugh Poulton is a specialist in Balkan and Turkish affairs. From 1984 to 1991 he was East European Researcher for Amnesty International at Amnesty's International Secretariat in London. He is a consultant on Turkey for Article 19 – the international centre against censorship – and is also a consultant on the Balkans for the Minority Rights Group. His publications include: *The Balkans: Minorities and States in Conflict* (MRG Publications, 1991 and 1993); *Who Are the Macedonians?* (Hurst & Co./Indiana University Press, 1995); *Top Hat, Grey Wolf and Crescent: Turkish Nationalism and the Turkish Republic* (Hurst & Co./New York University Press, 1997); *Muslim Identity and the Balkan State* (co-editor with S. Taji-Farouki, Hurst & Co./New York University Press 1997). He was also co-author with Daniele Joly and Clive Nettleton of *Refugees: Asylum in Europe?* (MRG Publications, 1992); and the writer and compiler of the East European section of *World Directory of Minorities* (Longmans/St James Press, December 1989).

Jens Reuter is a Senior Researcher at the South East Europe Institute in Munich, and a member of the editorial board of the journal *Sudosteuropa*. He studied Slavistics at the University of Hamburg, followed by postgraduate studies at the University of Belgrade. His publications include *The Albanians in Yugoslavia* (1982), and more than a hundred articles in journals and other publications. He broadcasts regularly on German radio and television on Balkan issues.

Nina Smirnova is senior researcher at the Institute of World History of the Russian Academy of Science in Moscow. Her field is the history of Albania and the history of international relations in the twentieth century. She has written articles on the history of Albania, Soviet foreign policy and international problems in the East Mediterranean and Balkans (including post-Dayton and Kosovo problems). Among her publications are: *Formation of the People's Republic of Albania* (1960); *A Short History of Albania* (1965, co-author); *Balkan Politics of Fascist Italy, 1936–1941* (1969); *Italian Politics in the Balkans 1922–1935* (1979); *A Short History of Albania* (1993, co-author).

Stefan Troebst was born in 1955 and educated at the Free University of Berlin (MA 1979, Ph.D. 1984 and habilitation 1995 – all in history). From 1976 to 1980 he studied in Sofia and in Skopje, from 1984 to 1992 he taught as assistant professor and associate professor Russian and East European history at the Free University of Berlin. In 1992–95, he served in the OSCE Missions to Macedonia and Moldova CSCE Spillover Monitor Mission in Macedonia, and in 1994–95 in the OSCE Mission to Moldova. In 1996 he was nominated founding director of the Danish-German 'European Centre for Minority Issues'. Since 1999, he has been Professor of East European Cultural Studies at the University of Leipzig. Among his books are *The Bulgarian–Yugoslav Controversy over Macedonia, 1967–1982* (1983, in German), *The 'Internal Macedonian Revolutionary Organization' and the Balkan Policy of Fascist Italy, 1922–1930* (1987, in German) and *Conflict in Kosovo: Failure of Prevention? An Analytical Documentation 1992–1998)* (1998).

Tom Winnifrith was born in 1938 and educated at Tonbridge and Christ Church, Oxford. Between 1961 and 1998 he taught at Eton College and the University of Warwick. In 1984 he was Visiting Fellow at All Souls College, Oxford. In 1987 he published *The Vlachs: The History of a Balkan People* (Duckworth, 1987, 2nd edition, 1995). In 1992 he edited *Perspectives on Albania* (Macmillan) and in 1995 produced *Shattered Eagles: Balkan Fragments* (Duckworths). He is currently engaged on a general history of the Balkans and a particular study of the Vlachs in Albania.

Alla Yashkova is Chief Research Fellow, Institute of International Economic and Political Studies, Russian Academy of Sciences, Moscow.

Introduction

As one of the states emerging from the collapse of the second Yugoslavia, between 1990 and 1995, the former Yugoslav Republic of Macedonia (FYROM) has attracted intermittent newspaper and other media coverage in connection with the protracted disputes about its name, but little scholarly study compared with the Balkan states which have been militarily involved in the ex-Yugoslav crisis in the last decade. Nevertheless, the territory of FYROM occupies an important strategic point in the southern Balkans, and the 'Macedonian Question' in its historic dimension has been one of the most intractable and difficult Balkan conflicts. It is re-emerging as a factor in the Kosovo crisis which dominated the region from 1998.

The years since 1991 have seen FYROM establish itself successfully in the formal sense, and gain diplomatic recognition under the name of the 'Republic of Macedonia' with some countries and 'FYROM' with others, but the state has existed in a climate of continual serious economic and political difficulties. Without substantial and continuous international financial aid through the World Bank and the International Monetary Fund (IMF), and specific programmes to stabilise the value of the currency against a German Mark benchmark, the economy would have collapsed. FYROM was at the heart of the struggle to maintain United Nations sanctions against Serbia, although it has been claimed that the Skopje government did not act in accordance with its international obligations towards Serbia and that very large quantities of goods, particularly oil, were transported across the FYROM-Serbian border between 1992 and 1995.

It is a matter of debate as to what extent a new Macedonian Question has emerged in the detritus of the second Yugoslavia, but it is clear that the new small state that has emerged after the national referendum voted for independence in September 1991 has faced many difficulties as a result of the protracted Balkan crisis and has suffered periods of severe internal ethnic tension and outbreaks of serious violence involving the 25 per cent Albanian national community. International attitudes to FYROM and its government has varied greatly but the decisive factor in the situation has been the effects of the surrounding Balkan crisis, particularly in Kosovo, and the fact that relations with neighbouring states have not generally been easy, with many outstanding difficulties in relation to the country's name (with Greece), border delineation, religion and cross-border trade during UN sanctions (with Serbia), national minority issues and education (with Albania), and language and national minority difficulties (with Bulgaria).

In this context a number of scholars and analysts from different national backgrounds were invited to contribute papers to this book in which some recent research on FYROM and its history could be made available to a wider audience. Debate about the new Macedonian Question has been largely seen through Anglo-American perceptions, post-Dayton, and this has inhibited some analyses. In some countries with a direct interest in the Macedonian Question, notably Bulgaria, it was difficult to publish much academic research on 'Macedonian' issues under communism, and thus Bulgarian contributions form an important section of the book. Ethnicity is also very important in FYROM, with as much as half the population belonging to national, ethnic, or religious minorities, and the papers of Dr Tom Winnifrith and Dr Hugh Poulton illustrate aspects of the ethnic minority problems in FYROM.

The purpose of this book is to contribute to informed debate about the Macedonian Question, and to illustrate current international attitudes towards the FYROM. For that reason it includes a reproduction of an important interview with President Kiro Gligorov, on the future, as well as material illustrating different national policy positions, such as the papers from Professor Nina Smirnova, from Moscow, and Dr Nina Dobrkovic, from Belgrade. An international relations approach is brought to bear by Dr Sophia Clement of the Western European Union, Institute of Strategic Studies, in Paris.

There is also some historical material, as recent history forms a very critical element in the current Macedonian consciousness and has been subject to intense ideological debate. The late Elisabeth Barker's paper sets out the traditional pro-Greek view of the British Foreign Office. Sir Reginald Hibbert's paper illustrates the difficult and controversial historical background to the position of the Albanians in western

Macedonia under communism. As an introduction to the main issues, I reprint my own paper 'The New Macedonian Question' from 1992, to outline the situation of the state when it came into being as an independent entity on the international scene.

I have not taken any editorial position on the very controversial issue of the correct nomenclature for the state, or the spelling of Kosovo/Kosova, and different terminology in papers has been retained in exactly the form submitted to the editor.

I would like to express my thanks to Dr Alex Pravda of St Antony's College, Oxford, who originally commissioned the volume for the Macmillan/St Antony's series. I also owe thanks to Tim Farmiloe at Macmillan and to Aruna Vasudevan and Keith Povey for expert and patient editorial assistance, and to the contributors who have found the time to write. In the last few years of the Balkan crisis severe pressures on time have been felt by most people in any way involved in trying to follow or interpret events. I am most grateful for the time they have given to write for this book.

I would also like to take the opportunity to thank Kyril Drezov, Miranda Vickers, Bob Churcher, Dragi Ivanovski, Professor Basil Kondis, Tim Judah, Sami Ibrahimi and Arben Xhaferi for many discussions of Macedonian matters over the years.

Much of my view of events has been gained while writing for *The Times* in Macedonia, and I am most grateful to the Editor, the Foreign Editor and Foreign Desk staff for their generous encouragement and support.

JAMES PETTIFER

Institute of Balkan Studies
Thessaloniki

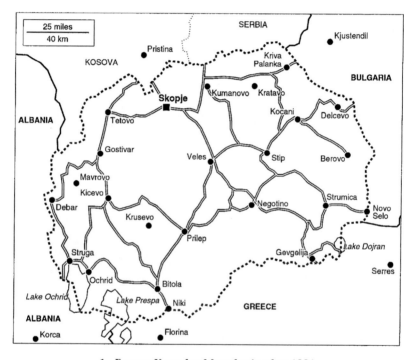

1. Former Yugoslav Macedonia after 1991

On the eve of the Russo-Turkish War

Bulgarian frontier proposed
by Treaty of San Stefano, 1878

Treaty of Berlin, 1878

2. Balkan frontier changes involving Macedonia

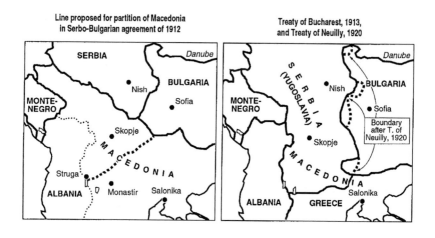

Line proposed for partition of Macedonia in Serbo-Bulgarian agreement of 1912

Treaty of Bucharest, 1913, and Treaty of Neuilly, 1920

Boundary of Macedonian People's Republic set up within Yugoslavia after the Second World War

2. Balkan frontier changes involving Macedonia

3. Balkan frontiers in 2000

Part I
The National Question in modern Macedonia

Chapter **1**

The origin of the Macedonian dispute[*]

Elisabeth Barker

The Macedonian question came into being when in 1870 Russia success-fully pressed Ottoman Turkey to allow the formation of a separate Bulgarian Orthodox Church, or Exarchate, with authority extending over parts of the Turkish province of Macedonia. This step quickly involved Bulgaria in strife both with Greece and with Serbia. The Greek Patriarch in Constantinople declared the new autocephalous Bulgarian Church to be schismatic, and the Greeks sharply contested the spread of Bulgarian ecclesiastical, cultural, and national influence in Macedonia. The Serbian government complained of Turkey's decision through eccle-siastical as well as diplomatic channels, and, after an interruption caused by Serbia's war with Turkey in 1876, also tried to fight Bulgarian influence in Macedonia. So began the three-sided contest for Macedonia, waged first by priests and teachers, later by armed bands, and later still by armies, which has lasted with occasional lulls until today.

This was not the result planned by Russia in 1870. What Russia wanted was to extend her own influence in the Balkans through the Orthodox Church and through support of the oppressed or newly lib-erated Slav peoples. She had the choice of Bulgaria or Serbia as her chief instrument in this policy; Greece was of course non-Slav and so less suitable than either. Of the Slav nations, Bulgaria was geograph-ically closer to Russia, and commanded the land approaches to Constantinople and the Aegean, and, through Macedonia, to Salonika. Also, Bulgaria was at that time not yet liberated from Turkey and so was more dependent on Russian aid and thus more biddable than Serbia. Serbia was more remote from Russia, and was then still far from

---

[*] Originally published in *Macedonia – Its Place in Balkan Power Politics* (London, Royal Institute of International Affairs, 1950) and reproduced with permission.

access to the Adriatic; she had already declared her independence and was thus less docile than Bulgaria; and with her alternating dynasties, she was liable at intervals to fall into the Austro-Hungarian sphere of influence. So Russia's choice naturally enough fell on Bulgaria. But this choice started, or revived, a bitter rivalry between the two Slav Balkan nations, which has ever since been a stumbling-block in the way of Russia's aspirations in the Balkans.

While the creation of the Bulgarian Exarchate is usually accepted as the origin of the Macedonian question, this, like almost everything else about Macedonia, is disputed. Some Serbian historians say that Bulgarian penetration of Macedonia had started some years earlier. Others find the root of the trouble in the San Stefano Treaty of 1878, by which Russia gave Bulgaria nearly all Slav Macedonia. Nationalist Bulgarians blame the Treaty of Berlin, in the same year, by which the great Powers took Macedonia away from Bulgaria. All these were clearly contributing factors in the Macedonian problem; but the fact remains that Russia's sponsorship of the Bulgarian Exarchate caused the first clash.

Macedonia: the country and the people

Other disputed questions are the exact area of Macedonia and the national character of the Macedonians. There has been no Macedonian State since the days of the Kings of Macedon in the fourth century BC Between that time and 1912, Macedonia belonged successively to the Roman Empire, the Byzantine Empire, the medieval Bulgarian and Serbian Empires, and the Ottoman Empire. Consequently its borders fluctuated. Some Serbian historians have therefore claimed that the Skopje region, in the north-west, is not part of Macedonia, but belongs to 'Old Serbia'. However, the usually accepted geographical area of Macedonia is the territory bounded, in the north, by the hills north of Skopje and by the Shar Mountains; in the east, by the Rila and Rhodope Mountains; in the south, by the Aegean coast around Salonika, by Mount Olympus, and by the Pindus mountains; in the west, by Lakes Prespa and Ochrid. Its total area is about 67,000 square kilometres.

It is mainly a mountainous or hilly land, producing cereals, tobacco, opium poppies, and sheep; there are chrome mines, and some lead, pyrites, zinc, and copper in Yugoslav Macedonia. In Greek Macedonia the plain north-west of Salonika is now a big wheat-producing area. Bulgarian Macedonia is rich in timber. But the main economic (and strategic) importance of Macedonia is that it controls the main north-south route from central Europe to Salonika and the Aegean down the

Morava and Vardar Valleys, and also the lesser route down the Struma Valley. The far less valuable east-west route from Albania and the Adriatic to the Aegean and Istanbul also runs through Macedonia. But it is above all the Vardar route which has made possession of Macedonia – most of which is backward and poor even by Balkan standards – so much coveted by rival claimants.

By far the most important town of this territory, in fact its only wealthy city, is Salonika. The next most important, a long way behind, is Skopje, capital of Yugoslav Macedonia. Otherwise the towns of Macedonia, whatever their historical interest or beauty, are small country market towns, such as Florina, Kastoria, and Seres in Greece; Bitola (Monastir), Veles, and Ochrid in Yugoslavia; Gorna Djumaja and Petrich in Bulgaria.

Until 1923, a bare majority of the population of Macedonia was Slav. This is now no longer true of Macedonia as a whole, because of the influx of Greek settlers into Greek Macedonia after the Greek-Turkish war. But in Yugoslav and Bulgarian Macedonia taken together, Slavs still form over three-quarters of the population. It is the national identity of these Slav Macedonians that has been the most violently contested aspect of the whole Macedonian dispute, and is still being contested today.

There is no doubt that they are southern Slavs; they have a language, or a group of varying dialects, that is grammatically akin to Bulgarian but phonetically in some respects akin to Serbian, and which has certain quite distinctive features of its own. The Slav Macedonians are said to have retained one custom which is usually regarded as typically Serbian – the Slava, or family celebration of the day on which the family ancestor was converted to Christianity. In regard to their own national feelings, all that can safely be said is that during the last eighty years many more Slav Macedonians seem to have considered themselves Bulgarian, or closely linked with Bulgaria, than have considered themselves Serbian, or closely linked with Serbia (or Yugoslavia). Only the people of the Skopje region, in the north-west, have ever shown much tendency to regard themselves as Serbs. The feeling of being Macedonians, and nothing but Macedonians, seems to be a sentiment of fairly recent growth, and even today is not very deep-rooted.

Their neighbours have, inevitably, had conflicting views about the Slav Macedonians. The Bulgarians have fluctuated between saying that all Slav Macedonians were Bulgarians and declaring that there was a separate Macedonian people, according to the needs or convenience of the moment. The official Serbian (or Yugoslav) policy up to 1941 was to say that all Slav Macedonians were Serbians, and to call Yugoslav Macedonia 'South Serbia'. However, between the two wars certain opposition politicians of Yugoslavia, such as Svetozar Pribiceviç, declared that the Macedonians were a separate people; and this theory is the basis of Marshal Tito's policy. The Greeks, in common speech, call their Slav Macedonian minority 'Bulgarians', but in official language 'Slavophone Greeks'. (When in September 1924, by the Kalfov-Politis Protocol, Greece prepared to recognise her Slav Macedonians as a 'Bulgarian' minority, she met with a strong protest from the Yugoslav government and abandoned the idea.)[1]

In addition to the Slavs, there are also in Macedonia Greeks (now about one-half of the total population of Macedonia as a whole), and lesser elements of Albanians, Turks, Jews, and the Vlachs, or Kutzo-Vlachs. (The Vlachs speak a form of Latin dialect akin to Roumanian, belong to the Orthodox Church, and are mainly shepherds living in western Macedonia. The Roumanian government took a lively interest in them at the beginning of this century, but few of them have ever played a very active part in Macedonian affairs.)

The Turkish census of 1905 of the three vilayets roughly comprising the territory of Macedonia obviously gave a greatly exaggerated number of Moslems, which is omitted here, but it is of interest for its estimate of the relative numbers of Greeks, Serbs, and Bulgarians, reckoned on a Church basis and not on a language basis:[2]

Greeks	.	.	.	.	648,962
Bulgars	.	.	.	.	557,734
Serbs	.	.	.	.	167,601

Perhaps one-half of the estimated number of 'Greeks' must at that period have been Slavs who had remained loyal to the Greek Patriarchate in spite of the wooing of the Bulgarian Exarchate and, to a lesser extent, of the Serbian Orthodox Church. What is significant is the preponderance of 'Bulgars' over 'Serbs': the Bulgarian Exarchate at that time had clearly kept the lead over the Serbian Church which it won in 1870.

In 1912, at the time of the Balkan Wars, a reliable estimate of the population, reckoned on a language basis, not a religious basis, was:

Slavs	.	.	.	.	1,150,000
Turks	.	.	.	.	400,000

Greeks	.	.	.	.	.	300,000
Vlachs	.	.	.	.	.	200,000
Albanians	.	.	.	.	.	120,000
Jews	.	.	.	.	.	100,000

The Greek–Turkish exchange of populations in the 1920s completely altered these proportions, because 348,000 Turks left and over 600,000 Greeks arrived in Macedonia. The 1928 Greek official census gave the following figures for Greek Macedonia.[3]

Greeks	.	.	.	.	.	1,237,000
'Slavophones'	.	.	.	.	82,000
Others	.	.	.	.	.	93,000

A reliable estimate of the position just before the last war, in Macedonia as a whole, was:

Greeks	.	.	.	.	.	1,260,000
Slavs	.	.	.	.	.	1,090,000
Others (Albanians, Turks, Jews, and Vlachs)		.	.	.	440,000

According to this estimate, the Slavs were distributed as follows: 750,000 in Yugoslav Macedonia, 220,000 in Bulgarian Macedonia, 120,000 in Greek Macedonia.

If this estimate is accepted, then, allowing for natural increase, the total population of Macedonia as a whole must now (1949) be close on 3 million. Of these about one-half are Greeks living in Greek Macedonia, and about two-fifths are Slavs living in Yugoslav and Bulgarian Macedonia and spilling over into the north-west corner of Greek Macedonia. The other elements live mainly in Yugoslav Macedonia.

Historical background of the dispute

The Slavs first came to Macedonia, where they found a mainly Greek-speaking population, in the sixth century AD. Before then the inhabitants of Macedonia had been under Greek influence from the ninth century BC until the second century BC; then they were under Roman influence, and from the fourth century AD onwards under Byzantine influence.

In the seventh century AD the Bulgars followed the Slavs into the Balkans, and soon started their struggle against Byzantium. In the second half of the ninth century, the Bulgarian, Tsar Boris, overran part of Macedonia, and in the early part of the tenth century the Bulgarian, Tsar Simeon, gained possession of the whole of it, except the Aegean coast. In the latter part of the tenth century, after a brief return to Byzantium, Tsar Samuel – whom Serb historians claim as the first 'Macedonian' Tsar[4] – won a far-reaching empire, including Macedonia; but it fell back into the hands of Byzantium. It was at this period that a Bulgarian Patriarchate was first established at Ochrid.

After that, Macedonia, or parts of it, were alternately under Bulgarian or Byzantine rule until the thirteenth and fourteenth centuries. Then the country came under the Serbian Tsars, of whom the greatest was Stephan Dushan, who made Skopje his capital. In 1346 the Archbishop of Serbia took the title of 'Patriarch of the Serbs and Greeks'. But on the death of Stephan Dushan the Serbian Empire broke up. The Turks invaded the Balkans; and in 1371 Macedonia came under Turkish suzerainty.

In 1459 the Turks suppressed the Serbian Orthodox Patriarchate and placed the administration of the Church under the Bulgarian Archbishopric of Ochrid. But in practice the Archbishops were by that time Greeks. In 1557 the Serbian Patriarchate was restored with its seat at Ipek; but in 1766 it was again suppressed. In 1777 the Bulgarian Archbishopric of Ochrid ceased to be an autocephalous church, and the Turks placed the Greek patriarchate in control of both Slav churches. Thus from this time until 1870 Greek clergy had spiritual control of the Orthodox population of Macedonia.

Nearly ten centuries of national-ecclesiastical wrangles, which the Turks had skilfully exploited, were the local background to the creation of the Bulgarian Exarchate in 1870. During the nineteenth century they had taken on an increasingly nationalist character, as the Serbs and Greeks achieved at least partial liberation from the Turks, and the Bulgarians experienced their national awakening in which individual Macedonians played a considerable part. At the same time the great Powers, fearing or hoping for the ultimate collapse of the Ottoman Empire, became intensely interested in the Balkans; and by 1870 Russia had chosen Bulgaria as the best channel for expansion of her influence. Thus the Macedonian dispute began.

It developed quickly. In 1872 the new Bulgarian Church acquired the 'eparchies' or additional ecclesiastical districts of Skopje and

Ochrid; this was in accordance with Article 10 of the Turkish decree of 1870 by which districts where two-thirds of the population wished to join the Exarchate might do so after proper investigation. In the same year the Greek Patriarchate declared the Bulgarian Exarchate schismatic. The Bulgarians, however, seized their chance to send Bulgarian priests, usually ardent nationalists, throughout Slav Macedonia, and to send Bulgarian teachers to set up Bulgarian schools. The Greeks, and later the Serbians, retaliated with the same methods. Serbia's effort was hampered by her war with Turkey in 1876 and by her subsequent marked unpopularity with the Turks; but she did her best.

Later the pioneer priests and teachers were backed up by armed bands, whom the Turks called 'komitadjis', or 'committee men'. These were unofficially sponsored by the governments or War Offices of Sofia, Athens, and Belgrade. Although the bands were theoretically formed to struggle against the Turks, they more often – Bulgarians, Greeks, and Serbs – attacked each other, and sometimes betrayed each other to the Turkish authorities.

The Macedonian dispute was injected with a large dose of venom by the Treaty of San Stefano in 1878, which Russia imposed on Turkey after the Russo–Turkish war. This gave Bulgaria enormously inflated frontiers which have haunted Bulgarian nationalist dreams ever since – even, perhaps, the dreams of Bulgarian Communists. It awarded her nearly all Slav Macedonia, including Vranje, Skopje, Tetovo, Gostivar, the Black Drin, Debar, and Lake Ochrid; a strip of what is now southeast Albania, including Korca; and, in what is now Greek Macedonia, Kastoria, Florina, Ostrovo, and a small strip of the Aegean coast west of Salonika. It was a startlingly large gift to receive even at Russia's hands; but before the year was out it was taken away again by the other great Powers, who compelled Russia to abandon San Stefano and to negotiate the Treaty of Berlin, which restored Macedonia to Turkey once again.

The Treaty of Berlin, while it provided for guarantees of religious liberties in Macedonia and elsewhere, left Bulgaria with a burning grudge and undamped ambitions. After 1878 she even succeeded in adding several more bishoprics to the Exarchate. In 1895, Macedonian refugees in Sofia founded a 'Supreme Committee' to organise the struggle for the 'liberation' of Macedonia, which, to the Committee, meant its annexation to Bulgaria. This Committee soon became closely linked with the Bulgarian government and Crown. Next year, however, a more genuinely Macedonian body was formed: the Internal Macedonian Revolutionary Organisation, led by two Macedonians, both nationalist-minded school-teachers, Damian Gruev and Gotse Delchev.

From the early days of IMRO there were always two trends, or two wings, in the movement. The one tended towards closest collaboration with the Supreme Committee, and through it with the Bulgarian War Office and the Bulgarian Tsar. This wing only used talk of Macedonian autonomy or independence as a cloak for its real aim of Bulgarian annexation of Macedonia. In ideological terms, it later developed into the extreme nationalist right wing of the movement; and, apart from a brief deviation to the left in 1924, it became the bitter enemy not only of the Communists but also of the left-wing Bulgarian Agrarian movement.

The other trend in IMRO was towards genuine autonomy or independence for Macedonia. In the early days of the movement, this wing preached brotherhood of all the peoples of Macedonia, not only Slavs but also Turks, Albanians, and Greeks,[5] and it tried to preserve a certain independence of the Supreme Committee and the Bulgarian War Office. Nevertheless Bulgaria was its main source or channel for arms and money; so this independence was limited. Later this trend developed into the left wing of the movement: after the First World War many of its members either became 'Federalists', advocating an autonomous Macedonia within a South Slav Federation, or else Communists, and the name of IMRO was left to the pro-Bulgarian right wing. Yet even then there continued to be left-wing tendencies within the rump IMRO.

IMRO at first worked in secret, organising and arming the population of Macedonia and setting up a kind of shadow administration of its own. Then in August 1903 it came into the open in the 'Ilinden' (St Elijah's Day) rising against the Turkish garrisons and officials in Macedonia. According to some accounts, this rising was forced by the Bulgarian War Office (acting on Russian encouragement) on the hesitant leaders of IMRO, who thought that the time was not yet ripe for open action. In any case, after initial successes the insurgents were ruthlessly crushed by the Turkish army. According to Bulgarian figures,[6] 9,830 houses were burned down and 60,953 people left homeless.

The rising at least succeeded in bringing about the somewhat ineffectual intervention of the great Powers in Macedonia. Russia and Austria-Hungary agreed in October 1903 on reforms for Macedonia, and got the other great Powers to consent to the creation of an international gendarmerie for the territory. Under this scheme, which led to considerable friction between the participants, all the great Powers except Germany took control of a gendarmerie zone in Macedonia.[7] In 1905 Britain tried to secure international supervision of tax collection in Macedonia, and this proposal was finally accepted, under heavy pressure, by Turkey. In the summer of 1908 Britain and Russia seemed on the verge of agreeing to a fresh scheme for reforms in Macedonia; but in July the Young Turk revolution broke out, and attempts by the great Powers to intervene in Macedonia were dropped on the grounds that the new rulers of Turkey were liberals. However, the Young Turks, after initial promises of progress, turned out to be extreme nationalists, and the lot of the Macedonians was somewhat worse than before the revolution.

In October 1908 King Ferdinand had, by agreement with Austria-Hungary, proclaimed the full independence of Bulgaria, while to the fury of Serbia, Austria had annexed Bosnia-Hercegovina. Great Power relations over the Balkans became extremely strained, but war was narrowly averted. The chief result of the crisis was to impel both Serbia and Bulgaria, for different reasons, into the arms of Russia.

Then in 1912 came a unique occurrence. The small Balkan Powers, Greece, Serbia, and Bulgaria, sank their differences over Macedonia, and, together with Montenegro, formed an alliance, defied the great Powers who said they would permit no change in the *status quo*, and drove the Turks out of Macedonia.

The factors which had helped to bring about this alliance were, first, that Russia had succeeded in temporarily reconciling Bulgaria and Serbia,[8] and then that Greece had found in Venezelos an unusually enterprising and broad-minded Prime Minister. The shakiest aspect of the alliance was the Serbo-Bulgarian Agreement of 3 March 1912 on the partition of Macedonia. Under this agreement, Bulgaria was to get all territory east of the Rhodope Mountains and the River Struma; Serbia was to get everything west and north of the Shar Mountains. As for the disputed area between, the two parties agreed on a line running from south-west to north-east, starting from Lake Ochrid, and running, between Skopje and Veles, to a point just north of Kustendil. Serbia undertook to make no claim south east of this line, while Bulgaria undertook to accept the line provided that the Russian Tsar arbitrated in its favour.

This line would perhaps have given the fairest settlement of Macedonia – based on partition and not autonomy – that has ever been proposed. The Bulgarians might have resented the loss of Skopje to Serbia, but they would have received reasonable compensation in the south-east half of Slav Macedonia where the population was most nearly Bulgarian.

The Greek-Bulgarian Treaty of May 1912 made no territorial arrangements, so that Greece's share of Macedonia was left undefined. It is interesting that none of the three Balkan States apparently ever thought that Macedonia, once liberated from the Turks, should be independent or autonomous. That may have been because after forty years of their three-sided cultural, ecclesiastical, and armed struggle for power in Macedonia, none of the three could imagine the existence of a genuinely independent Macedonia free from outside intervention.

The course of the fighting in the First Balkan War unfortunately wiped out the agreed Serb–Bulgarian south-west – north-east line in Macedonia. While the Bulgarians were busy conquering Thrace, the Serbs advanced beyond the line and occupied the main part of the Vardar Valley; and the Greeks took southern Macedonia and Salonika. Because the great Powers decided that Serbia must abandon the northern Albanian territory which she had also occupied, Serbia demanded more than her agreed share of Macedonia as compensation. Bulgaria demanded her agreed share of Macedonia and also claimed that the Greeks had advanced too far. The Russian Tsar was not asked to arbitrate. After war-like preparations by all parties, Bulgaria launched an attack. Serbia and Greece counter-attacked by mutual agreement, and Turkey and Roumania also set upon Bulgaria. Bulgaria was badly defeated and, by the Treaty of Bucharest of August 1913, managed to retain, of Macedonia, only the middle Struma Valley, the upper Mesta Valley, and a westward-jutting salient in the Strumica Valley. Serbia kept all the territory she had occupied; this, except for the Strumica salient, was the same as Yugoslavia acquired after the First World War.

The Treaty of Bucharest was inevitably as a bad blow not only to the Bulgarian government and people but also to the Macedonian 'Supreme Committee' and to IMRO, many of whose members had fought with the Bulgarian army. Bulgaria had lost all but a small corner of Macedonia; and Macedonia, though liberated from the Turks, was neither autonomous nor independent. Thus neither wing of IMRO had any satisfaction.

When the First World War broke out in 1914, it was clear that Bulgaria would eventually join the side which offered her the largest share of Macedonia. The Entente, which was allied with Serbia, found it difficult to make any handsome offer. In September 1915 they suggested that Bulgaria might be content with the territory east of the River Vardar, together with an exchange of populations. But this bid was not high enough and Bulgaria joined the central European Powers, who, according to some accounts, had already been working closely for some months with IMRO.[9]

Bulgaria occupied the whole of Serbian Macedonia and the eastern section of Greek Macedonia. Many Macedonians served in the Bulgarian Army and a number of IMRO's leading members (including Dimiter Vlahov, thirty years later a member of Marshal Tito's Government) became administrative officials in Macedonia. There was, apparently, no talk of Macedonian autonomy; it was generally assumed that Serbian Macedonia was simply annexed to Bulgaria. The Bulgarian authorities set to work 'Bulgarising' the Slavs of Macedonia, and incidentally forcing them to change their surname suffixes to '-ov'.

In 1918 the situation was again reversed. The central Powers were defeated. A well-known IMRO leader, Protogerov, then Commandant of Sofia, prevented Bulgarian army deserters (led by the Bulgarian army deserters (led by the Bulgarian Agrarian, Stambuliski) from invading the capital. But IMRO could not prevent Stambuliski from becoming Prime Minister of a defeated Bulgaria, which had lost not only all Serbian Macedonia as defined by the Treaty of Bucharest, but also the Strumica salient, and 'Aegean Macedonia' as well.

Thus at the end of the First World War, Macedonia was partitioned into three. A resentful Bulgaria was left with only a small corner (6,798 square kilometres); while Yugoslavia, with 26,776 square kilometres, and Greece, with 34,600 square kilometres, each had a large share; and Greek Macedonia then still had a large Slav-speaking population. It was not surprising that in these circumstances Bulgaria became the base for Macedonian terrorist activities which poisoned her relations with the new Yugoslavia, and to a lesser extent with Greece, for the next quarter of a century.

Notes

1. A. A. Pallis, 'Macedonia and the Macedonians, a Historical Study' (mimeographed publication issued through the Greek Information Office, London, 15 April 1949).
2. *Ibid.*
3. Pallis, 'Macedonia and the Macedonians'.
4. T. R. Georgevitch, *Macedonia* (London, Allen & Unwin, 1918), chap. III.
5. The first article of its rules and regulations was: 'Everyone who lives in European Turkey, regardless of sex, nationality, or personal beliefs, may become a member of IMRO.'

6. G. Bazhdaroff, *The Macedonian Question* (Sofia, Macedonian National Committee in Bulgaria, 1926), p. 13.
7. A. J. Grant and H. W. V. Temperley, *Europe in the Nineteenth and Twentieth Centuries* (London, Longmans, 1939), p. 452.
8. Grant and Temperley, *Europe in the Nineteenth and Twentieth Centuries*, p. 472.
9. J. Swire, *Bulgarian Conspiracy* (London, Hale, 1939), p. 133.

Chapter 2

The new Macedonian question*

James Pettifer

All Balkan territorial disputes have their mythologies; that of the Macedonian question is that of the most bloody, complex and intractable of all, in a small peninsula already well burdened. But it was also the conflict that, perhaps more than any other, socialist Yugoslavia seemed to have superseded. So what gave rise to some of the most acute political turmoil of the inter-war period, particularly the recurrent Macedonian assassinations and bombings, seemed to have been 'solved' by Tito's creation. It is in its way appropriate, then, that it is only with the final demise of Yugoslavia, symbolised by international recognition of the independent Croatian state, that the new Macedonian problem is emerging.

The purpose of this chapter is not to try to put forward any blueprint for 'solution' of the issue; that would be wholly inappropriate, as the outlines of the new 'Macedonian' state are only becoming apparent, and it is very far from clear what shape many aspects of its political and military orientation will take. All that is possible is to try to indicate what the basis of the old Question was, and to suggest some comparisons with the past and present; and in that light to try to see what the problems for the international community may be. There is every indication that the process of remaking the Balkans is spreading southwards; and the centre of gravity of events may soon focus on Macedonia, as it has done in the past, and it will be disturbing if international attention is distracted from this process simply because armed conflict between Serbia and Croatia has been brought to an end, at least at the time of writing.

---

* Originally published in *International Affairs* (London), vol. 68, no. 3 (1992) and is reproduced with permission.

Macedonia: the Eastern Question, and the shortage of Macedonians

In one sense, Macedonia throughout the nineteenth century was no different from its four immediate neighbours, Serbia, Greece, Albania and Bulgaria, in that all these peoples were struggling to throw off rule from Constantinople and the declining power of the Sublime Porte. In the different phases of the Eastern Question the standing of the different candidate nation-states waxed and waned, generally linked to the power of their larger non-Balkan backers and different diplomatic imperatives, arising in many cases from events far outside the Balkans themselves. Throughout the peninsula border issues were paramount, for as the distribution of population under the old Ottoman system of government was determined on the *millet* system, where religion rather than race or language was taken as the basis of administrative organisation, existing Ottoman governmental divisions often bore little relation to the aspirations of the majority of the inhabitants living within them.

But unlike Serbia or Greece, in Macedonia there was no basically homogeneous population that could form the basis of a new nation-state. There was, however, and still is, a plainly dominant majority in the cultural sense, in that there are more people of Slavonic origin living there than of any other group – but only within a patchwork of extreme complexity, with Turks, Greeks, Albanians, Vlachs, Pomaks and Gypsies living alongside the Slavonic majority; and, moreover, that majority is itself subdivided into Serbian, Bulgarian and 'Macedonian' elements.

Under the Ottoman regime no detailed statistics were kept of the Macedonian population, and substantial changes in numbers were caused by the Balkan wars of 1912 and 1913. But according to Foreign Office papers from 1918 there were in the ethnic territory of Macedonia, before 1912, about 1,150,000 Slavs, 400,000 Turks, 120,000 Albanians, 300,000 Greeks, 200,000 Vlachs, 100,000 Jews and 10,000 Gypsies. Although these figures would probably be disputed, then and now, by partisans of the different nationalities, there seems to be no reason why they should not be taken as at least a rough approximation of the position at that time.

Although there have been substantial changes since, they have not produced a more homogeneous population, merely changed the mixture. Given the problems with recent Yugoslav censuses, in which boycotts for political reasons have been common, figures now are no more exact than they were in 1912, but the main developments have been the near total disappearance of the Jewish community as a result of

Nazi persecution, a greatly reduced Vlach presence due to the heavy losses this community of pastoralists suffered in the second Balkan war, and subsequent assimiliation, a substantial increase in numbers of Gypsies, a very great increase in numbers of Albanians, a reduction in those of Greeks, a stable Turkish presence, a small immigration of northern ex-Yugoslav groups such as Croats and Montenegrins, and the open split of the Slavonic group into Serbian and Macedonian identities. There were also, until very recently, some people who preferred to regard themselves as Yugoslavs.

According to the 1981 Yugoslav census, probably the last where figures have any substance before the whole process was vitiated by political manipulation, the population of the Socialist Republic of Macedonia was 1,912,257 of whom 1,281,195 were Macedonians, 377,726 Albanians, 44,613 Serbs, 39,555 Pomaks, 47,223 Gypsies, 86,691 Turks, 7,190 Vlachs and 1,984 Bulgarians, plus a small number of people from six other ethnic groups. The main change since then has been the inexorable rise in Albanian numbers, which may now amount to as much as a quarter of the whole population, with a disproportionate age bias towards youth so that over the next 20 years or so the Albanian element is certain to increase further. The overall shortage of Macedonians is compounded by the fact that some ethnic groups, particularly the Vlachs, have tended to call themselves Macedonians if they have become urbanised, while retaining a *de facto* Vlach identity in cultural and domestic life, particularly if, until recently, they were country-dwellers.

What is most important about these figures is that they indicate a consistent and unresolved problem for any Macedonian state based on Skopje, whether before the First World War or now, in that a predominantly urban political elite of Macedonians is ruling over a country where they have almost no presence at all in very large rural areas (for example, the Albanian regions of western Macedonia), and that in nearly all these cases, like that of the Pirin Bulgarophile Slav population, the non-Macedonian minority is, or has been, wooed by the neighbouring nation-state. This is the origin of the famous Macedonian fear of the 'Four Wolves' which surround the country: Greece, Albania, Bulgaria and Serbia. Although now all four neighbouring states have said that they have no claim on Macedonian territory, there are substantial political parties in all of them, with the partial exception of Greece, who do have claims over Macedonian territory or who want a revision of the position of their compatriot minorities that would have a profoundly destabilising effect on the new Macedonia.

The original Macedonian question: the heritage of IMRO

The seminal date for the original issue was 1878, after the Treaty of Berlin had overthrown the short-lived 'Greater Bulgaria' established by the Treaty of San Stefano. Under the earlier treaty much of what is now Macedonia had been given to Bulgaria, but the great powers, fearful of the possibility that a Greater Bulgaria could dominate the whole peninsula, had subsequently changed their minds. The first phase of the question is dominated by the efforts of a revisionist Bulgaria to recover what was lost in 1878. At the same time Serbia was actively expansionist in the south, calling Macedonia 'South Serbia' and establishing Serbian schools and churches there. Greek policy followed a similar pattern dominated by the breach in Orthodox ranks many years before, caused by the establishment of the Bulgarian Exarchate in 1870. About 1,400 Greek schools existed by 1895 while Vlachs, speaking a language related to Romanian, had persuaded the Bucharest government to pay for over 30 Vlach language schools.

Underlying the vigorous cultural struggle for the allegiance of the population was a much deeper and longer history, on the Greek side at least. Although it is difficult for non-Greeks to understand, as the generally negative international reaction to Greek objections to EC recognition of Macedonian independence has shown, the existence of Macedonia as a part of Greece has a fundamental place in the Greek political psyche. Alexander the Great was a Macedonian and the period of his empire has a much greater hold on the Greek popular imagination than outsiders can easily appreciate. There is, of course, some dispute about the Greekness of the world of Alexander, and numerous volumes have been produced by partisans of the different nationalities to prove or disprove particular arguments. The best known statement of the Greek position is made by Dascalakis in his book *The Hellenism of the Ancient Macedonians*,[1] in which he sets out very fully the literary and archeological evidence as he sees it. Slav scholars usually concentrate their arguments on the passage in Plutarch where the ancient historian describes the struggles that took place between Alexander's successors, referring to the troops as 'shouting in Macedonian'. The Slav lobbyists usually conclude that this shows the existence of an autochthonous Macedonian people who were colonised by a Greek-speaking ruling class. And so on. Like many other academic disputes, the shortage of evidence means that both sides can continue their polemics more or less indefinitely. But in terms of practical political rhetoric, the disputes are very important and very much alive, particularly those aspects of them which threaten to disturb normal Greek assumptions about the nature of Greek identity throughout recorded history being based on the use of the Greek language. Another point which should be borne in mind when considering what may at first sight seem to be the exaggerated Greek response to the new state is the traditional Greek fear of instability and invasion coming from the north. Generally speaking, nearly all invasions of Greece from the time of the Slavs in the Dark Ages to the German and Italian motorised divisions of the Second World War have followed the same routes down through the northern mountain passes towards Athens, with similar results. For Greeks, the Macedonian problem awakens ancestral fears that had been conveniently forgotten for many years after the improvement of relations with Tito's Yugoslavia and the end of the Greek civil war. They are not, of course, fears of invasion at the moment, merely of chronic instability and involvement in Balkan feuds; but the fears are nonetheless real. The border of northern Greece with Albania, Macedonia and Bulgaria is very long, and the Greek army and police will be very stretched to defend it in the event of a breakdown of good relations with the states to the north.

So in terms of the neighbours of the new Macedonia, the heritage of the Internal Macedonian Revolutionary Organisation (IMRO) is represented by the creation of a new political vacuum as much as anything else. The type of Greater Macedonia that was envisaged by the nineteenth-century nationalists was a much larger state than the present one, with an opening to an Aegean port. The problem now is best summed up in one sentence, uttered to me by an inhabitant of Skopje not long after the independence referendum last autumn: 'What are we going to build a new state with? Tobacco plants?'

Whatever political complexion the new state may have, the underlying realities are likely to be dominated by the extreme economic weakness of the country, and it is apparent that many Serbs in Belgrade still feel that this critical weakness may mean that Macedonia eventually, or perhaps quickly, will have to come back towards some sort of new Yugoslav federation, led by Serbia, as the only means of Macedonian economic survival. There are few competitive modern industries, and it is unfortunate that agriculture is dominated by the production of a single crop, tobacco (and high-tar tobacco at that), which is already in oversupply within the EC. The actual condition of the soil is frequently poor, with over-cultivation and soil erosion common problems, and although extensive investment could generate substantial improvements in production, the means to accomplish this is not in sight.

Foreign exchange reserves to back the new denar are almost non-existent, and there seems to be a strong possibility that in the absence of a stable and internationally recognised Macedonian currency to replace the almost worthless ex-Yugoslav dinar, the currencies of the adjoining states will circulate in neighbouring Macedonian regions and become the *de facto* currency of those parts of Macedonia. There is some evidence of this happening already in the Pirin area adjoining Bulgaria. No great leap of the imagination is required to see the likely political consequences that flow from this, where the regions concerned start to look towards Sofia or Thessaloniki, rather than Skopje, for economic and political leadership. But whatever form this process takes, it is likely that one of the central respects in which the new Macedonian question will differ from the old will have to do with the primacy of economic survival. The Macedonia that IMRO envisaged in the nineteenth century would have consisted almost entirely of semi-subsistence peasants and pastoralists: and Macedonian tobacco was worth, proportionately, a good deal more then than it is now. That entity would not have had the pretensions of a modern industrialised state within Western Europe, which is perhaps the Achilles heel of the new nation. This is despite the fact that throughout the Yugoslav era, Macedonia was at the bottom of the federal heap in every way, in terms of wage or output levels, literacy, social and educational provision, or any other measure. The non-party government of experts at present in power in Skopje has in effect placed its salvation at Brussels' door. If no investment and economic help from the EC of the scale needed to transform the situation is forthcoming, then the policies of Macedonia's neighbours will be crucial in determining the future. The government sees this process as having two main stages, the first concerned with getting widespread international recognition of statehood, by the EC in particular, which the second, international investment, will follow. But in the absence of recognition, the power of Macedonia's neighbours will be decisive.

Albania, Greece, Serbia and Bulgaria: wolves or lambs?

It is not possible to set out in full detail the positions of all the different significant currents of opinion in all four of these countries towards the new Macedonian state; all that is attempted below is a general survey of the main factors that are likely to affect the situation in the immediate future.

Albania

In Albania, the formation of the new state has been welcomed, primarily because it is seen as a counterweight to Serbia and an irritant to Greece. Cultural relations were reasonably close for some time under Tito and the latter years of Yugoslavia, and although recently the Albanian government has taken up the human rights issues raised by the Albanian minority in Macedonia, as their position compares favourably with the very bad conditions endured by the Albanians in Serbian-ruled Kosovo, the issue has not been pursued very energetically. But Albanian nationalism is growing, particularly in the northern parts of western Macedonia adjoining Kosovo where Albanians dominate, in population terms. A referendum held in January this year produced an overwhelming majority for Albanian autonomy. The *de facto* border imposed between Kosovo and Skopje by the Yugoslav federal army has been strongly resented. There are also growing trade links with Albania proper, for despite the appalling problems of the Albanian economy, there is a reasonable amount of hard currency in circulation there, which can be used to pay for many Macedonian goods that with the collapse of inter-Yugoslav trade arrangements had become almost unsaleable. Quite sizeable quantities of wine, for instance, are being imported into Albania. But it should be noted that this trade, as elsewhere, depends on the availability of hard, or at least, respected currency, in the neighbouring state. It is also axiomatic that little if any of the revenue generated will find its way back to the government in Skopje, in any shape or form.

It appears that for the time being, at least, in terms of the regional dimension of the Macedonian issue, the Albanian government will try to achieve supportive and good relations with the new state. If hostilities develop between Albania and Serbia over Kosovo, which is a very real possibility and accounts for much of the current concern in Tirana over army re-equipment, Macedonia will become strategically important to both parties, and at the moment Tirana is unlikely to back the claims of the Tetovo-based Albanian parties in Macedonia too far. That said, relations in Macedonia between the Albanian minority and Skopje are poor, and worsening. The boycott of the original independence referendum by the Albanians in September 1991 was felt to be very much a stab in the back, and there have been calls in some quarters for the two Albanian parties to be banned. Although there are one or two Albanians at high levels in the new government, in general they are excluded from most important decision-making processes in Skopje. A particularly critical issue will be the composition of the new

35,000-strong Macedonian army which the government is in the process of creating. It appears that few, if any, Albanians will be allowed in senior positions. Since the parties representing ethnic Albanians are dissatisfied with the number of ethnic Albanian officers in the new army, they have called on the youth to boycott conscription. But by and large, Macedonia is not a central issue in Albanian politics at the moment, and this is likely to remain the case for the immediate future.

Greece

In Greece, the demise of Yugoslavia was accepted later and with more reluctance than in almost any other state in the world. Important Greek trade routes pass through Yugoslavia, and Yugoslav stability was important for many economic reasons. But the economic problem, critically serious for only a short phase of the Yugoslav crisis which resulted in the loss of most of a year's peach exports, pale into insignificance beside the emergence of the new proto-Macedonian state – a development which all Greek politicians would have regarded as unthinkable as recently as nine months previously. The problems regarding the ancient cultural heritage have been referred to above. A more potent heritage, in terms of recent history, is the legacy of bitterness from the civil war, in which many of the Slav-speaking minority of northern Greece became active communists and in particular were deeply involved in the guerrilla army. It has been estimated that there were as many as 40,000 Slav-speakers in the communist forces in the last phase of the civil war that ended in 1949. Many went into exile in Skopje, and have risen to influential positions. There is an element of revenge, here, in the view of some in Athens. Across the mainstream political spectrum it has been suggested that the left-wing side in the civil war was some sort of minority Slav conspiracy, rather than a mass movement that had widespread support throughout Greece only two or three years before. In addition to reopening a difficult international and regional issue, the new Macedonian question also risks reopening some of the wounds and unresolved internal controversies in Greece arising from the civil war and how it was won by the Right with foreign support. There are also difficult questions for the Greeks concerning human rights issues in relation to the treatment of the remaining Slav speakers left in Greece after the civil war. In the far north, the writ of Athens has seldom ever run easily, and turmoil and border problems of the kind now appearing may stretch the fabric of Greek democracy itself. There have already been accusations of quite serious human rights abuses against Greek security forces on the Albanian border. But equally, there is a growth of banditry in these regions, with armed gangs making raids into Greece, and a deterioration in the economy of already poor northern cities such as Florina. A strong mood of militant Greek nationalism is developing across the political spectrum, tinged with popular concern, at the apparent failure of the Athens politicians to deal with the Macedonian problem firmly enough in its early stages.

The official responses of the Greek government to the emergence of Macedonia are well known and have been well publicised in the last few months. The Greek approach has been to use whatever leverage it can within the EC to prevent recognition of a state called 'Macedonia' and to attempt to base diplomatic initiatives on the assumption that some sort of new Yugoslav federation may well emerge that will include Macedonia as a component part. In essence, this differs little from the previous policy of backing Serbia to the hilt, and there is a general correspondence between Athens and the main currents of Serbian thinking in Belgrade. The private visit made to Athens by the Serbian president in March this year to discuss the synchronisation of policy is very significant. But it must be very doubtful how much longer this policy can remain viable. The first major victim has been the Greek foreign minister, Mr Samaras, who was sacked in April this year by prime minister Mitsotakis for taking a hard line over Macedonian recognition, in line with the wishes of EC leaders eager for a settlement. But Mitsotakis miscalculated the degree of feeling against recognition among the Greek public and was forced into a vote of confidence in parliament which was only survived with some difficulty. With a majority of only two in parliament, and a substantial body of opinion in the New Democratic Party (ND) supporting the positions of Mr Samaras (particularly members from northern Greek constituencies), the Macedonian issue is clearly capable of bringing down the government. It should also be noted that the Greek President, Mr Karamanlis, is of Macedonian origin.

At some point in the short term, the Greeks will be forced into an open choice between the EC and Serbia, but it should not be assumed that the Greek public will easily back the European line: preparations for the Single Market, with the austerity programme monitored by EC officials in Athens leading to some quite dramatic rises in the cost of living, and a resurgence of support for the PASOK opposition, which would probably be returned to power if an election were held now, has increased the unpopularity of the EC in Greece.

But however the issue is dealt with in the short term in Athens, it is presumably clear in Brussels that without major external assistance the new Macedonia is likely to collapse economically, and there is no prospect whatsoever of international investment in a state that does not have diplomatic recognition, as the shadowy existence of the 'Turkish Republic of Northern Cyprus' has shown. The prospects for democracy would also be as poor. In the light of the developing crisis in Bosnia, there is no reason to suppose that the re-integration of Macedonia into a new Yugoslav federation is practicable. The federal army has been systematically withdrawing from Macedonia, and border posts, even with Albania, are now controlled by Macedonian officials. In so far as the federal army is the decisive force on the ground, it shows every sign at the moment of being willing to abandon Macedonia to its fate.

Unfortunately some early actions of the Skopje government have been insensitive to Greek concerns, especially the draft banknote design showing a prominent historic building in Thessaloniki as 'Macedonian', at least by implication.

Although there are well-founded rumours of splits in the Greek foreign policy establishment over Macedonia, it is hard to see what new policy could be formed without abandoning vital Greek positions, as Mr Mitsotakis discovered in April. The disputes with the EC have fundamentally affected public opinion, and he has little room to manoeuvre. In the immediate future, the most important developments affecting Macedonia are likely to be in Greece, as the government there attempts to find some compromise between European pressures and domestic viewpoints. As in other problem areas of the Balkans recently, the EC has on this issue often seemed deeply insensitive to the legitimate concerns of people about their cultural identity, to the detriment of the EC's political influence.

Serbia

In Serbia, the government does not at the moment appear strong enough to risk a confrontation with Skopje, in particular given the care with which the Macedonians have attempted to proceed in such a way as to avoid war. Although there is a single substantial Serbian enclave in Macedonia, at Kumanovo, the inhabitants do not at present seem to feel threatened and have not resorted to the proclamations of armed 'independent' Serbian 'republics' that have so bedevilled peace efforts in the north, although pro-autonomy referenda have been held in some places. Serbs have traditionally controlled some of the most prominent economic enterprises in Skopje, and in some cases seem to be turning themselves into honorary Macedonians, in order to benefit from the privatisation process. How long this uneasy equilibrium will last is doubtful.

The main dimension of Serbian policy is to allow Macedonia to become a dependent statelet; but if any of the surrounding powers, especially Bulgaria, increased their influence in Skopje dramatically, or took matters as far as territorial revision, then Belgrade would consider itself forced to act. At the moment Serbian interests are served by a policy of inactivity, with the hope in the background that Macedonia will fail to become a viable state and will turn to Serbia as its least offensive neighbour for protection. But Serbian leader Slobodan Milosevic has in the recent past allied himself with the advocates of a Greater Serbia including Macedonia, who claim that it is really 'South Serbia', exactly as it was described in the 1890s. The leader of the Serbian far Right, Vojislav Šešelj, has spoken in favour of a partition of Macedonia between Bulgaria and Serbia, with a few small areas given to Albania. The Serbian Orthodox Church considers its Macedonian co-religionists as renegades, and that the bishopric of Skopje should be Serbian. The Macedonian Church was to all intents and purposes set up by Tito.[2] And so on. Although at the moment Serbia is unable to pursue a forward policy towards Macedonia, that state of affairs could rapidly change.

Bulgaria

Bulgaria has traditionally been the power with the most direct designs on Macedonian territory. In the late nineteenth century quite sizeable sections of the Macedonian population fled to Sofia, and to this day many Bulgarian cities are made up of people of almost wholly Macedonian origin. Many scholars consider the Macedonian language to be basically a dialect of Bulgarian. In the 1956 census 187,000 people declared themselves to be Macedonians, despite political pressure from the regime not to do so.

The territory of the contemporary Macedonian state is, however, far from that of nineteenth-century irredentist ambition. The key element in Bulgarian irredentism then was the *Drang nach Saloniki*, the opening to the Aegean and the great port on the Vardar estuary. This would have transformed the economic and political potential of Bulgaria, to the detriment of Greece. It is a disturbing sign of the potential for this issue to re-emerge that the largest party in the current Macedonian parliament, the VPRO-DPMNE, the lineal descendant of IMRO, has as its policy the recovery of these territories, and although the influence of this party in Skopje has declined in recent months, it nevertheless still exists as a major force.

There are also mainstream political parties in Bulgaria which share this ambition. But the economics of it all are doubtful. Macedonia now has little to offer Sofia except people, land and many problems, and no revision of the Greek border could be achieved without a major war. Greece has made it clear that it would call upon its Western military allies to assist its defence of the status quo, although given the nature of the Balkan crisis in 1991–2 it is perhaps doubtful how readily many of them would do so, given that the whole exercise would be strongly reminiscent of many forms of great power involvement in Balkan disputes in earlier periods. Apart from the diplomatic dimension, there is in Greece a great legacy of popular bitterness from memories of the Bulgarian occupation of parts of Greece during the Second World War, and there is no doubt that any Greek government, of whatever complexion, would have overwhelming popular support for more or less any imaginable policy directed towards the defence of Greek territorial integrity. It should also be noted that wider Macedonian attitudes to Bulgaria were affected in a similar way by the Bulgarian occupation there in the Second World War. But Bulgaria was the first country to recognise the independence of Macedonia, and doubtless plans to involve itself deeply in its affairs. It remains to be seen how far the natural struggle for a regional sphere of influence will be seen by other neighbouring states as an attempt at economic and later, political and military, integration. It is also possible that the long quiescent notion of a Balkan Federation will re-emerge as an expression of Bulgarian policy.

A European question

Perhaps the central short-term question for Europe is how far it is going to allow a Serbian-Greek stranglehold on Macedonia to develop. When the EC did not recognise the new state on 15 January 1992, it allowed time for this pressure to develop. The 1991 policy of Macedonian President Gligorov has failed, to the extent that there is no sign of the emergence of a new Yugoslav confederation between the remaining republics. It is independence or nothing. The possibility exists that a viable, if poor, small state could develop with Skopje as a capital if sufficient EC assistance is forthcoming, and a willingness in Brussels and the other EC capitals to stand up to Greek pressure. There is certainly a government in Macedonia now which is deeply – if, some may feel, a little naively – committed to a Europe without borders. But the window of opportunity may not last long: external political and internal economic pressures may encourage disintegration and violence if the Macedonians are left to their fate within the ruins of the old Yugoslavia. So perhaps it is possible to conclude with the thought that while the classic features of the Macedonian question are beginning to reappear in terms of population and territory, the area of decision already extends to a wider Europe, which was not always so in the past, and that the single great power of the European Community has replaced the competing northern European powers of the late nineteenth century. Whether this will mean the issue can be resolved more easily, though, is extremely doubtful, as EC initiatives so far in the region seem to founder on the contradiction that a transnational organisation is a poor arbiter of the competing claims of new nationalisms.

Notes

1. C. Dascalakis, *The Hellenism of the Ancient Macedonians* (Thessaloniki, Institute of Balkan Studies, 1981)
2. It remains in schism with all other Orthodox churches, and is itself very divided in the Macedonian diaspora, particularly in Australia.

Chapter **3**

Policy and economy in Macedonia*

Jens Reuter

Historical survey

The present-day Republic of Macedonia, with its two million inhabitants, is a small country still striving for international recognition. The 1.3 million Macedonians who live in this country, together with about 430,000 Albanians, nearly 100,000 Turks and other minorities, are anxious not only about their difficult economic problems. There is also a traditional fear of the 'four wolves' surrounding this country – Greece, Albania, Bulgaria and Serbia.[1]

Greece claims a monopoly on the name Macedonia and denounces the Republic's right to use it as the name of the state. The failure by the European Community to recognise Macedonia to date has been a result of the influence of Athens. Albania maintains diplomatic relations with Macedonia, but bilateral relations between Skopje and Tirana have been complicated by the problem of the Albanian minority. Bulgaria has diplomatically recognised Macedonia, but still disputes the existence of the Macedonian nation. Official Serbia has indeed never expressed territorial claims to Macedonia's territory, but has so far failed to recognise the country. Some extreme Serbian nationalists, such as the leader of the Radical Party, Vojislav Šešelj, have openly demanded the division of Macedonia between its four neighbours.

Accordingly, as a result of the disintegration of Yugoslavia, we once again have Macedonia as the region of conflict, after it had seemed in the early 1950s that the traditional 'Macedonian Question' was no longer a problem. The region of Macedonia – known at the time as a geographical term with drifting borders and a variegated ethnic

---

* First published in *Balkan Forum* (Skopje), vol. 1, no. 3 (June 1993).

mixture – became an object of dispute following the Russo-Turkish War of 1877–8. According to the Treaty of San Stefano, the whole of Macedonia – that is, the territory of the present-day Republic as well as the two regions now forming parts of Bulgaria and Greece – was to be incorporated into Greater Bulgaria, which was constituted at the time. This Treaty had an explosive effect on the atmosphere in the Balkans, which was poisoned by expansionist greed and mistrust. Only three months later, the Berlin Congress revised this decision and left Macedonia within the borders of the Osmanli Empire. To be sure, Article 23 of the Treaty of Berlin envisaged some kind of 'autonomy', but in practice Macedonia was sub-divided into three vilayets (districts) and was directly administered by the Sublime Porte. The Turkish administration used the designation 'the three Vilayets' as a synonym for Macedonia. In the background was the fear that the designation Macedonia might awaken a desire for national independence. This precautionary measure should not lead present day observers to the conclusion that there had already been a Macedonian national consciousness in the population living in Macedonia. The church remained an essential unit of identification together with the village. The reasons for the insurrections organised at the time and the unrest in Macedonia were an anti-Turkish disposition, religious antagonism between Islam and Orthodox Christianity, and the diffuse feeling of a Slav, or Bulgarian identity. The Macedonian Revolutionary Organisation, established in Salonica in 1893, which later became known as VMRO (IMRO) after taking on its additional attribute 'Internal', played an important role. This organisation fought not only against Osmanli domination, but also against Greek and Serbian claims on Macedonia. In fact, at the time VMRO pursued the goal of establishing a Greater Bulgaria, as envisaged by the Treaty of San Stefano. As a result, the Slav-Macedonian consciousness which was present in a large part of the population remained fixed for decades on Bulgaria.[2]

Following the Balkan Wars of 1912–13, this territory on which heavy battles had been fought was divided. With Aegean Macedonia, Greece received more than half of the land, while Bulgaria had to satisfy itself with Pirin Macedonia, which was only 10 per cent of the total territory. The remainder of almost 40 per cent was assigned to Serbia as Vardar Macedonia. VMRO, which was again established following the First World War, opposed the division. Owing to its pro-Bulgarian position, it was exceptionally well received in Bulgaria until the early 1930s, while in Greece it almost never appeared on the scene. The main field of action was Yugoslavia, where it also cooperated with the Croatian

Ustashas. The assassination in Marseilles, where the victims were the Yugoslav King Alexander and the French Foreign Minister Barthou, was ascribed to these two organisations. In the 1930s there was a split within the ranks of VMRO. One, more influential wing of VMRO rejected the pro-Bulgarian orientation and proclaimed a distinct Macedonian national consciousness, wishing to combine the three parts into a single united and independent Macedonia. But this national consciousness did not include all Macedonians. The midwife to the Macedonian national sentiment was the Yugoslav Communist Party, which at the end of the Second World War established a Macedonian constituent republic. This act of the establishment of an individual nation with the right to a unified nation-state, resulted, according to Troebst,[3] in the anchoring of the new Macedonian national ideology in the people; all this, even though the Yugoslav Communist Party leadership had to give up its initially offensive Macedonian policy with regard to Greece and Bulgaria. The establishment of the Republic of Macedonia was later presented in Yugoslav statements as 'the final settlement of the Macedonian national question'.[4] In addition to the statehood thus won, the development of an individual literary language was of special significance. Philologists accepted the assigned task, sticking to the principle that the new language must differ as far as possible from Bulgarian. Historians also tried to present a picture of a nation which had always existed. The establishment of an autocephalous Macedonian Orthodox Church in 1958, which was not recognised by Greece, Bulgaria or Serbia, followed the same line.

Although in the period following the war there were continuing controversies concerning Macedonia between Yugoslavia on the one hand and Bulgaria and Greece on the other, we may say that the four decades between 1950 and 1990 were a period in which the Macedonian question was 'frozen', cemented through the East-West opposition and through the discipline of the blocs, but also as a result of the existence of a relatively strong Yugoslav state which, in fact, could not be offensive or aggressive in this field, but which was able to thwart the emergence of all potential aspirations towards Vardar Macedonia.

When the disintegration of the Yugoslav state was in sight, Macedonian nationalism began developing altogether unhindered. In 1990 there were again demonstrations and blockades of the border crossings to Greece, which were organised by young Macedonians. They described the reasons for their action through leaflets distributed to Western tourists stuck in the queue of vehicles. Even four decades after the Second World War and the end of the Civil War in Greece, they were still obliged to obtain visas for each visit to Greece. On the other hand, in spite of the Helsinki Declaration and the CSCE Conference, the recognition of any Macedonian minority in Northern Greece was denied. These activities were extremely unwelcome to the Yugoslav Foreign Ministry, as they represented a serious obstacle to the officially proclaimed process of establishing closer ties with the European Community.[5]

Visa requirements for all Yugoslav citizens take their roots from the Greek Civil War which lasted until 1949. The support of Yugoslavia for the Communists and the massive mobilisation of the Slav population in north-west Greece for 'the Macedonian liberation struggle' are still not forgotten in Athens. After the failure of the Communists, 67,000 refugee Slavs from Greece settled in Yugoslav Macedonia. Greece disputes the right of these emigrants even to a visit, unless they sign a document declaring themselves as 'Greeks of Greek origin'. It is understandable that the indignation of Yugoslav Macedonians was great: the refusal to recognise the Macedonian nation combined with discrimination against a large number of compatriots was a fruitful ground for nationalists. The Yugoslav political leadership had a clear position on this issue. It represented the view that the newly-established Macedonian nation had the right to be recognised by Greece. At the same time Belgrade tried to dissuade the Macedonians from making demands in the name of the 'Slavophones' inside Greece. This view was justified by the argument that it was not advisable for the Macedonians to open fronts of conflict on all sides.[6] In Bulgaria, too, Macedonian nationalism was aroused in the early 1990s. Some 10,000 Macedonians from the Pirin region gathered there and established the 'United Macedonian Organisation', which was named 'Ilinden' (OMO Ilinden) in reference to the 1903 Uprising.

The disintegration of Yugoslavia has revived the 'four wolves'. Without the protection of this 24 million state with an army of 200,000 soldiers, it no longer seems impossible that this Republic may be attacked. On the other hand, the former Yugoslav Macedonians are no longer disciplined by a centre, Belgrade. The dream of the unification of Macedonia divided into three parts can now be dreamt aloud, without fear of any reprisals. The most important and strongest proponent of this political direction is the Internal Macedonian Revolutionary Organisation, a party which has succeeded the old VMRO, but is decorated by the attribute 'Democratic Party for Macedonian National Unity' (VMRO-DPMNE). The movement which, according to its own figures, has over 100,000 members, has inscribed on its flag the slogan of 'spiritual and territorial unification of Macedonia'. The party openly demands that a new delineation of Macedonia's borders with Bulgaria, Albania and Greece be carried out. Although in the first free elections in November and December 1990 VMRO-DPMNE won 38 of the total of 120 seats in Parliament and thus became the strongest party, it failed to carry out its revisionist policy with regard to borders. Amendments I and II to the Constitution of the Republic of Macedonia, adopted by the Parliament in Skopje on January 6, 1992, clearly set out the following:

I.1. The Republic of Macedonia has no territorial pretensions towards any neighbouring state.

I.2. The borders of the Republic of Macedonia can only be changed in accordance with the Constitution and on the principle of free will, as well as in accordance with generally accepted international standards.

II.1. In the exercise of this concern the Republic of Macedonia will not interfere in the sovereign rights of other states or in their internal affairs.[7]

Internal political development after the disintegration of Yugoslavia

In November and December 1990, following 45 years of totalitarian rule, the first free elections were held. Some 1.3 million citizens with a right to vote were invited to elect 120 representatives to the unicameral Parliament. The parties which stood for election were divided into two groups: 'pro-Yugoslav' and 'national'. The first group included the former League of Communists, which was now renamed 'Party for Democratic Transformation' (SKM-PDP) and won 31 seats in Parliament. Also pro-Yugoslav in its orientation was (the communist) Alliance of Reformist Forces (ARF) (the party of the former Yugoslav Prime Minister Ante Marković), which succeeded in winning 19 seats. Thus the two transformed communist parties obtained almost half the seats and narrowly failed to achieve an absolute majority.

Among the parties with a national orientation, VMRO-DPMNE was the most successful. This party, which seceded from the Party for Pan-Macedonian Action (MAAK) in March 1990, became the strongest faction in Parliament with 37 seats. The Party for Democratic Prosperity (PDP), the national party of Albanians, who constitute about one-quarter of the population of Macedonia, won 25 seats. But it was not the only party of the Albanians. Apart from it, there were the

National Democratic Party (NDP) and the Union of the Democratic Youth (UDJ) which, however, remained insignificant.[8]

Stojan Andov, the President of the Alliance of Reformist Forces, was elected President of the Parliament. In late January 1991, the 73-year-old reformed communist Kiro Gligorov was elected President of the Republic. This politician, who was formerly Deputy President of the Yugoslav government and Federal Minister of Finance, won even the votes of VMRO. Ljupčo Georgievski of VMRO-DPMNE, at the time a little-known theatre director, was elected Deputy President of the Republic. The formation of the government proved to be extremely difficult. After two months of negotiations, a 'supraparty' government of experts was elected, at the head of which stood Nikola Kljusev, a prominent Economics Professor who was not a member of any party. His 23-member government, which was called an 'expert government', had only two ministers who were party affiliated. The government included three Albanians and one minister from the previous Communist government.[9]

On June 25, the Parliament adopted a 'Declaration of the Sovereignty of Macedonia', in which it opted for independence and territorial integrity, but also for the right to secession. It was decided that a referendum should be held concerning the question of remaining within or seceding from the Yugoslav federation. Kiro Gligorov, whose influence was far greater than that of the 'expert government' – so that people already spoke of a Macedonian presidential democracy – opted for a 'commonwealth of sovereign Yugoslav states'. This experienced politician knew that Macedonia, for security and for political and economic reasons, should be oriented at least towards a loose commonwealth with the other Yugoslav republics. About 50–60 per cent of Macedonia's trade was carried out with this region. Accordingly, Gligorov played on the card of an alliance of sovereign Yugoslav successor states – a commonwealth of states with a market economy, respect for human rights, common defence (an exceptionally important point for Macedonia) and a common foreign policy. As the survey of April 1991 showed, some 60 per cent of the Macedonian population opted for a commonwealth of sovereign successor states, while only the supporters of VMRO chose the option of an independent national state in all its aspects.[10]

The road to state independence which Macedonia later followed was virtually imposed on the Republic. After the attempt at the establishment of a new Yugoslavia based on the principle of equal cooperation failed, Macedonia had only two options left. It could either join the new Yugoslavia and thus be subjected to Serbian hegemony, or it could set off along the thorny road of state independence. Macedonian politicians from all parties have always stressed that they want to be partners with neighbouring Serbia, but not its subject. The skilful tactician Gligorov succeeded, through arduous negotiations, in procuring the withdrawal of the Yugoslav People's Army from Macedonia, which improved Macedonia's position with regard to Serbia.[11]

In July 1992 came the end of the Kljusev government. The economics expert was blamed for not having succeeded in his professional field. Parliament passed a vote of no confidence in him and his government by an overwhelming majority (there were only 2 votes against and 7 abstentions). But the attempt of VMRO to depose Kiro Gligorov failed. It is not without irony that the Kljusev government was held responsible for the economic failure which was chiefly an outcome of the blockade by Greece.[12]

The formation of the new government, as might have been expected, encountered a number of difficulties. Following two months of negotiations, a coalition of four parties was constructed, consisting of the Albanian Party for Democratic Prosperity, the Social-Democratic Union (the former Communists), the former communist Socialist Alliance and the Liberal Party (formerly Alliance of Reformist Forces). Its Prime Minister is 30-year-old Branko Crvenkovski, an engineer and computer specialist. The government includes, among others, five Albanian ministers and one Turk. The two women members of the government are an innovation in conservative Macedonia. The main purpose of the government is to achieve the international recognition of Macedonia. Branko Crvenkovski has bitterly concluded that only those three of the former Yugoslav republics in which there has been war – Slovenia, Croatia and Bosnia-Hercegovina – have received international recognition. Macedonia, on the other hand, where not a single bullet has been fired and from which the Yugoslav People's Army withdrew peacefully, must still await its recognition. This is difficult to understand, bearing in mind that the Badinter Commission, constituted of 5 Presidents of Constitutional Courts from Western countries, was clearly in favour of Macedonia's recognition. The Macedonian people, too, in September 1991, at the appropriate referendum, came out in favour of state independence with 95 per cent of all votes.[13] The lack of recognition is fertile ground for Macedonian and Albanian extremists. Macedonian nationalists consider the failure of recognition as proof that a peaceful and nonviolent policy shows no results, and it corroborates the secessionist aspirations of Albanian nationalists.[14] The Prime Minister has stated the other essential aims of his government to be the privatisation, as swiftly as possible, of the formerly state-owned property, and the harmonious regulation, as far as possible, of complicated inter-ethnic relations in the Republic. It is precisely this last task which has met with difficulties. On October 28, following a long and vigorous debate, Parliament adopted the Macedonian Citizenship Law. Only those persons able to prove residence in Macedonia for at least 15 years have the right to Macedonian citizenship. This provision has been a serious blow to the Albanians in Macedonia. It is estimated that about 150,000 Albanians have settled there during the last 15 years from Kosovo, Serbia and other regions. Not having citizenship, they will not only remain without any political rights, but also their right to ownership of land is now under question.[15]

The problem with Albanians

According to the results of the 1991 census, Macedonia has a total population of 2,033,964. Almost two-thirds of them, or 1.314 million inhabitants, are ethnic Macedonians, while the Albanians, numbering 427,313 persons, account for about 21 per cent of the total population. The political leaders of the Albanians strongly contest these figures. They say that the proportion of Albanians in the total population of Macedonia is 35 or even 40 per cent. In explanation they say that a large number of Albanians boycotted the 1991 census. The reason for this was the forms which were written in Macedonian and to which only a few explanations in Albanian were added. The second argument was that the commissions were composed of Macedonians only, so that the number of Albanians would be diminished by manipulation. The Macedonian side states that the Albanians used the boycott in order to conceal the fact that their number was much smaller than they claim.[16]

The region most densely populated by Albanians is west Macedonia. There, in the communities of Tetovo, Debar, and Gostivar they have an absolute majority, and in Kičevo a relative majority. In Kumanovo and Struga they are a strong minority of one-third and more than 40 per cent respectively. It is important to note that the said communities constitute a compact whole and border on Kosovo and Albania. Secession from the Macedonian state and cession to Greater Albania would accordingly be easier owing to the geographic circumstances. At the beginning of 1992, the recognised leader of the Macedonian Albanians, the head of the Party for Democratic Prosperity, Nevzat Halili, rejected the claim that his aim was secession. Nevertheless, in the meantime the Albanians took a step which was interpreted by many as the first step towards secession. They organised an unofficial referendum on territorial and political autonomy in West Macedonia. As always happens in such projects, the result corresponded to the expectations: the overwhelming majority voted for their own, autonomous region.[17]

Nevzat Halili has explained the referendum with the following words: 'By this we want to show to the world that the state recognition of Macedonia by the world community is premature, as the rights of our minority in this country are trampled underfoot'.[18]

Being left in the lurch by their Albanian compatriots over the exceptionally sensitive issue of international recognition has been difficult to tolerate for many Macedonians. Hence Macedonian politicians have pointed to the fact that the Albanians still have not built the right attitude to the Macedonian state. They do not have a developed sense of identification with this state and are constantly showing this. Hence they demonstratively express indignation at the legal institutions and the organs of administration by simply abandoning Parliamentary sessions or by refusing to pay taxes and duties for community services. Thus, for example, in 1990, only about 20 per cent of taxes and duties were collected in Tetovo.[19] On the other hand, the Albanians complain of alleged discrimination. They demand the status of a constituent nation, which is not provided in the Macedonian Constitution. Thus, for instance, its Preamble quotes 'the historical fact that Macedonia is constituted as a nation-state of the Macedonian people'. The Albanians, Turks and other minorities are simply guaranteed complete civil equality and coexistence with the Macedonian people.[20]

Another important point of conflict is the language. In connection with this, Article 7 of the Constitution says that the official language is Macedonian, written in its Cyrillic alphabet. Paragraph 2 sets out that in the communities where the majority of the inhabitants belong to a nationality, in addition to the Macedonian language and its Cyrillic alphabet, the language of those minorities is also in official use, in a manner stipulated by law.

The Albanians do not wish to be reconciled to this rather restrictive provision. They point out that even in the West Macedonian communities with a high participation of Albanians, i.e. in Kumanovo, Kičevo, Struga and Tetovo, there is instruction in Albanian only in elementary schools. In the school year 1989/90, Albanians students refused to accept their certificates because they were written in Macedonian. A petition addressed to the Macedonian Parliament and signed by

119,000 Albanians demanded the opening of schools and other educational institutions as well as a university with Albanian as the language of instruction. This idea, i.e. the organisation of a complete educational and instruction system in Albanian, has remained without a response from the institutions responsible.[21]

The Albanian members of the Macedonian Parliament submitted demands for the issuing of birth certificates in Albanian and for the right of Albanians to use their mother tongue before the courts. In February, the President of the Party for Democratic Prosperity, Halili, protested against the alleged discrimination against Albanians with regard to appointing personnel to public functions. Thus, for instance, the leading posts in the Republic were allegedly occupied exclusively by Macedonians.[22] At the same time he called upon the Macedonian government to recognise both the autonomy of the Albanians and the state independence of Kosovo, while he called upon Tirana not to recognise Macedonia as long as the Republic fails to fulfil these demands.[23] These demands clearly caused serious doubts about the loyalty of the Albanians towards the Macedonian state. The recognition of an independent Kosovo in conjunction with guarantees of territorial and cultural autonomy for the Albanians would not be far from an implicit invitation to bring the two sides closer and to their possible unification.

Macedonians also regard these demands by the Albanians in the field of politics, culture and education with particular distrust because they are troubled by a hidden fear that they may be suppressed by other nationalities. The Albanians have the highest birthrate in Europe and demographic estimates say that they may become a majority in Macedonia within three or four decades. This is even further strengthened by the fact that the Albanians differ greatly from the Macedonians in their lifestyle, in religion and culture. Intermingling, for instance, by concluding mixed marriages, is not considered desirable by either side.[24]

It is questionable whether the present coalition between the transformed Communists and the largest party of the Albanians may change anything with regard to the differences in principle between the two people groups. The head of the parliamentary group of the PDP Albanian party, Estref Aliu, said in November 1992 that it was not easy for his party to form a coalition with the reformed Communists. The danger of conflicts had not in any way been avoided considering the widespread prejudices and mistrust demonstrated in many places towards the Albanians. On the side of the Albanians there were also radical forces which rejected the policy of PDP and condemned it as a 'betrayal of the national cause of the Albanians'.[25]

In summary, we can conclude that Macedonia is indeed a multinational state, but this fact will hardly be or will never be accepted, especially by the supporters of VMRO-DPMNE. As this party is now in opposition, this only suits their Macedonian-nationalist agitation. The largest and by far the strongest party of the Albanians is tied through its responsibility in participating in the government, and can hardly present itself as being in favour of the 'Albanian cause'. In the adoption of the Law on Citizenship of the Republic of Macedonia it suffered a heavy defeat. The second field of problems, the use of Albanian as an official language and a language in education, from an Albanian point of view, seems to be a minefield. Serious conflicts may certainly be envisaged here. We can say that Macedonia's internal stability is most strongly threatened by these confrontations.

Economic situation

In November 1992, the Macedonian President Kiro Gligorov wrote an open letter to the Secretary General of the United Nations, Boutros Ghali. Among other things, he said that the main commercial routes of Macedonia were entirely blocked – to the north as a result of the embargo against the new Yugoslavia by the Security Council, and to the south as a result of the arbitrarily imposed economic blockade by Greece. The small number of roads to the west and east were inadequate and the network undeveloped, in winter even useless. Gligorov appealed to the United Nations to exert pressure on Greece so that Athens might halt its economic blockade against Macedonia. Macedonia, which has no access to the sea, depended on the use of the Greek port of Salonica.[26]

The devastating damage from economic blockades is even more obvious if we bear in mind that the economic power of Macedonia was fairly modest even in conditions of the unhindered transfer of goods. In the former Yugoslavia, like Montenegro and Kosovo, the Republic included some of the poorest parts of the country. In 1990, Macedonia contributed less than 6 per cent of the total gross social product of Yugoslavia, while it comprised 9 per cent of the population and 10 per cent of the territory of Yugoslavia.[27] The contribution of industry, concentrated in its capital, Skopje, was 41 per cent of the gross social product of Macedonia. It was followed by agriculture, accounting for 25 per cent of Macedonia's gross social product. Tourism and communications came next. Metallurgy, machine construction, chemistry, textile- and tobacco-processing appeared in relatively small enterprises, which were mainly directed towards the local markets. There was no Macedonian company which could acquire international significance. The general framework of conditions for the Macedonian economy are hardly favourable: the obsolete manner of production and the entirely undeveloped service sector will for a long time be a hindrance to the projected economic growth.[28]

Macedonian industry is neither modern nor competitive. Agriculture is dominated by a monoculture – tobacco. But Macedonian tobacco contains a large amount of tar, and accordingly has no chances on the European Community market, where there is already an excessive supply of this product. From a general point of view, the land is exhausted through the uncontrolled cultivation of the soil and erosion, so that huge investments are necessary for its improvement. The country does not have the necessary means at its disposal.[29] Foreign exchange reserves to back the newly-established *denar* are exceptionally modest. At present they amount to 59 million dollars, a somewhat symbolic amount in this context. In 1990, money orders from Macedonian workers working abroad still amounted to 168 million dollars, but owing to the unstable political situation, they fell to 8.6 million dollars in 1992. Yet the contribution of Macedonian workers working abroad is considerable to the albeit modest standard of living. Many families would by now have been lost without the money they are receiving from their relatives in Western Europe, which enters the country via unofficial routes. One can even say that the Macedonian population maintains its standards of living only through financial injections from foreign workers. The exceptionally optimistic estimates come from the fact that there is a total of one billion dollars in the hands of the population.[30]

1992 was anything but a successful year for Macedonia. The gross social product decreased by 15 per cent and investment by 24 per cent, while the real depreciation of salaries was 34 per cent. The young Prime Minister Branko Crvenkovski has given the following explanation of the depressing figures:

> The economic blockade to the north and south, which was imposed upon us, was a heavy blow to the economy and the citizens. As a result of Resolution 577 of the United Nations alone, the Macedonian economy has suffered damage to the extent of 1.3 billion dollars. The damage caused by the Greek embargo amounts to an additional 1 billion dollars.[31]

Sofija Todorova, Macedonian Minister of Development, says that even if Macedonia achieves international recognition, this will not mean the end of economic blockades. Macedonia will not be able in the near future to count on its traditional markets and communication routes. For a small country such as Macedonia, there is nothing more devastating than its state borders becoming also the borders of its economy.[32]

At the moment, for understandable reasons, Macedonia is unable to repay its foreign debts amounting to 288 million dollars. These difficulties will have to be surmounted through stand-by arrangements and through covering the old loans by taking out new ones. Macedonia's direct foreign debts total 1.2 billion dollars. Its share of Yugoslav foreign debts should be added to this figure.

Macedonia has so far received financial assistance of 100 million ECU (124 million dollars) from the European Community, which considering the economic difficulties of the Republic is only a drop in the ocean. In the words of Ljupčo Trpeski, Minister of Finance of the Republic of Macedonia, this year Macedonia hopes to be admitted to the main international financial institutions such as the International Monetary Fund and the World Bank. The Republic has up to now been denied any access to international financial markets owing to the lack of its international recognition, which has naturally had grave consequences for the Macedonian economy. The first breakthrough in this respect was achieved in December 1992. The European Bank for Reconstruction and Development agreed to Macedonia's membership. The country was admitted under the name 'the Former Yugoslav Republic of Macedonia'.[33]

Owing to the fact that Macedonia had always received financial support from the federation of the former Yugoslavia, some observers have supported the view that the Republic will be forced, because of its serious economic problems, to join the new Yugoslavia and thus be subjected to Serbia's hegemony. The present political leadership headed by Gligorov is determined not to follow this course. He plays on the card of assistance from the European Community and hopes to achieve the association of Macedonia within the European Community as soon as the problem of its international recognition is resolved.

The struggle for international recognition

In September 1991, the European Community set up the Badinter Commission. The Commission, named after its president, the former French Minister of Justice, established criteria for the international recognition of the former Yugoslav republics. The main points were respect for human rights and the rights of minorities and a consensus on independence confirmed at a referendum. Unlike Croatia, Macedonia satisfied all these criteria, so that, from a theoretical point of view, there were no obstacles to the recognition of this republic. The question became politically pressing in December 1991, when the recognition of Croatia was imminent. Under pressure from Greece, the European Community demanded on December 16, as a precondition for its recognition, that the Republic gave constitutional guarantees that it has no territorial claims. In addition, any kind of 'hostile propaganda' had to cease, including the use of a denomination which might imply territorial claims. This lengthy and obscure text did not indeed mention the term 'Macedonia', but it implicitly contained the demand for renouncing that name.[34]

The Parliament in Skopje reacted immediately and as early as January adopted three amendments to the Constitution which stated that Macedonia has no territorial claims against its neighbours, that it considered existing borders as inviolable and that it would not 'interfere in the sovereign rights of other states or in their internal affairs'.[35] But seen from the perspective of Athens these concessions were insufficient. Greece created such a picture among its partners as if the fate of the whole Greek nation depended on whether or not it would keep the monopoly on the name 'Macedonia'. Greece saw a threat and aggression in the use of that name, regardless of how this could be achieved by the two-million state of Macedonia with its army of 10,000. The preservation of the name Macedonia was designated by the Greeks as 'preservation of postcommunist neo-nationalism'. It is hard to understand why the Greeks resorted to a total economic blockade against its small neighbouring state.

When explaining their position with regard to the threat, the Greeks most often rely on quoting statements by the Macedonian-nationalist VMRO-DPMNE, which won a relative majority at the elections in Macedonia. Without any doubt, the radical wing of this party, which holds 33 of the 120 seats in Parliament, dreams about a Greater Macedonia with Salonica as its capital. The supporters of this party have already put into circulation appropriate geographical maps where the northern Greek province of Macedonia is also part of the Greater State which is to be established, together with Bulgarian Pirin Macedonia. The radical nationalist young people greet each other with the 'Macedonian salute', i.e. making a circle with the thumb and index finger of the left hand, symbolising the sun of Philip II with its sixteen rays. The other three fingers remain spread – they represent the three parts of Macedonia which are to be united. However, these as well as some other nationalist follies, such as, for example, the name 'Solunka' for one of the Macedonian plumb brandies ('Solun' is the Macedonian name for Salonica), should not be overestimated. The majority of VMRO-DPMNE is for respecting borders and speaks of a spiritual, not political unity of all Macedonians.[36]

Somewhat more serious is the fact that on the new state flag, instead of the old Yugoslav star, there is now the sun from Vergina, the sign of Philip II. There are also three waves on the state's coat of arms. This could symbolically mean: the Republic of Macedonia extends to the Aegean.[37]

On the other hand, the Macedonian Parliament decided, on December 10, 1992, to include the addition Skopje to the name of the state, so that its official name would be 'Republic of Macedonia (Skopje)'.[38] But this, too, was not enough to reassure Athens. The Greek fear of Macedonia is not, as a matter of fact, based on the threat by a small neighbouring state. There are also no longer any fears of a civil war which might break out in Northern Greece. The real fear is of the fierce enemy, Turkey, of which there are suspicions that it pulls the strings in Macedonia. Thus Greek politicians speak of a 'Moslem encirclement'. By this they refer to the fact that Turkey signed an agreement on economic cooperation and an agreement on military cooperation with Albania, whose population is predominantly Moslem by religion. The circle would thus be closed by the partly Moslem Macedonia, which, in the words of Evangelos Kofos, a specialist in the Athens Foreign Ministry, could become 'a pawn on the Turkish chessboard'.[39]

It is in this predominantly irrational fear, as it seems, that the motives of Greece lie when it tests the patience of the EC countries and shatters the bases for its future economic cooperation with Macedonia. But it is the states of the European Community itself that must be blamed for allowing themselves to be blackmailed as regards the Macedonian question. The Greek Foreign Minister made the signing of the Treaty of Maastricht conditional on accepting 'the special Greek interest concerning Macedonia' by the European Community. As a result of that, the statements of the European Community no longer referred to Macedonia but to 'Skopje'. At the same time, the Community proposed some compromise solutions such as 'New Macedonia' or 'Macedonia' for internal, and 'Skopje' for external use.

In January 1993 the following scandalous event took place. Uffe Ellemann-Jensen, the Danish Foreign Minister, presented the EC work programme of his government and said, among other things, that the European Community, as a hostage of the Greek right to a veto within the Council of Ministers, was unable to act with regard to the Macedonian question. Although the former Yugoslav republic of Macedonia in the meantime fulfilled all preconditions, it could not be recognised by the European Community because Athens continued to block all decisions as a result of the name dispute. In another statement, the Foreign Minister was even sharper saying that his personal impression was that the rest of eleven members of the European Community were fed up with the Greek policy of obstruction. The failure to recognise the Republic of Macedonia only because of demonstrating understanding for Athens, was a dark stain on the Community's foreign policy, which had to be removed. The sharp words of the Danish foreign minister were possible because he was to hold his post for only a few days more, but his statements nevertheless must have been a reflection of the mood in many parts of the European Community.[40]

It was perhaps these clear statements by the Danish Minister that made Greece deviate from its course. In early February, the spokesman of the Greek government, Vassilis Magginas, said that Greece was ready to accept a compromise solution achieved under international mediation. The mitigation of the Greek position was most probably also a result of the fact that France, Great Britain and Spain submitted to the United Nations Security Council a draft resolution for the purpose of Macedonia's admission to the UN. The name 'the former Yugoslav Republic of Macedonia' was envisaged as a provisional name in the resolution. Athens said that Greece had no objection to recognition under this name.[41]

Since at the beginning of February Italy, too, had expressed its readiness to establish diplomatic relations with Macedonia, victory in the struggle for international recognition may already be discernible. Up to this moment, the success in this field has been rather modest – Macedonia maintains diplomatic relations only with the following countries: Turkey, Russia, Bulgaria, Byelorussia, Lithuania, the Philippines, the Turkish Republic of Northern Cyprus, Croatia and Slovenia.

Conclusion

If we bear in mind endogenous factors which could undermine Macedonia's stability, then the Albanian problem must be mentioned in the first place. There must be serious doubts of the will of the Albanians to integrate within the Macedonian state. The lack of loyalty by many Albanians is also reflected in the fact that many of them have obtained passports in their 'mother country' of Albania. On the other hand, the Macedonian side, too, has made serious mistakes which have prevented the integration of the Albanians. This especially refers to the Macedonian Citizenship Law and the constitutional provisions in connection with the official and education language. One can reckon with the fact that Macedonian Albanians will feel more bound to Tirana and perhaps to the Kosovo leadership than to the Macedonian state.

The second endogenous factor which jeopardises the stability is the difficult economic situation. Without comprehensive foreign assistance, the Macedonian economy will find itself in collapse. If the European Community fails to provide prompt economic assistance, it seems that social unrest and political turmoil are predetermined.

The exogenous factors which jeopardise the stability of the country are the 'four wolves' – Greece, Serbia, Bulgaria and Albania. From a general point of view we may say that for the time being these four countries are holding each other in check, i.e. there is no immediate danger that one of Macedonia's neighbouring countries may intervene militarily there.

Very soon Greece will have to face how the other eleven member-countries of the European Community are abandoning the present political course with regard to Macedonia. The readiness of Athens for a compromise, which can already be discerned, is a result of the conclusion that one cannot hope to endure with a policy under the motto 'alone against the other eleven'.

In spite of a few militant articles in the Conservative press of the right, which even called for war against Macedonia, there is no danger from Greece. It is precisely the picture of Macedonia as 'the pawn on the Turkish chessboard' which will make Athens abstain from reckless steps.

As far as Serbia's policy is concerned, we may start from the position that Belgrade would be delighted to present itself as the guardian protecting Macedonia from the 'Albanian danger'. Relying on Belgrade will certainly have to be accompanied by economic concessions. Aggressive factors in Serbia are the Radical Party of the fascist Vojislav Šešelj and the influential Serbian Orthodox Church which has still not reconciled itself to the autocephaly of the Macedonian Church. But Serbia is so preoccupied with the military conflict with Croatia that it cannot think about military encroachment on Macedonia with its small Serbian minority.

Bulgaria has recognised Macedonia diplomatically, but still disputes the existence of the Macedonian nation and language. Yet there is great sympathy in Macedonia for the Bulgarian President Želju Zelev. He is seen as the personal guarantee of good Bulgarian-Macedonian relations. Macedonia in no way feels threatened by Bulgaria and hopes to build even greater good-neighbourly relations.

Albania is both economically and militarily weak and does not in the least present a danger to Macedonia. Yet there is the horrible scenario that Macedonia may be involved in a Balkan war exactly because of the problem with the Albanians. If there were an insurrection of the Albanians in Kosovo, where their concentration is 90 per cent against Serbian oppression, the mother country of Albania would not stand aside without taking any action, and thus Macedonian Albanians would also be more or less involved in the whirlpool of events. This leads to the conclusion that the greatest danger for Macedonia's security in the immediate future may come from the crisis region of Kosovo.

Notes

1. Cf. James Pettifer, 'Die neue Mazedonienfrage', *Europäische Rundschau*, vol. 20, 1992 (4), pp. 45–55.
2. Cf Ekkehard Kraft, 'Die Entstehung der mazedonischen Frage', *Neue Zürcher Zeitung*, February 13, 1992.
3. Stefan Troebst, 'Makedonische Antworten auf die "Makedonische Frage" 1944–1992: Nationalismus, Republiksgründung, Nation-Building', *Südosteuropa*, vol. 41, 1992 (7/8), pp. 423–42.
4. *Politička enciklopedija*, Belgrade 1975, p. 526.
5. Viktor Meier in *Frankfurter Allgemeine Zeitung*, June 22, 1990.
6. *Ibid., Frankfurther Allgemeine Zeitung*, August 7, 1990.
7. *Constitution of the Republic of Macedonia*, Skopje 1992, p. 56.
8. Cf Thomas Brey, 'Jugoslawien: Der Vielvölkerstaat zerfällt', *Osteuropa*, no. 7/1991, pp. 709–24.
9. Milan Andrejevich, 'Macedonia's New Political Leadership', *RFE/RL Report on Eastern Europe*, vol. II, no. 20, 1991.
10. *Ibid.*
11. Viktor Meier, 'Mazedoniens Unabhängigkeit nur halb gewollt', *Frankfurter Allgemeine Zeitung*, March 24, 1992.
12. *Neue Zürcher Zeitung*, July 10, 1992, and *Nova Makedonija*, July 10 and 11, 1992.
13. The referendum was primarily boycotted by the Macedonian Albanians, which constitute about 25 per cent of the total population.
14. *Borba*, November 21–22, 1992.
15. *Nova Makedonija*, October 29 and 30, 1992.
16. Duncan M. Perry, 'The Republic of Macedonia and the Odds for Survival', *RFE/RL Research Report*, vol. 1, no. 46, November 20, 1992, pp. 12–19. Compare with the figures quoted here: *Jugoslovenski pregled*, no. 1/1992.

17. *Nova Makedonija*, January 13 and 14, 1992.
18. *Die Tageszeitung* (Berlin), January 13, 1992.
19. Anton Parvanov, '"Albanian Syndrome" in the Republic of Macedonia', *National Problems in the Balkans* (ed. Krastjo Mancev *et al.*), Sofia 1992, pp. 140–58.
20. *Constitution of the Republic of Macedonia*, Skopje 1992, p. 3.
21. *Ibid.*
22. *Vjesnik*, February 10, 1992.
23. Cf Patrick Moore, 'The Albanian Question in the Former Yugoslavia', *RFE/RL Research Report*, vol. 1, no. 14, April 3, 1992.
24. Cf Duncan Perry, p. 17.
25. *Neue Zürcher Zeitung*, November 18, 1992.
26. *Borba*, November 20, 1992.
27. Information Service of *Frankfurter Allgemeine Zeitung*, July 1992, p. 25.
28. *Ibid.*
29. James Pettifer, 'Die Mazedonienfrage...', p. 49.
30. *Ekonomska politika*, January 25, 1990.
31. *Ekonomska politika*, January 25, 1990.
32. *Ibid.*
33. *Frankfurter Allgemeine Zeitung*, February 2, 1993.
34. *Neue Zürcher Zeitung*, June 21–22, 1992.
35. Compare the documentation in *Südosteuropa*, 11–12/1992, pp. 731–2.
36. *Ibid.*
37. *Die Zeit*, November 27, 1992.
38. *Nova Makedonija*, February 11, 1993.
39. *Ibid.*
40. *Das Parlament*, January 29, 1993.
41. *Süddeutsche Zeitung*, February 5, 1993.

Chapter 4

Macedonian identity: an overview of the major claims

Kyril Drezov

> Only those Macedonians who feel direct descendants of Philip and Alexander in unbroken continuity will remain eternally immune to the assimilation propagandas of the neighbouring states and will never betray the Macedonian race.

A programmatic statement of *Makedonsko Sonce*, the weekly organ of the World Macedonian Congress

In 1991 the former Yugoslav Socialist Republic of Macedonia became an independent state under the name 'Republic of Macedonia'. The identity of this state, its name, symbols, language and history, emerged as one of the most contentious issues in the Balkans. Even the most moderate Greek historians and politicians reject the use of the unqualified adjective 'Macedonian' in describing the state that has emerged north of their border, and its majority population and language. Bulgarian academics and politicians accept the name 'Macedonia' as a legitimate geographic and state designation, but unanimously reject the existence of a separate Macedonian nation and language before 1944, and many of them deny their existence even after that date. Even the most level-headed Serbian intellectuals remain sceptical about the historical existence of any fixed ethnic identity among Slavs in present-day Macedonia before the twentieth century. In turn, Macedonian intellectuals and politicians project the contemporary reality of their statehood, nation and language on to the nineteenth century and before, many of them going as far back as ancient Macedonia. All these 'schools of thought' are accepted in varying degrees by non-Balkan academics and politicians, who rarely remain even-handed and instead consciously or unconsciously take sides in the ongoing Balkan 'debate' on the Macedonian identity. To sum up, the emergence of the Republic of Macedonia in 1991 has unexpectedly given a new lease of life to the complex and ever-changing blend of history, geography, ethnography and psychopathology which since the end of the nineteenth century became known as the 'Macedonian Question'. This chapter will examine critically the four major interpretations of Macedonian identity coming from Greece, Bulgaria, Serbia, and the Republic of Macedonia.[1]

Greece

The Greek claim of exclusive copyright on the name 'Macedonia' is an attempt to cover up two problem areas that are extremely uncomfortable for modern Greeks: first, the identity of the ancient Macedonians, and second, the relatively recent (re)Hellenisation of much of Aegean Macedonia.

Who were the ancient Macedonians? The official Greek dogma is that the ancient Macedonians were nothing more than one of the many Greek tribes – and consequently Philip and Alexander were the 'unifiers' of Hellas. This flies in the face of the historical evidence that the ancient Macedonians were perceived by all Greek tribes as barbarians and non-Greeks and were violently opposed as such. Their likely ethnic and linguistic closeness to the Greeks could not sway Demosthenes (384–322 BC) to accept them as Greek. It could be argued that Demosthenes was blinded by his ferocious opposition to Philip, but Macedonians were viewed in a similar light by Isocrates, a supporter of Philip. His position was that the Macedonian royal family was Greek (their dynastic name 'Argead' imputed a false etymology to Argos in the Peloponese) but that their subjects were most certainly not.[2] Modern Greek historians are keen to buttress their claims about the essential Greekness of ancient Macedonians with linguistic arguments and archeological material from recent excavations of ancient Macedonian sites,[3] evidently forgetting that no contemporary exercises could posthumously change the opinions of Philip's and Alexander's contemporaries. To sum up, the complexity of Greek-Macedonian relations in antiquity does not fit the straitjacket of nineteenth and twentieth-century Greek nationalist propaganda, which has invariably projected on to antiquity the contemporary reality that a subdivision of the Greek people lives in geographic Macedonia.

Whether ancient Macedonians were originally 'Greek' or not makes virtually no difference to the contemporary Greek claim on Macedonia. Nor does it make any difference to the millennia of continuous presence of Hellenic culture in Macedonia, and to the role that the ancient Macedonians played in rooting Hellenic culture in their own native lands. The only things that can be said with any certainty about the ancient Macedonians is that they were not of Slavic origin, that whatever their ethnic origins they were active in spreading Hellenic culture throughout the world, and that they were completely Hellenised many centuries before the Slavs started to settle in the Balkans.

Aegean Macedonia: 75 years of Greek civilisation?

The catchphrase 'Macedonia – 4,000 years of Greek civilisation', one of the rallying cries of the 'anti-Skopje' campaign in Greece, covers up the fact that the ethnic Greek predominance in at least half of the territory of present-day Aegean Macedonia goes back to only 75 years ago, following the resettlement there of mostly Asia Minor refugees in the 1920s. The Greeks, like many other Balkan peoples, tend to view themselves only as innocent victims (of Turks, Bulgarians, 'Skopejans'), and find it difficult to accept the idea that a sizeable part of present-day Northern Greece (Macedonia and Thrace) was not 'liberated' earlier this century, but was, rather, conquered by the Greeks against the will of the local population, most of which was either slaughtered or expelled. The Greeks then concentrated on a complete Hellenisation of their new possessions. In this they were immensely successful thanks to the population exchanges with Bulgaria and, especially, with Turkey. As a result half of Aegean Macedonia's indigenous population – most Macedonian Bulgarians and all Macedonian Turks – were expelled from Greece and replaced by Asia Minor emigré Greeks. The Greek share of the population of Aegean Macedonia rose from 42.6 per cent (of which probably half were 'Slavophones') in 1912, to 88.8 per cent in 1926.[4]

Greek contributions to Macedonian nation-building

By denying the name 'Macedonian' to a Slav nation the Greeks refuse to face up to their own contribution to Macedonian nation-building:

(1) *The name Macedonia.* In the early 19th c. the modern Greeks with their Western-derived obsession with antiquity played a crucial role in reviving the classical name 'Macedonia' in the popular consciousness of the Balkan peoples. For a thousand years before that the name 'Macedonia' had meant different things for Westerners and Balkan Christians: for Westerners it always denoted the territories of the ancient Macedonians, but for the Greeks and all other Balkan Christians the name 'Macedonia' – if at all used – covered the territories of the

former Byzantine *thema* 'Macedonia', situated between Adrianople (Edrine) and the river Nestos (Mesta) in classical and present-day Thrace.[5] The central and northern parts of present-day 'geographic Macedonia' were traditionally called either 'Bulgaria' and 'Lower Moesia', but within a generation after Greek independence these names were replaced by 'Macedonia' in the minds of both Greeks and non-Greeks. In 1845 the Russian academic traveller Viktor Grigorovich registered a change in the title of the Greek bishop of Bitola – from 'Exarch of all Bulgaria' to 'Exarch of all Macedonia'; while travelling in the region he also noted that the exceptional popularity of Alexander the Great 'felt as if impressed from outside on the people, as those who mentioned his name often could not describe him without further reference to the teachers and their books on the subject.'[6] The massive presence of the Greek schools and teachers inevitably led to some 'Macedonization' of all Orthodox Christians, including the ones that were ethnically and linguistically non-Greek. A comparison of statements by three teachers of different generations would show how gradual and natural was this process: in 1816 and 1840 Kiril Peichinovich described the language of his books as 'the simplest Bulgarian language of Lower Moesia' and placed Skopje and Tetovo in 'Lower Moesia'; in 1851 Yordan Hadzhikonstantinov-Dzhinot (1818–1882) would still routinely speak about 'the Bulgarians of Lower Moesia' but at the same time put Skopje 'in the Albanian and Macedonian lands'; in 1862 the vehemently Bulgarian and anti-Greek Rayko Zhinzifov (1839–1877) knew no other name for his native land apart from Macedonia. In the 1860s Petko Slaveykov, one of the Bulgarian national revival leaders, was puzzled by the existence of compatriots who would deny that they were Bulgarian and would rather describe themselves as Macedonians, descendants of Philip and Alexander.[7]

(2) *The making of 'the Macedonian Slavs'*. The very term 'Slav Macedonian' was widely popularised by the Greeks since the 1890s in order to emphasise a separateness from the Bulgarian church, nation and state, and conversely, to stimulate closeness to the Greeks through a linkage with the ancient Macedonians.[8] These Slav Macedonians allegedly lacked any ethnic/national affiliations apart from their 'natural' religious links with the Greeks (the Greek definition for such hapless Slavic speakers – 'Slavophones' – has survived to this day in Greek Macedonia). It is hardly a coincidence that today the most fervent believers in the continuity between present-day and ancient Macedonians are the Slav emigrés from Greek Macedonia in Australia

and Canada – most of whom have undergone Greek schooling for several generations either in Greece or abroad. Ironically, although these emigrés are now vehemently anti-Greek and pro-independent Macedonia, they continue to mirror-image the Greeks in their obsession with antiquity and in downgrading the Slavness of contemporary Macedonians.[9]

Bulgaria

Bulgarians either deny the contemporary reality of a Macedonian nation and language, or – when they do acknowledge it – ascribe it entirely to Serbian, Comintern and Titoist propaganda. But this fails to take account of a natural withering-away of Bulgarian identity in Vardar and Aegean Macedonia in the 1920s–1940s, and also neglects the Bulgarian contribution to Macedonian nation-building.

A natural dying-out of Bulgarian identity?

Although it seems that before the 1940s the majority of the population in Vardar Macedonia professed some sort of a Bulgarian identity – as a legacy from medieval history and the Bulgarian national revival in the nineteenth century[10] – this same population at the very same time had also a very strong Macedonian identity – as a result of specifically Macedonian struggles for the fifty years preceding the 1940s. Once specifically Macedonian interests came to the fore under the Yugoslav communist umbrella and in direct confrontation with the Bulgarian occupation authorities, the Bulgarian part of the identity of Vardar Macedonians was destined to die out – in a process similar to the triumph of Austrian over German-Austrian identity in the post-war years.[11] Unlike Austria, however, which stopped being German but was constituted as an independent state, the nation-building process in Macedonia was distorted in at least two ways: (1) because of the Yugoslav dimension this process acquired some overt 'Yugoslav' (in effect Serbian) characteristics in alphabet and language, and (2) because of the firm communist control of the process (resulting in predilection to remove every obstacle by massive repression) everything linked to Bulgaria was forcibly and bloodily suppressed.

Bulgarian contributions to Macedonian nation-building

In the circumstances of the 1940s Yugoslav-inspired national 'Macedonism' was a natural outgrowth of the Bulgarian-oriented political Macedonism of the preceding decades. From a contemporary perspective there can be no doubt that the only lasting legacy of the late-nineteenth-century Bulgarian-Macedonian ideas about 'autonomy' or 'independence' of Macedonia (propagated often with violent means by IMARO – the Internal Macedonian – Adrianopolitan Revolutionary Organisation at the turn of the century – and by its successor IMRO – the Internal Macedonian Revolutionary Organisation in the 1920s–1930s) was the implanting of a very strong Macedonian identity (albeit initially a non-ethnic one) among Macedonian Bulgarians in the whole territory of 'geographic Macedonia', which no doubt facilitated their later 'Macedonisation' and deBulgarisation.[12] This process was not completed in the 1940s: the majority of Pirin Macedonians and the descendants of the pre-1944 Macedonian diaspora from all parts of geographic Macedonia have retained to this day their Bulgarian identity (coupled with a strong Macedonian regional identity), while the majority of Vardar Macedonians and the post-1944 Macedonian diaspora from Vardar and Aegean Macedonia nowadays consider themselves as belonging to a separate and non-Bulgarian Macedonian nation.

Until the 1940s Bulgarian academia and Bulgarian propaganda played a major role in countering Greek claims about the Greekness of ancient Macedonians, and – very similar to the present-day Skopje line – insisted either that they were a people totally separate from the Greeks (in more academic publications), or that they were Slavs or directly related to present-day Bulgarian-Macedonians (in popular propaganda).[13]

Serbia

Unlike Greeks and Bulgarians, in 1996 the Serbs completed the process of diplomatic recognition of the Macedonian name, state, nation and language to the full satisfaction of Skopje.[14] To the annoyance of Greece and the Greek diaspora, on 8 April 1996 FRY recognised Skopje under the name 'Republic of Macedonia' (similar to Bulgaria but unlike Albania, which recognised Skopje as FYROM in April 1993), and it also recognised 'the state continuity of Macedonia' since 1944. The latter was explicitly linked to the 1944 session of the 'anti-fascist assembly of national liberation of Macedonia' (ASNOM), which is also referred to in the Preamble of the present Macedonian Constitution and is considered offensive by the Greeks – because at this session ASNOM addressed Macedonians in Greece and Bulgaria about 'self-determination of the entire Macedonian people' and described Yugoslav Macedonia as a 'Macedonian Piedmont'. Belgrade also accepted the Macedonian formula that the document was prepared in two copies 'in Macedonian and Serbian languages' (a formula rejected by Bulgaria, which insists on a formula 'the official languages of both countries', thus avoiding an explicit mention of a separate Macedonian language).

While Serbian attitudes to Macedonian identity seem straightforward at the political level, difficulties remain at the academic level. The accepted view of even the most moderate Serbian academics does not deviate significantly from the early-twentieth-century theory popularised by the famous Serbian geographer and ethnographer Jovan Cvijic: that throughout the ages the Macedonian Slavs were devoid of any particular ethnic characteristics, and always represented a part of 'une masse flottant' that stretched between 'true' Serbs and 'true' Bulgarians – from Timok and Morava in the north-west to the Aegean and Iskar (a river east of Sofia) in the south-east. This theory confused two very different realities:

(1) In the nineteenth century a transitional territory between Serbs and Bulgarians existed not only between Nish and Sofia, but also between Nish and Belgrade: the conviction that only to the west of Belgrade Serbian language and culture were free of any Bulgarian influence prompted the great Serbian reformer Vuk Karadjic to base his 'authentic' Serbian language on the Hercegovina dialects.[15]

(2) Serbian national revival and statehood started decades before their Bulgarian equivalents, and as a result of that not only all 'transitional' Serbs between Belgrade and Nish were fully Serbianised, but Serbia could lay claim to the 'transitional' Bulgarians to the south-east of Nish as well. By the end of the nineteenth century Serbia had largely assimilated the 'floating' populations along the rivers Timok and South Morava (previously known as Bulgarian Morava), and turned its attention to Macedonia.[16] In 1906 Cvijic summarised his 'Slav Macedonian theory' in the following way: the Macedonian Slavs were an amorphous mass that could be easily made either Serb or Bulgarian depending on the strength of the relevant propaganda; 'the name Bugarin/Bulgarian with which the Macedonian Slavs usually call themselves is not an ethnographic name and does not mean that they are ethnic Bulgarians'; according to him all previous ethnographic maps were not based on linguistic material (Cvijic himself was not a linguist) but were coloured 'on the basis of the erroneously understood Bulgarian name, with which the Macedonian Slavs often call themselves'.[17] The problem with this

concept is that it defined the existing self-identification of the Macedonian Slavs as 'erroneous' (in 1914 the highly respected and impartial Carnegie international commission – created 'to inquire into the causes of the Balkan wars' – called Cvijic's term 'Slav-Macedonian' 'a euphemism designed to conceal the existence of Bulgarians in Macedonia'[18]). Thus Cvijic's approach in the beginning of the twentieth century is identical to the position of many Greek and Bulgarian politicians and academics in the 1990s, when they deny to present-day Macedonians the opportunity to express an 'erroneous' identity.

Republic of Macedonia

The strength of the Macedonian position is primarily based on a concrete political reality attested by all independent observers: nowadays the majority population of the Republic of Macedonia is firmly convinced that it forms a Macedonian nation and speaks a Macedonian language. Against this fact the protestations of many Greeks and Bulgarians that this self-identification is somehow inaccurate carry little weight. Self-identifications by definition mean only what the people themselves say – irrespective of whether they are historically 'accurate' or not. In the nineteenth century the Greeks changed their traditional self-identification as *Romaioi* into *Hellenes* (and the language from *Romaika* into *Hellenika*) – which represented a shift of emphasis from the Byzantine to the ancient Greek legacy. At the same time the Rumanians replaced the 'u' in their traditional name with 'o' in order to assert a more explicit link with ancient Rome. Both nations attempted respectively re-Hellenisation and re-Latinisation of their demotic speeches, and the Romanians also changed their alphabet from Cyrillic to Latin in the 1860s. Against this background the Macedonians can hardly be considered as an 'artificial' nation. Still, the reality of the present-day Macedonian identity by no means makes it a reality in previous times. After 1944 Macedonians have certainly copied other Balkan nations in streamlining and simplifying their historical pedigree. Moreover, the late coming of Macedonian nationalism makes it curiously indebted to the very propagandas that it so vociferously exorcises.

The 'link' to the ancient Macedonians

The explicit or implicit claims of present-day Macedonians that since Alexander the name 'Macedonia' has always denoted 'their land' are wildly inaccurate. The ethnic groups inhabiting the former territories of the ancient Macedonians and the adjacent lands hardly ever called them 'Macedonia' for a period of almost a thousand years before the early nineteenth century. In the Byzantine period the name 'Macedonia' applied to part of what is now Thrace, and the territory of the present-day Republic of Macedonia was the core of the Byzantine province of Bulgaria. Until the late nineteenth century the Turks did not even know that they were in occupation of a place called 'Macedonia'. The term 'Macedonia' was regularly applied to the territories of the ancient Macedonians only by Western travellers, cartographers and politicians after the Renaissance, and was widely re-adopted for local use first by the Greeks in the early nineteenth century.

Macedonians as the oldest Slav nation

The basic dogma of Macedonian historiography, namely, that there was an uninterrupted existence of a self-conscious 'Slav Macedonian' entity since the settlement of the Slavs in 6–7C AD to the present day, certainly ranks amongst the world's best-kept secrets for the last 15 centuries.[19] That SS Cyril and Methodius, St Clement, Tsar Samuel and every other significant personality hailing from these lands until the nineteenth century, self-consciously had a Macedonian identity, is something believed only in the Republic of Macedonia, in the Macedonian diaspora, and among the more gullible of their Western apologists. The same goes for the portrayal of Gotse Delchev's IMARO (The Internal Macedonian–Adrianopolitan Revolutionary Organisation) from the turn of the century as an 'ethnic Macedonian' organisation (the acronym VMORO/ IMARO has been routinely abbreviated in Macedonian historiography to VMRO/IMRO to avoid difficult questions about the presence in the same organisations of people nowadays described as 'ethnic Macedonians' from geographic Macedonia – together with 'ethnic Bulgarians' from the Adrianople region). In all these cases a present-day reality is projected wholesale into the past.

Conclusion

Despite all their differences one feature is common for all Balkan interpretations of the Macedonian identity – be they Greek, Bulgarian, Serbian or Macedonian: none of them recognises the importance of historical change, in either the past or the present, or both are evaluated exclusively in 'moral' terms. Thus, if ancient Macedonians were Greek, then no one other than contemporary Greeks has the right to use the Macedonian name – now or in the future. If Macedonian Slavs considered themselves Bulgarian at the turn of the twentieth century, this surely must have been erroneous: they must have been Serb, or at least halfway between Serbs and Bulgarians. If Macedonian Slavs once considered themselves Bulgarians, then they are Bulgarians nowadays as well. If nowadays they consider themselves Macedonians, then they must have been always Macedonians and, of course, will always be Macedonians. However, if the tortuous history of the Macedonian Question is any guide, it surely shows how fluid and unexpectedly changeable these identities can be.

Notes

1. In 1913, 'geographic Macedonia' was divided up among Greece (51%), Serbia, later Yugoslavia (39%) and Bulgaria (10%). Since 1991 the former Yugoslav and Serbian share became the Republic of Macedonia.
2. For Isocrates' opinion on the ancient Macedonians, see his speech 'Ad Philip', 105ff. Thucydides similarly listed the Macedonians amongst the Barbarians: Thucydides 2.81, 4.124 and 4.126. I am obliged to Dr Andrew Fear of the Department of Classics at Keele University for drawing my attention to these sources.
3. For a good summary of such arguments, see M. B. Sakellariou (ed.), *Macedonia. 4,000 Years of Greek History and Civilisation* (Athens, 1988), pp. 48–63. After an examination of the available evidence Prof. Sakellariou comes to a definite conclusion: 'the Macedonians were a Greek tribe' (p. 63). According to the same author the fact that all Greek contemporaries of Philip and Alexander thought otherwise was of little consequence: they were either 'mistaken', or 'enemies of the Macedonians' (*ibid.*, p. 54). For the role of archeology in legitimating the Greek position see also Loring M. Danforth, *The Macedonian Conflict: Ethnic Nationalism in a Transnational World* (Princeton, 1995) pp. 169–170, 172.
4. League of Nations statistics quoted from G. Zotiades, *The Macedonian Controversy* (Athens, 1961), pp. 39–40. According to Elizabeth Barker, at that time about half of the native Greeks in Macedonia were in fact Slavs belonging to the Constantinople Patriarchate. See E. Barker, *Macedonia. Its Place in Balkan Power Politics* (Royal Institute of International Affairs, 1950), p. 11.
5. For a detailed examination of the millenial 'migration' of the term 'Macedonia' see Koledarov's chapter in Francis William Carter, (ed.) *An Historical Geography of the Balkans* (London, 1977) and N. Andriotes *History of the Name 'Macedonia'* (Balkan Studies, Thessaloniki 1960); on the Byzantine *thema* 'Macedonia' see Sakellariou, p. 258, and the map on p. 319. About the nineteenth century Western tendency to view Macedonia as a 'natural region' in its classical borders see H. R. Wilkinson, *Maps and Politics. A Review of the Ethnographic Cartography of Macedonia* (Liverpool, 1951) pp. 1–3. Wilkinson's painstaking analysis of over 200 ethnographic maps of Macedonia of the nineteenth and twentieth centuries makes his book an indispensable reading for everyone who wants to orient himself in the web of mutually exclusive claims about Macedonia.
6. V. Grigorovich, *Ocherk puteshestviya po evropeyskoy Turtsii* (Moscow, 1877) pp. 95, 139. This is the second edition, reprinted in Sofia in 1978; the first edition was published in Kazan in 1848.

7. Slaveykov outlined the main arguments of the 'Macedonists': descendants of the ancient Macedonians; pure Slavs unlike the 'Tartar' Bulgarians; their dialects were different from the ones in 'Upper Bulgaria'; were unhappy about the domination of 'Upper Bulgarians' and their language; wanted to turn 'the local Macedonian dialect' into a literary tongue; wanted to separate from the Bulgarian Exarchate and restore the Ohrid Archbishopric as a separate Macedonian Church – see Slaveykov P.R. 'Makedonskiyt vapros'. *Makedoniya*, 18 January 1871, and two letters to Exarch Antim from 1874 (quoted from Hristo Andonov-Poljanski, (ed.) *Dokumenti za borbata na makedonskiot narod za samostojnost i za nacionalna drzhava, vol. I*, (Skopje, 1981) pp. 208–210, 219–220).

8. In the 1870s the preferred term was 'Bulgarophone Greeks' (Greeks who happened to speak Bulgarian). By the 1890s the term was already 'Slavs-under-Greek influence', or Slavophones see Wilkinson, *Maps and Politics*, pp. 69–75, 120–4, and the literature quoted there. The main reason for the change was the emergence in the 1880s of a concerted Serbian propaganda in Macedonia: the Serbs had redesigned the 'Bulgarophones' in Macedonia into some sort of unidentified Slavs, and this development proved extremely beneficial to the Greek propaganda as well.

9. See Danforth, op. cit., pp. 42–6, 72–8, 104–5, 160–3, 185–96, 239–47. An early example of Greek-oriented Slavs, or Bulgarophones, who preferred to call their language 'Makedonski' instead of Bulgarian, is given by Alan Upward in *The East End of Europe*, L. 1908. While his Greek interpreter described the language of someone local as Bulgarian 'the man himself said Makedonski ... it was Macedonian, the Slave form of Makedonski... And so the "Bulgarophone" villagers are no longer willing to admit that they speak Bulgarian ' According to Upward, they voluntarily created a new expression, and vowed that from that time onwards their dialect would be called 'Makedonski', until they freed themselves from it. The Athenian friends of the author were reportedly thrilled by this development – Ibid. pp. 204–205.

10. Until the 1830s personalities from would-be Macedonia played a leading role in the Bulgarian national revival. The major centres of Bulgarian church traditions, Rila monastery, Hilendar and Zograf, were all situated there. Father Paisi, the author of the first 'Slav-Bulgarian History' (1762) was born in Bansko, now in Pirin Macedonia, and his history was written mostly in Zograf on Mount Athos. Later, Bulgarians from Macedonia again played a major role in the establishment of a separate Bulgarian church in the 1860s–1870s.

11. The best and the most balanced account for the initial enthusiastic welcome of the Bulgarian troops in Vardar Macedonia and later dissatisfactions with Bulgarian authoritarianism and overcentralisation can be found in Steven Palmer and Robert King, *Yugoslav Communism and the Macedonian Question* (Archon Books, Hamden, Connecticut, 1971), pp. 63–5.

12. A telling account of similar processes under way among Macedonian settlers in the USA can be found in the 1980 *Harvard Encyclopedia of American Ethnic Groups*, p. 692: 'Although the Macedonian Patriotic Organisation (an American offshoot of the earlier IMRO founded in 1922) claims that Macedonians are Bulgarians, its activity is centred on Macedonia. Little is said about Bulgaria. Most of the Americans born of Macedonian Bulgarian

descent have hardly any knowledge of Bulgaria and increasingly identify themselves simply as Macedonians. The purely Macedonian policies of the Macedonian Patriotic Organisation have increased indirectly the Macedonisation of older, Bulgarian-oriented immigrants and their descendants'.

13. For the academic arguments see Gavril Kazaroff 'Quelques observations sur la question de la nationalite des anciens Macedoniens', *Revue des Etudes Grecques*, 23 (1910). In his influential *Macedonia: Its Races and Their Future* (1906), Brailsford describes how in Macedonian villages 'the legend that Alexander was a Greek' was confronted by 'the rival myth that Alexander was a Bulgarian'. (p. 103)

14. The border between Serbia and Macedonia is still not demarcated several years after the Yugoslav recognition of Macedonia, and there are valid suspicions that Milosevic deliberately keeps this problem open as a leverage for pressure on Skopje.

15. For an extreme Bulgarian view on the transitional Serb-Bulgarian territory see Misirkov 'O znachenii Moravskago ili Resavskago narechiya dlya sovremennoy i istoricheskoy etnografii Balkanskago poluostrova', *Zhivaya starina*, VII, 3–4 (Saint Petersburg, 1898). Misirkov was the first to claim that the Slavs in the Belgrade-Nish transitional zone were 'closer to the so called Bulgarian Slavs rather than to the Serbo-Croats'. In 1903 the same author published the pamphlet 'On Macedonian Matters' – the future Bible of Macedonian 'national separatism'. In 1907 Misirkov renounced separatism, and in several articles published in the leading Macedonian academic journal in Sofia expanded his earlier extreme views 'on the issues of the border between the Bulgarian and Serbo-Croat languages and peoples' – see *Makedonsko-Odrinski Pregled*, 1907, nos 2, 4, 5, 6. Misirkov changed his views several more times before his death in 1926, vacillating between extreme Macedonian separatism and extreme Bulgarian nationalism.

16. According to Wilkinson, until 1890 the Morava region 'had been universally considered as exclusively Bulgarian ... The new interpretation which indicated the population to be wholly Serbian could mean either that the Slavs in the region had never been Bulgarian or that the Bulgarians had lost their national traits within 12 years of incorporation into Serbia ... This concession in favour of the Serbs had important repercussions on the formation of the Serb hypothesis about the amorphous character of the Macedonian Slavs ... Cvijic no doubt was thinking of the Slavs of the Nish and Leskovatz areas who, before 1878, had been regarded as Bulgarians but who, after those districts became part of Serbia, had become good Serbians' (Wilkinson, op. cit., pp. 105, 149). See also J. Cvijic, *Promatranja o etnografiji makedonskih slovena* (Beograd 1906), p. 12 (English edition: J. Cvijic, *Remarks on the Ethnography of the Macedo-Slavs*, L. 1906).

17. Cvijic, *ibid.*, p. 9.

18. *Report of the International Commission to Inquire into the Causes of the Balkan Wars* (Washington, Carnegie Endowment for International Peace, 1914) publication no. 4, p. 158.

19. In 1981 a two-volume collection of 'Documents on the Struggle of the Macedonian people for Independence and a Nation-state' was published by

Skopje University, and later translated into English and Russian. It contains hundreds of valuable documents, but for the period between 6 AD and 1846 only two of them show *local* use of the term 'Macedonia' by seemingly *local* Slavs: in the beginning of 13th c. one person from the Ohrid region was called 'Macedonian by origin' in a local administrative act, and in mid-14th c. another person described himself as 'Bratan from Macedonia' in a church inscription – see Andonov-Poljanski (ed.), pp. 121, 130.

Chapter 5

IMRO + 100 = FYROM? The politics of Macedonian historiography

Stefan Troebst

I used to think that the profession of history, unlike that of, say, nuclear physics, could at least do no harm. Now I know it can. Our studies can turn into bomb factories like the workshops in which the IRA has learned to transform chemical fertiliser into an explosive.

Eric J. Hobsbawm, 1993[1]

Introduction

On 3 November 1893 in the Ottoman *Vilâyet* capital of Selânik, nowadays known as Thessaloniki, seven Christian Orthodox intellectuals, speaking the eastern variety of the southern Slavic tongue founded a national-revolutionary and conspiratorial organisation in opposition to the ruling Sultan with the title of the '(Internal) Macedonian Revolutionary Organisation', abbreviated as IMRO. Their goal was the establishment of their own state, first in the form of territorial autonomy within the Ottoman Empire as a step towards independence. One hundred years later, on 8 April 1993, the United Nations admitted a state called the 'Former Yugoslav Republic of Macedonia', shortened to FYROM, as its 181st member.[2] The strongest political party of this new UN member state, the 'Internal Macedonian Revolutionary Organisation – Democratic Party for Macedonian National Unity', abbreviated as VMRO–DPMNE, had deliberately chosen the name of the underground movement which was founded a century earlier.[3] So does today's FYROM represent the fulfilment of the political agenda of the IMRO that existed towards the end of the nineteenth century? Is there a direct link to the VMRO-DPMNE of the twentieth century? Are we now seeing the result of a belated process, lasting over one hundred years, from the foundation of a nation to the formation of a state?

The construction of tradition through the interpretation of history

While the liberal, nationalist and 'governmental' wings of the historiography of the new Macedonian state emphatically endorse the 'IMRO + 100 = FYROM' formula, their counterparts in the neighbouring states of Bulgaria, Greece and Serbia-Montenegro declare it to be invalid. From the perspective of Sofia, the IMRO of the turn of the century was a genuinely Bulgarian organisation aimed at the annexation of the three historical regions of the then Ottoman Macedonia – the Pirin Mountains, the Vardar River region and the Aegean Coast – to Bulgaria. Consequently the 100th anniversary of the founding of IMRO in 1993 was celebrated in Skopje[4] as well as in Sofia.[5] This explains why within today's alliance of anti-Communist parties in Bulgaria, the Union of Democratic Forces, there is an 'Internal Macedonian Revolutionary Organisation – League of Macedonian Associations'.[6] Partly similar, although differing in crucial issues, are the Athens and Belgrade perspectives: they, too, hold the anti-Ottoman IMRO to be an organisation dominated by Bulgaria; yet, they consider the new Macedonia state and its titular nation to be a genetically manipulated, artificial product out of Stalin's and Tito's nation-building 'test-tube'.

From the point of view of Bulgarian, Serbian and Greek nationalism, the 'Macedonian Question' of the latter part of the nineteenth and the early part of the twentieth centuries was a zero-sum game – and remains so even today: every weakening of one's own position means a strengthening of one or both rivals, each gain a loss for the opposing side. The appearance of an extra, fourth, player in the shape of Macedonian nationalism was a surprise for Sofia as well as Athens and Belgrade, something unforeseen in their world view.[7] 'What cannot be, should not be' was the mantra for 'thinking away' the problem. From the Bulgarian point of view, Macedonian nationalism was a Serbian (!) folly; from a Greek point of view, it was a short-lived will-o'-the wisp of Moscow provenance; and from a Serbian point of view, hopes for the reversibility of the new Macedonians into 'Southern Serbs' alternated with the suspicion of their – concealed – 'Bulgaromania'. When what was termed the 'new' Macedonian Question[8] emerged in 1991, neither Bulgaria nor Serbia nor Greece had come up with any counter-strategies. From Sofia,

Belgrade and Athens only haphazard cries of war and complaint were to be heard. Just as a stunned Romania watched the neighbouring Socialist Soviet Republic of Moldavia follow the path of modern nation-building and finally become a state – the Republic of Moldova – the countries bordering the now independent Republic of Macedonia stumbled over their own continuing concepts of nationalism. Yet, 'Once Rumanian, always Rumanian!' had as little meaning for central Bessarabia as had analogous postulates for Vardar-Macedonia. The Moldovan 'prodigal son' did not return repentantly to his Romanian 'father', nor did the 'Daughter Macedonia', 'kidnapped and raped' in 1913 by Serbia and Greece, return to the bosom of 'Mother Bulgaria' after her 'release'. In both cases, the 'parents' were unable to develop any sense of understanding. In a similar fashion, the ability for abstraction of the Greek political class was nothing like sufficient to understand that the Macedonian nation, this 'Stalinist-Titoist soap bubble', did not burst immediately. And Serbian nationalism was stunned by the fact that the 'amorphous, temporary construction' populated primarily by 'Gypsies, Bulgarians and Shiptars' on the territory of 'the historical Southern Serbia', did not collapse like a house of cards after the withdrawal of the Yugoslav National Army in March 1992.

These politically significant but naïve interpretations of the modern history of Macedonia from Serbian, Greek, Bulgarian, and – not least – Macedonian points of view, the diverging and similarly amateurish opinions of Turkish and Albanian national historiographies in relation to Macedonia, as well as the even less effective conceptions of history of Aromunians, 'Egyptian' Roma, Torbeshs and others – all suffer from one and the same distortion of perspective: they assume one single line of tradition that, however thin it may be, is considered to be decisive and is extended rigorously in both directions along the axis of time. Contemporary ideas are easily projected back into the past, just as historical facts are extrapolated into the present and then on into the future.[9] Historical, ideological or political discontinuities and breaks, even changes of ethnonational paradigms, have no place in such static, deterministic interpretations of history.

A striking example of this is the Russian-Ottoman Preliminary Peace Treaty of San Stefano (3 March 1878) providing for an independent Bulgaria. According to this agreement, Bulgaria's borders were the Danube, the Aegean Sea and Lake Ohrid – i.e. incorporating all three parts of historical Macedonia. Bulgarian national historiography turned this treaty into the fixed point in the system of coordinates of Bulgarian nationalism. In terms of history, it is a simple mistake, since the territorial shape of the various Bulgarian empires during the Middle Ages only partly coincides with the frontier lines drawn up in San Stefano. From a political perspective, however, the San Stefano myth was (and is) a stunning success. Having been the Bulgarian National Holiday up to 1946, San Stefano Day of 3 March was again proclaimed in 1990.[10]

Similar historiographic mechanisms are used by the neighbouring national historiographies which likewise do not necessarily mature with increasing institutionalisation and professionalisation. Only in the rarest cases are the creators of myths capable of flexibly coping with reality – e.g. bridging the gap between the mythical Bulgarian picture of the nineteenth-century Vardar region and the present state of mind of the inhabitants of the Republic of Macedonia. Neither can they bridge the gap between the Kosovo myth of Serbian nationalism and the Albanian domination in today's Kosovo. Here the newcomers to Balkan nationalism are clearly at an advantage as their newly created system of coordinates still allow for corrections. For instance, in the first programmatic blueprints of Macedonian national history from the 1940s, the decade from the foundation of IMRO in 1893 to the 'Ilinden Uprising' on 2 August 1903 (St Elias Day), and the subsequent 10-day 'Republic of Kruševo'[11], was identified as the birth date of the Macedonian nation.[12] Immediately, however, the new Marxist-Leninist paradigm of world history resulted in a redating by a couple of decades: nations, it was now proclaimed, are the product of capitalism, and the capitalist mode of production was applied in Ottoman Macedonian from the first half of the nineteenth century on.[13] Yet, as soon as an institutionalised form of historiography came into existence in the 1950s, Tsar Samuel's founding of empire in the late tenth century was described as the embryonic stage of Macedonian statehood, and the Great Migration of the Peoples with the arrival of the Slavs in the Balkans in the sixth and seventh centuries identified as the birth of the Macedonians. Moreover, in the early 1990s, this birth date was advanced even further, this time to the fourth century BC – i.e. to the days of Philip II of Macedonia[14] and his son Alexander the Great, known as 'Alexander the Macedonian' to the Slavic peoples. And finally, the rivalry of Greek nationalism instigated present-day amateur historians and archaeologists in Skopje to examine the hypothesis that today's Macedonians are descendants of an archaic people related to the Etruscans and Basques, one which is much older than the ancient Greeks. This is the reason why the relationship between the Macedonians and Greeks, as far as national historiography is concerned, is not dissimilar to that between the fairy-tale hare and the hedgehog.[15]

The interpretations of the ethnogenesis and formation of the South Slavs in the Macedonian region from prehistoric times until the present made by propagandists of history and professional historians in Athens, Belgrade, Sofia, Thessaloniki and other places diverge so much that they are completely incompatible. Moreover, the fact that these interpretations are all in tune with programmes of Macedonian, Greek, Bulgarian and Serbian nationalisms arouses the suspicion that the professional ethics of expert historians are being made – either voluntarily or otherwise – to fit the ups and downs of current politics. In other words, what appears under the label of 'scholarly research' is deceptively packaged: on the one hand, what is inside is not what the label describes – low-value 'politics' instead of high-value 'research' – and on the other hand, the weight of the box does not correspond to the information on the label; instead of the announced 'whole truth', one gets only a subjective fraction.

Nevertheless, it would be too rash were one to dispose of these products from the laboratories of rival national historiographies once and for all: after all, national historiography is the mainstay of any national agenda and therefore possesses a considerable source value. Furthermore, many members of the first generation of historians in the Balkans have solid technical training from mostly Habsburg universities; although their historical field of vision has been restricted by the blinkers of nationalism, their researcher's eye for detail often has not been affected.[16] Finally, the importance and effect of the competition among the national historiographies should not be underestimated as a corrective – what one historiography deliberately suppresses as unpopular because it does not fit into its own Procrustean bed of national history, the other one will bring to light with malicious glee.[17] Thus, while the interpretation of national history of Balkan provenance and its artefacts, as in the fairly tale of Cinderella, can be consigned to the pigeon's crop without hesitation, there is quite a pot to be filled with results that qualify for further use.

This concerns, above all, the organisational history of the various movements, societies, parties, underground groups, etc. which were subsumed under the name 'Macedonian' until the founding of the Republic in 1944, partly even until the founding of the state in 1991. Between 1950 and 1989, Bulgarian historical expertise, outstandingly well equipped with both financial and human resources, earned great admiration in this area. The competition from Skopje, poorly treated by both state and party, had to take a step back. Yet, a lack of quantity can be balanced out by quality as the example of two 'lone fighters' on the historical front line, Ivan Katardžiev[18] and Blaže Ristovski, shows.[19] Almost everything substantial written and – in Katardžiev's case, edited[20] – about the organisational forms and programmatic foundations of the Macedonian National Movement over the last forty years in Skopje flows from the pens of these two historians. In contrast to Ristovski's research which centres primarily on intellectual history, Katardžiev incorporates in his work the concrete political effects of the various building blocks of ideas surrounding Macedonian national identity.

Up to 1989, the interdependence between politics and historiography in the then 'Socialist brother states' of Yugoslavia and Bulgaria was immense, as the controversy over Macedonia and its history demonstrated. The status of this by no means 'academic' dispute rose at times so much so that the Yugoslav–Bulgarian relationship as a whole was temporarily exposed to strong tensions – to the point of possible military consequences. In 1973, a knowledgeable observer wrote:

> Not only has the Macedonian debate been the most extensive and most bitter, it has also been the least esoteric of the nationality debates between Communist parties. Although both sides generally stayed within the framework of historical debate, they have gone farther by specifically accusing each other of making territorial claims. The other historical debates between East European states have generally stopped short of this.[21]

At that time, the Yugoslav–Greek relationship was different since it had excluded the Macedonian problem throughout the 1949–91 period. Non-aligned Yugoslavia was politically too important for the NATO member Greece for historiographic debates of the Macedonian kind to cast a cloud over bilateral relations. The changes of scene in 1991 came all the more drastically: Bulgaria, the main opponent in the Macedonian controversy, made an attempt to style itself as the protector of Skopje, whereas Greece, along with Serbia, would have preferred that the new Macedonian state disappear from the face of the earth. At the same time, Athens set in motion a powerful propaganda machine, the written output of which was supposed to 'do away with' the unpopular fact that a state by the name of Macedonia existed.

Even while the hysteria of the Hellenes over Macedonia in 1991–6 is fading away, Greek historians still play the part of collective propaganda makers *in macedonicis*. The role of historians in Skopje and Sofia is very similar. Few of them are presently able to resist the strong pressure from the government or the opposition. In Greece, Macedonia and Bulgaria, historiography is still a direct political action whenever the ancient, medieval and contemporary history of Macedonia is involved.

The difficult phase B

Thirty years ago, the Czech historian Miroslav Hroch developed a three-phase model of national mobilisation of what he called the smaller European nations – 'Phase A, the Learned Interest', 'Phase B, the National Agitation' and 'Phase C, the Mass Movement'.[22] Macedonia shows itself to be a special case, not, however, an exception. Phase C is most easily identifiable as the critical decade between 1944 and 1953. In accordance with instructions from Belgrade, Communists within the partisan movement of the Vardar region of Macedonia returned to the sparse Macedonian ideology of the previous decades and purposefully and successfully began to propagate a new ethnoregional identity: the Macedonian Nation.[23]

The 'academic' Phase A of Macedonian nationalism is also relatively easy to date, – i.e. the decades prior to 1893. Phase B, the phase of agitation, however, is more difficult to identify: does it completely bridge the gap between Phases A and C – that is the period of time between 1893 and 1944? Yes and no. Yes, if the mere existence of such political factors propagating a separate Macedonian identity are judged to be decisive; on the other hand, the answer is no if the effectiveness of this sort of ethnoregional propaganda is included in the equation. Between the foundation of IMRO in 1893 and the establishment of the Vardar Macedonian partisan parliament, the 'Anti-Fascist Assembly of the People's Liberation of Macedonia' (ASNOM) on 2 August 1944, there were several Phases B which, however, proved to be 'misfires' that did not trigger any mass impacting Phase C. First, ASNOM which, according to the cast-iron logic of Macedonian nationalism, was appropriately named the 'second Ilinden', led to the foundation of a Vardar Macedonian constituent republic a year later in the 'new' Yugoslavia of Tito. The new republic provided the basis and starting point for a rapid nation-building. 1991 then acted as a litmus test for the existence of the Macedonian nation – as its 'third Ilinden'.

So which were the failed Phase B starts during the period of time from 1893 to 1944, and what were the reasons for so many misfires?

There are at least two failed attempts – the first the time-span from the foundation of the organisation in 1893 until the attempted uprising in 1903,[24] and a second the years from the Paris Peace Conference in 1919 until the final left-right split of the Macedonian movements in 1924. Whether or not there were any moves towards a Phase B during the 1930s is not clear at present.

The first unsuccessful attempt towards a Phase B within the Macedonian national movement during the decade between 1893 and 1903 is fully covered by western research.[25] It began with the foundation of IMRO and ended with the bloody failure of the 'Ilinden Uprising' in 1903. Half a dozen national–revolutionary organisations – partly in parallel or even in alignment with one another (more frequently, however, against one another, either within the Ottoman Empire, or from neighbouring states) – were pushing ahead for the separation of the Macedonian region from the crumbling empire. At that time, the question of what was meant by 'Macedonia' and 'Macedonian' in relation to Macedonian state-building and nation-building was problematic and therefore the cause of constant controversy, as was the definition of the final objective. In the view of various movements and organisations within the national–revolutionary movements inside the Ottoman Empire, the terms 'Macedonia' and 'Macedonian' could refer to at least two different ethnopolitical contents. On the one hand, they could have a regional connotation. This meant that anyone living within the area described as the Macedonian heartland of the 'three Vilâyets' – Selânik, Manastir and Kosova – was in this sense Macedonian. This would therefore include South Slav peoples, Aromunians, Turks, Albanians, Sephardim, Greeks, Roma, Yuruks, Circassians, Gagauz and Torbeši, among others. On the other hand, 'Macedonia' and 'Macedonian' could be understood in an ethnolinguistic sense, with territorial and denominational components: in this interpretation, Macedonians were only those who (1) spoke east-southern Slavic, and (2) were Christians. These problems of definition were in no way simplified by the fact that in the view of several Macedonian organisations, these two interpretations were compatible with each other – that there were Macedonians in a wide regional sense as well as a narrow ethnolinguistic sense, the latter being a subset of the former. The picture became completely confused at the turn of the century because of the Macedonian–Thracian duality. At that time, IMRO acted as a national–revolutionary movement not only in the 'three Vilâyets' but also in the Vilâyet Edirne in Thrace, a region which today is divided among Turkey, Greece and Bulgaria and which was (and is) characterised by a strong mix of Southern Slavs, Greeks, Turks, Armenians and Pomaks, among others.[26] The differentiation between a Macedonian and a separate Thracian national–revolutionary organisation first took place after the division of the remaining territory of the Ottoman Empire in Europe during the course of the Balkan Wars of 1912–13.[27] To complicate things further, regarding the term 'Macedonian', one has always to keep in mind the centres of Macedonian emigration in Europe and overseas, as well as the widespread Macedonian Diaspora. From the end of the nineteenth century, Orthodox Slavs emigrated from Macedonia to the Americas and later also to Australia. Ensuing situations of political, and then economic, crisis as well as the Greek Civil War of 1946 to 1949 led to a Macedonian emigration to almost all European states, so that nowadays 'Macedonia' is not just found in Prilep and Berovo, Valandovo and Kumanovo, but also in Toronto and Indianapolis, Szeczin and Gothenburg, Buenos Aires and Berlin, even in Tashkent and Sydney.[28]

The forms of the much searched-for solution to the 'Macedonian Question' also differed from period to period, and from organisation to organisation. The term 'autonomy', for example, was seen as an unfortunate but necessary preliminary stage for unification with Bulgaria by pro-Bulgarian groups in the Macedonian spectrum – following the model of the short-lived autonomy in East Rumelia.[29] The Macedonian politicians who cooperated with the young Turks interpreted the term in the sense of a self-administrated province inside and under the protection of the Ottoman Empire. The same applies to the different concepts of Macedonian independence: when the IMRO of the inter-war period spoke of an independent Macedonia, they meant a second Bulgarian state; when the Partisans during the Second World War spoke of liberation, they meant shaking off Bulgarian occupation and returning to a restored but federalised Yugoslavia with a constituent republic that included, besides Vardar Macedonia, also Pirin and Aegean Macedonia.

The second beginning of a Phase B in the Macedonian national movement took place, as indicated, in 1919. The successful instrumentalisation of Macedonian organisations by Imperial Germany with the aim of persuading Bulgaria to enter the First World War, as well as the participation of the same organisations in the Bulgarian occupation of Vardar Macedonia and parts of Serbia, turned the defeat of Bulgaria in 1918 also into a defeat for Macedonia.[30] The kaleidoscope of Macedonian political organisations was again well shaken up by events. The result was an overall consensus that the unstable post-war arrangements for the Balkans drawn up in Paris in 1919–20 should be revised. 'Autonomy' for Macedonia was substituted for the concept of 'independence'.[31] Alongside the building of an inherent 'IMRO state within a state' in the Bulgarian territory of Pirin Macedonia, there were attempts to snatch the territory of Vardar Macedonia from the newly established Kingdom of the Serbs, Croats and Slovenes – from 1929 onwards known as Yugoslavia – by means of guerrilla warfare.[32] Diplomatically and logistically, IMRO leaned upon Italy and the new Soviet Union for support as the weakened war-time ally Germany did not react to approaches by the Macedonian guerrillas.[33] The level of coordination between the left- and right-wing organisations in Macedonia and the level of mobilisation of the groups targeted was considerable. The compromise reached was, however, of a generational nature: it collapsed within a few years when the pre-war generation within IMRO was replaced by young hardliners. In 1924 a deep ideological divide opened up within the Macedonian movement. Questions about means and aims became unimportant.[34] Reduced to an element of the Moscow-dominated Communist International, the so-called United IMRO (UIMRO) lost contact with its surroundings as outside control increased,[35] and the Mihailovist and Shandanovist right wings of IMRO, forced into the service of Fascist Italy, National-Socialist Germany, and even the Yugoslavia of the Karadjordjeviches, wiped each other out in bouts of fratricidal violence. The liberal-federalist organisations, as represented by the 'Macedonian Federal Émigré Organisation'[36] (MFEO) and the unpolitical union of the veterans of the 1903 uprising, the 'Ilinden Organisation',[37] (IO) were now caught between the millstones of the great rivalling Macedonian organisations.

The protagonists of the autochthonous new beginnings of a Macedonian movement in the Vardar Macedonian region of Yugoslavia during the second half of the 1930s, such as the 'Macedonian People's Movement' (*Makedonski naroden pokret* – MANAPO) founded in 1935,[38] were then absorbed during the Second World War by the career opportunities offered by the Bulgarian occupation regime and by the newly emerging Partisan movement. From 1943 onwards the Communist–Yugoslav symbiosis of Belgrade provenance dominated the Communist–Macedonian alliance shaped by Skopje. In two steps, in 1944 and 1949, the non-Communist as well as the not decidedly anti-Bulgarian protagonists of Macedonian consciousness were ruthlessly eliminated. However, the relative and repressive tolerance of the Titoist system can be seen in the fact that memory

of the non-Communist alternatives in the Macedonian movement survived until 1991 and was passed on. Outlining this problem, the
German historian Heinz Willemsen notes that this was a process not
free of conflict:

> The relationship between the victorious Partisans in 1944 and the
> tradition of the Macedonian movement within the Ottoman Empire
> was by no means as unbroken as it has seemed to be since the
> 1970s. Many of the founders of the Republic were not like the
> Communists of the 1920s part of the tradition of the Macedonian
> movement. This led to a great dispute with the older and tradition-
> ally pro-Bulgarian generation within the party during the Partisan
> War of 1941–44. In this controversy, the group of pro-Yugoslav
> members who were 10–20 years' younger than the pro-Bulgarians
> came to assert itself. This group also included present-day president
> Kiro Gligorov. Originating mostly from the regional rudimentary
> middle class, many of them had studied in Belgrade or Zagreb.
> There they had quickly joined a movement related to the
> Communist Party of Yugoslavia, the so-called 'progressive students'.
> After 1944 they threw themselves with great energy into the project
> of Macedonian nation-building.[39]

In a study on the different layers of *identité macédonienne*, the French
historian of the Balkans, Bernard Lory, has pointed to territorial, linguistic, religious, historical, cultural and political components, as well
as to other factors crucial to identity such as *identification á la terre*, and
identité diasporique. He has also dealt with a specific form of affinity
held by the ethnonational and ethnoreligious groups within the
modern-day Republic of Macedonia and has referred to this complicated phenomenon by the apt term *identité oecuménique*.[40] And with
reference to Fredrik Barth's emphasis of borders being the strongest
factor for the identity of an ethnic group,[41] he stressed that this bundle
of identifiers is open to enlargement. As difficult as a positive
definition of Macedonian consciousness still remains, its definition *ex
negativo* is all the more simple: in political terms clearly non-Greek,
non-Serbian, non-Bulgarian and non-Albanian, whereas in terms of
culture, having a Serbian, Albanian, or even Bulgarian origin is perfectly compatible with an 'ecumenical' Macedonian identity.

   The social processes during the difficult transition to the independence of the early 1990s had the effect of bringing about the appearance of a right-wing Macedonian nationalist movement in Macedonia

in the form of the VMRO-DPMNE. Yet, the lines of division do not run between the Macedonian majority and the non-Macedonian minorities in the country. In fact, since 1992 a coalition government made up of post-Communists and moderate Albanians faces an anti-centralist, anti-Communist and predominantly youthful front that at least partially coordinates its activities and whose two pillars are the VMRO-DPMNE and the radical Albanian party. The dominant left-right divide and the – politically secondary – difference between the titular nation and the minorities present cross-cutting cleavages with strong generational characteristics.

1991: The point of no return

Not coincidentally, the year 1991 in the Republic of Macedonia saw the new popularity of a Partisan song that originated in 1941 in the Prilep region and was inspired by an anti-Ottoman predecessor, *A bre makedonče* ('Hey, Little Macedonian'):

> Hey, little Macedonian,
>> Where are you heading to?
> War is waiting for you,
>> War for freedom
> For Macedonia,
>> the subjugated country.
> So that today's tyrants
>> finally understand:
> The name of Macedonia will never perish.[42]

Although the song was heroic and its content apt for the year in which the independence of the country was declared, it failed to capture the general and rather gloomy mood. Not surprisingly, the Macedonian summer hit of the following year, *Sviri mi cigane* ('Play for me, Gypsy') by Rosana Sarik-Todorovska[43] adopted a much less warlike, melancholy tone: 'today we are happy and healthy, tomorrow we may not be so'. For even though the Yugoslav National Army had just left the country, the fear of war was growing. This was caused by the Serbian aggression against Bosnia-Herzegovina and the influence of Greek blockade measures. It was not until the involvement of the international community – first from September 1992 onwards via the Spillover Monitor Mission of the Conference on Security and Cooperation in Europe (CSCE, today OSCE), then from January 1993 via a blue-helmet contingent of the

United Nations Protection Force (UNPROFOR) and, finally, in the form of admission into the United Nations in April of the same year – that any kind of stability prevailed in this region.[44] Since then, the Republic of Macedonia, a.k.a. FYROM, has proved itself to be a constructive political factor in the southern Balkans – in stark contrast to its northern and southern neighbours and despite the expectations of many experts. Eric J. Hobsbawm is therefore right in observing:

> It was not the 'Macedonian Question', well known to scholars as leading to battles between rival experts in a half-dozen fields at international congresses, which provoked the collapse of Yugoslavia. On the contrary, the Macedonian People's Republic did its best to stay out of the Serb–Croat imbroglio, until Yugoslavia was actually collapsing, and all its components, in sheer self-defence, had to look after themselves. (Characteristically enough, its official recognition has been hitherto sabotaged by Greece, which had annexed large parts of Macedonian territory in 1913).[45]

A popular pose of militant national movements and their 'ethnic entrepreneurs'[46] is standing against the rest of the world with their backs to the abyss. In a position like that, one can rightly demand an unanimous declaration of support by followers. In this respect, the protagonists of Macedonian nationalism have been lucky twice – in the 1940s as well as in the beginning of the 1990s. Both times, the impulses for political mobilisation for and public identification with the Macedonian national cause came from external forces – first by Bulgarian and then Greek nationalism. At the end of the Second World War, between the hammer of the Bulgarian regime and the anvil of the Macedonian partisans, a majority of the Christian Orthodox population of Vardar Macedonia had opted against Bulgarian national identity; and in 1991, in the face of Greek scorn, malice and hatred, as well as Milošević's campaigns against Slovenia and Croatia, a majority opted for political independence and thus for Macedonian national identity.[47]

In 1969 Mathias Bernath had prophesied with appropriate caution

> that the existence of an almost fully developed nationality in Vardar Macedonia is today a hypothesis which needs to be taken seriously, and which tomorrow will be an irreversible fact, provided there is no change in the mutual territorial assets of both Yugoslavia and Bulgaria during the course of the next two generations.[48]

The course of events since then has proved him right. Nevertheless, our title equation 'IMRO + 100 = FYROM', as propagated above all by Skopje's politicised historiography, is not only simplifying but also inaccurate: the Republic of Macedonia is not so much the result of years of systematic work by a Macedonian national movement, but a by-product of the implosion of post-Titoist Yugoslavia. What is more, neither the IMRO founded in 1893 nor the different organisations under the same name in the inter-war period were pursuing a coherent programme providing for the formation of an independent Macedonian state in the Vardar region and the building of a new and ethnically homogeneous Slavic nation of the Macedonians. As the degree of sovereignty of the new Republic of Macedonia is increasing, it can be expected that there will be a similar increase in the sovereignty of Macedonian, Bulgarian, Serbian, Greek and other Balkan historians who deal with the history of the Macedonian region from antiquity to the present – and especially with the crucial hundred years between 1893 and 1993.

Notes

1. Eric Hobsbawm, 'The New Threat of History', *New York Review of Books*, vol. 40, no. 21 (16 December 1993), pp. 62–4, here p. 63.
2. The 'Former Yugoslav Republic of Macedonia' is a misleading name, since the Republic of Macedonia is an existing, not a former one. 'Former' as well as no longer existing are the Socialist Federative Republic of Yugoslavia (SFRY) and its constituent part, the Socialist Republic of Macedonia (SRM), whereas the Serb-Montenegrin Federative Republic of Yugoslavia (FRY) still exists. With tongue in cheek, though convincingly, Norman Davies has opted for replacing FYROM by the historically more correct, yet considerably longer, abbreviation FOPITGROBBSOSY: 'Former Province of Illyria, Thrace, Greece, Rome, Byzantium, Bulgaria, Serbia, the Ottoman Empire, Serbia, and Yugoslavia'. Cf. Norman Davies, *Europe. A History* (Oxford and New York: Oxford University Press 1996), p. 135.
3. Georgievski, Lupčo: 'VMRO-Demokratska Partija za Makedonsko Nacionalno Edinstvo (1893–1993), sledbenik na ideite na VMRO', in Aleksandar Trajanovski *et al.*, *Zlatna kniga 100 godini VMRO* (Skopje, 1993), pp. 249–55. Cf. also Branislav Sinadinovski, *VMRO-DPMNE. Od vizii do stvarnost* (Skopje, 1993).
4. For the three wings of Macedonian historiography cf. *partes pro toto* their contributions to the 1993 anniversary: Ivan Katardžiev, *Sto godini od formiranjeto na VMRO – sto godini revolucionerna tradicija* (Skopje, 1993); in Trajanovski, 'Zlatna kniga 100 godini VMRO', and 'Sto godini od osnovanjeto na VMRO i 90 godini od Ilindenskoto vostanie. Prilozi od naučen sobir održan na 21–23 oktomvri 1993', Ksente Bogoev *et al.* (ed.) (Skopje, 1994).
5. *100 godini Vŭtrešna Makedono-Odrinska Revoljucionna Organizacija*, Dobrin Mičev and Dimitŭr G. Gocev (eds) (Sofia, 1994).

6. Milena Mahon, 'The Macedonian Question in Bulgaria', in *Nations and Nationalism*, 4, (1998), pp. 389–407.
7. Georgi D. Matzureff, 'The Concept of a "Macedonian Nation" as a New Dimension in Balkan Politics', PhD thesis (Washington, DC, 1978) and Stefan Troebst, Makedonische Antworten auf die 'Makedonische Frage' 1944–1992 'Nationalismus, Republiksgründung und *nation-building* in Makedonien', in *Südosteuropa*, 41 (1992), pp. 423–42. Cf. also John Shea, *Macedonia and Greece: The Struggle to Define a New Balkan Nation* (Jefferson, NC: McFarland, 1997) and Ivan Katardžiev, *Sosedite i Makedonija – včera, dnes, utre* (Skopje: Menora 1998), pp. 24–84.
8. James Pettifer, 'The New Macedonian Question', *International Affairs*, 68 (1992), pp. 475–85. Cf. also Pettifer, 'Macedonia: Still the Apple of Discord', *The World Today*, 51 (1995), pp. 55–58; Misha Glenny, 'The Macedonian Question: Still No Answers', *Social Research*, 62 (1995), pp. 143–60; and Sabrina P. Ramet, 'All Quiet on the Southern Front? Macedonia Between the Hammer and the Anvil', in *Problems of Post-Communism* (November–December 1995), pp. 29–36. For a critique of the concept of a 'new' Macedonia Question, see Viktor Meier, 'Von der mazedonischen zur griechischen Frage', *Europäische Rundschau*, 23 (1995), pp. 17–24.
9. For recent anthropological interpretations of this situation cf. Keith S. Brown, 'Of Meanings and Memories: The National Imagination in Macedonia', Ph D thesis, Department of Anthropology, University of Chicago (1995). Cf. also Brown, 'Seeing Stars: Character and Identity in the Landscapes of Modern Macedonia', *Antiquity*, 68 (1994), pp. 784–96; Jonathan M. Schwartz, 'The Petrified Forests of Symbols: Deconstructing and Envisioning Macedonia', *Anthropological Journal on European Cultures*, 4 (1995), pp. 9–23; Schwartz, Listening for Macedonian Identity: Reflections from Sveti Naum, in *Beyond Borders. Remaking Cultural Identities in the New East and Central Europe*. (Boulder, CO: Westview Press, 1997), pp. 95–110; and James Krapfl, 'The Ideals of Ilinden: Uses of Memory and Nationalism in Socialist Macedonian' in John S. Micgiel (ed.), *State and Nation Building in East Central Europe: Contemporary Perspectives* Ed. John S. Micgiel (New York. NY Institute on East Central Europe. Columbia University, 1996). 297– .
10. Cf. Andrej Pantev, 'Otkŭde idva treti mart', *Kultura* (Sofia), 9 (9 March 1991), p. 11; and Stefan Troebst, 'Fluchtpunkt San Stefano. Nationalismus in Bulgarien', *Die Neue Gesellschaft/Frankfurter Hefte*, 37 (1990) 5, pp. 405–414.
11. For the significance of the Kruševo myth and the modern Kruševo monument cf. Brown, 'Of Meanings and Memories'.
12. Kiril Nikolov, *Za makedonskata nacija* (Skopje 1948).
13. This 'heretic' view was repeated as late as 1971 by the 'liberal' leader of the League of Communists of Macedonia. Cf. Krste Crvenkovski, *Sojuzot na komunistite na Makedonija i demokratizacijata na opštestvoto* (Skopje, 1971), p. 144.
14. Vasil Tupurkovski, *Istorija na Makedonija – Filip II* (Skopje, 1995).
15. Cf. *partes pro toto* two recent authoritative publications from Skopje and Saloniki: Georgi Stardelov, Cvetan Grozdanov, Blaže Ristovski (eds), *Macedonia and Its Relations with Greece* (Skopje: Council for Research Into South-Eastern Europe of the Macedonian Academy of Sciences and Arts 1993); Basil Kondis, Kyriakos Kentrotis, Spyridon Sfetas and Yiannis D.

Stefanidis (eds), *Resurgent Irredentism. Documents on Skopje 'Macedonian' Nationalist Aspirations (1934–1992)* (Thessaloniki: Institute for Balkan Studies, 1993).

16. Emil Niederhauser, 'Vasil Zlatarski und seine osteuropäischen Berufskollegen' in Mito Isusov *et al.* (eds), *Sbornik včest na akademik Hristo Hristov. Izsledvanija po slučaj 70 godini ot roždenieto mu* (Sofia, 1989), pp. 204–15.

17. The most extreme among the many illustrative examples of this scientific-ethically questionable fact is probably the way in which an inscription found in Bitola in 1956 from the early eleventh century on Tsar Ivan Vladislav was dealt with by the authorities in the Yugoslav Macedonia. Originally exhibited in the local museum, the stone witness was locked away once Bulgarian archaeologists became aware of the epithet *samodŭržec bŭlgarski* ('Bulgarian autocrat') for the Tsar. Cf. Stefan Troebst, *Die bulgar-isch-jugoslawische Kontroverse um Makedonien 1967–1982* (Munich, 1983), p. 223.

18. Ivan Katardžiev, 'VMRO and the Macedonian Liberation Movement After the First World War', in Balkan Forum, 1 (1993), pp. 137–50; Katardžiev, *Borba do pobeda*, 4 vols (Skopje, 1988); Katardžier, *Borba za razvoj i afirmacija na makedonskata nacija* (Skopje, 1981); Katardžiev, *Po vrvicite na makedon-skata istorija* (Skopje, 1986); Katardžiev, *Sto godini od formiranjeto na VMRO*; and *Sosedite i Makedonija – včera, dnes, utre* (Skopje, 1998). Cf. also Voislav D. Kuševski, 'D-r Ivan Katardžiev – naš istaknat istoriograf i opštestvenik (Po povod 60-godišninata od raganjeto)' *Istorija*, 32 (1986), pp. 1–17; and Katardžiev, 'Selektivna bibliografija na objaveni trudovi na d-r Ivan Katardžiev', *Istorija*, 32 (1986), pp. 19–24.

19. Blaže Ristovski, 'The National Thought of Misirkov', in Balkan Forum, 4 (1996), pp. 129–70; Ristovski, *Krste P. Misirkov (1874–1926). Prilog kon proučuvanjeto na razvitokot na makedonskata nacionalna misla* (Skopje, 1966), Ristovski, *Makedonskiot narod i makedonskata nacionalna svest*, 2 vols (Skopje, 1968); Ristovski, *Dimitrija čupovski (1878–1940) i Makedonskoto naučno-literaturno drugarstvo vo Petrograd*, 2 vols (Skopje, 1978); Ristovski, *Makedonskiot stih 1900–1944. Istražuvanja i materiali*, 2 vols (Skopje, 1980), Ristovski, *Projavi i profili od makedonskata literaturna istorija*, 2 vols (Skopje, 1982); Ristovski, *Kočo Racin. Istorisko-literaturni istražuvanja* (Skopje, 1983); Ristovski, *Makedonskiot narod i makedonskata nacija*, 2 vols (Skopje, 1983); Ristovski, *Makedonskiot folklor i nacionalnata svest*, 2 vols (Skopje, 1987); Ristovski, *Portreti i procesi od makedonskata literaturna i nacionalna istorija*, 3 vols (Skopje, 1989–1990).

20. Ivan Katardžiev (ed.), *VMRO (Obedineta). Dokumenti i materijali*, 2 vols (Skopje, 1991–2); Ivan Katardžiev (ed.), *Makedonskata nacionalno-politička misla megu dvete svetski vojni*. Prilozi, (Skopje, 1991).

21. Robert R. King, *Minorities under Communism. Nationalities as a Source of Tension among Balkan Communist States* (Cambridge, Mass., 1973), p. 219.

22. Miroslav Hroch, *Social Preconditions of National Revival in Europe. A Compa-rative Analysis of the Social Composition of Patriotic Groups among the Smaller European Nations* (Cambridge, 1985).

23. H. R. Wilkinson, 'Jugoslav Macedonia in Transition', *The Geographical Journal*, 118 (1952), pp. 389–405; Stephen E. Palmer, Jr. and Robert R. King,

Yugoslav Communism and the Macedonian Question (Hamden, Conn.: Archon Books, 1971); Jutta De Jong, 'Die makedonische Nationswerdung – eigenständige Integration oder künstliche Synthese?', in Klaus-Detlev Grothusen (ed.), *Jugoslawien. Integrationsprobleme in Geschichte und Gegenwart* (Göttingen, 1984), pp. 163–77; Stefan Troebst, 'Yugoslav Macedonia, 1943–1953: Building the Party, the State and the Nation', in Melissa K. Bokovoy, Jill A. Irvine and Carol S. Lilly, *State-Society Relations in Yugoslavia, 1945–1992* (New York NY, 1997), pp. 243–66. Disappointing in this regard is a recent book, which explicitly set out to 'examine how Tito fostered a separate Macedonian consciousness', but failed to do so: Poulton Hugh, *Who Are the Macedonians?* (London: Hurst 1995) (back cover).

24. Jutta De Jong, *Der nationale Kern des makedonischen Problems. Ansätze und Grundlagen einer makedonischen Nationalbewegung (1890–1903). Ein Beitrag zur komparativen Nationalismusforschung* (Frankfurt/M. and Bern 1982), pp. 16, 290–1. However, another leading expert, Fikret Adanïr, proposes a completely different view. He states that the turn of the century brought about the coinciding of Phases A, B and C and from here demonstrates the inappropriateness of Hroch's Phase Models in the case of Macedonia. Cf. Fikret Adanir, 'The Macedonians in the Ottoman Empire, 1878–1912', in Andreas Kappeler, Fikret Adanir and Alan O'Day (eds), *The Formation of National Elites* (Aldershot, 1992), pp. 161–91, here p. 170; and Kappeler *et al.*, 'The Sociopolitical Environment of Balkan Nationalism: The Case of Ottoman Macedonia, 1856–1912', in Heinz-Gerhard Haupt, Michael G. Müller and Stuart Woolf (eds), *Regional and National Identities in Europe in the XIXth and XXth Centuries* (The Hague, London and Boston, Mass., 1998), pp. 221–54.

25. Fikret Adanir, *Die Makedonische Frage. Ihre Entstehung und Entwicklung bis 1908* (Wiesbaden, 1979); De Jong. *Der nationale Kern des makedonischen Problems;* Duncan M. Perry, *The Politics of Terror. The Macedonian Revolutionary Movements, 1893–1903* (Durham, NC, London, 1988).

26. Konstantin Pandev, *Nactionalnoosvoboditelnoto dviženie v Makedonija i Odrinsko 1878–1903* (Sofia, 1979).

27. See Katrin Boeckh, *Von den Balkankriegen zum Ersten Weltkrieg. Kleinstaatenpolitik und ethnische Selbstbestimmung auf dem Balkan* (Munich, 1996).

28. Cf. Ivan Katardžiev, *Makedonija i makedoncite vo svetot* (Skopje, 1996); Loring M. Danforth, *The Macedonian Conflict. Ethnic Nationalism in a Transnational World* (Princeton, NJ, 1995); Lillian Petroff, *Sojourners and Settlers: The Macedonian Community in Toronto to 1940* (Toronto, 1995); Peter Hill, *The Macedonians in Australia* (Carlisle, WA, 1989); Risto Kirjazovski, *Makedonskata politička emigracija od Egejskiot del na Makedonija vo-istočnoevropejskite zemji po vtorata svetska vojna* (Skopje, 1989); Lars Baerentzen, 'The "Paidomazoma" and the Queen's Camps, in Lars Baerentzen, John O. Iatrides and Ole L. Smith (København, 1987), *Studies in the History of the Greek Civil War 1945–49*, pp. 127–57; Mieczystaw Wojecki, 'Ludność grecko-maćedońska na Dolnym śląsku', *Sobotka, śląski kwartalnik historyczny*, 1 (1980), pp. 83–96.

29. For the historiographic echoes in Sofia cf. Dimitŭr G. Gocev, *Idejata za avtonomija kato taktika v programite na nacionalnoosvoboditelnoto dviženie v Makedonija i Odrinkso 1893–1941* (Sofia, 1983); and Kostadin Palešutski, 'Avtonomnoto načalo v bŭlgarskoto nacionalno-osvoboditelnoto dviženie v

Makedonija', in *Bŭlgarija 1300. Dokladi na Tretija kongres na Bŭlgarskoto istoričesko družestvo, 3–5 oktomvri 1981*. T. 3: *Institucii i dŭržavna tradicija* (Sofia, 1983), pp. 287–92.

30. Wolfgang-Uwe: Friedrich, *Bulgarien und die Mächte 1913–1915. Ein Beitrag zur Weltkrieges- und Imperialismusgeschichte* (Stuttgart, 1985).

31. IMRO, in particular, firmly believed in the feasibility of this concept, and had already started to design postal stamps for an independent Macedonian state. Cf. Max Demeter, Peyfuß, Nataša Vittorelli, Pro Macedonia. 'Briefmarken-entwürfe für ein unabhängiges Makedonien in der Zwischenkriegszeit', in Walter Lukan and Peter Jordan (eds), *Makedonien. Georgraphie – Ethnische Struktur – Geschichte – Sprache und Kultur – Politik – Wirtschaft – Recht* (Vienna, 1998), pp. 185–202. On other symbols of IMRO statehood cf. Stefan Troebst, 'Nationalismus und Gewalt im Osteuropa der Zwischenkriegszeit. Terroristische Separatismen im Vergleich', *Berliner Jahrbuch für osteuropäische Geschichte*, 1 (1996), pp. 273–314.

32. Ivan Katardžiev, *Vreme na zreenje. Makedonskoto nacionalno prašanje megu dvete svetski vojni (1919–1930)*. 2 vols (Skopje, 1977).

33. Stefan Troebst, *Mussolini, Makedonien und die Mächte 1922–1930. Die 'Innere Makedonische Revolutionäre Organisation' in der Südosteuropapolitik des faschis-tischen Italien*, (Cologne and Vienna, 1987); Troebst, 'Die "Innere Makedonische Revolutionäre Organisation" und die Außenpolitik der Weimarer Republik (1919–1933), in Wolfgang Gesemann, Helmut Schaller and Kyrill Haralampieff (eds), *Einundzwanzig Beiträge zum II. Internationalen Bulgaristik-Kongreß in Sofia (1986)*, (Neuried bei München, 1986), pp. 387–420; Troebst, 'Macedonia heroica': Zum Makedonier-Bild der Weimarer Republik, *Südost Forschungen*, 49 (1990), pp. 293–364.

34. Ivan Katardžiev, 'VMRO and the Macedonian Liberation Movement after the First World War', *Balkan Forum*, 1 (1993), pp. 151–64.

35. Andrew Rossos, 'Macedonianism and Macedonian Nationalism on the Left', in Ivo Banac and Katherine Verdery (eds), *National Character and National Ideology in Inter-war Eastern Europe* (New Haven, Conn., 1995), pp. 219–54.

36. Kostadin Palešutski, 'Sŭzdavane i dejnost na Makedonskata federativna organizacija (1920–1923 g.)', in *Izvestija na Instituta po istorija na Bŭlgarskata komunističeska partija*, 66 (1990), pp. 40–74; and Darinka Pačemska-Petreska, 'Makedonskata federativna grupa vo Viena i vesnikot "Makedonsko soz-nanje" vo periodot 1923–1925 godina', in *Glasnik na Institutot za nacionalna istorija*, 31 (1987), pp. 117–133.

37. Kostadin Palešutski, 'Ilindenskata organizacija (1921–1924 g.)', in *Izvestija na Instituta po istorija na Bŭlgarskata komunističeska partija*, 61 (1988), 84–116.

38. For basic information on this completely under-researched group see Kiril Miljovski, *Makedonskoto prašanje vo nacionalnata programa na KPJ (1919–1937)* (Skopje, 1962), pp. 140–54; and Dimitŭr G. Gocev, *Mladežkite nacionalno-osvoboditelni organizacii na makedonskite bŭlgari 1919–1941* (Sofia, 1988), pp. 64–70.

39. Heinz Willemsen, 'Politischer Konflikt und gesellschaftlicher Wandel in der jugoslawischen Teilrepublik Makedonien: "Funktion und Wandel des make-donischen Nationalismus 1944–1953"', (Bielefeld, 1997), p. 3 (ms) – with reference to Ivan Katardžiev, 'Makedonskite politički sili i istoriskoto nasled-stvo na makedonskiot narod', *Istorija*, 26–27 (1990–1), pp. 7–28).

40. Bernard Lory, 'Approches de l'identité macédonienne', in Bernard Lory and Christophe Chiclet (eds), *La Republique de Macdoine* (Paris, 1998), pp. 13–32. Cf. also Feroz A. K. Yasamee, 'Nationality in the Balkans. The Case of the Macedonians', in Gunay Göksu Özdoğan and Kemâli Saybaşili (eds), *Balkans. A Mirror of the New International Order* (Istanbul: 1995), pp. 121–132.
41. Fredrik Barth, 'Introduction', in Fredrik Barth (ed.), *Ethnic Groups and Boundaries. The Social Organisation of Culture Differences* (Oslo, 1969), pp. 9–38.
42. Blaže Ristovski, 'Kako e nastanata pesnata "A bre makedonče"', in Blaže Ristovski, *Makedonskiot folklor i nacionalnata svest*, 1, pp. 349–54.
43. 'Sviri mi cigane', music, text and arrangement by Tode Novačevski. Version referred to here is the A-side of cassette no. 1 of 'Folk hitovi na godinata "92"', Makedonska Radio-Televizija, MP 21120 (Skopje, 1992).
44. Alice Ackermann, 'The Former Yugoslav Republic of Macedonia: A Relatively Successful Case of Conflict Prevention in Europe', *Security Dialogue*, 27 (1996), pp. 409–24; Stefan Troebst, 'Präventive Friedenssicherung durch internationale Beobachtermissionen? Das Beispiel der KSZE-Spillover-Monitormission in Makedonien 1992–1993', in Gerhard Seewann (ed.), *Minderheiten als Konfliktpotential in Ostmittel- und Südosteuropa* (Munich, 1995), pp. 282–331.
45. E. J. Hobsbawm, *Nations and Nationalism Since 1870. Programme, Myth, Reality* (Cambridge, 1992), p. 166.
46. For the term 'ethnic entrepreneur' cf. Joseph Rothschild, *Ethnopolitics: A Conceptual Framework* (New York, 1981), pp. 2–3. This term is based on Max Weber's *politischer Unternehmer* ('political entrepreneur'). See Max Weber, *Wirtschaft und Gesellschaft. Grundriß der verstehenden Soziologie*, 5th edn Tübingen, 1985), pp. 830–1, 843–8, 860.
47. Cf. A. Hatschikjan Magarditsch, 'Macedonia: Variable Balances, Fragile Structures', in Balkan Forum, (1996), pp. 127–44; Stefan Troebst, 'Von der "Mazedonischen Frage" zur "Albanischen Frage". Der Balkan am Ende des 20. Jahrhunderts. Vier vorläufige Schlußfolgerungen', in Valeria Heuberger, Arnold Suppan and Elisabeth Vyslonzi (eds), *Der Balkan. Friedenszone oder Pulverfaß* (Frankfurt/M. and New York, 1998), pp. 127–38; Troebst, 'Macedonia: Powder Keg Defused', *Radio Free Europe/Radio Liberty Research Report*, 3 (28 January 1994), pp. 33–41; and Troebst, 'An Ethnic War That Did Not Take Place: Macedonia, Its Minorities and Its Neighbours in the 1990s', in David Turton (ed.), *War and Ethnicity: Global Connections and Local Violence* (Rochester, 1997), pp. 77–103.
48. Mathias Bernath, 'Das mazedonische Problem in der Sicht der komparativen Nationalismusforschung', *Südost-Forschungen*, 29 (1970), pp. 237–48, here p. 244.

Chapter 6

Yugoslavia and Macedonia in the years 1991–6: from brotherhood to neighbourhood

Nina Dobrković

In the last few years the name of Macedonia has appeared quite frequently among the primary issues within the crisis in the Balkans. For years it was little known world-wide, except for its ancient heritage and Alexander the Great, but the name of this pleasant region has out-grown its geographic connotation and gained very significant political importance. Macedonia, one of the former Yugoslav republics, slipped rather easily away from the common state, but it faced other very serious problems with regard to its fundamental political (name and emblems) and economic future.

At the beginning, it had a problem – there seemed to be no legal, political, or any other substantial obstacles to recognising this former Yugoslav republic as an independent state, but it could not take a name of its own choice. Greece protested against the use of the name 'Macedonia', seeing it as an assault on its own ancient history and his-torical inheritance, as well as a sign of possible territorial pretensions of the new state. An interim solution was found, however: Macedonia was admitted to international organisations under the name of the Former Yugoslav Republic of Macedonia (FYROM).

Important as relations with the neighbouring states always are, for this newly created state the relations with Greece and Yugoslavia became specially important – with Greece because it prevented full normalisation of the international status of Macedonia, and with the new FR Yugoslavia because Macedonia had to settle all the problems in its relations with the neighbour with which it used to have a common constitution and wider nationality. This northern neighbour of Macedonia had a problem of status, too. The new federation of Yugoslavia (often called 'rump-Yugoslavia') was not really fully accepted internationally and the country was often named as Serbia and Montenegro (its two federal units) in order to show that it was not yet defined (which, of course, was a reflection of a number of political and legal questions that had to be solved, first of all with regard to continuity and succession of the previous Yugoslavia). In practical terms, however, it was Serbia that was always considered to be more influential and with a more important and decisive role, both internally and internationally; and it is Serbia that is Macedonia's neighbour.

In the troublesome years 1990–6, relations between Yugoslavia and Macedonia were very much influenced by the crisis and civil war in the territory of former Yugoslavia. Undoubtedly, these relations represented an important segment of the general situation in the Balkan region. When these two countries established diplomatic relations in April 1996, this certainly was an important landmark in the overall improvement of the situation in the Balkans that started with the signing of the Dayton Agreements in December 1995. For Yugoslavia and Macedonia this should put an end to a rather awkward relationship between the two countries that prevailed since the breakout of the Yugoslav crisis and the disintegration of Yugoslavia.

I

The crisis in Yugoslavia in 1991 and the subsequent disintegration of the country seem to have caught most international analysts, diplomats and politicians by surprise.

One should not forget, though, that from time to time there used to appear analyses with gloomy prospects for this country – especially at times of crisis in bloc relations, and particularly with regard to prognoses that were trying to envisage what would happen after the death of Yugoslavia's charismatic leader Tito. All these were nurtured by certain ethnic, political, cultural or geo-strategic features that did make Yugoslavia a somewhat unique phenomenon in Europe (and the Balkans) in times of bipolarism, and that gave rise to warnings about the political fragility of this country. They all seem to have had as their starting point the presumption that Yugoslavia was a rather 'artificial creation' (an expression that was very much used by most nationalists with a separatist orientation during the crisis in the 1990s), a political result of historical circumstances that did not provide for a natural bond of its many nations, and one that was not seen to be a possible 'melting pot' for all the ethnic and national groups living within its frontiers. From time to time there were predictions of its falling apart (to mention just one given by Zbigniew Brzezinski in the 1980s, or the report, i.e. analyses, made by the American CIA in 1990[1]). All these messages mostly were not received with utmost interest – neither in the world (which did not pay too much attention to them, treating them mainly as analytical speculations), nor in Yugoslavia itself (where they were generally rejected and understood as artificial simplifications, as a proof of the world's poor understanding and superficial knowledge, and as primarily politically motivated).

Generally speaking, however, Yugoslavia was nonetheless regarded as a stable country that was gradually paving its way toward European standards and frameworks; among the socialist countries in Europe Yugoslavia was seen as one that was first in line to join European institutions. Occasional crises – although under national and ethnic symbols and rhetoric – were mainly seen as ideological, and a consequence of the socialist system within which the country was trying to find its own path toward modernisation. On the other hand, in the whole period after the Second World War in Yugoslavia there developed a feeling that the outside world was generally hostile to the country and its achievements and was trying by all means to destabilise it – these internal crisis were, thus, explained as induced from the outside.

Therefore, when the country fell apart (and it happened one decade after Tito's death in 1980) during a bloody civil war, it came as a surprise. First, it was generally believed that armed clashes in Europe belonged to history. Second, there was also the belief that existing institutional mechanisms (like the CSCE, i.e. OSCE, and of course the UN) offered, sufficient possibilities to guarantee that disputes would be solved by political means. Third, it was also generally believed that after the end of bipolarism the international community acquired capacities to cope efficiently with disputes and conflicts and to impose standards of good behaviour upon states (the experience from the Gulf war strengthened this view). Fourth, integration tendencies in Europe were so apparent that it was surprising to see political entities going against this tendency. Finally, it was also generally presumed that at this particular point of time in Europe national issues could not be of such importance so as to lead to armed conflicts.[2]

However, it was precisely national issues that, at the end of the 1980s and the beginning of the 1990s, came to the forefront of political disputes in Yugoslavia, and it was those national issues that led to the disintegration of the country through civil war – and all this happened in a European country that for many years was (despite those mentioned pessimistic warnings) seen as a possible model for nations living within one state.

Once present on the surface, however, the national issues in Yugoslavia provoked much international attention, and – as a consequence – international involvement. They certainly gave rise to speculation on the possible future behaviour of some of the ethnic and national groups if the leaders of the individual republics failed to find a general solution for the state's political system – something that was becoming more and more probable.

In this regard analysts have been mainly pointing at relations between Serbs and Albanians as the spark that is most likely to set on fire the Yugoslav multi-national federation, and possibly the Balkan powder-keg; they had in mind occasional demonstrations in the region of Kosovo and – more recently – turmoil and civilian disobedience provoked by constitutional changes (in 1990) that deprived Kosovo of most of its autonomous prerogatives granted by the 1974 Constitution. But they certainly also had in mind that developments in neighbouring Albania – namely, the political changes in a country that after years of isolation opted for democratic development and joining European trends – in the context of which the demands of the ethnic Albanians in Kosovo (i.e. Serbia) and in Macedonia acquired a special role. With regard to the Kosovo problem and the status of the region, it was obvious that some of the Yugoslav republics (first of all, Slovenia and Croatia) were using the situation to pursue their own political aims – and that, certainly, made this whole Kosovo question additionally complicated.

There was also much attention paid to the relations between the Serbs and Croats, a relationship that was historically well known as a troublesome one, and one that was seen as crucial for the future of the entire country and, eventually, the region. This attitude stemmed from the understanding that Serbs and Croats represented the two biggest ethnic groups in Yugoslavia whose consent was essential for the creation and the very existence of Yugoslavia. In view of the proportion of the Serb population within Croatia, it was presumed that any clashes between them could develop into serious turbulence. Their relationship was burdened by bad memories from the Second World War, which especially in the 1990s were at the same time both influential (particularly with regard to the resistance of Serbs against the disintegration of Yugoslavia, and the possibility of using that resistance in the political field) but also neglected (particularly by the international community). Actually, the impossibility of solving the Serbian–Croatian dispute over issues pertaining to the future political organisation of the country essentially led to the outbreak of the civil war in the summer and autumn of 1991.

Practically speaking, it was the developments among the leaderships of Serbs, Croats, Slovenes, and the ethnic Albanians, that were seen as constituting the core of the solution of the Yugoslav crisis, with the role of Serbia (and, hence, the Serbs) as very special, since it was this republic that so persistently opposed the others; rather little mention was made of the other nations and ethnic groups in the country, as if it were presumed that they would follow the decisions of those that were holding a more 'important' role. However, their stances and status gained in importance as soon as it was more than clear (at the end of 1991) that Yugoslavia would cease to exist within its existing territory and frontiers. The international community decided that the internal, administrative borders of the former Yugoslav republics should be recognised as international borders of those republics that would apply for international recognition as independent states – a solution that certainly did seem technically clean and easy to define, and therefore convenient and easy to implement. Obviously, such a solution was also motivated by the aforementioned general standpoint that at this point in history national issues (hence, to be an ethnic minority), with obligations under the OESC Final Act, should not become a major problem. As became clear afterwards, matters to do with ethnic geography, and ethnic memories in ex-Yugoslavia, were not that simple, and in certain political context (i.e. a set of historic, ideological, cultural, religious, sociological or international circumstances) are difficult to handle.

In any case, for some national and ethnic groups in the former Yugoslavia this was an opportunity to gain a new historical status – one of a 'state-building' nation – and to get into the position to create their own national state. Especially in Serbia, which was very vehemently trying to prove that it is absolutely necessary to preserve Yugoslavia[3] (bringing this aim to a status of 'to be or not to be'), this was met with very negative feelings – disappointment with the international community, disapproval, rejection, cynicism, denial. The essence of all criticism – apart from the argument that the disintegration of the country would disperse the Serbs and imply injustice – was that some of these republics and respective nations have never existed as a state, or did centuries ago (like Slovenia and Croatia), and now achieved only such status after the successes of the Serbian army in the Second World War. For others, it was said that they not only did not have a state, but that they obtained the status of a nation only thanks to the leaders of socialist Yugoslavia (like Macedonians and Muslims). From these statements the conclusion was drawn that these nations, or the republics, have no right to be independent states, and certainly not without the consent of Serbia.[4]

II

In this respect the case of Macedonia was a special one within the context of the Yugoslav crisis in general: it was the poorest among the Yugoslav republics, with a weak economy that was very much dependent on others and on the Yugoslav market – hence, many analysts thought independence would be rather risky; it was a multinational republic in the troublesome surrounding of the Balkans, with a nation established only half a century ago; and yet, it was the only former Yugoslav republic that managed to disassociate itself from Yugoslavia without war!

For Serbia – the republic which most analysts were accusing of reluctance to accept any solutions except its own – the case of Macedonia was very different from relations with the other republics. The reasons for this were mainly of a historic nature. One should not forget that the territory of the former Yugoslav republic Macedonia came under the jurisdiction of Serbia after the Balkan Wars against Turkey (1912–13); it was treated (geographically and politically) as Southern Serbia, and it was not until after the Second World War that Macedonia became a separate administrative entity. The existence of a separate, Macedonian nation, was recognised during and immediately after the war; within the triumphant atmosphere of liberation and radical social changes this was not questioned, although there have never ceased to exist opinions (large-scale ones) that this was part of the Serbian national entity and that the Macedonian language was artificially 'created' and therefore contributed to the division within the Serbian nation.

Thus, when Macedonia decided to apply to the European Community's Arbitration Commission for international recognition of independence, in Serbia this was met with surprise. Even more: in the generally tense situation which existed in the former Yugoslavia, when it was quite clear that Slovenia and Croatia would gain independence, this Macedonian move was seen as a kind of disloyalty. Generally speaking, with all over-simplification implied, Serbia expressed not only political but also emotional feelings about every republic's application for independence, seeing them as a kind of betrayal – of the notion of a common motherland, of historic achievements, of the sacrifices made for this country, and, hence, of Serbia and everything it did for the Yugoslav people in the two World Wars.

In the relatively short, but highly turbulent time-span 1990–6 the relations between Macedonia and Yugoslavia have undergone different phases. Expectedly, however, they coincide with phases in the development of the crisis in the former Yugoslavia and of the war that broke out in some of its republics. Maybe less expectedly, they depended very much on what was going on in bilateral Yugoslav-Greek relations. However, one must stress that for both Macedonia and Yugoslavia, it was mainly the Serbian attitude and actions that marked the overall affairs in Macedonian–Yugoslav relations.

No doubt that a separate phase of these relations covers the period from the outbreak of the internal political crisis in the former Yugoslavia till the end of 1991, when Macedonia applied for recognition of independence (a possibility opened for all Yugoslav republics by the European Community). After that, in the few months between the recognition of Macedonian independence up to May 1992, when the UN introduced sanctions against FR Yugoslavia (Serbia and Montenegro), Yugoslav–Macedonian relations went through a period of adaptation to the new situation. From June 1992 till the suspension of these sanctions in November 1995, Yugoslavia and Macedonia developed a very special relationship in which Macedonia helped Yugoslavia to mitigate the effects of sanctions (of course, this was to the benefit of the Macedonian economy as well). However, this was a period in which there were also a few peaks of deteriorating relations between Yugoslavia and Macedonia – and practically all were in connection with the Yugoslav desire to stress its friendship with Greece, the country which tried to get as many allies as possible in its conflict with Macedonia. Actually, in Yugoslav–Macedonian relations it was usually the Yugoslav side that 'dictated' the quality and level of relations; as in its relations with other (neighbouring) countries, Macedonia has also exercised patience in its relations with Yugoslavia. After the suspension of sanctions in November 1995 and the signing of the Dayton Agreements in December 1995, a way was opened for establishing relations on a new footing. In April 1996 Macedonia and Yugoslavia established diplomatic relations and opened new prospects for intensifying contacts between their peoples.

In the whole period after the recognition of Macedonia's independence it was never really clear why Yugoslavia did not decide to establish diplomatic relations with Macedonia earlier than April 1996. It was the only republic of the former Yugoslavia with which Serbia and Montenegro not

only did not have armed conflicts, but also did not have any serious political disputes over questions that emerged in relations with the other
republics when they decided to break up with Yugoslavia. Of course, this
gave rise to different types of speculation with regard to the true intentions of Serbia (or, Yugoslavia); all the more so because official explanation was either missing, or rather unconvincing (for instance, that the
question of the name had to be settled first).

The fact was, however, that there was some tension in Serbian–
Macedonian relations. It was most certainly provoked by the disintegration of Yugoslavia, but actually, from today's perspective, it is quite
easy to identify the first signs of tension in the mid-1980s. At that time
the Macedonians raised their voice against the general, long-lasting
atmosphere of celebration of the anniversary of the Balkan Wars
(1912–13) against the Turkish occupation. The general approach was to
praise the Serbian Army as the liberation force, and nobody spoke dif-
ferently over decades. Now, almost as a surprise (at least for the public,
especially the one in Serbia), from Macedonia came an intervention:
yes, it was said, these wars liberated Macedonia from the Turks, but
only to replace them with the Serbs and to make Macedonia part of
Serbia (in the Kingdom of Serbs, Croats and Slovenes, which was
created in 1918 and later changed its name to Kingdom of Yugoslavia;
this was Southern Serbia).

In the initial stages of the crisis which was an introduction to the
break-up of SFR Yugoslavia, Macedonia did not insist so much on independence and sovereignty, as was the case with Slovenia and Croatia.
Nonetheless, its leadership did support options that were presumed to
be leading to a decentralised state, a loose federation, a confederation
and all the other proposals that met with fierce disagreement from
Serbia. Nowadays it seems rather unimportant, but Macedonia really
did not speak too much of leaving Yugoslavia, and in the meetings of
the leaders of the six republics Macedonian President Kiro Gligorov
was always stressing the need to find ways to accommodate the different positions of the Yugoslav republics. Although in January 1991 the
Macedonian Parliament (Sobranje) adopted the Declaration on independence (according to which the option of leaving Yugoslavia and
proclaiming independence was made possible), it also adopted the
Platform for talks on the future political order in Yugoslavia. It was in
May 1991 that it became clear that Macedonia would opt for sovereignty if Slovenia and Croatia did so.

Kiro Gligorov and Alija Izetbegoviç, the president of Bosnia-
Herzegovina (another republic that in the initial stages of the Yugoslav

crisis did not insist so much on independence), in June 1991 even tried to put forward a document of principles that would enable the continuing existence of Yugoslavia, but with a changed political system. The other republics rejected this platform. Later on, in the course of the crisis, some analysts pointed to the stances and efforts of these two leaders; in times of heightened nationalist emotions in Serbia, however, any discussion in this respect would start and end with the conclusion that these were not sincere efforts, but mostly covert political activity with the only aim being to leave Yugoslavia.

On the other hand, it is rather difficult to escape the impression that neither Bosnia-Herzegovina nor even Macedonia felt very secure about the idea of achieving independence. Of course, one could argue about whether or not they wanted it, but it could be said that neither of these two republics was sure that this would work. At the time of very intense situations in Yugoslavia, both of them did show signs that they might remain in a federation without Slovenia and Croatia. Reasons for this were of a rather practical nature. Bosnia-Herzegovina was a nationally immensely mixed area, and with a very large portion of the Serb population, which very clearly showed no willingness to live separated from its mother republic and feared a possible renewal of the genocide in the Second World War. On the other hand, the Muslim population also did not seem to have any strong feelings about a sovereign national state, maybe because of the number of Muslims living in Serbia and Montenegro, as well as because of traditional ties with the Serbs,[5] or maybe because they never had a state of their own. Macedonia was also a republic of a mixed ethnic composition, with the dominant nation, the Macedonians, being a young nation, officially recognised after the Second World War. It was also a republic with a poor economic performance and therefore with weak prospects of independence.[6]

However, in view of the widespread fear that Serbia was rejecting all proposals for compromise solutions because it wanted to have a state in which it would clearly dominate and impose its ideological and political views, both Bosnia-Herzegovina and Macedonia decided to join Slovenia and Croatia in the drive to independence. In the view of the events after 1991, it seems that Serbia has made a serious mistake in not giving a hand to these two republics by making it easy for them to stay in a common state. It is not hard to see that such a state, with four federal units, might be of benefit to Serbia as well.

Once independent, Macedonia found itself in an awkward position. Out of its four neighbours, none was friendly to the new state:

Yugoslavia (or Serbia, as the immediate neighbour), because Macedonia left Yugoslavia, and thus annulled the historic successes of Serbia; Bulgaria, because it never stopped thinking about Macedonians as Bulgarians; Greece, because it could live with Macedonia as part of Yugoslavia, but not with a separate state under this name, and not being ready to recognise either the name of the state, or a Macedonian nation – either in Macedonia, or in Greece; Albania, because it was unsatisfied with the way in which Macedonia has treated its Albanian population.

As is known, Greece managed to postpone the recognition of Macedonian independence within the European Community,[7] additionally complicating the situation in the region. On the other hand, Bulgaria was the first to recognise the new state, but with a clear standpoint that this does not mean recognition of the Macedonian nation, nor of a Macedonian language. However, Yugoslavia did not recognise Macedonia, for reasons that were not quite clear and gave rise to speculation about possible territorial aspirations, or the possibility of making it join new Yugoslavia. Yugoslavia itself should by no means have problems with the Macedonian name – after all, it was its own republic under the very same name.

In Macedonia itself, this situation was seen (especially by the very nationalistic oriented VMRO-DPMNE) as a creation of a Greek–Yugoslav anti-Macedonian 'axis', and as probably confirming the notion that Macedonia might be the biggest political victim of the Yugoslav crisis (with Bosnia-Herzegovina undoubtedly being the biggest general and war victim of this crisis). Non-recognition by the important foreign countries, and non-admission to international organisations (it became a member of the UN in the spring of 1993), had adverse economic effects: primarily because of the lack of access to international financial support.[8]

In the Serbian press it was frequently being written that Macedonia would have a hard time in attempting to survive as an independent state. The decision of Macedonia to try to do so was implicitly presented as an irrational one, and one that will imply big costs. It was clear that Macedonian–Serbian relations were at a low level, and this was attributed to 'foreign factors' which wanted to destabilise the region in order to weaken its states and peoples, and in order to be able to dominate them. There were accusations also in some political circles in Macedonia; it was said that they actually do not want genuine Macedonian independence, but rather subordination to traditional enemies of the Macedonian people, and specifically mentioned those who are in favour of the creation of Greater Bulgaria.[9]

On the part of Yugoslavia not much was being done to change this image of its possible intentions, and certainly there was no official reaction to extremist statements. Moreover, there were more signs indicating to the contrary. One of the most prominent nationalist leaders in Serbia, Vojislav Šešelj, often spoke against Macedonian independence, and of the historic rights of Serbia over this territory. In the Assembly of Serbia he was very vehement on this subject, and even spoke of two army divisions that could occupy Macedonia.[10] The Serbian Orthodox Church also revived the old question of independence of the Macedonian Church – in itself, this should not be a major problem, but in the prevailing internal and surrounding difficulties it exacerbated the tensions. Serbian President Slobodan Miloševiç also added to the problem – in June 1992 in an interview he spoke about his offer to Greece to form a federation;[11] on the other hand, in winter 1992–3 he also spoke about good neighbourly relations between Greece and Yugoslavia.

It is interesting that all this happened at a time when it was logical to presume that Macedonia was of vital interest to Serbia and Yugoslavia. It was the time when the UN sanctions against Yugoslavia were imposed, causing great trouble for the country's economy. In this situation Macedonia represented the 'safety valve' – everybody in both Yugoslavia and Macedonia (and probably in the international community) knew that a large-scale smuggling channel was being developed along the Macedonian–Yugoslav (Serbian) border.[12] Of course, it goes without saying that this was beneficial to the Macedonian economy, too; one should not forget that the international community did not provide for any compensation for the countries affected by the embargo against Yugoslavia, and among those countries Macedonia was, no doubt, particularly vulnerable. In such a situation, the Yugoslav attitude was particularly confusing.

The press and the media in both countries did not contribute to an improvement of the situation. The most widely read Serbian newspapers wrote about the injustice done to the Serbian people and their sacrifices during turbulent years of Balkan history; of course, this was at a time of general nationalist euphoria that was a characteristic also of other former socialist countries in Eastern and South-East Europe. In Macedonia, on the other hand, the media sent messages about Serbian aspirations toward the new state, about its wish to join the new Yugoslav federation and to dominate the Macedonian people.[13] On both sides there were, though, politicians and analysts who opposed such approaches – unfortunately in those hectic days, they were not given much room or importance, and they did not have very much influence,[14] as if it were in the state interest to suppress such attitudes. It is interesting to note that calls for an easing of tensions in bilateral relations were frequently issued from the top in Macedonian – its president Kiro Gligorov – whilst in Serbia calls for tolerance and understanding of the new situation were coming mainly from opposition circles and the media.

III

And still, in all these tense circumstances, with war going on in parts of Croatia, and with one becoming all the more probable in Bosnia-Herzegovina, Macedonia was the only republic from which the Yugoslav Peoples Army withdrew peacefully. This certainly was a surprise, especially in view of the stance taken by prominent Serbian nationalists with regard to the Macedonian national and state status. Much of the tribute for such a resolution with the Army must be paid to Macedonia's President, even though the Army withdrew after removing everything possible from the barracks. Still, Macedonia had its victims in the emerging civil war – the first victim within the army was a young soldier serving in Split (Croatia) in 1991, who was killed in demonstrations against the Yugoslav Peoples Army.

This attitude with regard to the Army's withdrawal, and the obvious agreement to the fact that no serious military equipment would be left in the newly created state after the withdrawal of troops, officers and their families, was rather unusual. It meant giving up part of what normally would constitute the common assets of the former common state, and in which Macedonia would be entitled to some share.

As was seen later, it was a wise orientation – firstly, it took away the danger of war, and secondly, it fitted very well into what later was established as the concept of defence for Macedonia. It was a concept that was differed in the extreme from what other Balkan states opted for. Unlike other Balkan states, which have always done their best to acquire armaments and equipment, Macedonia made a different choice. It obviously had concluded that with its income and the state of its economy it could not provide for an army that could really compete with those of its neighbours (one should not forget that Greece is also a member of NATO). So, it oriented itself toward something that could be called 'self-demilitarisation' and 'protecting itself by military weakness'.[15] At one point, when it was planned to deploy international troops (the UN Blue Helmets) in some parts of the former

Yugoslavia, plans encompassed Macedonia, too. Moreover, US troops also came under special provisions. Finally, Macedonia applied to join the 'Partnership for Peace', a NATO programme for organising connections of the alliance with the former socialist countries.

All these were met with suspicion in Serbia and Yugoslavia. It was often stressed that such moves led to losing state sovereignty. It was also said that by doing so, Macedonia was not only subordinating itself to foreign countries, but that it was also endangering Serbia and Yugoslavia, by bringing foreign troops into its vicinity. Macedonia was stressing that, on the contrary, all these Macedonian decisions were a proof of an orientation toward the international community and Europe, and the system of collective security as the basis of its defence.[16] The Macedonian army is nowadays a force consisting of some 14,000 soldiers (with 25–40 per cent being professional soldiers), equipped with light weapons (due to budgetary restrictions, but also to the UN embargo with regard to import of arms to the entire territory of the former Yugoslavia)[17] and with the task of guarding the state borders of Macedonia. At the time of the withdrawal of the Yugoslav Army it was necessary to create an armed force, which could not be easily and quickly accomplished; initially, the borders were guarded by the police force.

IV

When, finally, in April 1996, Macedonia and Yugoslavia signed the Agreement by which the two states paved the way for the normalisation of their relations, this came both as a surprise and as an act that had been awaited for many years. It is interesting that even when it was clear that something was going to happen in this regard, it was still postponed. Again, there was much speculation about the reasons. Was it because the two states could not get what they both wanted in the political and legal fields? Was it because of Greece and its still unresolved dispute with Macedonia over the name? Or was it something from the general state of affairs among the former Yugoslav republics?

It is interesting that in the media in Serbia this act was presented to the public in different ways: as a victory of the policy of Yugoslavia (judged for instance by the emphasis given to the fact that Macedonia recognised the continuity of Yugoslavia), as an act to which Yugoslavia was more or less forced because of the Dayton agreements, or as a natural development between the two states.

One thing was sure – the provisions of the Dayton agreement did contribute to this decision of the Yugoslav government. It was mainly their decision that enabled this Agreement on normalisation, since it was always clear that Macedonia was in favour of a normalisation of relations with its northern neighbour. On the other hand, regardless of other considerations, Yugoslavia hesitated also because it did not want to jeopardise its relations with Greece – a country that in the crisis years was considered to be the only true ally.

Although Greece and Macedonia had made certain steps in the direction of normalisation of their bilateral relations in the autumn of 1995, the signing of the Agreement between Macedonia and Yugoslavia was met with very negative feelings in Greece. Explanations from Yugoslavia that this was a necessity if Yugoslavia wanted to normalise its relations with members of the European Union and to open the process of its re-integration into the international community did not help very much. In Greece this was understood as betrayal.

Macedonia recognised Yugoslavia's continuity from 1918 (an issue that in Yugoslavia's official international policy and diplomatic activity was given highest priority), and Yugoslavia recognised Macedonia under this name, and its continuity from 1944. For both countries these were important achievements with regard to their relations with third countries (Yugoslavia's relations with other former Yugoslav republics; Macedonia's relations with other countries and international organisations in which it is referred to as FYROM). Yugoslavia seemed surprised by Greek reactions, saying that this actually meant assisting Greece in its relations with other members of the European Union, and was also a contribution to solving the situation in the Balkans.[18]

This Agreement between Macedonia and Yugoslavia, as we said, was an important sign of the beginning of a new period in the bilateral relations of the two countries. It will most certainly make all future arrangements on economic cooperation easier, something that for both countries is very important. Their economies are complementary, and this is an important reason for further economic cooperation; one should not forget that for years Serbia was the main economic partner of Macedonia (47 per cent of Macedonia's economic exchange), and in the present economic position of Macedonia[19] it is important to do everything to help the economy.

Practically, there do not seem to be any conflicting issues between the two countries, though there might be some open questions – border demarcation, the problem of succession of the common state, the position of Serbs in Macedonia. With regard to the border, this is an issue that is not treated as important, because it is obvious that these issues have been dealt with. The problem of succession will be handled within the international conference in which all the former Yugoslav republics will have to present their standpoints.[20] With regard to the status of Serbs in Macedonia, this will have to be treated within bilateral contacts, and of course within the internal laws and regulations in Macedonia. In Serbia, there were frequent accusations that Serbs in Macedonia (some 2.1 per cent of the population, both in 1991 and in 1994) were not treated well;[21] one of the main arguments was the fact that they are not mentioned as a national minority in the Macedonian Constitution as is the case with other national groups.[22] The explanation given by Kiro Gligorov was that this was so because the Macedonian constitution was adopted at a time when the former Yugoslavia was still in existence, and mentioning them as a national minority in a situation when they are state-building people in Yugoslavia, could be understood as an offence.[23]

Some reforms will be necessary – schools for Serbs, care of national monuments and developing media in the Serbian language. On the other hand, Macedonia has certain demands with regard to the monastery Prohor Pčinjski which is on Serbian territory. During the Second World War it was the site of the conference that represented the foundation of today's Macedonian nation and state, and Macedonia wants to respect fully the memory of this event.

The general improvement of relations has yet to be developed through concrete forms of cooperation. Progress has been slow, to the surprise of many individuals and institutions involved. Thus, for instance, there were expectations that one of the first decisions would be to allow travel without passports (just with identification cards); although simple to implement, such a decision was not made. On the other hand, both countries are sensitive with regard to things said and done. Thus, Mr Gligorov's rather favourable speech concerning the Croatian army (on the occasion of his visit to Croatia in April 1996) could not meet with approval in Serbia; nor could his statement in the Council of Europe (in May 1996) in which he did not put into balance the Serbian contribution to the emergence of the Macedonian nation with what was described as the Macedonian role in the liberation war in the region and in Yugoslavia (or, at least how this was interpreted). On their side, Macedonia and Macedonians are still very sensitive about the way Yugoslavia is treating them – there is still fear of possible hegemonic aspirations.[24]

There is a problem that might be seen as one shared by Macedonia and Yugoslavia – that of the Albanian population. In both countries, there is a significant Albanian minority. In Serbia, however, the Albanians have a separate administrative unit, the autonomous province of Kosovo, whilst in Macedonia they do not. However, both countries at the moment do not see a solution to the problem with regard to Albanian demands for autonomy or independence. Speculation suggested that they could jointly deal with this issue, or, that resolution in one country might help solve the problem in the other.

Nonetheless, the signing of the Agreement on normalisation of relations between Yugoslavia and Macedonia will contribute to the solution of the general situation in the Balkans – one that is still very fragile and needing a lot of attention and care.

Notes

1. David Binder, 'Yugoslavia seen breaking up soon? CIA paper predicts action in 18 months and adds civil war is likely', *New York Times*, November 29, 1990.
2. Rita Jalali and Seymour Martin Lipset, 'Racial and Ethnic Conflict', *Political Science Quarterly*, Winter 1992–3, pp. 585–606. The authors argue that until recently it was generally understood that ethnicity reflects conditions of traditional societies with limited communications; Marxists saw socialism as the end of tensions, non-Marxists that industrialisation and modernisation would bring an end to ethnic tensions.
3. It should not be forgotten that there was a large number of Serbs living for centuries outside Serbia – first of all in Croatia and Bosnia-Herzegovina, but also in Montenegro (some are arguing that Serbs and Montenegrins are of the same ethnic origin), and in Macedonia. Therefore, the creation of Yugoslavia in 1918 was by some historians and politicians understood as a victory of an old dream, i.e. of the aim to have all Serbs in one state.
4. It is interesting that there was practically no mention of the very simple fact that all nations in history at some point in time were creating their states for the first time; this lack of understanding of historic development, or even a non-historic feeling, is interesting, especially when compared with the very dominant role of historical argumentation in the whole course of the Yugoslav crisis when history and long ago events were the main sources and motives of the contemporary behaviours.
5. In this context, it should be mentioned that there is much discussion with regard to the national origins of the Muslims. It is mostly accepted that they are mainly Serbs who at times of Turkish occupation converted to Islam. Although this was centuries ago, and despite the fact that they have developed a specific culture and tradition of their own, on the basis of which they were recognised as a nation in socialist Yugoslavia, there are those (especially in Serbia) who deny the existence of such a separate nation.
6. John M. Fraser, *Yugoslavia – What Went Wrong?*, The Norman Paterson School of International Affairs, Occasional Papers 4, 1993, pp. 7–10.
7. It is worth mentioning that this was one of the first examples of inconsistent behaviour of international factors in the Yugoslav crisis. Macedonia and

Slovenia were the only republics to meet the criteria for independence, said the report of the Arbitration Commission of the EC (headed by R. Badinter). And yet it was Slovenia and Croatia that were recognised, while Macedonia was not. These were times of crisis in the European Union (after German reunification and its behaviour with regard to the Yugoslav crisis), and the unity of Europe was of paramount importance to EU leaders.

8. Duncan M. Perry, 'The Republic of Macedonia and the Odds for Survival', *Radio free Europe – Research Report*, No. 46, November 1992, pp. 12–19.
9. *Politika*, February 28, 1992.
10. *Borba*, April 30, 1992.
11. *Frankfurter Algemeine Zeitung*, June 9, 1992.
12. It would be interesting to analyse the effects of sanctions also from this aspect. It was well known that the countries neighbouring Yugoslavia did participate in activities contrary to the UN resolution. This situation created a specific smugglers' economy in Yugoslavia, promoting criminalisation of the society. No doubt all these could have been put under tighter control by the international community; the question would be – why was it not done?
13. Dragan Nikolić, 'Soliste raštimovanog orkestra' (Soloists of a badly tuned orchestra), *Borba*, March 21, 1992. Dragan Nikolić, 'Varvari u bermudskom trouglu' (Barbarians in the Bermuda Triangle'), *Borba*, April 30, 1992.
14. Interview with Kiro Gligorov, *NIN*, January 22, 1993.
15. Zlatko Isaković, 'Macedonia and Security in the Balkans', *CSS Survey*, 5–6 (1996), pp. 1–11.
16. Interview with Kiro Gligorov, *Naša Borba*, September 15, 1993.
17. Interview with Kiro Gligorov and Blagoj Hanožiski (Minister of Defence), *Intervju*, July 4, 1995.
18. Branislav Marinković, 'Vruć krompir iz Atine' ('A hot potato from Athens'), *Intervju*, April 19, 1996.
19. Ksente Bogoev, and Nikola Uzunov, 'Perspectives of the Republic of Macedonia', *Balkan Forum*, 1 (March 1996), pp. 63–113.
20. The Macedonian stance is analysed in Todor Džunov, 'Succession of States, Citizenship and the New Legal Order of the Republic of Macedonia', *Balkan Forum*, No. 4 (December 1994), pp. 199–230.
21. Svetska srpska zajednica (The World Serb Community) organised in the autumn of 1996 a seminar on the position of Serbs in Macedonia; this was the second meeting of the kind – the first was organised on Serbs in Slovenia, in July 1996. Papers presented to the conference were mainly critical of the way that the Serbs and the Serbian culture and cultural and historic heritage were treated in Macedonia.
22. *Novi ustavi na tlu bivše Jugoswlavije* (new Constitutions in the territory of the Former Yugoslavia). Medjunarodna politika, Pravni Fakultet i Fakultet političkih nauka, Beograd, p. 135.
23. Interview with Kiro Gilgorov, *NIN*, January 22, 1993.
24. Zoran Andonovski, 'Sa srpskim ukusom u ustima' ('With a Serbian Flavour in the Mouth'), *Nova Makedonija*, cited from *Tanjug, Crveni Bilten*, 13 April 1995.

Chapter 7

The unrealistic dreams of large states[*]

Kiro Gligorov

Eighty-year-old president Kiro Gligorov, who in a way symbolises Macedonia as an independent state, cannot run for president for a third time at the parliamentary elections, in 1999. The Republic of Macedonia Constitution does not envisage this and Gligorov himself does not wish to, regardless of suggestions that he could legally be enabled to run, if the Constitution were 'creatively' interpreted. Assessing that the forthcoming parliamentary elections could have historical significance in respect of maintaining the foundations of the young Macedonian state, the continuity of the peace policy and equidistance with all neighbouring states might depend on which political party wins the elections, we asked Mr Gligorov for an interview, to hear his opinion on the best possible course of events from the viewpoint of the long-term consolidation of Macedonia's foundations and survival as an independent state.

Q: When do you think the parliamentary elections will take place?
KG: I cannot answer that question precisely because it is being discussed by all parties in Macedonia. Prime Minister Branko Crvenkovski, as the chairman of the Social-Democratic Alliance, is in charge of the issue. Certain opposition parties have been urging early elections for a year now. They first tried to persuade and pressure the parliament into reaching such a decision, but failed. And that was the only way to decide on early elections, as it implies the previous dissolution of the existing parliament. I am not going into the problem of whether that is a good way to

---

[*] First published in the Belgrade weekly *Ekonomiska Politcia*, 25 August 1997. Interview conducted by Vladimir Golikov.

call early elections, but that is what the Constitution envisages and it must be observed. By including this provision, the authors of the Constitution highlighted the importance of the parliamentary system and the civic state.

Q: Early elections as a form of political struggle can be initiated by the ruling circles as well. If I recall well, this has already happened in Macedonia.

KG: In some states, the Cabinet has the right to call for the early dissolution of the parliament, if it assesses that would be the best way for it to make use of its advantages. In other states, the decision on early elections is taken by the head of state or parliament speaker, if the president is unable to, if he assesses that the parliament is unable to pass certain relevant regulations and that its composition must change.

Q: Neither is possible under the Macedonian Constitution. The Constitution does provide the unique option of the parliament dissolving itself.

KG: Our case is specific because it envisages the parliament's decision on self-dissolution. This has advantages and weaknesses. The advantage is that it allows a favourable structure of elected MPs enough time (four years of term in office) to implement a Cabinet programme.

Q: The Coalition Alliance for Macedonia won the previous elections. The strongest coalition party was Social-Democratic Alliance. The coalition broke up after the Social-Democrats disagreed with Stojan Andov's Liberal Party, but this did not prevent the parliament system from functioning. How was this possible?

KG: The coalition's break-up also prompted the demands for early elections with the explanation that the people had voted for the coalition at the previous elections and that the new elections would show whom they would entrust with power now. One should bear in mind that there are three large party groups in Macedonia – Social Democratic Alliance, VMRO and Democratic Party of Albanians – which absorb most of the electorate. There is also a series of minor parties vying for votes. If one views each of them individually, one can hardly expect any of them to win enough votes to rule the state by itself. As the electorate is so divided, all of them are forced to create coalitions so they can assume power. That has been our fate since the first parliamentary elections. I do not expect any radical changes in that respect. This, of course, does not mean there will be no changes in the relations of political forces. It is difficult to predict today whether some other party will prevail.

Q: When are the regular parliamentary elections due?

KG: Regular elections should be held next October. The opposition had urged elections last spring and now insist they be held in late autumn. Certain parties think that deadline is too short because the election laws have not been passed and the voters have not received their election IDs which are guarantees that their legitimacy will not be disputed, a regular complaint by the election losers.

Q: Do you think the changes in the political strength of certain parties, for instance the predominance of the largest opposition party (VMRO), will not radically change Macedonia's policy?

KG: I cannot claim that for sure. Some parties have mostly crystallised their policies. At the time Macedonia was gaining its independence, the parties with more prominent national orientations and concern for the people's fate, accused others of just waiting for the moment to return Macedonia into a tri-partite, quadri-partite or some other kind of Yugoslav federation. Some still have such ambitions, but the major parties in Macedonia do not. This is why such accusations are not as relevant now as they used to be.

Q: Nationally-oriented parties now motivate their actions by social reasons, claiming widespread dissatisfaction with the grave economic situation. At one point, they were said to be increasingly assuming the attributes of civic parties.

KG: Those are parties which are predominantly nationally oriented. Their moves show that things are not exactly the way they present them. Some of these parties are more oriented towards our eastern neighbour, Bulgaria. Other, ethnic Albanian parties converge on the general idea of uniting all Albanians in one state. Some of these parties openly articulate such ideas, others do not. I think all of them share common goals, manifested through the events which ensued after the university at Tetovo, teaching in Albanian, was banned in Macedonia.

Q: How do you assess the Albanians' recent refusal to take down Albania's state flags in the municipalities they rule, which resulted in an intervention by the Macedonian state police?

KG: You must bear in mind that a law has been passed banning the flying of alien flags on public institutions, except during official holidays set forth in a law, or during private celebrations or fetes. It must be clear that, according to the latest census conducted at the insistence of Albanians and in the presence of European institutions, 22.9 per cent of the overall population registered as Albanian. That is a smaller percentage than they previously claimed, when they made up as much as 40 per cent of the population and that, together with all other nationalities, they were the majority of the population! What is at issue here is to turn part of Macedonia's territory into an autonomous region to approach the ultimate goal of independence and secession from our state.

Q: In the context of assessing Macedonia's future, how do you view the different stands of certain parties, including extremist opinions, on your policy of involving the Albanians and their parties in the power structures, including the possibility that they rule the municipalities where they won the elections?

KG: I think that every Macedonian Cabinet should include representatives of the majority Albanian party. Even if a party were able to rule Macedonia by itself after winning a majority of votes at elections, which I think is virtually impossible, it should never dare do that without a coalition with a party representing the Albanian national minority. That pertains to other national minorities, too. We have already had a Cabinet with one or two members of Turkish descent.

Q: Are the rumours true that the events which ensued after the Law on Flags was passed were due to the gaps in the legislative system?

KG: We realised that new judges should be appointed in the legislative system, all the way to the Constitutional Court and the Council of the Court, without restricting their mandates, under the condition that they do not commit crimes which would lead to their dismissal. Their inalienable task is to observe that the Constitution and law are implemented. After their proposal on flying flags was turned down by the parliament, the Albanians appealed to the Constitutional Court, which ruled that flying foreign flags was out of the question. The judges were even more rigid than the law because they maintained that foreign flags could not be flown under any circumstances. They suggested that the Cabinet should implement that decision. The Constitutional Court decision is final, as there is no higher court which could overrule it, and it was a matter of time and of a way to implement that.

Q: You thought the problem of foreign flags would be resolved when the law was passed and its constitutionality confirmed?

KG: You understood correctly; without legal and constitutional authority, nationalities used flags freely in Macedonia. They did not do that before Macedonia gained its independence; no foreign flags were flown although Albanians held leading municipal and republican posts. Of course, we could not contemplate banning foreign flags, but we realised that flags of a foreign state cannot be flown on public institutions symbolising the authorities. Matters became complicated when the Albanians won majority votes in 23 out of 126 municipalities, notably Tetovo and Gostivar. In them, the two strongest Albanian parties united (the Party of Democratic Prosperity and the Independent Democratic Party which set up the Democratic Party of Albanians) and flew the Albanian flag alongside the Macedonian one; in Gostivar, they also flew the Turkish flag. This had caused fierce public reactions.

Q: I presume Albanian demands do amount to flying Albania's flag in Macedonia?

KG: Albanians are doing everything they can in the parliament and outside it to much more clearly articulate their demands on the Macedonian state. In general, their demands imply the non-acceptance of the Macedonian Constitution, under the explanation that they had not voted for its adoption. Also, they want a new Constitution to be drafted, with the Albanians and Macedonians sitting at the same table to agree what kind of state they want and with the idea that the state should be bi-partite. What this state would be called, whether it would be a federation or something else, is a separate issue. They also demand that the Albanian minority exercises autonomy in the municipalities in which it is the majority population. They also want Albanian to become the second official language in Macedonia, which is unprecedented in our history. Their third demand is to ensure proportional participation of Albanians in all state, judiciary, military and other institutions. Bearing all this in mind, the move we made on flags was meant to draw a red line to show how far another state can go (Albania, Turkey, Serbia or any other state) in protecting the interests and rights of national minorities. We wanted to show when demands for rights turn into interference in a state's internal affairs.

Q: Was the police intervention based on the Constitutional Court decision the only option?

KG: The public was of the opinion that the problem could be resolved the way the Constitutional Court decided. As soon as the parliament passed the law – I was out of the country at the time – the Cabinet decided to take down the Albanian flags the next morning in the Gostivar and Tetovo municipalities. All measures were taken to implement the court decision and avoid the danger of clashing with citizens. That's what happened in Tetovo, but there was unrest in Gostivar, and several thousand citizens rallied. Albanians in Gostivar offered resistance in the afternoon, which had acquired undesirable proportions. They first threw rocks, and fired shots from apartment blocks, while the police cordon had persistently, without changing shifts for 48 hours, protected the municipalities so the foreign flags would not be raised again. Two Albanians were killed in the clashes.

Q: This gave reason for the Albanians in Macedonia to send protests to foreign embassies, the European Union, European Parliament, OSCE, the Council of Europe, the US Congress, etc. What were the international reactions?

KG: There was no support, because the police did not show aggressive intentions towards Albanians. On the contrary, the police suffered blows and ten policemen were lightly or seriously injured. There was no call for those attacks, because not one country in the world allows foreign flags on its public institutions. Also, Albanians were allowed to fly them on all other occasions (religious holidays, local state holidays, weddings, baptisms). Albania's flag was flown during the St. Elias holiday in some municipalities, while the Gostivar and Tetovo authorities decided not to fly any flags on that day.

Q: I presume the Albanians had their own draft Law on Flags. What did they suggest?

KG: Their leader, Mr Djaferi, suggested that all nationalities fly the flags of their states in the municipalities they run, that Macedonians have their own flag and that there is a separate, common state flag! Accepting such a proposal would mean allowing the existence of seven or eight official flags in Macedonia. This would cause great confusion on which flag is the state flag. All this was thought up to introduce the flag of the state of Albania as the official one in our state.

Q: The problem of flags in Macedonia might be viewed in the context of flying the old Macedonian flag at the St. Elias national holiday celebration in Krusevo. VMRO opposition followers had *en masse* flown the old banner which Macedonia had replaced with a new one after Greece complained.

KG: That flag has been used as VMRO's party flag for a long time, by the Macedonians in the diaspora and our emigrants. VMRO claims the current flag was imposed on us as a state symbol and that the old one with the 16-point star belongs to us, Macedonians. Recently, when I was visiting the USA, representatives from all municipalities with Macedonian churches (US, Canada and Australia) came and asked why we were not using the old flag. I replied that we Macedonians have never used that flag in our recent history and that we should not be slaves to hypotheses that we are direct descendants of Alexander the Great. This flag was discovered in the late 1970s close to the grave of Phillip II of Macedonia in Greece, although we still dispute whether that was the site where it was found. The fact is that the flag was present in a much broader region, by far exceeding the boundaries of present-day Greece. The flag's origin is linked to the Sun God Ra and was seen in Orthodox parts of Ancient Egypt, where ex-Secretary General of the UN Boutros Boutros Ghali comes from which were under the auspices of or in a kind of symbiosis with the Greek church. There were such flags in Orthodox churches in Albania and Macedonia (it was flying in the portal of a Prilep church), which proves it was a general symbol of the Mediterranean. The Greeks' appropriation of it as their symbol helps the thesis that the whole history of Macedonian kings is actually part of their broader history. The crowning proof that it belongs to them is the allegation that the disputed flag was found on the grave of Philip II of Macedonia. In other words, the Greeks consider it a symbol of ancient Greece.

Q: I presume that was the reason for accusing Macedonia that it wanted to annex part of Greek history, that you and Greece began haggling over whose nation is more ancient...

KG: Not only that, there were allegations that all this proved our territorial pretensions, that we wanted to annex parts of Greece where the grave was found to our state. None of our attempts to prove we have no territorial pretensions succeeded and we had to change our Constitution, to record that we did not have aspirations towards any of our neighbours. Even before our referendum on independence, I personally said on TV that Macedonia is possible as a state only within its present borders and that any other intention would be an venture in which we could lose what we had achieved in the Second World War, which was the basis for setting up an independent state, which became a UN member. At the time, many people warned me not to do that, fearing revolt, clash and destabilisation. I thought I should do that for a number of reasons, above all so that we could distance ourselves from all slogans in the ex-Yugoslavia and elsewhere about the need to create a Greater Croatia, Greater Serbia, Greater Albania. I include in such attempts what some of our eastern neighbours today advocate – the creation of a Greater Bulgaria and annexing Macedonians as part of their nation. Also, I believed that our people should view our state realistically, that they should be aware of the time they were living in and which are the ways to resolve problems wherever nations are divided. And, we are not the only divided nation, although we could serve as the most drastic example. The Croatian nation is also divided, even the Serbians, and Hungarians.

Q: Macedonia made a compromise on its flag and it was replaced by a new one. There have recently been rumours that a compromise could be reached with Greece on the name of Macedonia, one of the possibilities being to call it Nova Macedonia (New Macedonia). Are the rumours on compromise founded?

KG: No. We refused that proposal a long time ago, during Mitsotakis's government. We rejected it via mediator Cyrus Vance and said they had no grounds to try and resolve the problem through a UN Security Council resolution. We still think so. Giving a state a name would be a precedent for a nation, which would suffer unpleasantness if it woke up one morning and found it was not called by its name.

Q: During the St. Elias national holiday on August 2, you experienced unpleasantness from the opposition VMRO, who whistled, trampled on the Macedonian flag, tried to throw bottles, and pour water at you during your speech.

KG: It was too late by the time I found out that VMRO was drafting a script for the Ilinden fete, at which I and other senior guests headed by the Prime Minister were to take part. True, the presence of VMRO members, who organised camping in Krusevo ahead of the fete was interpreted by some as their capitulation, while others, knowing their nature, knew they would use every opportunity to create situations which resembled demonstrations and occasional incidents and political attacks (they said Ilinden would be celebrated by those who until recently did not recognise that national holiday) and tried to have their leader Ljupco Georgijevski address the rally. True, the VMRO did not try to seize the microphone from the head of state, but it was evident that all of it was well prepared by the militant nucleus of the party, members and sympathisers willing to do anything. My speech was accompanied by fierce noise, spitting, one woman wanted to throw a beer bottle at me. They are now charged by the district attorneys for inciting unrest and endangering the state and its president.

Q: Which election scenario would be best in terms of the state's consolidation and survival, as Macedonia had won this status by a policy of peace?

KG: First, election laws which all parties or, at least, the strongest parties agree should be passed. This is necessary so that no one tomorrow complains that the system was imposed, which is always a good excuse for losing the elections. That happened at the previous elections when the opposition parties boycotted the second round under the incomprehensible explanation that it was all a direct state forgery. This happened despite the presence of representatives of all parties who monitored what was happening and signed the records. They realised, however, that their expectations that they would win for certain would not be fulfilled. That's what they expect now as well.

Q: The presidential elections are to be held in 1999. Would you accept a 'creative' interpretation of the Constitution which would allow you to run for the third time?

KG: Opposition parties think the elections should be held earlier, simultaneously with parliamentary elections. I believe we are a serious state; that implies loyalty to the Constitution and giving up changes and interpretations for day-to-day politica needs.

Q: Should the constitutional limit that the presidential candidate must be over 40 years of age be abolished?

KG: The Constitution should not be amended in that respect either, no matter who the candidate may be.

Part II
Ethnic minorities

Chapter **8**

Non-Albanian Muslim minorities in Macedonia

Hugh Poulton

The ethnic minority situation in Macedonia has and remains perhaps the most complex in any region of the Balkans. Macedonia was among the last areas in the Balkans to undergo the transition from Ottoman control to incorporation into successor states. Consequently many Muslims (Turks and others) moved to these areas, escaping from the encroaching new states which saw them as an alien remnant from the Ottoman period, and joining those Muslims already living there.

The Ottomans ruled the area for over five centuries and there were inevitably some people who accepted the religion – Islam – of the new Ottoman rulers. These were the majority of the Albanians, large groups of Slavs especially the Pomaks (Islamicised Slavs) of the Rhodope mountains, and the Bosnians in what later became central Yugoslavia, and others. However, the Ottoman rulers were, in the Balkans, essentially non-assimilative and multi-national without the technological and institutional facilities for integrating and unifying the subject peoples, unlike in Western Europe where states were able, for the most part, to transcend regional loyalties and lay the foundations for the new 'nation states'. As a result the peoples of the Balkans managed to retain their separate identities and cultures as well as, for many of them, returning a sense of a former glorious history when they controlled a particular area, which with the national awakenings of the nineteenth century they once more claimed – often at the expense of their neighbours who likewise made historical claims to the territory in question.

The *Millet* system

The Ottoman conquest saw the arrival of large numbers of Turkish and Turkic-speaking settlers as well as the arrival of Islam into the Balkans.

The arrival of Islam was also especially significant as the Ottoman Empire was an empire ruled by Islamic precepts for most of its existence. In line with these, the empire was, until attempted changes beginning with the *Tanzimat* reforms in the mid nineteenth century, divided not along ethno-linguistic lines but by religious affiliation – the *millet* system. The Christian and Jewish populations were accepted, as traditionally so in Islam, as 'people of the book'. The common ancestry of the three religions here helped this tolerance – a tolerance illustrated by the acceptance of large numbers of Jews, especially Ladino-speaking Sephardic Jews who were expelled from Spain in the sixteenth century. Many of these people settled in Salonika which subsequently became predominately Jewish. For Muslims, there was no official differentiation by language or race. The concept of being a 'Turk' as used in modern parlance was, until the end of the nineteenth century, alien to the Ottoman elites who saw themselves as Ottomans (*Osmanli*) rather than 'Turks' which had the connotation of being uneducated peasants. Indeed the language of state, Ottoman Turkish, was not the everyday language of the vernacular. A requirement of high office in the Ottoman Empire was firstly to be a Muslim, and secondly to know Ottoman Turkish.[1] Ethnicity was not a factor *per se* and many Grand Vezirs and high officials were from originally Albanian or Muslim Slav or other Ottoman Muslim populations.

Thus the Ottoman state was an Islamic state and the population was divided by religious affiliation and the whole system preceding the *Tanzimat* was based on the separation of the groups – even to regulations as to the colour and type of clothing each religious group could wear. As noted above, all Muslims were officially recognised as equal first-class citizens in the Muslim *millet*. Other 'peoples of the book' were organised into their own separate *millets* – members of the Jewish faith in one, members of the Armenian Church in another, etc. Faith not ethnicity or language was the differentiator.[2]

Despite their origins, perceived or real, the *millets* became accepted and the leaders of the different *millets* had wide jurisdiction over their flock who were bound by their own regulations rather than by the *Shariat* (Islamic Law). The different *millets* were treated like corporate bodies and allowed their own internal structures and hierarchies – indeed the Ottoman state encouraged this by dealing exclusively with the heads of the different *millets* as opposed to the individual members. Included with these structures were the educational systems for the different religious communities. Thus the religious community – the *millet* – was the prime focus of identity outside of family and locality. This has had the enduring result of a confusion in modern times between the concepts of citizenship, religion and ethnicity. For Muslims in the Empire, the Muslim community – the *umma* – was the prime focus of wider loyalty and group identity.[3] As such, the sense of differentiation within this group was relatively weak. Conversely there was, and remains, a tendency for non-Muslims, especially Orthodox Christians to view all Muslims as 'Turks' – the exception here being the Albanians, both because of their numbers and because Muslims today constitute a majority of Albanians in the region, and thus they are seen as a Muslim people like the Turks. Conversely, the Slavs in the southern/central Balkans (and the Greeks) saw themselves as an Orthodox people and thus the Muslim Slavs were often not regarded as part of the new 'nation' (whatever that nation was considered to be). Due to the *millet* legacy, they tended to be seen as 'Turks' by their fellow Slav speakers and not as Greeks or Bulgarians or whatever. However, the modern era has seen these groups caught between the concepts of modern nationalism whereby the mother-tongue is often a (if not *the*) primary differentiator, and the *millet* heritage – especially in an environment of urbanisation and modernisation where religious ties are often weakened. The situation regarding these smaller non-Albanian Muslim groups in Macedonia is the primary focus of this chapter.

The defeat of the Ottomans in the First Balkan War saw their expulsion from the whole area of Macedonia. However the victors fell out over the spoils and in the Second Balkan War Bulgaria was defeated by its erstwhile allies (as well as the Ottomans and Romania). The end result of this internecine fighting was that Macedonia was partitioned, with Serbia and Greece gaining at the expense of Bulgaria: the latter's gains being reduced to the area around the Pirin mountains. In all three areas, large Muslim minorities remained.

Greek Macedonia

In the area under Greece's jurisdiction, the above-mentioned process reached its apogee in the Balkans. The Muslim population was expelled *en masse* to Turkey in the great population exchanges of the early 1920s following Greece's defeat in Asia Minor and the setting up of the modern Turkish state. In these exchanges, religion rather than ethnicity or language was the criterion, so that virtually all Muslims in Greece were seen as 'Turks' and conversely all Orthodox peoples in Anatolia were viewed as 'Greeks' regardless of whether they could even speak the relevant language. The main exceptions to this early form of ethnic cleansing were the Muslim community in western Thrace which was allowed to remain in exchange for the Orthodox community in Istanbul and the islands of Gokceada and Bozcaada.⁴ Thus the Muslim population of Aegean Macedonia effectively left *in toto* for Turkey.⁵

Bulgarian Macedonia

In Bulgaria, a similar process occurred, whereby all Muslims were seen initially as alien remnants of the Ottoman period – this despite the situation whereby perhaps as many as half of the inhabitants of the new Bulgarian state were Muslims.⁶ As a result, large-scale emigration of Muslims – both Turks and others – from Bulgaria to initially the Ottoman Empire and then later to the Turkish republic occurred. However, many Muslims remained, and due to their high birth rate the number of Muslims in Bulgaria has remained approximately at one million. In the Pirin region they live mostly in the Mesta valley and the majority of these were Muslim Slavs – known in Bulgaria as Pomaks – as well as some Roma (Gypsies). The Pomaks in Bulgarian Macedonia are on the western edge of the Pomak areas of the central Rhodope. Although the bulk of Bulgaria's Pomak population live outside of Bulgarian Macedonia, they were subject to the same pressures by the state as those outside in the central Rhodope. Therefore, it would be instructive to briefly look at the changing situation of the whole Pomak community in Bulgaria.

The situation regarding the Pomak community of Islamicised Slavs living predominately in the central Rhodope mountains is illustrative of changes in national identity, especially of minorities, whose distinctiveness from the majority is based almost exclusively on their religious adherence and traditional related customs. The state has oscillated between viewing them on the one hand as aliens who should be encouraged to go to the Ottoman Empire/Turkey, and on the other as a group who should be assimilated, forcibly if necessary, into the Bulgarian nation. During the Balkan Wars there were compulsory conversions of Rhodope Pomaks to Orthodox Christianity, as well as massacres. This policy of forced conversion and name-changing from Islamic forms to 'Bulgarian' ones was soon abandoned. In the 1920s and 1930s there was a movement among some of Bulgarian's intellectuals to view religion as not being of paramount importance and thus to view the Pomaks as part of the national body, and *Rodina*, a cultural-educational organisation, was established in 1937 to further this aim. The Koran was translated into Bulgarian and a Rhodope Mufti separate

from the central Turkish one was set up. In 1942, the practice of christening all new-born children with 'Bulgarian' names was introduced
and the National Assembly brought in a law to facilitate the changing
of names of adults many Rhodope Pomaks, either voluntarily or under
pressure, changed their names. The Communists initially changed all
this and in October 1945 a decree restored old Muslim names.[7]
However, following the rise of Todor Zhivkov in the 1950s,
Communist Bulgaria progressively pursued a policy of homogenisation
of its minorities and the Pomaks were subject to severe pressure to
assimilate and become part of 'the unified Bulgarian socialist nation'
(see below).

Pomak numbers, as is often the case regarding minorities in the
Balkans, are hard to accurately assess. They were in the late 1980s estimated to number in excess of 250,000[8], and live in compact settlements in the Rhodope mountains and down the Mesta valley in the
Pirin region. Similarly as in Greece where the two communities in
many ways overlap across the Rhodope mountains, the Pomaks live
further to the west. However there is some overlap and intermarriage.
Where they have cohabited villages, campaigns against Pomaks, which
tended to pre-date similar ones against ethnic Turks, have been applied
to both groups at the same time. Since 1948, the Bulgarian authorities,
even before the Zhivkov regime, have made repeated attempts to
induce the Pomaks to change their names, renounce their faith and
become integrated into the then socialist Bulgarian state. Some Pomak
activists and their families were forcibly resettled in 1952 to other areas
of the country. However the most brutal campaign was in the period
1971–3 when the authorities tried to force the Pomaks to change their
names by obliging them to choose new ones from a list of 'official'
Bulgarian names.[9] This campaign was in many ways a prototype for
the larger campaign which was to come against the ethnic Turks in the
mid-1980s and prompted similar violent resistance in instances.

There appears to have been a number of reasons behind these extraordinary campaigns. These included the high birth-rate of minorities,
as shown by the high birth-rate in areas where ethnic Turks, Pomaks
and Roma predominated, while the rest of the country as well as the
country as a whole suffered negative rates. In addition, adherence to
the Islamic faith was seen by the authorities as a key factor inhibiting
loyalty to the communist government.[10] As such, the Zhivkov regime
undertook a full-scale campaign to homogenise Bulgarian society by
force within a few generations and turn all its inhabitants into model
socialist Bulgarian citizens. Interestingly, when the campaign turned

fully to the ethnic Turks in December 1984, the official line was that they were not ethnic Turks at all but descendants from forcibly Islamicised Bulgarians (i.e. Pomaks) who were now 'spontaneously' and 'voluntarily' reclaiming their identity as Bulgarians.

Both campaigns despite the brutality and hardship were failures. Indeed the failure of the campaign against the ethnic Turks led to the mass exodus of 1989, the collapse of the agricultural economy and the fall of Zhivkov himself. It is possible that in an earlier part of the century such heavy-handed repressive tactics may well have paid off to some extent over a long period. The example here perhaps is Greece, where policies which while not so brutally violent were nevertheless in the long term pursued rigorously and with the same goal – homogenisation – and with a large degree of success regarding non-Muslim minorities. Again in Greece, Muslim minorities have proved far harder to assimilate than Christian ones, hence the Zhivkov regime's attempt to close mosques and stamp out Islamic practices like circumcision.[11]

Following the fall of Zhivkov the entire minority situation turned around. The Pomaks along with the ethnic Turks were allowed to reclaim their original names[12] and freely practise Islam. The December 1992 census preliminary results on ethnic breakdown gave 7,272,000 ethnic Bulgarians (85.8 per cent), of whom 143,000 (2 per cent) were Pomaks; 822,000 ethnic Turks (9.7 per cent), of whom, 9,000 (1.1 per cent) were Christian; and 288,000 Roma (3.4 per cent), of whom 60.4 per cent were Christian with 39.2 per cent Muslim. Bulgarian was given as the mother-tongue of 86.3 per cent of the total, with Turkish accounting for 9.8 per cent and Romany for 3 per cent. Bulgarian was given as the mother-tongue of 28,000 ethnic Turks, 19,000 Roma and 24,000 from other ethnic groups.[13]

In the new period the Pomaks have to some extent had their imposed isolation – due to inhabiting inaccessible closed border regions between Bulgaria and Greece and Yugoslavia – lifted. As such, in Bulgaria there is a marked tendency for polarisation of those who move to the towns and, by losing their religious identity, become associated with the Bulgarian majority. This drift from the countryside has been aided by a catastrophic drop in the price of tobacco – a staple crop of the Rhodope – which has seen many Pomaks destitute and unemployment levels in all minority areas shoot up.[14] On the other hand there were those who were becoming Turkified helped by shared religion. Regarding the latter there was a radical element among the Party for Rights and Freedom (DPS) – the main ethnic Turkish political grouping and at times a government coalition partner – who called for Turkish education among the Pomaks for this very purpose.[15] Slav Bulgarians have accused local officials for forging census results so as to inflate the number of Turks, and criminal proceedings have begun against them. The accusations continued and were repeated by the Bulgarian Socialist Party (BSP) – the successor to the Bulgarian Communist Party and which retook control in 1994.[16] The Democratic Party of Labour, headed by Kamen Burov, set up in December 1992 to defend Pomak interests, was very close to the DPS.[17] It appeared at that time that the Pomak minority in Bulgaria was gradually dividing itself between those who saw themselves as Bulgarian and as Turkish respectively. Since then the number of those claiming to be Turks has dropped dramatically and some observers see the beginnings of a possible move towards the creation of a separate 'Pomak' identity[18] similar to that which has occurred in Bosnia with the adoption of the term 'Bosniak' to denote Slav Muslims there.[19] The basis for this view seems to be the large numbers (65,000 as per the 1992 census) who declared themselves 'Muslims', 'Pomaks', 'Bulgarian Mohammedans' and the like. On the other hand, the use of terms like 'Bulgarian Mohammedans' – a term used by the Zhivkov regime to denote Pomaks (and later ethnic Turks as well) and one which a practising Muslim would be very loathe to use – perhaps merely illustrates the present temporary confusion over national self-identification of such groups, rather than a process like that in Bosnia where a larger and more dominant group has previously been recognised as a separate 'nation' of Yugoslavia and which has been cemented during the course of a war.[20] The chair of the Supreme Muslim Council in Bulgaria, Nedim Gendzhev,[21] alleged in late 1996 that Pomak youths, some of whom were from around Gotse Delchev in the Pirin region, were being 'illegally' trained by the Muslim Brotherhood Foundation in radical Islamic training camps in Algeria and Saudi Arabia, and that armed training of such Muslim youths was taking place under such foreign auspices near Gotse Delchev as well as in the central Rhodope area.[22]

Regarding emigration to Turkey, Pomaks, as noted above, have along with other non-Turkish Balkan Muslim groups often joined the waves of emigration to Turkey in the last 100 years and more following the collapse of the Ottoman Empire in the region. However it was noticeable that during the mass exodus of 1989 when the authorities freely gave tourist passports to ethnic Turks, they were not so freely issued to Pomaks. Despite huge numbers – perhaps as many as half – of the ethnic Turks returning from Turkey when the reality of life there did not match up to expectations, emigration continued. Again many Pomaks tried to take advantage of this but were usually weeded out by the Turkish embassy issuing visas who gave would-be applicants a rudimentary Turkish-language test. Since those days all emigration has become harder and in 1993 only 70–80 cases of divided families were allowed to emigrate officially to Turkey.[23] However, many continue to come as tourists, and stay. Those who have come to Turkey and who are not ethnically Turkish soon become assimilated into the mass of the Turkish nation.[24]

The Republic of Macedonia (ROM)

The national self-identification of by far the largest Muslim group in what became Yugoslav Macedonia, the Albanians, has remained solid, with the exception of a brief period in the 1950s when large numbers of them identified themselves as Turks so as to take advantage of the then emigration agreement between Tito's Yugoslavia and Turkey (see below). In contrast, that of smaller groups continues to fluctuate. The apparent confusion over the identity of different Muslim groups in the case of ROM demonstrates further that in the Balkans religion has often been of paramount importance in ethnic differentiation.

Torbeši and 'Muslims'

The Muslim Slav Macedonians are known as Torbeši, Pomaks, Gorans or Poturs, and will be referred to as Torbeši in this chapter. In former 'Yugoslavia', the term 'Muslim' was used to describe descendants of Slavs who converted to Islam during the Ottoman period and, it should be stressed, was *not* applied to the mostly Muslim Albanians, or the wholly Muslim Turkish minorities. The Muslims were recognised as a 'nationality' of Yugoslavia in 1961, and as a separate 'nation' in 1971.[25] Although a large majority of these Muslims spoke Serbo-Croat and lived mainly in Bosnia-Hercegovina or the Sandžak area on the Serbian/Montenegrin border, there were some 40,000 or so Muslims in Yugoslav Macedonia, who mostly spoke Macedonian. These were descendants of the Slav population of Macedonia who had converted to Islam during the Ottoman period. Thus they should perhaps have been differentiated from the Serbo-Croat-speaking Muslim Slavs. To further complicate the issue, Muslim sources in Sandžak claim that many of the Torbeši are recent Serbo-Croat speaking arrivals: taking advantage of the emigration agreement in the 1950s with Turkey they left Sandžak for Turkey, and on their way there settled in Macedonia.[26]

As with the Pomaks in Bulgaria, the Torbeši have in the past often identified closely with fellow Muslims, and especially with Turks. However, the authorities, both of former Yugoslavia and ROM, have been worried by the penetration of Albanian nationalism among them by way of, among other things, Albanian-speaking hodzhas. The numbers of the Muslim Slavs has fluctuated greatly in past censuses – 1,591 in 1953; 3,002 in 1961; 1,248 in 1971; and a dramatic rise to 39,555 in 1981. This last figure presumably includes many who had previously declared themselves Turks (see below).

In 1970, the Torbeši formed themselves into an association, the republican community for cultural and scientific events of Macedonia Muslims, and held their first cultural meeting at the monastery of Saint Jovan Bigorski in western Macedonia. The organisation, which was set up with the blessing of the authorities, claimed that since the war over 70,000 of their number had been assimilated by other Muslim groups, especially the Albanians.[27] If this was indeed the case, the rise in their numbers reflected in the 1981 census demonstrates that the founding of the association and its subsequent prorogation of a specifically Macedonian Muslim Slav identity was a great success.

In spite of this apparent success, there persisted indications that the Torbeši remained susceptible to assimilation into the Muslim (Albanian) majority in the Yugoslav republic of Macedonia. This demonstrates the fact that in the Balkan context Islam is often a more powerful unifying factor than ethnicity. The fears of the Torbeši community came into the open in 1990 when Yugoslavia was entering its final phase. On 13 August 1990, Riza Memedovski, chairman of the Torbeši organisation, sent an open letter to the Chairman of the Party for Democratic Prosperity of Macedonia (PDP: the predominately ethnic Albanian party based in Tetovo) on the subject of this 'quiet assimilation'. He accused the PDP of abusing religion for political ends through the attempted 'Kosovoisation and Albanianisation of western Macedonia'.[28] The same concern was voiced by the Council of Elders of the Islamic Community of Macedonia, on 6 November 1990.[29] This tendency for Torbeši to lean towards the ethnic Albanians was underlined by apparent support for the PDP among Slav Muslims. In the second round of elections in Macedonia on 25 November 1990, the PDP complained that in Slav Muslim villages in western Macedonia inhabitants were prevented from voting for the PDP by members of the nationalist parties in the Front for Macedonia National Unity (FMNU), the militia organs, and even by members of the electoral commissions.[30]

The tension felt by the authorities in the Yugoslav republic of Macedonia over possible assimilation of the Torbeši and Slav Muslims by non-Slav groups like the Albanians or the Turks has continued since the emergence of Yugoslav Macedonia as an independent state. Most recently, tensions have risen in relation to Torbeši and Muslim refugees from Bosnia-Hercegovina. While the Yugoslav Macedonian authorities actively encouraged smaller Muslim groups (like the Turks and the Torbeši) to identify themselves as such out of a fear that these groups were becoming Albanianised, the ROM authorities now appear nervous of possible leverage by Turkey, currently the main regional power. A number of Torbeši in the Debar region have indeed requested schooling in Turkish rather than Macedonian; the authorities turned down this request.[31] In early January 1993 the presidium of the official Torbeši state body, the Republican Community of Islamicised Macedonians, issued a statement stating that the Democratic Party of Turks in Macedonia (DPTM) was behind the 'pan-Turkish ideas' exhibited in the Moša Pijade school, which was at the centre of the controversy and was demolished on 28–29 December 1992.[32] The DPTM for its part told the mission of the Conference on Security and Cooperation in Europe (CSCE) in January 1993 that the status of the Turkish minority was under threat.[33] Construction of a refugee village in the Skopje suburb of Djorče Petrov with the help of finance from Germany to house the influx of Muslims fleeing Bosnia-Hercegovina, was halted after protests and demonstrations by local inhabitants in February 1993.[34] The authorities appeared wary of recognising the Serbo-Croat Muslims as a distinct people, and in spite of the old legacy they continue to be unrecognised. First attempts to set up a branch of the Party of Democratic Action (PDA: the party of Bosnian President Alija Izetbegović) were met with obstruction from the ROM security forces.[35]

Thus in the late Yugoslav period the authorities, worried at the assimilation of the Muslim Slavs by the Albanians, in 1970 set up a Torbeši organisation specifically to counter this threat. In spite of the apparent success measured by the rise in the number who identified themselves as 'Muslims' in succeeding censuses, the threat of assimilation remained. Such threats continued after the break-up of Yugoslavia and the emergence of an independent Macedonia. The picture is further complicated by the presence of Serbo-Croat-speaking Muslims (as opposed to the Macedonian-speaking Torbeši), whose numbers have been increased by the arrival of refugees from Bosnia. The ROM authorities appear reluctant to recognise these 'Muslims' as a distinct people separate from the Torbeši. As in Bulgaria, the crux of the matter lies in the question of to whom, in national terms, do these relatively small groups of Slav Muslims belong. Is their sense of separateness sufficiently developed to resist the attractions of the shared Islamic faith of larger, well-defined, national Muslim groups like the Albanians or Turks? Is it strong enough, in the case of the Torbeši, to resist the pull towards the majority Slav Macedonians arising out of the shared language? Can they indeed survive as a separate 'national' group?

The picture is further complicated by those calling themselves Gorans who live in some communities in the hills in western Macedonia and over the Sar Planina in Kosovo. These Muslims speak a mixture of Macedonian, Serbo-Croat and some Arabic, and as their name indicates (*gora* means hill or forest) live in upland regions. They see themselves as separate from the Torbeši and traditionally would marry only within their own community. However, in most respects they share many customs with the Torbeši, and perhaps illustrate further the problems of small Muslim groups whose identity was tradi-tionally based primarily on religion and narrow village communities, in the modern world. If there is a question on the survival of the Torbeši as a distinct national group, then this doubly applies to the Gorans.

Turks

Most of the Turks of former Yugoslavia lived in Macedonia. Remnants from the long Ottoman occupation, they numbered 101,292 in former Yugoslavia according to the census of 1981. Out of these, 86,691 lived in Macedonia, where they constituted 4 per cent of the population. In the census of April 1991 they numbered 97,416, i.e. 4.79 per cent of the population of the new republic (ROM). Assessing the true number of minorities like the Turks and others in Macedonia continues to be problematic. The census of 1948 gave a figure of 95,940 Turks, while that of 1953 recorded 203,938. By the next census seven years later, however, the number had fallen to 131,481. These major fluctuations were due essentially to external events. In the immediate post-war period, the Turks were regarded as suspect, thanks to the friendship between Turkey and the West. In January 1948, seventeen Macedonian Turks were tried as members of 'Judzel', ostensibly a terrorist/espionage organisation. The trial received extensive publicity within Macedonia in order to intimidate the Turkish minority. As a result, many Turks declared themselves to be Albanians in the 1948 census. However by 1953, following the break with Albania after the Tito-Stalin split, it was the Albanians' turn to be seen as suspect. Consequently many Albanians declared themselves to be Turks: of the 203,938 in the 1953 census, 32,392 gave Macedonian as their native tongue, and 27,086 gave Albanian. The number of declared Albanians fell from 179,389 in 1948 to 165,524 in 1953.

The period from 1953 to 1966 also witnessed the extensive emigration of Turks from Yugoslavia to Turkey. Some 80,000 emigrated according to figures from Yugoslavia's statistical yearbooks; over 150,000 according to some Turkish sources. However, some of these emigrants were unable to speak any Turkish, and were in fact either Muslim Albanians or Slavs who were claiming to be Turks to escape from communist Yugoslavia.[36]

In the 1971 census there were 108,552 declared Turks. By the census of 1981 this number had dropped to 86,690. This decline was the more surprising given the high birth-rate of ethnic Turks in Macedonia which would have been expected to result in an increase of some 20,000 during the decade from 1971 to 1981, instead of a decrease of over 20,000. It appeared that many who had previously declared themselves to be Turks were now calling themselves Muslims, while others were declaring themselves to be Albanians or Roma.[37]

The communist authorities, worried at the rise of Albanian nationalism in the 1980s, asserted that many Turks in Macedonia had been Albanianised under pressure. According to the director of the Macedonian Republic Bureau of Statistics in Skopje,[38] this was especially pronounced in Tetovo, Gostivar, Struga and Kičevo regions. In September 1987 the Macedonian League of Communists Central Committee Presidium construed the expansion of Albanian nationalism as one of the main reasons behind the emigration of Turkish families from the Gostivar municipality.[39] The Albanians apparently claimed that 'these were not Turks', but 'Illyrians turned into Turks' who were now 'returning to their flock', i.e. rejoining the Albanian mother nation.[40] In a like manner, Nevzat Halili, then leader of the Party for Democratic Prosperity (PDP: which was the main Albanian political grouping in Macedonia) called on Torbeši and Roma to declare themselves Albanians.[41]

Like the Albanians, the Turks were a recognised 'nationality' of former Yugoslavia, and from the outset were allowed educational and cultural rights. In the first school year under the new Yugoslav republic of Macedonia in 1944/5, there were 60 primary schools using Turkish as the language of instruction, with 3,334 pupils. In 1950/1 there were over 100 such schools with more than 12,000 pupils and 267 teachers.

As a result of emigration to Turkey, by 1958/9 the number had dropped to 27 schools (26 primary and one secondary), with just over 6,000 pupils and 219 teachers. While the number of primary schools had increased to 53 by the end of 1988, the number of pupils remained more or less the same.[42] As for the Albanians of Macedonia, the Turks had their own television and radio programmes and a newspaper (*Birlik*), as well as various cultural organisations. The main political movement for the Turks in Yugoslav Macedonia was the communist-controlled Democratic Alliance of Turks in Macedonia. With the advent of democracy in Yugoslav in 1990, its break-up, and the subsequent emergence of independent Macedonia, this organisation was superseded by the DPTM.

The Roma (Gypsies)

Yugoslav had one of the largest Roma populations in Europe, with important links with emigrant Roma groups in France, Germany, the United States, Australia, etc. As is the case elsewhere in the Balkans, the Roma community comprises both Muslims and Christians. In areas like Macedonia where Ottoman rule lasted longest, the majority of Roma are Muslim: as such they constitute a significant Muslim community. It is instructive to look briefly at the situation of the Roma within Yugoslavia as a whole, before concentrating on their position in Yugoslav Macedonia and subsequently ROM. Initially, the estimated 850,000 Roma of Yugoslavia were in the main ignored as a group by the authorities throughout communist Yugoslavia. This is illustrated by the manifesto issued by the communists in 1944 urging the people of Macedonia to join Tito's partisans. This called on Slavs, Albanians, Turks and Vlachs to join the struggle, but made no mention of the numerous Roma, who remained firmly rooted at the bottom of the social scale. This began to change in the 1970s as Yugoslavia evolved its complicated system of national rights entrenched in the 1974 Constitution. From 1981 they had (in theory) nationality status on an equal footing with other national minorities like the Albanians, Turks or Hungarians. However in practice this status was not uniformly applied by the Yugoslav republics: while Bosnia-Hercegovina and Montenegro granted them 'national minority status', the other republics (including Yugoslav Macedonia) placed Roma in the lower category of an 'ethnic group'. In spite of this, there were advances. Yugoslavia was in the vanguard of the movement to introduce Romani education, with the breakthrough initially occurring in the Albanian-populated region of Kosovo in the 1980s, and from 1983 Romani has been used in some state schools as the teaching medium for the first four grades, and regular Romani programmes have been broadcast. A modified version of the 32-letter Romani alphabet was used, so that it could be as widely understood as possible,[43] and in May 1980 the *Naša Kniga* publishing house of Skopje brought out the first Romani grammar to be written entirely in the Romani script and orthography.[44] Throughout former Yugoslavia the most significant development was in Macedonia. Following the devastating earthquake of 1962, the Romani town of Suto Orizari (known as 'Šutka') was established just outside Skopje. This has some 35,000 inhabitants, its own elected council, and a member of parliament.

In spite of these advances, the majority of Roma have continued to live well below the economic average. There has been discrimination in the workplace, with many Romani men unemployed and Romani women employed in the lowest of menial occupations. Only a few Roma have benefited from university education, and entered the professions. In former Yugoslavia half the Romani earners were industrial workers, and 20 per cent were farmers, many owning their land. The rest were self-employed artisans, and small-scale traders.

Even though they had thus gained substantial recognition, the Roma continued to be unwilling to identify themselves as such, due to the persistent stigma attached to this. This is encapsulated in the use of the pejorative term 'cigane'[45] by which they continue to be widely known. In Macedonia the number of Roma in the various censuses remained more or less static until the census of 1981, when it rose dramatically from 24,505 in the previous census of 1971 to 43,223. This reflected their more developed official status, and a consequent relative decline in the stigma. The last census of April 1991 recorded 55,575 Roma in Macedonia, i.e. some 2.73 per cent of the total population of just over two million. However, the real figure is certainly much higher, and Roma leaders themselves claim some 200,000 in Macedonia.

Many Roma have declared themselves to be Macedonians or Turks. For a long time, however, the former communist authorities alleged that they were being subjected to Albanianisation: this was particularly the case, the authorities claimed, in relation to the Muslim Roma, who comprise the vast majority. This was consistent with the view of many Macedonians that the Albanians constituted the main internal threat. The claim of Albanianisation was again made on 1 August 1990 by the presidium of the republican committee for nurturing the ethnic and cultural traditions of Roma in the Socialist Republic of Macedonia (an official body set up by the communist authorities), which accused the

PDP of persistently manipulating Roma on an Islamic basis. On 1 September 1990 the Macedonian Romani community called on all Roma to stop declaring themselves to be Albanians simply because they share the Islamic faith, and decided to celebrate 11 October (a Macedonian public day) with the first republican festival of the cultural achievements of Roma in Macedonia.[46] This illustrates well the continuing tendency of Balkan Muslim communities like the Muslim Roma to be drawn towards larger Muslim groups with a more developed national identity. It also demonstrates that the authorities have made efforts to prevent such assimilation, viewing it as a means of strengthening the most 'problematic' Muslim minority, namely the Turks in Greece, and the Albanians in Yugoslav Macedonia and later in FYROM.

'Egyptians'

Given the problems faced by the Roma, and the ethnic uncertainty of many Muslim citizens (a legacy from Ottoman times, when religion and not ethnicity was the main factor of differentiation), especially in areas dominated by highly organised and nationalistic Muslim Albanians, it is perhaps not surprising that unusual national claims appear from time to time. In Macedonia in 1990 the 'Egipcani' Association of Citizens was set up in Ohrid under the leadership of Nazim Arifi,[47] with the support of approximately 4,000 inhabitants of Ohrid and neighbouring Struga, who renounced being Roma in favour of being Egyptian.[48] A sister association was soon established in Kosovo, and by September 1990 the associations claimed 100,000 'descendants of the Pharaohs' in Kosovo, and between 20,000 and 30,000 in Macedonia. The associations petitioned the former Yugoslav Federal Assembly and the Serbian and Macedonian national assemblies to include the separate category of 'Egyptian' in the 1991 population census:[49] this was achieved in the 1991 Macedonian census. The phenomenon of Roma claiming to be Egyptians has not become widespread, however, and is unlikely to develop, in spite of claims of recently uncovered documents in the Vatican Library showing that Egyptians came to Macedonia between 306 and 337 AD in the shape of 150,000 infantry troops and 150,000 horsemen, which are claimed to be the forerunners of the Macedonian 'Egyptians'.[50]

Notes

1. Modern scholars give credit for the first establishment of Turkish as the base of the official language, at least as far as Anatolia is concerned, to the Karamanids who created in the thirteenth century a strong polity on the

ruins of the Seljuk Sultanate. See M. Önder, 'Türkçenin Devlet Dili Ilanini Yildönümü', *Türk Dili*, vol. X (1961), p. 507, quoted in David Kushner, *The Rise of Turkish Nationalism 1876–1908* (Frank Cass, 1977) p. 90. However this was not synonymous with demotic Turkish as spoken by the mass of the population.

2. There remains uncertainty over the origins of the *millet* system. Many trace the system back to the presumed appointment by Mehmed II, the conqueror of Istanbul, of Patriarch Gennadias, Bishop Yovakim of Bursa and Rabbi Capsali as hereditary leaders of the respective Greek, Armenian and Jewish communities. However others like Benjamin Braude say that the term '*millet*' was really a set of mostly local arrangements which varied from place to place and that there is much evidence to say that the authority vested in the leaders was both personal rather than hereditary/institutionalised, and varied in its territorial extent. E.g. the Greek Patriarchates of Jerusalem, Alexandria and Antioch retained their autonomy at least in canon law, while for the Armenians, the see of Istanbul became 'over the centuries... a sort of de facto patriarchate, but its ecclesiastical legitimacy was grudgingly recognized, if at all'. See Benjamin Braude in Bernard Lewis, *Christians and Jews in the Ottoman Empire*, (New York, 1982), pp. 72–82, and the review article 'Remembering the Minorities' by Andrew Mango in *Middle Eastern Studies*, vol. 21, no. 4 (October 1985), pp. 118–40. The Jews never had a single patriarchal leader for the whole community.

3. The 'imagined community' of Benedict Anderson: see his *Imagined Communities: Reflections on the Origin and Spread of Nationalism* (London, Verso, revised edition, 1991).

4. Other Muslim groups like the Muslim Albanian Chams did remain in Greece until the period after the Second World War when they were expelled to Albania and their mosques burnt.

5. In Atatürk's Turkey of this period there was a full-scale state-orchestrated campaign to create Turkish citizens out of the Turkish-speaking mass of the peoples as well as the other disparate Muslim groups of Anatolia, and those who had previously come to Anatolia fleeing 'Christian' rule either from the Balkans or from the Muslim areas of the Russian Empire. The Muslim Slavs, Vlachs, Greeks, etc. rapidly assimilated into the Turkish-speaking mass. For more details on all aspects of this, see H. Poulton: *Top Hat, Grey Wolf and Crescent Turkish Nationalism and the Turkish Republic* (London, C. Hurst, 1997).

6. See Wolfgang Höpken, 'From Religious Identity to Ethnic Mobilisation: The Turks of Bulgaria Before, During and Since Communism', in Hugh Poulton and Suha Taji-Farouki (eds), *Muslim Identity and the Balkan State* (London, C. Hurst, 1997).

7. See Boriana Panaiotova and Kalina Bozeva, 'The Bulgarian Muslims ("Pomaks")', in The Committee for the Defence of Minority Rights, *Minority Groups in Bulgaria in a Human Rights Context* (Sofia, October 1994).

8. Local authorities gave a figure of 268,971 at the end of 1990.

9. For more details see H. Poulton, *The Balkans: Minorities and States in Conflict* (MRG Publications, London, 1991 and 1993), pp. 111–15.

10. This was clearly set out in an article in *Filosofska Misul* – an official publication published in Sofia. See Poulton, *ibid*, pp. 124–5 for the full text.

11. While some showcase mosques were kept open and 'tame' Muftis paraded before foreign visitors, spouting the Zhivkov line of no ethnic Turks, the reality in the countryside was one of frequent mosque closure and persecution. See Poulton, *ibid*, chapters 10–12 for more details.
12. This despite some obvious moves by the Lukanov government to try and split the two groups and only allow restoration to ethnic Turks whose names were changed at a later date.
13. *BTA*, 4 December 1992, and *Bulgarian Radio*, 5 December 1992.
14. Interestingly, the Pomaks do not seem to participate in 'trader tourism' and associated black-market activities, but are well featured as members of the building community building dachas and the like for the new elite. See Yulian Konstantinov, 'Strategies for Sustaining a Vulnerable Identity: The Case of the Bulgarian Pomaks', in Hugh Poulton and Suha Taji-Farouki (eds), *Muslim Identity and the Balkan State* (London, C. Hurst, 1997).
15. *BTA*, 14 December 1992. In one case reported of schoolchildren and parents asked to complete forms stating ethnicity before 10/10/92, some 2,729 (23 per cent of all schoolchildren in the area) had claimed to be Turkish whereas in 1991 none had. In another case, 1,174 out of a total of 1,721 identified themselves as Turks – see *Duma*, Sofia, 23, 27 and 28 November 1992, and *Trud*, Sofia, 15 December 1992, both quoted in R. Nikolaev, 'Bulgaria's 1992 Census: Results, Problems and Implications', *RFE/RL Research Report*, vol. 2, no. 6 (1993).
16. See proceedings of the 41st Congress and resolution from delegates from Kardzhali, Haskovo and Smolyan opposing forcible Turkicisation of Pomaks, as well as *BTA*, 3 and 6 June 1994.
17. *BTA*, 12 January 1993.
18. See Boriana Panaiotova and Kalina Bozeva, 'The Bulgarian Muslims ("Pomaks")', in The Committee for the Defence of Minority Rights, *Minority Groups in Bulgaria in a Human Rights Context* (Sofia, October 1994).
19. A crucial factor here is the terrible persecution the Bosnian Muslims have suffered in the recent war, due to being Muslim – a factor which has immeasurably helped to cement a national consciousness.
20. War has often been a crucial factor in promoting national identity.
21. Nedim Gendzhev remains a controversial figure. He was chief Mufti during the Zhivkov era and an official apologist for the 'regeneration' process against the ethnic Turks when force was used to assimilate them, and Islamic practices were severely curtailed. In the initial period after the fall of Zhivkov it seemed that he was totally discredited, but he has made something of a comeback by claiming that he had no choice but to support the campaign at the time. He has also, with limited success, set himself up as a rival to the ethnic Turkish-dominated DPS in claiming to represent the Muslim community in Bulgaria.
22. *Trud*, Sofia, 1 November 1996.
23. Figures from Turkish Foreign Ministry, interview August 1994.
24. It is interesting to compare the ease of assimilating these non-Turkish-speaking Muslims who have come to the country by choice, with the problems Turkey has had in assimilating the large Muslim Kurdish population in the southeast of the country.

25. In former Yugoslavia the communist authorities' nationality policy always officially espoused the slogan 'brotherhood and unity'. In reality, however, it evolved from a Serb-orientated polity under Aleksander Ranković's control of the all-powerful security apparatus, to a three-tier system of national rights, which was enshrined in the 1974 Constitution (see Chapter 1) For the genesis and development of official recognition of the *Muslims* as a separate 'Nation', see Poulton, *The Balkans*, ch. 4.
26. The 1950s emigration agreement which lasted till Ranković's fall in 1966 in theory referred only to Turks. Due to the *millet* system and the strength of Islam as a binding factor in identification cutting across national boundaries, however, many non-Turkish Muslims took advantage of the agreement and went to Turkey. They have become peacefully assimilated into the Turkish majority there. The Sandžak Muslims claim that some 29 villages in Macedonia are completely settled by Muslims from Sandžak – see *'State Terror Against the Muslims in Sanjak'*, paper presented to the Vienna Conference on Human Rights, June 1993, p. 6. They appear to be Muslims who were caught in transit when the agreement ended and remained in Macedonia.
27. *Duga*, Belgrade, 8 May 1982.
28. *Tanjug* (the official Yugoslav news agency, Belgrade), 13 August 1990.
29. *Tanjug*, 6 November 1990.
30. *Tanjug*, 27 November 1990.
31. *Tanjug*, 30 September and 29 December 1992.
32. *Tanjug*, 4 January 1993.
33. *Tanjug*, 22 January 1993.
34. *Tanjug*, 20 and 22 February 1993.
35. A. Sebestyen, 'Walking the Tightrope in the Balkans', *New Statesman and Society* (London, 9 September 1994).
36. Paul Shoup, *Communism and the Yugoslav National Question* (New York, 1968), pp. 181–2; Stephen Palmer and Robert King, *Yugoslav Communism and the Macedonian Question* (Hamden, Connecticut, Archon Books, 1971), p. 178.
37. In the April 1991 census the figure had risen slightly to 97,416, or 4.79 per cent of the population. A further complicating factor in assessing the number of small minority groups in Yugoslav Macedonia was the rise from 3,652 to 14,240 between 1971 and 1981 of those declaring themselves to be 'Yugoslavs' rather than as belonging to a particular ethnic group (although the percentage of such people was still relatively low in comparison with other republics in former Yugoslavia).
38. *Duga*, Belgrade, 8 May 1982.
39. *Tanjug*, 21 September 1987.
40. *Duga*, Belgrade, 8 May 1982. The Albanians hold that the Illyrians are the forerunners of the Albanians.
41. M. Andrejevich, 'Resurgent Nationalism in Macedonia: A Challenge to Pluralism', *RFE/Report on Eastern Europe* (Munich, 17 May 1991). Unofficially 98 per cent of Albanians in Macedonia are Muslim – in the April 1991 census, households were asked to declare their religious as well as their national affiliation.
42. R. Kantardziev and L. Lazaroski, 'Schools and Education', in M. Apostoloski and H. Plenkovich (eds), *The Socialist Republic of Macedonia* (Skopje, 1974), p. 110.

43. *Tanjug*, 12 January 1980.
44. *Tanjug*, 30 May 1980.
45. This term has negative connotations and its usage is comparable to the use of the word 'nigger' to refer to coloured people.
46. *Tanjug*, 1 September 1990.
47. For a full discussion of the phenomenon of 'Egyptians' in Macedonia and Kosovo, see Ger Duijzings, 'The Egyptians in Kosovo and Macedonia' (forthcoming) which expands and revises his article on the topic first published in Dutch in *Amsterdams Sociologisch Tijdschrift*, no. 18 (1992), pp. 24–38.
48. *Tanjug*, 6 August 1990.
49. *Tanjug*, 24 September 1990.
50. *Tanjug*, April 1991, in BBC SWB EE/1043 B/17, 11 April 1991.

Chapter 9

The Vlachs of the Republic of Macedonia

Tom Winnifrith

The number of Aroumanians or Vlachs recorded in the 1994 Macedonian census was 8,467 people. This figure was obtained with some difficulty from B. Hunter, *The Statesman's Year Book* (London: Macmillan, 1996, p. 843). Other sources are confusing. H. Poulton in his excellent summary of the Vlachs of Macedonia points to a decline from 8,669 in 1953 to 6,392 in 1981 and suggests that this is due to assimilation, but elsewhere gives the figure of 7,190.[1] R. and B. Crampton even more confusingly lump together Aroumanians (Vlachs) with Roma (gypsies) and supply a figure of 2.7 per cent for the 1991 census, the last to be carried out when Macedonia was part of Yugoslavia.[2] Elsewhere I have seen the figure of 0.4 per cent for the 1991 census,[3] and this from a total population of around two million would produce about 8,000 Vlachs. Statistics before the Second World War are confusing because there was no separate identity for Macedonia, and Vlachs tended to be lumped together with the Romanians of Eastern Serbia.[4]

For what they are worth these figures give a fairly consistent picture. The assimilation noted by Poulton was reversed when it became more politically correct to proclaim that one was part of a minority culture. In censuses before 1991 some Vlachs would be keen to proclaim themselves as Yugoslavs, always a popular refuge for small and potentially vulnerable minorities.[5] Thus the fluctuations are easy to explain, and they are not very marked. Nevertheless every Vlach I have spoken to in Macedonia regards the census statistics as damned lies, and maintained that the actual number of Vlachs was far higher.

In my writings on the Vlachs I have always been cautious about exaggerated claims for the number of Vlachs in the Balkans. In my first book, written before I had a chance to visit Vlach communities in

Albania and Romania, I was clearly at fault in putting the total number for all Balkan countries as low as 50,000.[6] One basis for this figure was an examination of the five Vlach communities near Bitola which had a population of ten thousand in the days of Wace and Thompson (see note 11) but are now down to a thousand. Wace and Thompson thought there were half a million Vlachs in the Balkans, and I decimated them accordingly, not paying sufficient attention to the fact that people who have moved from villages like Gopeš, now deserted, and Nižepolje, where there has been extensive emigration to Australia, do somehow manage to preserve their culture and identity even in the unpromising surroundings of high-rise flats in big cities.[7]

Nevertheless, at the risk of making myself unpopular with Vlach friends in Macedonia, many of whom live in such high-rise flats, I do not think the census figures are all that inaccurate. I count as a Vlach someone who thinks of himself or herself as a Vlach and who regularly speaks the language, even if only at home. Clearly there are some in both categories who for one reason or another did not count themselves as Vlach in the 1994 census. I met one such individual in my short stay in 1996. She had declared herself a Macedonian as a good Macedonian patriot. Another group who might well not register as Vlachs are the Vlach-speaking wives and children of Macedonian husbands. Macedonia is still a male-dominated society, and therefore conversely there may be Vlach husbands of Macedonian wives who may have registered their families as Vlach although the children learning to speak at their mother's knee may not be able to speak more than a few words of their father's language.

Competence in Vlach covers a wide range. At one end of the scale there are monolingual speakers, of whom I have met a few, old and female, but this is a group that is unlikely to survive into the next century.[8] We also have quite a large group who have learnt the odd word, or are creditably trying to learn more than the odd word, but it is difficult to see how these can count as real Vlachs. Cornish counts as a minority language, because of the number of people in this category, and Irish counts as a strong minority language, but in fact nobody really speaks Cornish and very few speak Irish.[9] Even among those who have a fair command of Vlach there are gradations of fluency. Interestingly and embarrassingly when speaking on the Vlach programme for Macedonian television I worked my way through two interpreters. Both spoke English a great deal better than I spoke Vlach, but sadly it was their Vlach which let them down. One said he spoke the wrong kind of Vlach, coming from Beala on the Albanian border and speaking Farsherot Vlach. Another was the daughter of a Macedonian mother and Vlach father; her father (and grandfather) had had no truck with the mother's knee, but her Vlach was rusty as a result.

If we were not too fussy about what constituted competence in Vlach or what constituted the feeling of a Vlach identity we might get up to a figure of 15,000 Macedonian Vlachs. I would prefer 10,000, which with a total population in 1994 of just under two million, would make 0.5 per cent of the Macedonians belong to this minority. Much larger figures of a quarter of a million rely on a vague knowledge of Vlach ancestry. But this is a very unreliable criterion. Bulgarians, Greeks, Serbs, Albanians, Gypsies and Turks could use the same criterion to inflate their numbers, so that the population of Macedonia would not be two million but ten million. Under the same criterion the Queen of England would be a German, and I and practically every presidential candidate in the United States would be Irish, although Senator Dukakis would of course be both Greek and Vlach.[10]

Ten thousand does not seem a very large number and 0.5 per cent does not seem a very large percentage. In other Balkan countries the number is larger, but the percentage is smaller except in Albania. Numbers are equally hard to calculate with an equally wide variation both with official statistics and optimistic Vlach estimates. A figure of between thirty and fifty thousand Vlachs in each of Romania, Albania and Greece would probably please neither the Vlachs nor official quarters. The total population of Greece and Romania clearly makes the Vlachs a very insignificant percentage, and even in Albania we are only up to one per cent. Moreover there are difficulties in all three countries for the Vlachs which are not present in Macedonia. Albania has many economic problems, and the preservation of minority cultures and languages is not a high priority. Greece claims that all Vlachs are Greeks, and that there are no minorities in Greece. In Romania the Vlachs are late arrivals, and the process of assimilation is easy because of the similarity in language. There are Vlach associations in all three countries, but most in Greece take a very pro-Greek line, and in Albania there is a division of loyalty between those who favour Greece and those who favour Romania.[11]

For closer parallels with the Vlachs of Yugoslavia we have to look nearer to home. The number of Gaelic speakers in Scotland is probably between 30,000 and 50,000 if we use the same stern criteria that I have applied to the Vlachs. This is between 0.05 and 0.1 per cent of the population of the United Kingdom, and 0.5 and 1 per cent of the population of Scotland. Regular users of Irish form about one per cent of the population of Ireland.[12] The two languages receive a great deal of support from the government. Bilingual road signs and books on and in Gaelic can be found as far south as Fort William and as far east as Inverness. There is a new programme for teaching schoolchildren through the medium of Gaelic. In the Western Isles outside the main centres of the population the road signs are only in Gaelic. Remote communities on the mainland and the islands have been enabled to survive through new roads built with money from the European Community. Of course the language is still in a precarious position, but at least efforts are being made to preserve it.

And so are efforts being made in Macedonia to preserve Vlach. There is an established educational programme, initially handicapped by lack of textbooks and some resistance on the part of pupils, faced among other difficulties with the task of forming a different alphabet. There are radio and television programmes to which I listened and on which I appeared, although I could not help feeling that my appearance on two separate occasions was a sign that there was a slight shortage of material. There are Vlach writers and poets and singers, many of whom I met. Macedonia is a country with a high reputation for poetry, but publication is difficult in these hard times.[13]

There are also Vlach associations in most of the major cities of Macedonia, not only the obvious ones near Vlach villages like Bitola and Ohrid and Štip, but also in Skopje, and as far north as Kumanovo. Under the Communists there was a great tendency, encouraged by the government, to move from picturesque but remote villages to practical if ugly housing estates on the edge of big cities. It would be natural if this process of uprooting led to the forgetting of Vlach culture and language, but the existence of Vlach associations in most towns in Macedonia suggests that this process has not happened, as indeed it has not really happened in even more unpromising places like Manhattan and Melbourne. Apparently it is only in the western part of Macedonia in towns like Gostivar and Tetovo that Vlach associations have not been started. I met a fanatical Vlach from Tetovo in Kruševo which is the nearest approach to a Vlach town in Macedonia. He gave me some extraordinary figures for the number of Vlachs, and declared that Alexander the Great was undoubtedly a Vlach because in the Himalayas people spoke languages which had many words in common with Vlach.[14] I therefore did not wholly believe his explanation that there were many Vlachs around Tetovo who had unfortunately been assimilated. However it is possible that in those areas of Macedonia such as Tetovo where Albanians form a majority, Vlachs have seen the disadvantages of forming a separate splinter group and made common cause with the Macedonians.

There are advantages for the Vlachs in being so widely scattered. Again one thinks of Scotland where the Gaelic speakers have a good redoubt in the Western Isles, something of a presence in Skye, scattered pockets in other parts of the islands and on the western coast, but in the rest of Scotland and the United Kingdom, whose taxpayers help pay for the road signs, the Gaels are nowhere. There are of course Gaelic associations and a fine tradition of Gaelic scholarship in Glasgow and Edinburgh, but little enthusiasm for the Celtic fringe in Dumbarton or Dumfries, let alone Doncaster or Dover. In Ireland the position is roughly the same, except that there is slightly more interest in the position of Irish over the whole of the country, and the Western redoubts in Donegal, Galway and Kerry are remote from each other as well as the world, and indeed speak a different kind of Irish from each other. I have seen people in a bar in Donegal, briskly dismissing the Irish programme on television as not our kind of Irish before turning over to the BBC.

I hope the equivalent briskness is not shown by the Macedonian Vlachs in spite of possible dialect differences in an equally scattered population. The thin spread of Vlach speakers in Macedonia means that they can never really be a political force. It would be just possible with some gerrymandering to carve out a parliamentary constituency near Bitola including Kruševo and the Pelister villages in which a Vlach candidate might achieve a respectable vote, although it is difficult to see what such a candidate could offer, nor would there be any chance of victory, since even if all Vlachs moved to Kruševo they would barely form a majority. Wisely therefore the Vlachs have not tried to form a political party, only a cultural association. Other minorities do have political parties and representation in parliament, albeit not much above token representation. The Vlachs have done better. Three Cabinet Ministers are Vlachs, and they have achieved the remarkable success in education, media and publishing that I have outlined.

It would be nice to say that just as Macedonia is ideal for the Vlach minority, so this Vlach minority is ideal for Macedonia and indeed an example for any multi-ethnic state, asking and receiving cultural privileges, but making no political demands for independence or union with another state. There is no harm done if citizens of the United Kingdom support Ireland at football, or go to Gaelic evening classes; planting bombs for the IRA is another matter. Vlachs, always a cautious race, seem intent on following the former path, and, though this may be disappointing to those anxious to find in minorities a source of journalistic excitement, the Vlachs of Macedonia do not seem set to give many thrills.

But it would be wrong to be entirely optimistic. The Republic of Macedonia has many problems. I attended in September 1996 the celebrations in Skopje of the fifth anniversary of Macedonian independence. It was a curiously muted affair. The spectators did not quite seem to know what they were celebrating or what cause they had for celebration. The empty shops and the complete absence of tourists told their own tale. The trains to and from Skopje used to be late and full of *gastarbeiters* and backpackers; now they are punctual and empty. The situation is apparently even worse in the tourist area near Lake Ohrid. Through no fault of its own Macedonia has become isolated from Serbia and Greece, and thus isolated from Western visitors. All this cannot be good for Vlachs.

Sadly, as was seen in the former Yugoslavia, economic difficulties heighten ethnic tension. It is difficult to see how in spite of their caution the Vlachs can totally avoid this tension, and indeed the privileges awarded to them may actually exacerbate it if larger but less privileged minorities create trouble. The Albanians have of course their own television programme, and I spent happy hours in my Skopje hotel watching bad westerns dubbed into Albanian. But they are less happy about political representation and educational opportunities, in particular over the demand for an Albanian university. One sometimes feels that the Vlachs have been granted their privileges in the same way, and for the same reasons, that someone about to be made bankrupt is punctilious about paying the milkman.

Unlike the Albanians, Vlachs do not and cannot demand their own university. It is rather sad that at university level little work is being done to ensure the preservation of Vlach history or research into the Vlach language. There is a certain amount of investigation into folklore.[15] Events in the past fifty years have not helped. It cannot be easy to remember one's past if one has had to change from being an itinerant herdsman to living in a high-rise flat. Many Vlachs were rich merchants. The fortunes and families of such merchants have been dissipated, and an investigation into these families would be difficult, painful and even unpopular. The Macedonian term for Vlach, particularly used for the rich merchants as opposed to the poor herdsman, is *Cincar*; it is a word with a slightly derogatory meaning. The rich *Cincars* were not popular because they were suspected of hoarding their wealth.

From the end of the Second World War Macedonians were taught a version of history that combined dialectal materialism with a fierce if slightly spurious nationalism. This view of history is still shown in the museums of Skopje and Kruševo, which combines being a Vlach town with being a shrine of Macedonian nationalism, as the Ilinden rising of 1903 took place there.[16] It must be difficult for Vlach intellectuals to get away from this view which represents Macedonian history as the struggle of a heroic people to escape first from the Turk and then from the bourgeoisie, and there is a tendency for the Vlachs to see themselves on the side of the people, even though they were on occasions on the side of the Turks and members of the bourgeoisie. The true history of the Ilinden rising has never really been written; it is true that among the leaders of the rebellion, Goče Delčev was partially and Pitu Guli wholly of Vlach descent, and that many Vlach houses in Kruševo were destroyed, but as in most Balkan battles some people were on one side, some on another, some on neither and some on both.[17]

Recent history is painful and difficult to disentangle. Written records are lost or scattered or written in a variety of foreign tongues. It would take a great deal of time to make an objective study of these records. Not surprisingly the average Macedonian Vlach tends to shy away from the recent past and to concentrate on remoter eras in which it is easy to build theories to show how the Vlachs were the original inhabitants of Macedonia. Almost all the Vlachs I talked to subscribe to this theory; one can, pointing to the star pattern on the houses in Kruševo and noting its resemblance to the star of Vergina, the symbol of Alexander the Great, say that here was proof that Alexander was a Vlach.

The star has of course been a bone of contention with the Greeks, and the Macedonian flag has been changed accordingly. The Vlachs appear to agree with the Greeks and disagree with the Macedonians in asserting that the Slavs were late arrivals on the scene, but then insist that it was they who are the original autochthonous people.

This assertion is a variation on the old Balkan game of 'we got there first', played in Transylvania between Romanians and Hungarians, in Kosovo between Serbs and Albanians, and in Macedonia between almost everybody. It is a silly game. We are not going to hand over London to the Welsh, and the Americans are not going to yield their United States to the descendants of various native American tribes. In the Balkans there have been so many invasions that it would be quite impossible for any indigenous group to maintain its identity. Curiously the Macedonian Vlachs are right in claiming some kind of continuity for their Latin speech. In northern Macedonia and southern Serbia the *lingua franca* was Latin under the Roman Empire until the time of Justinian, himself a Latin speaker. The Slav invasions began at the end of Justinian's reign, and by the beginning of the seventh century most of the Balkans was full of Slavs. The Latin-speaking Vlachs are in some sense the descendants of the population who survived the Slav invasions. Latin of course did not arrive in the Balkans for more than a hundred years after the death of Alexander, but the Macedonian Vlachs have more claim to continuity than either the Romanians or the Pindus Vlachs, where under the Roman Empire there was either a very brief Latin presence or no presence at all, and in Byzantine times no record of a Latin presence until well after Justinian.

This excursus into ancient history is necessary because it unfortunately puts the Macedonian Vlachs at variance with their Greek and Romanian cousins. Both Greece and Romania are countries with the traditions and resources to produce reasonable historical and linguistic scholarship, and both sets of scholars have laboured ingeniously to prove that Vlachs are either Greeks or Romanians.[18] Indeed this is the accepted tradition of the Vlachs in those countries. The Macedonian theory, as yet unsupported by the full apparatus of scholarly books and articles and brought into discredit by wild claims about Alexander the Great, has much to commend it. There was a tradition of Balkan Latinity with Scupi (Skopje) as its centre. With the Slav invasions and the collapse of the Danube frontier Latin speakers moved from this centre northwards to Romania and southwards to the Pindus mountains, possibly joining other Latin speakers in the process. These movements have continued throughout history from north to south and vice versa, with some Latin speakers being assimilated and turned into Greeks and Slavs, while other Latin settlements were renewed by fresh arrivals. Only the rise of nationalism in the nineteenth century and demand for a national myth, national schools and a national language put an end to this, with the result that there a rapid decline in the number of Vlach speakers.[19]

After visiting Macedonia in early September 1996, I attended a Vlach congress in Freiburg, Germany, in late September. This was attended by Vlachs from Romania, Greece, Albania, Serbia and Macedonia with members of the Vlach diaspora in Europe and America, and a few interlopers like myself.[20] In the past at these congresses Greek Vlachs have been attacked for their views, but on this occasion Greek Vlachs were listened to courteously, although the Greek speakers invited disagreement by listing a host of Greek words in Vlach and saying that the Pindus mountains were the centre of Vlachdom. Romanian speakers were treated with less courtesy, being for instance asked for a translation into Vlach.[21] The pro-Greek Albanian speaker attacked the Romanian ambassador in Tirana. The Macedonian delegates were listened to with great respect, and even won some praise from the Greeks who clearly however disagreed with their views and even with the achievements in education and the media that were outlined to them.

Provided that the Macedonian Vlachs can achieve enough backing from their own government and from other Vlach communities there is no reason why these achievements should not continue. As I have shown, both kinds of support are precarious. It might be that as an exemplary minority being treated in an exemplary way the Macedonian Vlachs should appeal to some international foundation. This would enable them to improve their educational textbooks, do more research into their history and counter absurd nationalist claims which do such damage. In a way the Vlachs are perfect Balkan citizens, able to preserve their culture without resource to war or politics, violence or dishonesty. In my last book on the Vlachs I drew attention to a Vlach family from the village of Nižepolje near Bitola.[22] The name of the family was Babo, but falling under Serbian, Bulgarian (in the war) and then Macedonian rule they had in turn adopted the name of Babović, Babov and Babovski, and it was under these names that three brothers had emigrated to Australia from whence they returned to visit their mother who had spent the first twelve years under Turkish rule, and who spoke to me enthusiastically in Greek. Albanian is also spoken in the village which seemed to me in 1990 to be a very happy place in spite of its multi-ethnic past and present. I would hope that these rare gleams of Vlach happiness would be allowed to continue in the future.

Notes

1. H. Poulton, *The Balkans: States and Minorities in Conflict* (London, 1994), pp. 47–96.
2. R. and B. Crampton, *Atlas of Eastern Europe in the Twentieth Century* (London, 1996), p. 257.
3. *The International Year Book and Statesmen's Who's Who* (East Grinstead, 1996), p. 397.
4. W. Markert, *Osteuropa Handbuch: Jugoslavien* (Koln, 1954), gives a total of 102,953 Vlachs in the 1948 census, but only 9,511 of these are in Macedonia. In the 1921 census for the whole of Yugoslavia, Romanians and Vlachs are lumped together as 231,068, and in 1931 as 137,879.
5. *Veliki Geografski Atlas Jugoslavije* (Zagreb, 1987) is a mine of information, now sadly out of date, about ethnographical statistics in various parts of

Yugoslavia. Five per cent of the population declared themselves as Yugoslavs; it is tragic to note that 21.2 per cent was the percentage in Vukovar and 15.9 per cent in Sarajevo. In the two areas of Eastern Serbia where Bulgarians were in a majority, there was also a high percentage of Yugoslavs, and the same phenomenon can be found in areas where there were substantial minorities of Czechs, Slovaks, Ruthenians, Italians and even Istrian Vlachs. It looks as if Yugoslav became a convenient umbrella to hide a dubious or disputed identity. In Macedonia only 0.97 per cent of the population registered as Yugoslav, but this was more than twice the number of Vlachs. Some of the latter almost certainly registered as Yugoslavs or Macedonians, here slightly more politically correct than Yugoslavs, but Macedonia's other minorities would feel the same pressure.

6. I apologise for this error in the second edition of *The Vlachs* (London, 1995).

7. The total population of Gopeš, Nižepolje, Megarovo, Trnvo and Malovište is under a thousand, and not all are Vlachs. On the other hand I have met many Vlachs from these villages in Bitola, some rather confusingly owning both a flat in the town and a little cottage in one of the villages.

8. I have met monoglot Vlachs in Greece in the 1980s, but never in Macedonia.

9. *The Times* of 26 October 1996 says that a third of the Irish population speak some Irish and 4 per cent are fluent in it. But fluency is something different from regular use. I prefer the gloomier views of R. Hindley, *Death of the Irish Language* (London, 1990), and some gloomier correspondence and articles in *The Times* of November 1996.

10. This view that one is a Vlach because one has Vlach ancestors is in itself perfectly harmless, and involves no fascist theories of race provided that one does not carry it to extremes, in which case except in a few very isolated instances all people would be of all races. But it is very common in the Balkans, and leads to some very dangerous assumptions, as for instance the view among Greeks that all members of the Orthodox Church in Albania are really Greeks, some of whom have forgotten how to speak Greek.

11. There are in fact two Vlach associations in Albania, promoting different views. Before the First World War, as recorded by Wace and Thompson in *The Nomads of the Balkans* (London, 1914), most Vlach villages had the same two parties.

12. A more gloomy figure of 20,000 for regular speakers of both Scottish and Irish Gaelic would make Vlach in Macedonia stronger than the former and almost as strong as the latter. A figure of 30,000 to 50,000 might be more reasonable. The population of Scotland is about 5 million, of Ireland 3.5 million.

13. I was given several slim volumes of poetry and cassettes of songs by Mr Dina Cuvata. He like other Vlach poets and singers also works in Macedonian. There are films about Vlachs to be found in the Macedonian television station, including work by the famous Vlach pioneers of photography, the Manaki brothers.

14. I think this extraordinary theory springs from a confusion between the Himalayas and the Alps, where Romantsch does have obvious links with Vlach.

15. C. Liaku-Anovska, *The Origin of the Vlach Story-Tellers* (in Macedonian) (Skopje, 1995), is doing good work in this field.
16. The museum in Skopje is well maintained but with few visitors, and that at Kruševo is very much a shrine to Macedonian nationalism. There is more information about Vlachs in the former. Unlike the equivalent museums in Tirana there have been few changes made since the collapse of communism.
17. Compare the very different treatment of Ilinden in, for example, D. Dakin, *The Greek Struggle in Macedonia* (Salonica, 1966), and Bulgarian Academy of Sciences, *Macedonia: Documents and Material* (Sofia, 1978). Macedonian historians give another kind of picture. As well as Kruševo the Vlach villages of Neveska (Nymphaion) and Klisoura, both in Greece, were centres of the uprising, but this is partly because they were strategic points.
18. For a not very up-to-date account of recent Romanian and Greek scholarship on the Vlach problem, see *The Vlachs* (London, 1987), pp. 42–4.
19. Vlach schools never really got off the ground, especially in Macedonia, where after the First World War the Serb-dominated Yugoslav government did not even, as Greece did, allow Romanian schools. The first Vlach school was founded at Trnovo in the nineteenth century, but even on Mount Pelister Greek schools were always stronger.
20. The Vlach association at Freiburg produces a magazine *Zborlu Nostru* and has biennial conferences with delegates from all over the world. Held under the auspices of the perfectly respectable Romanian department of Freiburg University it combines scholarly papers, an opportunity for Vlachs to meet each other, and, regrettably, a good deal of controversy, although I saw less evidence of this on the last occasion.
21. *Shattered Eagles: Balkan Fragments* (London, 1993), pp. 48–9.
22. It is partly in this hope that I have written this chapter, although such is the situation in the Balkans that it will probably engender more heat than light. Even the name 'Vlach' is likely to cause misunderstanding, but it seemed preferable to the obscure and slightly degrading 'Cincar', or the confusing 'Aroumanian' or 'Macedo-Romanian'. I am grateful to the many Vlachs who helped me in Macedonia and for invaluable assistance rendered by Bill Macalister, James Pettifer and Gaynor Kennard.

Chapter **10**

The Albanians in western Macedonia after FYROM independence

James Pettifer

The Albanians in western Macedonia are probably the least known part of the Albanian nation in the Balkans, and when the second Yugoslavia began to disintegrate in 1989–90, little or no international attention was given to their position in the future remaking of the Balkan peninsular. Eyes and minds were focused on the crisis in relations between Croatia and Serbia, and the departure of Slovenia from the federation. In the following year, in September 1991, the old Socialist Republic of Macedonia left the collapsing federation peacefully, and although it was well known that the Albanians and other minorities in former Yugoslav Macedonia were very dissatisfied with their subordinate status to the Slav-speaking majority, there was no reason to believe that the position of this group, about 25 per cent of the total population, would give rise to critical problems for the future of the new state that was striving for independence and international recognition.

Albanians had been forced to accept the Titoist definitions of a 'Macedonian' identity within Yugoslavia, on the basis of Partisan victories in the area in the Second World War.[1] The long years of isolation of Hoxhaist Albania and its poor relations with Titoist Yugoslavia had serious repercussions for the Macedonian Albanians, as towns such as Debar had close family and cultural and economic links with Albania prior to 1939. An atmosphere of Albanian political marginalisation and practical impotence was current for these long years, along with general international indifference to the repression of Albanians and the serious human and cultural rights problems under Titoism.

The view of the international community ignored the strong radical and nationalist traditions in this community, living mostly in the west of the country in towns such as Tetovo and Gostivar, and in Skopje itself, and the fact that in the second Yugoslavia, these communities had resisted severe cultural and political repression, particularly in the Rankovic era, and after Tito's death. In the 1980s a better-educated elite had begun to develop, and the old insularity of the communities had been broken down by work as *gastarbeiters* in Germany and elsewhere. Islam had been an important issue, with the Macedonian communities known for their Islamic commitment, and the early years of the Tito period had seen severe repression of Islamic religion and religious institutions by the state, with vandalism and destruction of important Islamic libraries, such as that of the Bektashi *tekke* in Tetovo, and the expropriation of Islamic religious buildings for secular use. Roads were built by the Titoists over Muslim cemeteries in Tetovo and Gostivar.

Another factor which influenced external diplomatic views of FYROM was the long-running and serious crisis in Kosova, in neighbouring southwest Serbia over the Sar mountains, where in 1981 and 1989 there had been widespread violence and which has remained under martial law ever since. As the situation of the FYROM Albania's was not as bad as their Kosova compatriots, their interests tended to be overlooked completely in the international arena.[2] The diaspora of Macedonian Albanians has never been as numerous, well organised or vocal as the Kosovar diaspora, particularly in terms of newspapers and other media.

This situation has now fundamentally changed, and the internal political landscape of FYROM is in many ways dominated by the 'Albanian factor' in politics. Albanians are seen as having a practical veto over the future of the state. This has come about both by the internal dynamics of the FYROM itself, and in relation to the deepening Kosovo crisis.[3] The original catalyst for growing Albanian radicalism came before the September 1991 referendum, in 1990, when 2,000 Albanians marched through the western town of Tetovo and demanded independence and unity with Albania. The march was broken up by paramilitary police, and it was apparent to politically aware Albanians that they were unlikely to see much change in their position in a new state. This view was reinforced under the new constitution of the FYROM, which removed the rights of minorities to proportional representation on public bodies, a measure that had given Albanians at least some influence in the running of the old Yugoslav socialist republic. The FYROM constitution was put forward when the nationalist Internal Macedonian Revolutionary Organisation VMRO-DPMNE was the largest party in parliament and bears much of the stamp of their thinking. In 1992 there was growing political and inter-ethnic tension as the war in the northern Balkans unfolded, FYROM failed to obtain general international recognition and the economic crisis worsened markedly. About 65 per cent of the trade of the old Socialist Republic of Macedonia was with Serbia and Bosnia, and the war and UN economic sanctions dealt a hammer blow to the southern Yugoslav economy.

The years 1992–3 saw the founding of new parties in the Albanian communities, and the increasing incapacity of the political elite to form a stable administration under President Kiro Gligorov. In September 1992, the Conference on Security and Cooperation in Europe, CSCE, had sent a 'spillover mission' to FYROM, under the leadership of American diplomat Robert H. Frowick, which concluded that the state was in serious danger of being drawn into the ex-Yugoslav conflict.[4] Border tension increased, with many difficulties arising from the imposition of United Nations sanctions against Serbia, and increasing difficulties with Greece. Large demonstrations were held in Greece to protest about proposed international recognition of the state under the name 'Republic of Macedonia', and it was becoming clear that the promised smooth start to the FYROM states' life was unlikely to materialise. Ethnic relations within FYROM had deteriorated sharply in November 1992 when Skopje paramilitary police fired on a mostly peaceful protest in the Bitpazar area of the town, killing four Albanians.[5]

During this period the leadership of the Albanians had been dominated by ex-communist politicians, like most other ethnic groups, but 1993 saw new forces emerging, and serious political struggle began within the main Albanian party, the Party for Democratic Prosperity, PDP, about its future. The younger politicians articulated a radical agenda, with a freemarket economic policy accompanied by strong nationalist rhetoric. In June 1993, the key Tetovo PDP city committee fell under radical control, and other party branches quickly followed. Outside powers were beginning to take a greater interest in the Macedonian crisis, and the Albanians began to be seen as a potentially secessionist force, both by the Interior Ministry and the government in Skopje, and by foreign states concerned with the Balkan crisis generally. In November 1992, after the Bitpazar killings, leading Albanian politicians had begun to question whether it would be possible to share positions in the government with the 'Macedonian' majority.[6] In turn this produced increasingly interventionist policies from the European Union countries, particularly Britain, which was deeply involved with trying to continue the Yugoslav political project, and to keep FYROM together as a state, with the hope that it might one day reintegrate with Yugoslavia. It was clear by the following year that at the London Conference on ex-Yugoslavia, considerable pressure was put on President Gligorov by British Foreign Minister Douglas Hurd, and other leaders, to keep FYROM as close to Serbia as possible with a view to its future possible reintegration within a future Yugoslav federation, once the northern Balkan wars were over. This option remained open for the country, despite the independence decision in 1991, and was privately favoured by many of the Skopje elite. Considerable practical help was given to the Skopje Ministry of the Interior by British and French government intelligence and security experts who were very active in FYROM in 1992–3. British policy was the decisive influence in Skopje in this period, with President Gligorov having a further meeting with Hurd to discuss security issues in May 1993.[7] But inter-ethnic relations continued to deteriorate, and Britain and the other EU powers involved in advising the Gligorov government did not address themselves to the serious human rights problems suffered by the Albanians and other minorities. In practice this meant important material support was given to the Interior Ministry security apparatus at a time when it was rent with political divisions, and a purge of pro-IMRO nationalists in the Interior Ministry was taking place. They were replaced by pro-Serb, pro-Yugoslav, figures who remained in control of the Ministry until Autumn 1998.

The culmination of these undemocratic developments came in November 1993, when several prominent Albanians were arrested by Ministry of the Interior police and charged with attempting to overthrow the state and set up a secessionist Albanian state called 'Illyrida'. Those held included the Albanian Assistant Minister of Defence, Husein Haskaj, and a number of other prominent individuals. It was claimed that large caches of arms and ammunition had been found in their office premises. Considerable efforts had been made to portray all the Albanians as secessionist in this period, and it was widely believed in Skopje and elsewhere that foreign governments certainly knew of the arms plot and were involved in it.[8]

These machinations of the anti-Albanian leaders of the Gligorov government and of the Interior Ministry failed in terms of influencing internal Albanian politics in a more conservative direction, as in the first months of 1994, the radical forces won a vote to control the old PDP, but were forced by legal controls to leave and form a new party, the PDP (Sh). This situation has remained until the time of writing in 1998, with two Albanian parties competing for popular support in elections, as well as other small nationalist-oriented or Islamic groups. The radical PDP (Sh) is led by Menduh Thaci and Arben Xhaferi, and is now much the larger party, controlling the main local government bodies in all Albanian towns except Skopje, while the 'pro-Gligorov' PDP under Abdurman Haliti has its remaining significant support among the more integrated Albanians in the FYROM capital. In the November 1994 elections, there were widespread and well-substantiated allegations of ballot-rigging in favour of the 'moderate' PDP, and independent journalists and international observers covering the election regarded the CSCE report as an apologia for electoral manipulation.[9] The PDP politicians in Haliti's party have been willing to remain in parliament, and to take government jobs, and all post-1992 governments have had some Albanian representation, although generally in tokenistic positions, often as 'Assistant Ministers', without offices or staff, to Slav-speakers and never involving posts in the Defence or Foreign Ministries, or, above all, in the key Interior Ministry which most independent observers see as the source of all real power in FYROM. The Interior Ministry has a strong residual pro-Belgrade orientation after the purge of IMRO sympathisers and other alleged pro-Bulgarian personnel in 1993.[10]

Foreign influence over the government has remained very strong, with a small committee of European Union and American ambassadors acting in a highly interventionalist way over many policy and practical issues. This takes place under the symbolic leadership of President Gligorov. As the FYROM government is wholly dependent on external funds from these countries for survival, it is usually possible for Skopje policy to be manipulated in any direction the foreign ambassadors see fit, including the reduction in Albanian influence over the government wherever possible. The EU diplomatic community has a function in Skopje akin to that of colonial governors on dependent territories, dispensers of largesse from the mother-country, in this case the European Union and the international financial institutions, and guardians and defenders of the local law and order authority, in FYROM the ex-communist-dominated Interior Ministry.

As a result, unsurprisingly, relations with the Albanian political leadership has been a continual source of difficulty, with the local British and French and other EU officials in Skopje tending to be highly pro-Macedonian in their outlook and policies, and for long periods having little contact with any Albanian leaders other than the leader of the 'moderate' PDP, Mr Abdurman Haliti. This has remained the case until recently, when the overwhelming political dominance of the PDP (Sh) in most communities, with about 70 per cent of the Albanian vote in the autumn 1996 local elections, has led to the inclusion of PDP (Sh) leader Arben Xhaferi in some political consultations. The party generally is still regarded as 'beyond the pale' by many foreign organisations and diplomats in Skopje, many of whom rarely, if ever, visit the Albanian-inhabited areas in the west of FYROM.

Culture and education have been key areas of struggle for the FYROM Albanians, and given the near total absence of higher education in the Albanian language, and the steep decline in the number of Albanian secondary school teachers, has brought many conflicts with the government. An Albanian-language university was established in Tetovo in 1995, with some viable faculties in disciplines such as physical education, computer science and pharmacology, but the university has not achieved external recognition, and it is regarded as illegal by the Skopje authorities. By 1998, student numbers have reached over 4,000. It has been subject to continual harassment by the Skopje police, and it remains to be seen what its future will be. Attempts have been made since 1994 to establish an Albanian language pedagogical faculty in Skopje university, but this has been attacked by Slav-nationalists and it is equally uncertain what future it will have, or even if it will come into existence at all. The proposals have also been opposed by some of the radicals in Albanian political parties who have a commitment to the Tetovo institution.

Intercommunal tension tended to rise further during 1996–7, as it became clear to the Skopje government that the university in Tetovo had established at least a foothold in FYROM pedagogical life, and that secessionist rhetoric was becoming common among Albanian politicians, and not only those in the more radical parties. Under pressure of events, the two PDPs have often moved closer on practical issues in the recent period. A key factor in the last two years has been the collapse of the Berisha regime in Albania and the development of the Kosova crisis.

Political events in Albania had played little part in the world of the FYROM politicians since the intervention of President Sali Berisha in the PDP leadership struggle in 1993–4 on the side of the radical forces, but this was no longer the case in late 1996. The government crisis caused by the collapse of the pyramid banks was beginning to have wider regional repercussions, with knock-on effect in FYROM such as the collapse of the large FYROM savings bank, TAT, based in Bitola. Tens of thousands of Macedonians lost their savings when their money in TAT was diverted to Albanian pyramid banking schemes.

When the Albanian uprising began at the beginning of 1997, the areas of Albania such as Dibra which were near the FYROM border were deeply affected. Weapons which had been seized from Albanian armouries in the popular uprising began to find their way across the border, and became a factor in FYROM politics. The border itself became a problematic barrier in many places, with the absence of any guards or Interior Ministry police on the Albanian side, and for a time in spring 1997 the Podgradec sector was controlled by paramilitary groups. The influence of organised crime and drug dealing organisations in both Albania and FYROM has also increased at this time, with some overlap between the two social forces. The United Nations Preventative Peacekeeping Force, UNPREDEP, which had been deployed in FYROM for the last four years[11] was impotent to affect these difficult events. It had been regarded locally as having played a useful role in reducing ethnic tension in the early days of its deployment, and the initial UNPROFOR force of American and Nordic troops had been seen as fair to the Albanians. But local Albanian opinion is now often critical of the force. It is seen as ineffectual, too close to the government, and the mixed troop contingents who replaced the US soldiers as often openly anti-Albanian. The mandate of the force is concerned with border security and only recently have most FYROM citizens appeared to realise how little power it has to influence internal developments within the country.

This UNPREDEP impotence was demonstrated in the fighting that broke out in Gostivar in July 1997 when three Albanians were killed after FYROM paramilitary police stormed the town hall in a dispute over the right to fly the Albanian flag.[12] The Mayor of Gostivar, Mr Rufi Osmani, was arrested and charged with various anti-state offences under the old communist penal code legislation that is still in force in FYROM. He was subsequently sentenced to a long gaol sentence. The Mayor of Tetovo, Mr Adem Demiri, was imprisoned for the same reason in June 1998.

Under the old Yugoslav constitution it was possible for the Albanians and other national minorities to fly their flags on certain specific public occasions, but this right was removed under the post-communist FYROM constitution. The fact that such bloody ethnic violence could erupt on such a small symbolic pretext, illustrates the basic insecurity and instability of the 'Macedonian' FYROM state, where the new national identity has to be enforced in a highly coercive way on the Albanian minority. The United Nations Special Human Rights Rapporteur in the Balkans, Elizabeth Rehn, commented in her report on the Gostivar events that excessive force was used by the police against the Albanians, and the long gaol sentence and summary nature of the trial illustrates how far FYROM has to come before it breaks with the legacy of the communist past and the rule of law applies to the Albanians as much as to the Slav-speaking majority. The fact that some Albanians used weapons in these exchanges contributes a new element of destabilisation to the FYROM situation. If it is generally believed that the Albanians are armed in FYROM, as appears to be the case in Skopje security circles, more and more openly coercive methods of social control will be seen to be legitimate, extending the spiral of declining human rights, protest, repression and then intercommunal violence.

A key issue in the winter of 1997–8 was the prospect of spillover from the crisis in Kosova, where ethnic Albanians had become increasingly militant, and given that there are many links between the more radical Albanian leaders in Kosova and FYROM. A key figure is PDP (Sh) leader Arben Xhaferi, who is from a Kosova family with some Turkish links, but many other militants in FYROM were educated at the now-defunct University of Pristina in the old Yugoslavia. A tactic of the Skopje authorities in the period of the PDP power struggle in 1993–4 was to portray the new radical leaders as Kosovar 'outsiders' who had no proper role in the deeply culturally conservative communities in western Macedonia. This propaganda was repeated during the autumn 1994 election, when it was a key EU priority to boost the PDP and to restrict the influence of the PDP (Sh) radicals. It had some success then with the very conservative Muslim imams in Tetovo and elsewhere, who appear to have believed, wrongly, that the new party was in some way secularist, and possibly antipathetic to religion. It is ironic that all Albanian political leaders in FYROM have been under pressure from Islamic powers to become more 'Islamic' and reports have surfaced of attempts by pro-Iranian and other groups to supply weapons and military equipment to the Albanians. The curious paradox perhaps illustrates the extreme cultural conservatism and rather isolated provincial nature of western Macedonian Islamic life more than any specific political juncture. It is perhaps worth noting that the Islamic parties that do exist in FYROM, on Bosnian lines, have gained very little support, even in deeply Islamic towns such as Gostivar, and political life in FYROM among the Albanian and Turkish-speaking Moslem minorities remains firmly secular. Where Islamic bodies have succeeded in recovering their religious buildings from the state, it has often been difficult to assemble enough popular support to open them on a properly functioning basis although new mosques are being built in some places which are well supported such as the rural vicinity of Tetovo.

The next great challenge for the Albanians in FYROM will come with the retirement of President Kiro Gligorov from politics, linked to the continuing struggle for human and cultural rights and a fair electoral system against the Interior Ministry and the old police apparatus. In January 1998 Gligorov announced during a visit to Moscow that he was intending to leave politics after the next elections.[13] It is clearly the hope of the EU and the United States that the Albanians will cease to be a radical force in FYROM politics and that VMRO can also be persuaded to abandon its pro-Bulgarian links and adhere eventually to the FYROM state. There is as yet no firm evidence to suggest that either will be the case, and centrifugal tendencies in FYROM politics are likely to continue. VMRO leaders have moved closer to Bulgaria and to Russia after a period of intense inner-party struggle in 1997, which culminated in the purging of important non-vrachovist figures such as Alexander Dinevski from the leadership.[14] If the main Slav-opposition party follows this path, where much of its political impetus and identity comes from links with a neighbouring state which has historically had designs on its territory, there will be every reason for secessionist trends within the Albanian polity to grow, and the final crisis of Skopje/FYROM central authority will begin.

An important aspect of the crisis in Skopje which has not received very much attention in the West is the growth of organised crime as a major force in society, with rampant corruption in Skopje. Some of this was linked to the problems with United Nations sanctions against Serbia, but it did not disappear with the end of UN sanctions. The privatisation process has provided rich pickings for the Skopje 'Macedonian' elite, both Macedonian and 'Yugoslavist', i.e. Serbian, while the general impoverishment of the population continued, with stated unemployment at about 30 per cent but probably nearer 50 per cent. National income remains at only about 1,000 dollars a year per capita and is falling. Recently, there has been a dramatic rise in the drug trade, as Skopje is on the heroin route from Turkey to the Adriatic coast and Italian mafia cartels. Albanian and Bulgarian mafia groups are involved in this lucrative business, and the funds generated are beginning to affect the politics and culture of FYROM, as has occurred in other places, and among other Balkan ethnic communities. The culture of weapons and violence that it engenders is a threat to normal stable political life everywhere, as the uprising in Albania showed in spring 1997.[15]

In the final analysis, it is clear that the future of the FYROM Albanians cannot be considered in isolation from the development and resolution of the Albanian national question as a whole. In 1997 and

1998 a guerilla organisation, the Kosova Liberation Army, began operations against the Serbian forces in Kosova, and there has been increasing violence in FYROM, with bombings of police stations, major arms caches found and a general climate of intensified government repression. Some KLA leaders come from Macedonia. It is not clear whether the Kosova Liberation Army operates in FYROM, in the formal sense, although the KLA claimed responsibility in January 1998 for bombings of police stations in Prilep and Kumanovo. With Kosova descending into chaos and violence it will be very difficult, if not impossible for the FYROM Albanians to escape involvement in events. A major fear for the FYROM government is Albanian refugees from Kosova destabilising the state. In an effort to prevent this, an agreement was signed in February 1988 to control the movement of refugees through Kosova and FYROM for them to go to Albania. This 'corridor' avoids running through the Albanian inhabited areas of FYROM and it is difficult to avoid the impressions that the Gligorov government is anxious to avoid the creation of informal border breaches in the northwest and the Šar mountains that could threaten the delineation of the boundary between the two Albanian communities, so bringing a Greater Albania much closer as a political prospect. The election result of November 1998 bears out these underlying trends, with a united coalition of the two ethnic Albanian parties working together to establish complete political dominance in the western FYROM constituencies. It remains to be seen whether the new VMRO-led government will be any more successful in integrating the Albanians into FYROM than its predecessor.

Notes

1. The Yugoslav Partisan movement was deeply involved in the Macedonian Question, and the outcome of these struggles determined political realities in the wider region for many years afterwards. There are numerous books on the general crisis in Macedonia at this time, but little detailed research on the Albanian resistance in Macedonia. See the contribution of Sir Reginald Hibbert in this volume, and his book *Albania's National Liberation – The Bitter Victory* (Pinter London, 1991); also *Struggle for the Balkans* by Tito's emissary to the Partisans, Svetozar Vukmanovic-Tempo (Merlin Press, London, 1990). Tempo's account of contemporary events in Macedonia is very strongly disputed by Bulgarian historians. See the memoirs of Tsola Dragoicheva, *Pobedata* (Sofia, 1979). The official view of the current Skopje government of the Partisan movement then can be found in *Istoria na Makedonska narod*, Skopje, 1988. Most of the wartime section of this highly contentious volume is taken up with Greek-related issues.
2. For an account of events leading up to the Kosova crisis, see *Between Serb and Albanian – A History of Kosovo* by Miranda Vickers (C. Hurst, London,

1998). Also, Noel Malcolm's *Kosova: A Short History* (London, Macmillan 1998). A good picture of official attitudes towards the problem can be seen in the report of the head of the CSCE Mission in Skopje, Mr Norman Anderson, to the CSO meeting in Rome in November 1993 (OSCE office, Prague, July 1995) In this document, FYROM is discussed almost exclusively as a problem of Greek–FYROM relations.
3. See *Who are the Macedonians?* by Hugh Poulton (London, 1994).
4. Document No. 282 of the Conference on Security and Cooperation in Europe, Prague, 16 September 1992, 'CSCE Spillover Mission to Skopje'.
5. See *The Observer*, London, 7 November 1992.
6. See *Daily Telegraph*, London, 8 November 1992.
7. Interview with Ministry of Interior official, January 1997.
8. See story written by James Pettifer in *The Economist*, London, 20 November 1993. Some of those involved have disappeared, while others were soon released from prison and have gone into exile. There have been various allegations in the Skopje press over the years about the nature of the plot, and the subsequent events, but no conclusive evidence has been put forward to link it with any Albanian group.
9. There was major conflict between European Union governments and the United States over this issue and the American head of the CSCE Mission in Skopje, Mr Norman Anderson, resigned soon after the report was published. The Americans were unhappy with the degree of official manipulation of the vote legitimised in the report. The document was rewritten numerous times by British Foreign Office staff to bring the result into line with 'policy'. See analysis of the election in *The World Today*, Chatham House, RIIA, London, March 1995, also *'East European Newsletter*, London, vol. 8, no. 2, November 1994.
10. Interview with Ministry of the Interior official, January 1997.
11. UNPROFOR was deployed in January 1993 on the basis of a United Nations Security Council decision in December 1992. The first US troops arrived in July 1993, at the time the first committed by the US to a UN-run operation. See 'Macedonia – Handle with Care', by James Gow and James Pettifer, in *Jane's Intelligence Review* (London, 1993).
12. Report in *The Times*, London, by James Pettifer, 12 July 1997. The Nigerian and Ukrainian UNPREDEP observers ran away into the countryside when shooting started in the town. See report by Amnesty International, London, February 1998 for information on human rights abuses committed by the paramilitary police.
13. *Nova Makadonika*, Skopje, 28 January 1998.
14. See *Australian Macedonian Herald*, Melbourne 23 September 1997.
15. It is not clear how far small arms transfers from Albania to FYROM Albanians accelerated in 1997–8, but there are many stories in Skopje newspapers which suggest there are sizeable quantities of small arms and ammunition stored in the western FYROM countryside. The Kosova Liberation Army (KLA) is starting to operate in FYROM and has claimed responsibility for explosions in December 1997 and January 1998. As the war developed in Kosova in Spring 1998, further KLA activity and recruitment in FYROM has been reported. See story in *The Times* by Antony Loyd, 6 July 1998. For an analysis of the role of organised crime, see 'The Albanian Uprising' by James Pettifer, in *Labour Focus on Eastern Europe* No. 57, Oxford, 1997.

Chapter **11**

Status and rights of nationalities in the Republic of Macedonia[*]

Gjorgi Caca

I

The status and rights of national minorities (this latter term, which has been generally accepted both in scholarly work and theory, and in the documents of the United Nations Organisation, has, in the Constitution of the Republic of Macedonia, been replaced by the word **'nationalities'**) is a subject of interest and study in both scholarly work and theory, as well as of policies and state organisation, especially in the countries where, in addition to the nation which has created the state, there are also members of peoples which have their own states outside the state in which they live in the capacity of minorities.[1]

The issue of the status and rights of nationalities (in conformity with the terminology of the Constitution of the Republic of Macedonia, which actually means national minorities) is not a problem of modern political thought and state policies. It dates back as far as the Middle Ages, starting from the protection of religious minorities, and comes to the fore after the First World War, when the League of Nations paid special attention to it, although without any visible results. It became particularly topical and crucial after the Second World War, when the United Nations Organisation started to pay considerable attention to this issue over a period of several decades.

As a result of decades-long consultations, negotiations and agreements of the special commission and certain bodies of the Organisation, at the beginning of December 1992, the United Nations General Assembly finally adopted the Declaration on the Rights of Persons Belonging to National or Ethnic, Religious and Linguistic Minorities.[2] This Declaration

---

[*] First published in *Balkan Forum*, Skopje, vol. 4, no. 2 (June 1996).

is the most thorough document referring to all kinds of minorities, that is to say nationalities.

This Declaration first of all determines the duties and obligations of the states towards all kinds of minorities (i.e. nationalities), and then states the individual and collective rights of these minorities (i.e. nationalities).

Thus, the basic and most important duties and obligations of the states are: protection of the existence of the national or ethnic, cultural, religious and linguistic identity of minorities on their respective territories and promotion of conditions for development of this identity; the adoption of adequate regulations and other measures with the aim of realising these goals. In accordance with these obligations on the part of the state, the Declaration explicitly states the measures and activities which should be undertaken in order to realise the rights of minorities. Particularly important among these activities is the duty of the states to cooperate with each other and, especially, to exchange information and experience, in order to promote mutual understanding and confidence.

The Declaration states the individual and collective rights of minorities in a separate provision, the most important among them being the following: the right to have their own culture, confess and express their own religion and use their own language in private and public life, freely and without any intervention or other form of discrimination; the right to participate effectively in cultural, religious, social, economic and public life; the right to take part in decision-making of relevance to the minority to which they belong or the region in which they live at the national and, when appropriate, at the regional level, in a manner accordant with the national legislation; the right to establish and foster without any discrimination, freely and peacefully, links with other members of their group and with persons belonging to other minorities, as well as to maintain relations with citizens of other states outside the border, with whom they are related on a national or ethnic, religious or linguistic basis.

The summary of the most significant decisions of the Declaration points to the conclusion that the status and rights of nationalities on all bases and their realisation are a special concern of the world community expressed through its universal organisation. This concern, expressed through the Declaration, is adequate and proportionate to the general attitude of the United Nations Organisation towards human freedoms and rights, full human equality and the exclusion of any kind or form of discrimination. The specific character of the rights of nationalities, according to the general attitude of the UN towards human rights, is a result of a tendency towards preventing and eliminating the potential danger of treating the members of nationalities as second-class citizens, and especially of their assimilation by the majority people, that is to say nation.

II

The above-stated intentions and aims have been subject to constitutional and legal standardisation in the Republic of Macedonia since its proclamation as a state at the First Session of ASNOM on 2nd August 1944, including its current Constitution as a sovereign and independent state.

II. 1. With the *Declaration on the Basic Rights of the Citizens of the Democratic Republic of Macedonia*, adopted at that first session, all the rights of a free national life were secured to the national minorities in Macedonia.

II. 2. In accordance with Article 12 of the first Constitution of the Republic – the *Constitution of the People's Republic of Macedonia*, proclaimed on 31st December 1946 – national minorities in the People's Republic of Macedonia enjoyed the right to and protection of their cultural development and the free use of their languages.

II. 3. In the *Constitution of the Socialist Republic of Macedonia*, the dual term 'nationalities–national minorities' was used for the first time, and this essentially broadened the regulation of the previous Constitution. The introduction of this parallel term was not motivated by psychological and emotional reasons only. It had a crucial significance. It eliminated the potential possibility of treating nationalities as second-class citizens because of their capacity as a minority.

This Constitution, in Articles 72–75, determined the status of nationalities (according to the present constitutional terminology) in the following manner:

(a) Members of the nationalities–national minorities living in the Socialist Republic of Macedonia were equal in everything and had equal rights and duties to those of the Macedonians.

With this, these members were completely equalised with the Macedonians as a constitutive nation of their state within the then federation.

(b) The social and political communities (i.e. the Republic, districts and municipalities) took care that members of certain nationalities–national minorities were present in their representative bodies, at the same time taking care of the structure of the population in their region.

(c) Every nationality–national minority was guaranteed the right to freely use its language, express and develop its culture and establish institutions and organisations which provide these rights to it.

(d) In places inhabited by nationalities–national minorities, the education of their members was realised in schools or classes and educational institutions where the instruction and education were carried out in the language of the respective nationality–national minority, and the conditions regarding the realisation of this right were regulated by law.

(e) In the municipalities, that is the districts, inhabited by a larger number of certain nationalities–national minorities, the decisions and other more important acts of the municipal and district assemblies were also announced in the language of the nationality–national minority.

(f) All inhabitants of the nationality heterogeneous regions in the SR Macedonia had an equal right to use their own language in administrative and juridical procedures.

The public signs in these regions were bilingual.

(g) The statute of the municipality, that is the district, in accordance with the general conditions determined by law, determined the closer conditions and procedures which ensured the realisation of the rights of the members of nationalities–national minorities.

II. 4. The *Constitution of the Socialist Republic of Macedonia of 1974 (Articles 177–183 and Constitutional Amendment XLIII)* basically retained the resolutions of the previous Constitution with certain objectifications and amendments, which were a result of changes in the social and political set-up of the country (in conformity with the changes in the SFRY) and, especially, of the mention (for the first time in the constitutional text) of two nationalities – Albanians and Turks – in the definition of the Republic.

The regulations stated in Chapter 11, 'Equality of nationalities', contained the following decisions:

(a) The Macedonian people and nationalities in the Socialist Republic of Macedonia are equal and have the same rights and duties. Municipalities and the Republic ensure that nationalities be proportionally represented in the municipal assemblies and the Assembly of the Socialist Republic of Macedonia, and be adequately represented in their bodies.

This decision was a consequence of the one-party system and was in accord with the electoral system of that time.

(b) In the Socialist Republic of Macedonia the Macedonian language and its Cyrillic alphabet were in official and public use.

Members of the nationalities had a right freely to use their language and script and express and develop their own culture and establish organisations for this purpose.

Members of the nationalities had the right to instruction in their language, in accordance with the Constitution and as determined by law.

Municipalities and the Republic took care of the development of education, as well as the development of the press, radio, television and cultural activities in the languages of nationalities.

(c) In regions inhabited by members of the nationalities, the languages and scripts of the nationalities were equal in public and social life with the Macedonian language.

In municipalities inhabited by members of the nationalities, the decisions and the more significant acts of the assemblies of the municipalities and the organisations of associated labour and other self-management organisations and communities were also announced in the languages of the nationalities.

Public signs in these regions were in the languages of the nationalities as well.

(d) Members of the nationalities had a right to use their own language and script in the realisation of their rights and duties, as well as in procedures in state bodies and publicly authorised organisations.

(e) The law and the statute of the municipality closely determined the conditions and procedures which ensure the realisation of the rights of nationalities, as well as the manner and conditions in which equality of the languages and scripts of nationalities with the Macedonian language and script is implemented, in the regions also inhabited by nationalities.

The manner and conditions of implementing the equality of the languages and scripts of nationalities with the Macedonian language and script on the territories also inhabited by nationalities were determined by the general acts of the organisations of associated labour.

(f) The assemblies of municipalities on the territories of which there are members of nationalities, and the Assembly of the Socialist Republic of Macedonia formed a commission for inter-ethnic relations. The Commission followed and surveyed the realisation of the equality of nationalities and their other rights determined by the Constitution and law, and proposed measures for their implementation. The Commission for inter-ethnic relations was composed of an equal number of members of the Macedonian people, and of the Albanian and the Turkish nationalities.

II. 5. This Constitution and its Chapter V, 'Human and Civil Freedoms, Rights and Duties', established for the first time the rights of the ethnic group with its Articles 221 and 222 and the Constitutional Amendment XLVIII, in the following manner:

(a) Members of the ethnic groups living in the Socialist Republic of Macedonia are equal with the Macedonian people and the nationalities and have the same rights and duties.

Municipalities and the Republic ensure that the members of the ethnic groups be proportionately represented in the assemblies of the municipalities and the Assembly of the SR Macedonia, and be adequately represented in their bodies.

(b) Members of ethnic groups have the right to freely use their language, express and develop their culture and establish organisations with this purpose.

The municipalities and the Republic take care of the development of the radio, television, press and cultural activities in the languages of the ethnic groups.

III

The decisions of the *Constitution of the Republic of Macedonia* concerning the nationalities basically manifest a certain continuity with regard to the former decisions, with some appropriate modifications because of their adaptation to the new political system, especially as they are expressed in political pluralism, as well as their coordination with the already mentioned United Nations Declaration, the draft of which was available during the preparation of the Constitution and its legislation.

The status of nationalities in the present order of the Republic, besides having the full equality as citizens, is also characterised by their specific rights which are in the nature of a certain privileged position, which cannot and should not be the basis for its misuse in the form of national chauvinism, autonomism or separatism.

This Constitution contains regulations which refer directly or indirectly to the rights of nationalities, as well as regulations which are the basis for their detailed provision and realisation. These rights are determined as individual and as collective, i.e. as rights which are realised by the member of the nationality as an individual in his/her life and work and as rights realised by the collectivity of a certain nationality. Both of these kinds of rights are regulated and established by the Constitution in the following manner:

III. 1. The Preamble of the Constitution determines the status of nationalities in both of its sections.

The section determining the character and the capacities of the Republic of Macedonia proclaims: 'starting out .., the historical fact that Macedonia has been constituted as a national state of the Macedonian people where full civil equality and permanent coexistence of the Macedonian people and the Albanians, Turks, Vlachs, Romanies and other nationalities living in the Republic of Macedonia is ensured.'

The section of the Preamble determining the aims of the legislation of the Constitution establishes the following aims with regard to the nationalities: 'to guarantee the human rights, civil freedoms and national equality; to ensure peace and coexistence of the Macedonian people with the nationalities living in the Republic of Macedonia'.

These determinations of the Preamble are a dual basis: first, for the regulations of the Constitution referring to nationalities and, second, for their status, togetherness and coexistence with the Macedonian people in their single unitary state, based, among other things, on their equality as citizens. This is where the meaning, the content and the essence of the thought expressed by the President of the Republic, Kiro Gligorov, .lies: 'Nothing can be solved by force and restrictions, by fear from the rights of others. A broad view is needed which should rest on the European views of inter-ethnic relations. Understanding, sensitivity, and permanent concern for inter-ethnic relations are of the greatest importance for our peace, the future economic and social growth and, above all, for the security of our Republic.'[3] These indications refer equally to the members of nationalities and to their political parties and other forms of association and to their leaders, as well as to the Macedonians. Therefore, unreasonable maximalist requests can lead only to inter-ethnic intolerance which is not far from the danger of inter-ethnic conflicts.

The Preamble broadens the former list of nationalities in the Constitution. Thus, in addition to the Albanians and the Turks, it now includes the Vlachs and the Romanies as a significant portion of the total population of the Republic and opens up the possibility for other nationalities living in the Republic of Macedonia.

III. 2. Article 48 of the Constitution of the Republic of Macedonia expresses the essence of the rights of the members of nationalities, their scope, range and manner of realisation in conformity with the basis of these rights.

According to this regulation 'Members of nationalities have a right freely to express, foster and develop their identity and national attributes.

'The Republic guarantees the protection of the ethnic, cultural, linguistic and religious identity of the nationalities'.

'Members of the nationalities have the right to establish institutions for culture and art, as well as scholarly and other associations for the expression, fostering and development of their identity.'

'Members of the nationalities have the right to instruction in their language in primary and secondary education, as determined by law. In schools where education is carried out in the language of a nationality, the Macedonian language is also studied.'

This regulation at the same time determines the rights of the members of nationalities and the obligation of the Republic to guarantee the protection of these rights.

The freedom of expressing, fostering and developing the identity and the national attributes of nationalities is multi-faceted and complex. This freedom is, first of all, not conditioned by the number or the majority of a certain nationality in a certain territory or place. Members of the nationalities as individuals can exercise this right without any restrictions, at any place and on every occasion. Identity is also expressed in the right and the freedom of expressing the national identity in official records, such as, for instance, the census and the other activities of the state, and in everyday communications when the issue of national identity is in question.

The fostering of identity is realised in the circle of the family, education of the children, and in various forms of activities of the members of nationalities. The forms suitable for this purpose are those indicated by this Article and realised in practice: institutions of culture and art (cultural and artistic societies, theatres in the languages of nationalities, radio and TV programmes in these languages, publication of newspapers and journals), scholarly and other associations (scholarly societies, scholarly and expert meetings and other similar activities).

A subject of these activities is also the presentation, cultivation and promotion of the folklore of the respective nationality, the study and the deepening of the history of the nationality, especially that connected to their life in the Republic and coexistence with the Macedonian people in the past, the present and the future, the use and the development of the language in oral communication and through various forms of literary work – poetry, prose, novels, short stories, plays, anecdotes, sayings.

The framework of this identity also includes the expression of religious affiliation, the performance of religious rituals in religious institutions and at home, the maintenance and fostering of religious and other customs characteristic of the nationality and its religion.

National attributes can be expressed similarly to the above-stated manner in situations based on the tradition and its modernisation. Among the ways of expressing national attributes, in addition to those already mentioned, are the national costume of the members of nationalities in everyday life and, especially, their religious and other ceremonies of private and public character (weddings, circumcision, christening, funeral ceremonies and customs, etc.).

One of the most visible manifestations and proofs of the identity and the attributes of nationalities is the free use of their language. Besides the above-stated means of realising this freedom, as well as the right to mutual communication of the members of nationalities in their own languages, their right to petition state bodies, the public services and other forms of social and public activity in their own language is also important. The bodies of the republic are obliged to accept petitions and statements in the language of the nationality to which the petitioner belongs. The state bodies, public services and other institutions are obliged to provide translation in every form of communication with the members of nationalities when they petition them in their own language.

However, this right of the members of nationalities does not mean the establishment and introduction of multi-lingualism in the Republic, for, in accordance with Article 7, Paragraph 1, of the Constitution of the Republic, 'the Macedonian language, written using its Cyrillic alphabet is the official language in the Republic of Macedonia.' This means that the acts of the state bodies, services and other institutions are in Macedonian, although petitions of the members of nationalities can be in their own language. Oral communication with the bodies is also performed in this language, and the bodies are obliged to provide an interpreter if the individual wants to speak in the language of his or her nationality.

The right of the members of nationalities to instruction in their own language in primary and secondary education is an expression and confirmation of their right to free use of their language. The law which determines the manner of realising this right should also prescribe the conditions for its effective realisation in the interest and for the benefit of the pupils. The obligation that in these schools the Macedonian language should be studied as well is of primary interest to the members of the nationality. By studying and speaking Macedonian, which is the official language in the Republic, they will be able, in linguistic terms as well, to get any job in the Republic, especially in the regions where there are no members of their own nationalities or their number is insignificant and where their language is not used in public communication. Besides, if they speak Macedonian they will be able to enrol and follow lectures at any of the faculties of the universities in the Republic where the instruction is in Macedonian. Faculties and universities in the languages of the nationalities are not envisaged, for completely justified reasons. If they do not study the Macedonian language in primary and secondary education, the members of nationalities will put themselves in a position of linguistic and professional ghettoisation. After all, they will render impossible their own official and other communication with the Macedonians, who have no obligation to speak the languages of nationalities.

The Constitutional obligation of the Republic to guarantee the protection of the ethnic, cultural, linguistic and religious identity of the nationalities is multi-faceted and complex. It should be realised in normative, functional, organisational and financial directions. The overall aim of these directions should be the provision of the realisation of this identity.

Normatively, bases and conditions should be created for this realisation, and bans, sanctions, and even punishments should be envisaged for every attempt, activity or action directed at violating the expression of this identity.

The functional direction includes the activity of all state bodies, in conformity with their authorities determined by the Constitution and the laws, towards taking direct measures for the protection from and prevention of violations and injuries of any kind – verbal, physical or psychological.

The organisational direction must be expressed equally towards the institutions of nationalities and the general institutions in and of the Republic, especially those acting in the interest of the Republic as a whole and the Macedonian people in general.

The financial direction basically comprises granting financial support to the relevant institutions in accordance with their activity and the material capabilities of the Republic.

This protection at the same time refers to prevention of the misuse of the constitutional rights of nationalities on the part of their members in the form of creating associations and institutions the activities of which , overtly and covertly, are directed at incitement to national hatred and intolerance. Finally, the activities of the state should also be expressed in its international policies and relations with the mother-countries of the nationalities, with the aim of establishing effective links and relations of the nationalities with their native peoples. In this, the relations must be established in accordance with international norms and without any interference of the mother-countries in the sovereignty and internal relations and affairs of the Republic.

III. 3. Article 7 of the Constitution is of particular political and functional importance for the status and the rights of nationalities. According to it:

'The Macedonian language, written using its Cyrillic alphabet, is the official language in the Republic of Macedonia.'

'In the units of local self-government where the majority of the inhabitants belong to a nationality, in addition to the Macedonian language and Cyrillic alphabet, their language and alphabet are also in official use, in a manner determined by law.'

'In the units of local self-government where there is a considerable number of inhabitants belonging to a nationality, their language and alphabet are also in official use, in addition to the Macedonian language and Cyrillic alphabet, under conditions and in a manner determined by law.'

This Constitutional regulation introduces bi- or multi- lingualism in the units of local self-government on the basis of the criterion which expresses the numerical proportion of the nationalities and the Macedonians in these units. This proportion is expressed in two dimensions (expressed arithmetically): a majority and a significant number. The concretisation of these dimensions, that is the numerical proportion of the nationalities and the Macedonians as a basis for the use of the language and the script of the nationalities, will have to be determined by the envisaged laws, possibly in such a way that the number of members of the nationality will be considered as a majority if it exceeds 50 per cent of the total population in the unit, and as a significant number if it exceeds 25 per cent or is 30 per cent, but is certainly considerably below 50 per cent of the population.

For the details of establishing of bi- or multi-lingualism in the units of local self-government, the Constitution envisages two laws: in cases where the members of nationalities are the majority only the manner of the realisation of this right needs to be determined, and in cases where the members of nationalities are in a significant number prescription of the conditions and the manner of implementation is envisaged. This difference in the range and the subject of legal standardisation has been established because of the difference in the conditions arising from the different number of members of the nationalities.

The use of this Article of the Constitution as a basis for the numerical proportion of the Macedonians and the members of nationalities requires official statistical data from the census and the citizenship records of the Republic of Macedonia. In this way, all arbitrary and approximative estimations and unfounded and unconfirmed claims regarding the number of members of the nationalities, motivated by political and nationalist aims towards imposing decisions on the Constitution, will be eliminated.

The location of the equal use of the Macedonian language and the languages of the nationalities, together with the Cyrillic alphabet and the scripts of the nationalities, in the units of local self-government (municipalities – Article 114) makes completely indisputable the conclusion that it does not refer to the Republic as a whole or the city of Skopje as a separate unit of self-government, which means that the Republic and the city of Skopje are not multi-linguistic territories or regions.

This location is very important as an additional argument for the justifiability of the indisputable theoretical , scholarly, constitutional and legal premises that the right to a parallel use of the languages and scripts of the nationalities, and their other specific rights determined by the Constitution, does not mean an equalisation of the nationalities with the people which as a nation has organised itself and constituted a state, where all the citizens are equal and where sovereignty derives from the citizens and belongs to the citizens (Article 2 of the Constitution of the Republic of Macedonia).

The significance of this difference between the nation and the nationalities within a single state, regardless of its set-up and with full respect for its character as a civil state, consists of the fact that nationalities living in a state outside their mother-country as 'national, ethnic, cultural, religious and linguistic minorities' (Article 1 of the Declaration on the Rights of Persons Belonging to National or Ethnic, Religious and Linguistic minorities, 2/) have no right to create their own state within the state in which they live or to separate from it and create a separate state of their own or join their native national state.

Nationalities in any form and on any grounds which, as minorities (according to the generally established and accepted terminology), live in a state outside their mother-countries, do not have a right to the self-determination as was proclaimed towards the end of the First World War by the President of the United States of America at that time, Woodrow Wilson, and established and adopted by the documents of the world organisations. In the state where they live, they enjoy and exercise full rights as citizens, but have no right to create their own state outside their mother-country. This generally adopted standpoint and accepted decision was not and still is not denied by the former existence of two states of the German people, which have been united into a single state, and of the people of Korea which live in two states. The creation of these states at the end of the Second World War or following the end of the Korean War was a result of the balance of powers at that time and the forceful imposition of decisions based on the arguments of power, and not on international law.

The creation of states of certain peoples cannot be considered as nationalism with elements of chauvinism, because this process was and is not to the detriment of other peoples, but a form of expressing and realising the statehood of every people.[4]

Therefore, the announcements made by official representatives of the mother-countries of the nationalities living in the Republic of Macedonia that, for instance, 'the Albanians in the Republic of Macedonia are not a minority, but a people according to their number', or by a member of the Albanian nationality in Kosovo that 'there is no peace without self-determination for the Albanians as for all the other peoples of the former Yugoslavia',[5] are not only, in scholarly terms and according to the standards of international law, unfounded, but are also harmful: first of all, for the stability and the inter-ethnic relations in the state where these nationalities live, and then for the friendly and good-neighbourly relations between states.

The above-stated facts about the nationalities equally refer to the nationalities which were formerly denoted as ethnic groups – Romanies and Vlachs – although they have no mother-countries outside the state in which they live and of which they are the citizens.

III. 4. The meaning of inter-ethnic relations in the Republic as one of the important bases for its stability, development and progress is also confirmed by the constitutionally formed Council for Inter-Ethnic Relations – Article 78 of the Constitution. According to this Article, the Council consists of the President of the Assembly and two members each from the ranks of the Macedonians, Albanians, Turks, Vlachs and Romanies, as well as two members from the ranks of other nationalities in Macedonia; the President of the Assembly is President of the Council; the Assembly elects the members of the Council; the Council considers issues of inter-ethnic relations in the Republic and makes appraisals and proposals for their solution; the Assembly is obliged to take into consideration the appraisals and proposals of the Council and to make decisions regarding them.

The creation, the authority and the attitude of the Assembly towards this Council confirms the truth that inter-ethnic relations in the Republic in which, in addition to the Macedonians, there are also other nationalities, are a highly important element of the harmonious life as a prerequisite for its stability and general progress and development. The composition of the Council is a sufficient guarantee for the successful realisation of its function, and the duty of the Assembly to make decisions on the basis of its appraisals and proposals expresses the indispensability of a serious and responsible treatment of this issue.

The existence of the Council and its activity does not mean that it is an instrument for solving crisis situations. On the contrary, it should effectively prevent the appearance of such conditions and, if they should still occur, it should actively participate in their successful resolution.

III. 5. The free expression of national identity, established by Article 8, Paragraph 1, Point 2 of the Constitution of the Republic of Macedonia, has two meanings: first, no one can or should influence or put pressure on anybody to declare themselves as members of a certain nationality, that is to say – people; and second, the individual does not have to declare him or herself as a member of any nationality or people. The second meaning represents liberation of the individual from the national heritage on the basis of his or her birth, for which they have no credit or guilt. The expression of national identity, however, is not related to citizenship, meaning that even a person who has not expressed his or her national identity can be a citizen.

IV

The domain of the status and rights of nationalities also includes the status of the Macedonians living outside the Republic of Macedonia. According to Article 49 of the Constitution of the Republic of Macedonia and Constitutional Amendment II, 'the Republic cares for the status and rights of those persons belonging to the Macedonian people in neighbouring countries, as well as Macedonian expatriates, assists their cultural development and promotes links with them'.

In this, 'the Republic shall not interfere in the sovereign rights of other states and their internal affairs.'

'The Republic cares for the cultural, economic and social rights of the citizens of the Republic abroad.'

The concern of the Republic and its activity in this regard is not a moral obligation. It is a duty of the state in which the Macedonian people has organised itself and constituted a state towards the members of the Macedonian people who, because of the forceful partition of Macedonia, remained outside their mother-country, as well as towards Macedonian expatriates who, because of political and economic circumstances, or reasons, have left Macedonia.

The concern of the Republic for the Macedonians and its citizens abroad is conditioned by their status and their domicile. First of all, it refers to the members of the Macedonian people in the neighbouring countries, then to Macedonian expatriates and, finally, to citizens of the Republic abroad, regardless of their nationality.

The basic aim regarding the first and the second categories is the maintaining and stimulation of their national feeling of belonging to their own Macedonian nation from the state of which they are separated or which they have left; that is, they are not included in it because of border partitions. The subject of this concern is the status and rights of these Macedonians in accordance with international law and the documents of the international organisations, especially of the United Nations Organisation, referring to national minorities. It is realised through the relations of the Republic of Macedonia with the neighbouring countries in which there are members of the Macedonian people, through various agreements and arrangements for cooperation, in which the accent is placed on anti-discriminatory measures and acts. The subject of these agreements and arrangements is mainly cooperation in the fields of education, culture and art, and fostering of traditions and historical truths, as an expression and confirmation of the national feeling of these Macedonians. Of special importance for the character and the content of this concern is the constitutional determination of the Republic that it will not interfere in the sovereign rights of the neighbouring states and in their internal affairs. This means that the concern of the Republic absolutely excludes any territorial pretensions and confirms its determination for the unchangeability of borders.

The assistance to the cultural development of the members of the Macedonian people in the neighbouring countries and Macedonian expatriates is versatile and should be realised through the activity of state bodies, non-governmental organisations, various associations of citizens and other forms of organisation, and the Macedonian Orthodox Church. The forms this takes can be visits paid to these Macedonians, the organisation of various manifestations in the places

and states where they live, participation in and attending of their celebrations and other forms of gathering, sending of newspapers, journals, books, cassettes, the establishment and creation of libraries and
every other kind of communication. A highly suitable form is also
these people's stay in the Republic in the form of private visits or
attending celebrations, and organised meetings with them.

The promotion of links with these people requires permanent
contact and communication, in which they should be informed about
conditions and events in the Republic, and also their interest in invest-
ing in the Republic of Macedonia and other forms of economic cooperation of mutual interest.

The concern of the Republic for the cultural, economic, and social
rights of the citizens of the Republic abroad refers to its citizens who are
temporarily employed or have temporary residence abroad. This concern
can be direct – by assisting the activities of their associations – and indirect – by concluding and implementing various conventions with the
respective states, especially in the domain of economic and social rights,
such as employment, living and working conditions, social security,
health care and pensions. In this respect, what is important for these
people is the psychological aspect as an expression of their relatedness
with their mother-country, but also of this state's concern for them.

All the above-stated norms of the Constitution of the Republic of
Macedonia regarding the status and rights of nationalities point to the
indisputable conclusion that they are in conformity with the international standards regarding this status and these rights, and some
of them even envisage a higher normative standard.

The practice of their implementation so far also points to the indisputable conclusion that they are real and applicable in their essence
and basic content. This conclusion is also confirmed with regard to the
Albanian nationality as the most numerous among all nationalities
living in the Republic. It is expressed through their presence in the
Assembly of the Republic of Macedonia and the responsible functions
they have in the state administration and the other institutions of the
system. Compared to the past, the conditions regarding this presence
point to the fact that this nationality has never been so strongly represented in the Assembly, the government and the other state bodies.

These statements indicate that the maximalist requests of some representatives and leaders of the parties of this and other nationalities not
only exceed the frameworks of the Constitution and the generally

accepted world standards, but also represent rude violations of the Constitution and a breach of these standards. These requests are not only dysfunctional, but are also an indication of the deterioration of inter-ethnic relations, and a serious impediment to the constitutional order of the Republic and the activities of its institutions. On the other hand, the aversion of some political parties and their members to the legitimate and constitutionally founded requests of certain nationalities, especially the Albanian, mean a breach of the democratic relations and the system of the legal state, in which all citizens are equal and in which the rights of nationalities are inviolable within the constitutional framework.

However, a serious defect of the overall and consistent realisation of the rights of nationalities established by the Constitution is that some of them are not operational within the proposed laws. The failure to pass these laws, as a consequence of the balance of powers in the Assembly of the Republic , is a source of inter-ethnic disputes, which have a negative effect on the further development of the initiated democratisation of the country in the conditions of political pluralism and full respect for the basic freedoms and rights of the individual and the citizen, also recognized by international law.

Notes

1. (a) *Pravna Enciklopedija* (Encyclopaedia of Law), Savremena administracija (Modern Administration), Belgrade, 1979, pp. 659–70; (b) *Politička Enciklopedija* (Political Encyclopaedia), Savremena administracija, Belgrade, 1975, pp. 531–4, 604–7; (c) *Sociološki leksikon* (Sociological Lexicon), Savremena administracija, Belgrade, 1982, pp. 336, 381, 387–8; (d) *Protection des minorités*, Nations Unies, New York, 1967; (e) Kemal Sejfula, *National Minorities in the Socialist Republic of Macedonia*, Jugoslavija, Belgrade.
2. Declaration on the Rights of Persons Belonging to National or Ethnic, Religious or Linguistic Minorities, *Balkan Forum*, vol. 1, no. 2, Nova Makedonija, Skopje, 1993, pp. 41–4.
3. Constitution of the Republic of Macedonia, ed. Assembly of the Republic of Macedonia, 1991, exposition of the President of the Republic Kiro Gligorov at the formal session of the Assembly of the Republic of Macedonia, on the occasion of the declaration of the Constitution on November 20, 1991.
4. Vojin Dimitrijevič, 'The Ethnic Understanding of the Post-communist Nation-State', *Balkan Forum*, vol. 1, no. 2 (March 1993), Nova Makedonija, Skopje, pp. 59–68.
5. Interview with Leonida Mertiri, representative of Albania in Macedonia, *Nova Makedonija* newspaper, Skopje, 19th March 1993; and Mark Krasniči, 'There is No Peace without Self-Determination of the Albanians', *Nova Makedonija*, March 21, 1993.

Part III
Historical perspectives

Chapter 12

IMRO groupings in Bulgaria after the Second World War

Ivanka Nedeva and Naoum Kaytchev

It is difficult, indeed, to grasp the post-World War II history of the Internal Macedonian Revolutionary Organisation (IMRO), or rather, what remained of it after the communist takeover in Bulgaria in September 1944. Firstly, the numerous Macedonian refugees in Bulgaria had, ever since the end of the nineteenth century, formed a variety of cultural organisations: the majority maintained legal societies concerned primarily with cultural functions while the illegal IMRO operated as a leading political body, challenged after the 1920s by the pro-Yugoslavian, later pro-Soviet, breakaway faction of 'Protogerovists', and more importantly, by the Comintern followers, united until the mid-1930s in the UIMRO, and afterwards directly in the Bulgarian Communist Party (BCP). Therefore the actual IMRO presence in post-war Bulgaria could be outlined only within the complicated interrelationship between the legal societies and the competing Macedonian political circles. Secondly, the sources pose other kind of problems: since an illegal organisation was bound to become an object of attention of the secret services, the bulk of the relevant records is kept in hardly accessible security archives.

Nonetheless some research has already been done – mainly on the destruction of the IMRO groupings in the late 1940s.[1] Open files in the Bulgarian central state archive provide sufficient evidence on the legal societies. Furthermore, some of the old IMRO activists had survived: authors' interviews with them were invaluable for clarification of the picture. A sufficient base exists to present a concise story of the IMRO in Bulgaria after the Second World War. The IMRO activities in Yugoslav and Greek parts of Macedonia will not be examined here.

The fate of IMRO groupings in Bulgaria was important not only in domestic terms for the authorities. Until 1950 Macedonia was still a key burning question in Balkan politics. It dominated Yugoslav–Bulgarian, Yugoslav–Greek and Bulgarian–Greek relations. The new victorious Yugoslavia under Tito energetically established its new People's Republic of Macedonia (PRM) with the proclaimed Macedonian nation as its constituent element; Belgrade self-confidence was high enough to insist on incorporation of Bulgarian and Greek Macedonia into the new republic. Hence, both the prolonged Bulgarian–Yugoslav federation negotiations (1944–8) and the Civil War in Greece (1946–9) were dominated by the unregulated Macedonian future.[2] After 1950 this question was frozen by the Cold War realities, yet it continued to preoccupy the foreign ministries in Balkan capitals. Hence, the activities of IMRO groupings in Bulgaria were bound to have wider international repercussions.

After the 1934 military coup in Sofia the original IMRO was bloodlessly disbanded at a formal level. Contemporaries were surprised to discover how peacefully the once state within a state, and the horror of Balkan governments, put down arms and dispersed as a formal organisation.[3] Yet politicians and journalists continued to consider IMRO as a factor for over a decade. This notion was taken for granted by historians (who still are tempted to treat IMRO as existing until the late 1940s[4]) and was reinforced by the sudden resurrection of an organisation labelled with the same four capital letters in post-communist Bulgaria.

In fact, between 1934 and 1990 no formal political organisation existed in Bulgaria under the name IMRO. There were only loose groupings of former activists and young enthusiasts maintaining informal links. They talked rather than acted: after 1934 their sole major action was the organising of the Bulgarian *Ohrana* battalions in the far away western districts of Greek Macedonia in 1944. Even then the German and Bulgarian support was essential.[5] Nevertheless they still seemed to be a prospective party – were they to receive firm leadership and foreign backing they could have played a major role in future Balkan conflicts. However, throughout the war their leader Ivan Mihailov remained in exile – first in Poland, then in Croatia, with his old friend Ante Pavelich – and his followers in Macedonia were prevented from independent action.[6] No Great Power was really attracted by IMRO's offers. Britain and France were reserved if only because an independent Macedonia entailed a weakening of their allies in the region – Greece and Yugoslavia.[7] Moscow counted on its own communist branches in the Balkans and could only combat the main rival for the souls of the Macedonians. Only the Germans were sympathetic, yet they preferred to cooperate with the Bulgarian government. While the

Sofia regime was stable, Berlin kept Mihailov as a reserve card. It was only toward the end of the war, in the spring of 1944, when his supporters were activated to counter the ELAS offensive through *Ohrana*.[8] Finally, in early September Mihailov was brought to Skopie and invited to preside over a puppet Macedonian republic. He refused the suicidal entanglement and fled to Vienna, to his life-long emigration.[9]

On 9 September 1944, when the communist-dominated Fatherland Front established its rule in Bulgaria, ten years had past since the time when the communist structures in Macedonia were being ruthlessly suppressed by IMRO. Hence, the organisation's activists were not the first target group to be persecuted. Instead, the new authorities hurried to deal with the 1941–4 officials of the 'non-party' authoritarian regime. Only where local communists had a long enough memory were the IMRO men massacred. In the town of Nevrokop (Gotse Delchev), for example, about two dozen of them were slaughtered during the first month of communist rule.[10] In other places the IMRO men (or 'mihailovists', as they were labelled in the official jargon) were arrested, imprisoned or interned. On a national scale, however, the new 'People's Militia' initially overlooked IMRO men who generally refrained from collaboration with the pre-1944 regime.

While Mihailov left for Vienna, two other important figures stayed in the country: Georgi Nastev and Vladimir Kourtev – Mihailov's colleagues in the last, 1932–4 Central Committee of the organisation.[11] Since they were engaged in IMRO for several decades and had an intimate knowledge of its structures and mechanisms they were considered as its natural leaders. During the first months of communist rule, while the authorities were busy dealing with the previous powerholders, it appears that Kourtev, Nastev and their followers were content to survive the repressions in semi-legality and refrained from any collective activities.

However, after the summer of 1945 some important developments took place. The Fatherland Front split faction on Agrarians and Social Democrats formed an opposition to the hitherto one-party regime. Although they were discriminated against and barred from power some greater plurality was bound to take place. The IMRO men took advantage and began to meet and discuss with each other the current political developments. Unfortunately for them the State Security[12] was now able to pay attention to their activities: it recruited some agents among the former IMRO ranks and tapped all meetings. Later, its inflated reports were used by the public prosecutors to build up a case against some monstrous organisation called IMRO. It was claimed that Vladimir

Kourtev, Georgi Nastev and Kosta Rizov re-established the Central Committee of IMRO in December 1945. The first undertook the political side, the second the organisational side, and the third the youth work. Another man was responsible for student activities. This team (the Sofia centre) allegedly activated the dispersed 'mihailovists', did some organisational work with students and secondary-school pupils, created two armed groups in the town of Sveti Vrach (Sandanski), and got in touch with some army officers and opposition leaders.[13]

In fact, whether the grouping constituted itself as a formal organisation or not is actually a moot point. The contemporaries at the time were sceptical about the official accusations. Probably the former IMRO men just commented on the current political turnabouts, condemning authorities in both Sofia and Belgrade and their communist-sponsored new Macedonian republic within federal Yugoslavia. More interestingly, some evidence points to the fact that the authorities not only monitored but even inspired these activities. Peter Semerdziev claims that State Security managed to recruit the first IMRO man, Kourtev, manipulating through him all 'mihailovist' activities in 1945–6.[14] This proposition is supported by the memories of the then director of police Rusi Hristozov:

> With the help of our Soviet comrades, after 1945.... we managed to place the work of People's Militia on, as it is called, a scientific basis. Then we learned how to build an apparatus of agents, and information apparatus, how to work with enemy elements, how to fuel them with information, with external surveillance, with inside agents; it was not by chance that as early as 1945 we succeeded in the former IMRO-supremists. Vancho Mihailov escaped to Italy; we failed to capture him, but his men like Zhoro [i.e. Georgi] Nastev, Kourtev, Begamov and others stayed. We managed to insert our collaborators among them.[15]

Furthermore, recent research suggests that IMRO leaders initiated negotiations with the leading communist politician, the interior minister Anton Yugov. Kourtev lived legally in Sofia and was free to proclaim that agreement with authorities was concluded and a list of imprisoned former IMRO men was prepared for their release. During the winter and spring of 1946 a number of contacts between IMRO men and communist representatives took place.[16]

One such meeting was scheduled for 8 June 1946. A dozen IMRO leaders gathered, including Kourtev and Nastev, yet they were visited not by negotiators but by police officials instead. The outcome of the rendezvous was more than tragic for Mihailov's followers: all were arrested, the majority of them subsequently killed. This action was a signal for a nationwide police campaign which brought about 150 arrests of IMRO men. One of Kourtev's lieutenants, Kiril Drangov, refused to surrender and shot himself.[17]

The motives for the alleged short-lived communist flirtation with IMRO men are still not clear. Some international considerations might have been decisive: the authorities were not sure what kind of Balkan configuration might emerge in the next period, Kourtev's men had promising experience and influence in the Yugoslav and Greek parts of Macedonia. It was only towards mid-1946 the Soviet, and respectively Bulgarian, policy-makers ultimately resolved to follow the track of large-scale cooperation with Belgrade on the Macedonian issue. In early June 1946, while the police were arresting the IMRO activists, in Moscow Stalin praised the Yugoslav Macedonian policy and instructed the Bulgarian prime minister Georgi Dimitrov to follow the Yugoslav line by giving autonomy to Bulgarian Macedonia and by fostering the Macedonian national consciousness in the population. Two months later the BCP plenum followed suit: it resolved to establish a cultural-educational autonomy in Pirin Macedonia where special Skopje officials were supposed to execute some key functions. Obviously, Sofia adopted Moscow's reliance on Yugoslav and Greek communists; in this situation Kourtev's help was not considered indispensable: he could be sacrificed for the sake of good relations with Belgrade. Some evidence suggests that in June anti-IMRO action was carried out on Yugoslav's request and with the active involvement of the special Serbian intelligence representative with the Bulgarian State Security, Lieut.-Col. Ivan Bozhovic.[18]

Another line of explanation is connected with the internal political situation. After all, 1946 was the peak year of the scanty post-1934 Bulgarian democracy. However discriminated against and persecuted Agrarians and Social Democrats might have been, the sole existence of a legal organised opposition was unprecedented in a state where the political parties were banned for more than a decade. Bulgaria was heading towards the October general elections which would bring a substantial opposition minority in *Sabranie*, the Parliament – this in a country where neither opposition parliamentary fractions nor legislative assembly itself had existed on a regular basis since 1934. Hence, the ruling communist party was busy trying to prevent other political groups from joining the opposition. The negotiations with Kourtev, therefore, could be regarded as a part of their efforts to isolate the opposition.[19] However, in general the communists preferred to see IMRO as, to put it in Hristozov's words, 'a very dangerous potential enemy, which the opposition was prepared to use against our authority',[20] and decided at some point to eliminate it. In addition they hoped through forged IMRO-Agrarian connections to discredit and intimidate their election opponents.

The third line of argumentation, the most obvious and simple one, could claim that BCP never staked any serious political hopes on IMRO; early 1946 talks were routine police work with the sole aim of discovering the scope of IMRO groupings and their subsequent liquidation. As far as IMRO motives are concerned, they were dictated by political opportunism. Kourtev and his colleagues realised that after 1944 no conditions for successive illegal anti-government activities existed and sought contacts with the authorities.

Be that as it may, the IMRO men met disastrous fates. The destiny of the leading 13 figures, including Kourtev and Nastev, is still unknown – probably they were killed by either the Sofia or Skopje secret services. Another 22 men from the lower ranks were prosecuted in the official show trial in August 1946. One of them, Kosta Rizov, was sentenced to death *in absentia* – he was taken out of the central Sofia prison to disappear forever. The rest received various lengths of prison sentence. Others were interned or imprisoned without any court proceedings. The August trial was a widely publicised action with transparent political goals. The prosecuted were forced to make confessions on alleged links with the legal opposition or with some army officers. The authorities aimed at going on the offensive against the opposition, at justifying their own police repressions and distracting public attention from the purges in the army.[21]

The action was part of a wider strategy to intimidate the opposition and to establish one-party communist rule. Within a year these objectives were achieved. After 10 February 1947, when the peace treaty with the Allies was signed, the road to arbitrary dictatorship was open: the opposition Agrarian party was banned, its deputies ousted from *Sabranie*, and its leader Nikola Petkov put on trial and hanged. In other words, by the end of 1947 the headquarters of all traditional non-communist-dominated circles (i.e. pre-1944 regime establishment, former rightist organisations, bourgeois liberal parties, Agrarians, etc.) were wiped out. What remained was to crush some local nests of discontent and resistance.

The case with IMRO was part of the same story – the 1946 action had destroyed its headquarters in Sofia. Since all old leaders were either murdered or jailed, the old hierarchy of seniority virtually ceased to exist. Moreover, since the middle-rank activists were repressed or at least earmarked by the authorities, they were forced to conform with the new realities. Now the main concern for the authorities was the young generation – men in their early twenties, who hitherto either had had no involvement in IMRO-connected activities or had been just members of the pro-IMRO societies in the secondary schools. Those youngsters from Pirin Macedonia who for one reason or another were classified by the authorities as 'unreliable' and, accordingly, barred from access to higher education or to respectable jobs, promised to pose problems. Since they still enjoyed the energy of youth and freedom from the constraints of structured adulthood, they were inclined to express their discontent in actions. Initially these were caused primarily by personal motives to counter official discrimina-tion, but as far as both the authorities and the bulk of observers tended to put political labels on all anti-government manifestations, they were classified as 'mihailovist'. Some men, like a cluster of Nevrokop gymna-sium pupils in April 1947, tried to form armed resistance groups, while others, like several Bansko youths in August 1948, simply attempted to cross the Greek border and flee overseas.

Some managed to escape to Greek refugee camps; from there, after passive (or, probably in some cases, active) cooperation with Greek-American military intelligence, they went to the West, mainly to the USA and Canada. In the New World they joined the emigrant Macedonian Patriotic Organisation (MPO) which continued to work, under Mihailov's indirect guidance, for the old IMRO's goal: an independent unified Macedonian state, dominated by its Slavic Bulgarian population. Currently some of them (for instance, Borislav Ivanov and Pando Mladenov) are still key activists of the present-day MPO.

However, as a rule, in the late 1940s–early 1950s, Bulgarian State Security kept a close eye on the risky group in the Pirin region; by use of agents it was able to neutralise most actions in their beginning. Several trials were organised against the new young resisters to the totalitarian regime; jails and camps witnessed the reinforcement of the old 'mihailovist' groups of prisoners.

What followed in the subsequent decades was an elaborated system of keeping the former IMRO members and their heirs at the social periphery. Until the end of the 1950s direct repressions predominated: through imprisonments and exiles former organisation members were segregated from the core of society.[22] Afterwards more refined methods of discrimination prevailed; the targeted group was simply barred from respectable careers and forced to keep a low profile.[23] Small wonder that after the decades of disgrace and disappointment traditional IMRO circles wished to forget the painful personal past and longed for better adaptation in the society. In the late 1970s, with the communist hold on Bulgaria stronger than ever, the IMRO groupings seemed at the point of extinction.

Yet in the turbulent aftermath of Zhivkov's regime an institution-alised IMRO heir was not slow to emerge. On 10 November 1989 the longest survivor of the East European dictators was forced to step down, a month later an opposition newspaper under the traditional inter-war name 'Makedonia' came into being, two months afterwards the organisation claiming IMRO inheritance was founded, and within thirteen months it adopted the old name in its title.

This spectacular resurrection was largely due to two major previous developments: firstly, the old league of the Macedonian refugees in Bulgaria was preserved after 1944, and, secondly, the regime itself, in its later years, encouraged a nationalistic attitude toward the past, and, to a certain extent, toward the present.

Ever since the end of the nineteenth century Macedonian emigrants in Bulgaria maintained their own legal societies, named usually as brotherhoods. These were concerned primarily with preserving the social cultural pattern of the native region, and with helping the refugees adapt to their new dwelling places through mutual support. As far as politics was concerned, in the inter-war years the brotherhoods tended to back the illegal IMRO and its strategy. However, the rank and file preferred to refrain from active political involvement.

Hence, after 1944 new rulers chose not to ban these societies but to change their leadership and impose the new ideology on them. The initial takeover took place by mid-September 1944: the new authorities proclaimed the old bourgeois National Committee of the Macedonian Emigration dissolved and replaced by a new one. Party people like Hristo Kalaidzhiev, Angel Dinev and Georgi Denishev took charge.[24] This was the beginning of five years of turbulence for the brother-hoods' political facade. They were exposed to various experiments: arranging 'The First Free Congress of the Macedonian Emigration'; dis-solution and reconstitution into 'cultural-educational societies' admit-ting only those who 'feel themselves as Macedonians and stay at people-democratic positions';[25] pro-Yugoslavian leadership; radical anti-Belgrade turnabout and condemnation of the 'Tito–Kolishevist agents'; chairmanship of the BCP's Politburo member, etc.

The final stabilisation came in the early 1950s: under the old communist veteran Hristo Kalaidzhiev the Union of Macedonian Cultural-Educational Societies (UMCES) was converted into an auxiliary extension of the BCP's machine with no politics of its own; the activists were prepared to accept any twists of the party line.

The BCP policy was equivocal on the troublesome question of the nationality of the Slavic population of Macedonia. After the Yugoslavian breakaway from the Soviet Bloc in 1948 the separate Macedonian nationhood continued to be proclaimed officially. The population in Pirin region was still classified as of Macedonian nationality – a notion affirmed by the 1956 census. Kalaidziev instructed his followers; 'As we fought against being considered as a Bulgarian minority, we should fight wholeheartedly and decisively against Titoist attempts to label us as a Yugoslav minority... We must prove that Macedonians in Bulgaria are absolutely free.'[26] However, the Skopje authorities were brutally attacked for anti-Bulgarian actions; their official language was named not as 'Macedonian', but as 'Kolishevist' and '*serboman*' (the traditional pre-1944 qualification for pro-Belgrade opportunists in Yugoslav Macedonia). The implication was that the separate Macedonian nationality had real freedom and future only under the Soviet-Bulgarian socialist aegis, not under the Yugoslav revisionist one. Yet this was a shaky foundation for a successful rule over the country. Hence, some quiet corrections were made: when Macedonian emigrants openly proclaimed their Bulgarian consciousness, like the joint member did at an annual conference of Veliko Tarnovo's Macedonian society in April 1951, they were tolerated (hitherto they would have been persecuted). When the Macedonian student section in Sofia went too far in adopting the new Macedonianist approach, its leadership was changed under UMCES direction.[27] Finally, on 3 March 1958, on the celebrations of the 80th anniversary of Bulgaria's liberation, a Politburo member Encho Staikov proclaimed that 'In accordance with this treaty [San-Stefano] the Bulgarian people were liberated and united in one state...[i.e. including the majority of Macedonia]. But at the Berlin Conference, Bulgaria was torn to pieces... destroying the just cause of the Peace of San-Stefano....' The speaker praised the Bulgarian policy towards the Turkish minority but failed to mention any Macedonian one. Henceforth the Bulgarian nationhood of the Macedonians within Bulgaria was adopted.[28] When in the following year the Macedonian society in Gabrovo still used the old terminology in a letter to the UMCES, Sofia reacted instantly: 'We draw your attention to the expression "Macedonian minority in the town"... Settlers from Macedonia in Bulgaria are not a "national minority".'[29]

The party line on the current Balkan-Macedonian politics was simpler: while any solution coming from the capitalist West or revisionist Yugoslavia was rejected, Soviet-Bulgarian ones were glorified. There were no difficulties in preparing the desired history cocktail on the inter-war years either: while IMRO and their followers, 'mihailovists', were ceaselessly condemned, their rivals – Comintern adherents – were eulogised. However, despite the changing political rhetoric, the rank and file of the Macedonian societies continued to be concerned mainly with the traditional social functions such as adaptation in the society through commemorating the old regions, communities and life patterns. In this respect their attitude was rather conservative; it was modelled in the non-socialist past which the new authorities so passionately wished to obliterate. As Kalaidzhiev noticed, the traditional pre-1944 celebration events, 'Ilinden and the day of Gotse [Delchev] are popular and our actions are well-accepted [by the masses]. However, the action, ... commemorating the Macedonian victims of the fascism, those who died defending the common front with BCP and the friendship with USSR, is not so popular'.[30]

The UMCES continued through the decades as an organisation with diminishing functions; in 1977 it was finally disbanded and the societies converted into 'Macedonian cultural-educational clubs' under the Fatherland Front umbrella. Yet what survived was virtually an institutionalised structure where conservative-minded people gathered to worship the Bulgarian-Macedonian cause and early pre-1918 IMRO (in combination, of course, with the formal compulsory socialist festivities).

This took place in a country where authorities increasingly revised the former communist anti-national stance and opted for a more patriotic policy. They began to realise that the traditional internationalist ideology had limited application in complicated South East European politics (as so brilliantly demonstrated by Romanian–Hungarian or Greek–Turkish disputes) and was of small use for upholding their country's interests in the region. In addition, since the internationalist rhetoric had less and less appeal to the masses, 'patriotic education' had to be strengthened to give ideological legitimacy to the government. The steady propagation of Bulgarian 'grandeur', past and present, culminated in the 1980s with large-scale celebrations of the 1300th anniversary of the Bulgarian state which was combined with periodical anti-Yugoslav outbursts in the learned journals, and, more rarely, in the newspapers. True, Zhivkov was more than cautious on the Macedonian issue: his Balkan policy was principally defensive.

Bulgarian minorities everywhere, especially in the neighbouring states like Serbia, were forgotten.[31] The nationalist re-writing of history rarely covered the years after 1918, and the post-1944 period was banned for any logical discussion or research and subjected to the party's ideological dogma. Yet the general mood was in a nationalist[32] direction; it was bound to have some effect even on such ossified structures as the Macedonian societies.

Indeed, by the mid-1980s a group of Macedonian communist reformers began to insist on a more nationalist approach towards the past. No doubt they enjoyed some protection from a portion of the party elite. Most public was the case of Ivan Aleksandrov – a junior administrator in the apparatus of the Central Committee of the BCP – who while giving public lectures in the Macedonian club in Sofia ceaselessly wrote reports to Zhivkov, advocating a more bold nationalistic approach.[33] He went as far as to rehabilitate Mihailov on the grounds of his invaluable contribution to the Bulgarian nation. If some strict temporal watershed is to be outlined, it is 4 June 1985 when a new chairman of the Sofia Macedonian Cultural-Educational Club 'Gotse Delchev' was elected. The post, which hitherto was an honorary sinecure for old communist veterans, was now filled by the young historian Dimitar Gotsev[34] – being born in Yugoslav Macedonia, he overtly praised the inter-war IMRO of Todor Aleksandrov and Ivan Mihailov. Under his leadership further patriotic revision was carried out: every week various lectures on Macedonian history took place, Aleksandrov went ahead with his public revelations[35], and professional historians felt free to speak more overtly, breaking the traditional communist taboos. For example, the young scholar Georgi Parvanov was bold enough to refute in an open public debate a retired senior security service officer for his historical novels which praised regional pre-1912 IMRO breakaway left-winger Yané Sandanski at the expense of the organisation's mainstream.[36] People like Parvanov and Aleksandrov were welcomed by the rank and file of the Macedonian clubs, who perceived IMRO either as a symbol of its own strong youth years or as a genuine representative of the patriotic ideas which came to the fore in the 1980s. In addition, some old IMRO survivors joined the club thus providing continuity for the organisation.

What is more, apart from the ideological developments, organisational changes took place. The Macedonian club in Sofia hitherto was made up of a dozen or so sections traditionally based on the principle of the refugees' regional origin (i.e. the Skopje section, the Salonica section, and so on) which helped to conserve and save them but it entailed also their segregation on the periphery of mainstream Bulgarian society. In 1986–7 a new structure was established. A youth section emerged to attract students from Sofia and Veliko Tarnovo universities, inspired by the patriotic rhetoric of the 1980s (who usually had no kin relation with IMRO and even with Macedonia). Thus in the late 1980s the Macedonian Cultural-Educational Club 'Gotse Delchev', formally a secondary branch of the BCP's hollow public extension named the Fatherland Front, was in practice a potentially strong political nucleus for focusing attention of the various nationalist-minded Bulgarian circles.

Hence, the post-1989 developments were hardly a surprise. In late 1989 the youth section began to publish a newspaper, *Makedonia*. Macedonian societies emerged in towns like Blagoevgrad and Petrich. On 5–6 January 1990 the Restoration Congress of the UMCES was held; on 15–16 December 1990 another congress adopted the name IMRO – the Union of Macedonian Societies (IMRO-UMS).[37]

The first statute, adopted in January 1990, stipulated that it aimed at 'the spiritual unity of the Bulgarians, wherever they might be'. The December congress claimed the inheritance of the old IMRO and the Macedonian brotherhoods while the aim was ambiguously formulated as 'the complete and irreversible solution of the Macedonian question, based on the historical truth, political justice and international human rights agreements'[38] The vague redaction was a compromise between different persuasions: old veterans implied the old notion of a unified independent Macedonia, other members the traditional slogan of San-Stefano Bulgaria, while the realists envisaged the break-up of Yugoslavia and secession of the Republic of Macedonia.[39] In February 1993 the amended statute redefined the organisation's goal as a 'defence, saving and resurrection of Bulgarianism in Macedonia. The Organisation's principal interest,' the statute went on, 'is the complete solution of the Macedonian question as well as the general progress of the whole Bulgarian people.'[40] Obviously, Mihailov's old scheme for a unified independent Macedonia was abolished, although IMRO-UMS supported the Republic of Macedonia in its secession from Yugoslavia, as well as in the embittered international dispute with Greece. Though at the bottom of the members' hopes lies the traditional vision of the unified (San-Stefano) Bulgaria, the official statements accept the Paris–Helsinki border status quo and claim that the organisation's aims would be achieved through European unification. The current key objective is to ensure through democratisation favourable conditions for people with Bulgarian social and political consciousness in the

Republic of Macedonia, which is regarded as a prospective second Bulgarian state. IMRO-UMS maintains various links with the Albanian Bulgarians, pro-Bulgarian groupings in the Republic of Macedonia like IMRO–Tatkoviska Partia, (IMRO-TP) and Macedonian-Bulgarian emigrant organisations in the West, most notably MPO.[41]

Though the organisation initiated a number of demonstrations and other street actions, initially it refrained from active involvement in the current domestic politics, for its statute proclaimed it as a 'non-party' organisation. In addition, its conservative character – as well as the collective leadership, an uneasy coalition of nationalist ex-communists (like the chairman Gotsev), old IMRO veterans (vice-chairman Stoyan Boyadzhiev) and representatives of the young generation not bound by any former political attachment (secretaries Evgenii Ekov and Krasimir Karakachanov) – prevented it from any rapid comprehensive transformations. Thus in the early 1990s it was essentially a non-party pressure group with no say in everyday politics.

However, some changes slowly took place. By mid-1992 Dimitar Gotsev resigned due to alleged health problems; henceforth IMRO-UMS gradually took the road to active political involvement. Under Stoyan Bojadzhiev until March 1995, afterwards under the triumvirate of co-chairman (Raina Drangova, Evgenii Ekov, Krasimir Karakachanov), it gradually began to transform itself into a political party. In 1994 a coalition agreement with the mainstream right-wing Union of Democratic Forces was signed and two IMRO MPs were elected (Evgenii Ekov and Anatoli Velichkov). Later on, through shared ballots a number of local councillors and mayors were elected. IMRO-UMS also backed in the 1996 elections the new Bulgarian president Petar Stoyanov. In domestic politics IMRO-UMS stands for a number of specific issues: it opposes the Turkish-dominated Movement for Rights and Freedom in Southern Bulgaria (in the region of the Rhodopes mountains), and lobbies for refugees from southern parts of Macedonia and Thrace, who still await government compensation for their properties left in Greece.

It is difficult to judge the organisation's actual current influence. Its individual electoral possibilities are considered as minor ones, yet as a centralised well-organised structure with over 150 branches[42] all over the country it should not be underestimated, especially since all other 1990s nationalistic Bulgarian political enterprises (National Democratic Party, National Radical Party, Constitutional Forum, Fatherland Party of Labour, Patriotic Block, etc.) turned out to be short-lived. True, compared with Romania Mare or the Party of the Romanian National

Unity, with Šešeli's Serbian Radical Party or with the mainstream Greek parties, IMRO-UMS is a minor electoral force. For the Bulgarians, unlike their neighbours, have so far shown limited enthusiasm for nationalistic policies. Yet IMRO-UMS appears as a durable and influential body, perhaps because it opts for a moderate version of nationalism, i.e. the Bulgarian traditional national agenda. It is still considered to be potentially an important player in future political developments, as it has been for most of the time during this century.

Notes

1. The leading Bulgarian authority on this subject is Dobrin Michev who had special access to the security service's files. His publications include: Dobrin Michev, *Makedonskiyat Vapros i Balgaro–Yugoslavskite Otnosheniya* [Macedonian Question and Bulgarian–Yugoslav Relations] (9 Septemvri 1944–Yuni 1946) (Sofia, 1994); 'Usiliyata na Yugoslavskata Komunisticheska Partiya da Ovladee Makedonskite Bezhanski Organisatsii v Balgaria' [Efforts of the Yugoslav Communist Party to Gain Command over Macedonian Refugee Organizations in Bulgaria] (9 Septemvri 1944–Yuni 1946), *Makedonski pregled*, 14 (1991), no. 1, pp. 33–4; 'Protsesat sreshtu VMRO 1946' [The Process against IMRO 1946], in Dimitar Gotsev and Dobrin Michev (eds.), *Sto Godini Vatreshna Makedono-Odrinska Revolyutsionna Organizatsia* [100 Years Internal Macedonian–Adrianople Organization] (Sofia, 1994); 'Makedonskiyat Nauchen Institut' [Macedonian Scientific Institute] (9 Sept. 1944–May 1947), *Makedonski pregled*, 14 (1991), no. 4, pp. 49–74.See also Petar Semerdzhiev *BKP, Makedonskijat Vapros i VMRO* [BCP, the Macedonian Question and IMRO (Sofia, 1990).
2. Voluminous literature on the subject includes Evangelos Kofos, *Nationalism and Communism in Macedonia* (Thessaloniki, 1964); Milcho Lalkov, *Ot Nadezhda kam Razocharovanie: Ideyata za Federatsiya v Balkanskiya Yugoiztok* [From Hope to Disappointment: Federation Idea in the Balkan South-East] 1944–1948 (Sofia, 1994); Georgi Daskalov, *Balgaro-Yugoslavski Politicheski Otnosheniya* [Bulgarian-Yugoslav Political Relations] 1944–1945 (Sofia, 1989). For a detailed bibliography see Ivanka Nedeva, 'Amerikanskata Istoriografiya za Mezhdubalkanskite Otnosheniya' [American Historiography on the Inter-Balkan Relations] 1944–1948, *Istoricheski pregled*, 1982, no. 5, pp. 91–104.
3. Elizabeth Barker, *Macedonia: Its Place in Balkan Power Politics* (London, Royal Institute of International Affairs, 1950), p. 44.
4. Michev, 'Protsesat...', p. 205.
5. *Ohrana* is a Bulgarian word for guard. On it, see Dobrin Michev 'Balgarskite Dobrovolcheski Druzhini v Kostursko, Lerinsko i Vodensko pres 1944 godina' [Bulgarian Voluntary Units in Kostur (Kastoria), Lerin (Florina) and Voden (Edessa) Regions during 1944], *Voennoistoricheski sbornik*, 56 (1996), no. 3, pp. 38–57.; Ioannis Koliopoulos, *Leilasia Fronimaton: To Makedoniko Zitima stin Katehomeni Ditiki Makedonia* [The Robbing of Allegiances: The Macedonian Question in the Occupied Western Macedonia] (1941–1944) (Thessaloniki, 1994).

6. Stephen Palmer and Robert King, *Yugoslav Communism and the Macedonian Question* (Hamden, Conn., 1971), pp. 64–5, 81, 114.

7. Elizabeth Barker, *British Policy in South-East Europe in the Second World War* (London, 1976), p. 185.

8. Michev, 'Balgarskite Dobrovolcheski..'; 'Protsesat…', p. 204.

9. Kostadin Paleshutski, *Yugoslavskata Komunisticheska Partiya i Makedonskiyat Vapros 1919–1945* [The Yugoslav Communist Party and the Macedonian Question] (Sofia, 1985), p. 320.

10. Semerdzhiev, *BKP, Makedonskijat Vapros*, pp. 14–17.

11. Ivan Mihailov, *Spomeni*, vol. 3, (1967), p. 555.

12. In the state hierarchy the State Security (*Darzhavna sigurnost*) was a special department for political surveillance, intelligence and counter-intelligence. Together with the Department of People's Militia (i.e. conventional police) it formed a General Department of People's Militia (*Glavna Direktsiya na Narodnata Militsiya*) within the Interior Ministry.The head of both State Security and General Department of People's Militia was Rusi Hristozov (TsDA (Tsentralen Darzhaven Arhiv) [Bulgarian Central State Archive], Memory N 3012 (Rusi Hristozov), pp. 180–7).

13. Michev, 'Protsesat…', pp. 205–9.

14. Semerdzhiev, *BKP…*, pp. 97–9.

15. TsDA (Tsentralen Darzhaven Arhiv) [Bulgarian Central State Arhive], Memory N 3012 (Rusi Hristozov), p. 122.

16. Michev, 'Protsesat…', pp. 206, 212–13.

17. *Ibid.* Kiril Drangov's father, Lieut.-Col. Boris Drangov, was a well-known figure in the early-twentieth-century Bulgarian–Macedonian revolutionary organisations. He was famed for exemplary behaviour as a Bulgarian army officer and after his death on the Salonica front during the Great War he was canonised in military circles. Temporarily forgotten, his canonisation was renewed by the late communist and post-communist Bulgarian army. Kiril Drangov's daughter, Mrs Raina Drangova, is presently (November 1996) a co-chairman of IMRO-Union of Macedonian Societies (IMRO-UMS).

18. TsDA, Memory N3012, 74.; Robert King, *Minorities under Communism. Nationalities as a Source of Tension among Balkan Communist States* (Cambridge, Mass., 1973), p. 66. Michev, 'Protsesat…', pp. 212–14.

19. This version is supported in Semerdzhiev, *BKP…*, pp. 96–7. One of Kourtev's men, Stoyan Boyadzhiev, advances another hypothesis: the communists were afraid of their *Zveno* allies, traditional IMRO's foes and projected the special pro-communist anti-*Zveno* organization (authors' interview with Mr Boyadzhiev).

20. TsDA, Memory N3012, p. 141.

21. Michev, 'Protsesat…', 214–20; Semerdzhiev, *BKP…*, p. 93; Stoyan Boyadzhiev, 'Nova Makedonska Borba' – Edna Pochti Neizvestna Makedonska Revoljutsionna Organizatsia' [New Macedonian Struggle – A Virtually Unknown Macedonian Revolutionary Organisation], *Makedonski pregled* 18 (1995), no. 4, p. 110.

22. No documented qualitative analysis of these persecutions has been made yet. According to Dimitar Gotsev's assessment, the number of imprisoned self-confessed IMRO-ists did not exceed a few hundred (authors' interview with Mr Gotsev).

23. The destiny of Mr Stoyan Boyadzhiev, the current honorary chairmen of the IMRO-UMS, could be instructive to this point. In the mid-1930s he had been a chairman of the Macedonian student society *Shar* in Sofia, in 1941–44 he was an editor of the Skopje newspaper *Tselokupna Balgaria* (Unified Bulgaria), in early 1946 he served as a liaison between Kourtev and the British embassy. He was sent to prisons or labour camps several times, the last one as late as 1959–60. Afterwards this former judge and assistant-professor in law was forced to earn a living as a low-paid electric technician (authors' interview with Mr Boyadzhiev).
24. TsDA, Memory 800 (Hristo Kalaidzhiev), 76; Michev, 'Makedonskiyat Vapros...', p. 175; Michev, 'Usiliyata...;, 33–34.
25. TsDA, 299/1/4, f. 126, application form for membership in a Macedonian cultural-educational society. The 299 file in the Bulgarian Central State Archive contains an important selection of UMCES papers.
26. TsDA, 299/2/1, f. 34–36, Minutes of the Central Leadership of the UMCES, 22 Nov. 1951.
27. TsDA, 299/2/2, f. 65–67, Minutes of the meeting of the Macedonian Cultural Educational Society 'Dame Gruev', Veliko Tarnovo, 16 April 1951; 299/2/1, 80–87, Minutes of the Central Leadership of the UMCES of the proceedings held together with the leadership of the student section and the representatives of the Comsomol's Central Committee, 7 March 1954.
28. On Macedonian policy of Bulgaria during the 1950s and 1960s see King, *Minorities under Communism*, pp. 58–71, 187–218.
29. TsDA, 299/3/16, f. 36, Central Leadership of UMCES (Macedonian Cultural Educational Society) in Gabrovo, 15 May 1959.
30. TsDA, 299/2/1, f. 28, Minutes of the Central Leadership of the UMCES, 6 Sept. 1951.
31. Fresh insight into late 1970s–early 1980s inter-Balkan relations is offered by the Bulgarian ambassadors at the time: Nikolay Todorov, *Poslanikat-Istorik: Svidetelstvo za Balgaro – Gratskite Otnosheniya prez 80-te gg.* [The Ambassador-Historian: Evidence on Bulgarian–Greek Relations in the 1980s] (Sofia, 1996); Raiko Nikolov, *Diplomatsiya na Chetiri Ochi: iz Dnevnika na Edin Balgarski poslanik v Yugoslaviya* [Four Eyed Diplomacy: from a Diary of a Bulgarian Ambassador in Yugoslavia] (Sofia, 1995). The latter is especially instructive on Macedonia as a central problem in Bulgarian–Yugoslav relations.
32. Using the terms 'nationalist' or 'nationalism' the authors do not imply any pejorative element. Rather, nationalism is regarded as an instrument for modernisation, 'a movement for moral regeneration' John Hutchinson, *The Dynamics of Cultural Nationalism* (London, 1987), pp. 13–14 or 'the realpolitic phenomenon'. In other words, it is 'neither good, nor bad' (Georg Brunner, *Nationality Problems and Minority Conflicts in Eastern Europe* (Gutersloh, 1996), p. 28).
33. Aleksandrov and Zhivkov', 'Signal Memo on the Situation in Pirin Region, on the Nature of the Sandanism and Macedonianism, on the Perspectives of the "Macedonian" nation', 1 July 1985; 'Statement on the Bulgarian National Character of the Macedonian Liberation Movement and on the Advance of the Serbian Macedonianism', by Aleksandrov; 1984. 'The Facts on the Flowing out of Our Historical Heritage to Yugoslavia' by Aleksandrov, 26 March 1986. [Ivan Aleksandrov's private archive].

34. IMRO-UMS archive, memorial book of the Cultural-Educational Club 'Gotse Delchev', entry of 4 June 1985.
35. Some of Alexandrov's lectures were issued by the Macedonian club as a pamphlet (Ivan Aleksandrov, *Za Novo Mislene i Nov Podhod po Nyakoi Vaprosi ot Balgarskata Istorija* [For a New Approach and a New Thinking on Some Questions of the Bulgarian National History] (Sofia, 1988) which, however, was withdrawn from distribution by the authorities. Aleksandrov himself was dismissed from the CC of BCP and forced to retire.
36. IMRO-UMS archive, memorial book of the Cultural-Educational Club 'Gotse Delchev', entry of 13 June 1989. Parvanov's critique of the novels by Kostadin Kyulyumov, the former counter intelligence officer, was published: Georgi Parvanov, 'Za Dostovernostta na Edna Istoricheska Trilogiya' [On the Reliability of One Historical Trilogy], *Vekove*, 18 (1989), no. 2, pp. 81–5.
   Mr. Parvanov switched to a political career in the postcommunist period. By November 1996 he was a vice-chairman of the ruling Bulgarian Socialist Party.
37. Krasimir Karakachanov, *VMRO: 100 Godini Borba za Makedoniya* [IMRO: 100 Years of Struggle for Macedonia] (Sofia, 2 rev. edn. 1996), pp. 187–188.
38. *Ustav i Platfoma na VMRO – Sayuz na Makedonskite Druzhestva* [Statute and Platform of the IMRO – Union of Macedonian Societies] (Sofia, 1990), 3–4.
39. Authors' interview with Mr Krasimir Karakachanov.
40. *Ustav i Platfoma na VMRO – Sayuz na Makedonskite Druzhestva* [Statute and Platform of the IMRO – Union of Macedonian Societies] (Sofia, 1994), p. 3.
41. Authors' interview with Mr Krasimir Karakachanov; a brief survey of IMRO-UMS activities is also offered in Hugh Poulton, *Who are the Macedonians?* (London, 1995), pp. 160–2.
42. Mr Nikolay Kanchev, the IMRO-UMS secretary, stated to the authors that by December 1996 the organisation comprised 213 societies.

Chapter **13**

Albania, Macedonia and the British military missions, 1943 and 1944

Reginald Hibbert

The British officers who were parachuted into Albania by the Special Operations Executive (SOE)[1] in 1943 to assist the anti-Axis resistance did not come under the same staff section in SOE Cairo as those who were parachuted into neighbouring Macedonia. The latter counted as 'Yugoslav'. There was no special provision for border regions or minority areas. Briefings about Albania and the Albanians were poor. Officers were told that they were destined for Albania only a few weeks before being sent in. There was no opportunity for any useful language training. At that time only a handful of people who had lived in King Zog's Albania knew anything about the country. One of them, Mrs Margaret (Fanny) Hasluck, coordinated intelligence in the Albanian Section at Rustum Building in Cairo, but she was more knowledgeable about ethnography (in the Edith Durham tradition) than anything else. There was no instruction in Albania's short and troubled history and none in wider Balkan history. The bitter problems of relations between Albanians and Slavs (Serbs) in Kosovo, western Macedonia and southern Montenegro, or with Greeks in southern Albania (northern Epirus), were not mentioned. The officers were told to keep clear of politics and concentrate on promoting resistance to the Italian occupiers until September 1943, and thereafter to the Germans. All of this was a natural consequence of the improvisations of wartime.

The Communist Party of Yugoslavia (CPY) had established a regional committee for Kosovo and Metohija, the Kosmet Regional Committee, in 1940. The aim was to mobilise support among the Albanian population of Kosovo, and this led to the process by which the Communist Party of Albania (CPA)[2] was brought into being between November 1941 and March 1943. At this point Tito's close colleague Tempo (Svetozar Vukmanovic-Tempo)[3] appeared on the Albanian scene. He was the main

184

delegate of the CPY and the General Staff of the Yugoslav National Liberation Army for Macedonia. His concern was to create and coordinate resistance movements among the Albanians of southern Serbia (Kosovo) and western Macedonia, together with a Macedonian resistance movement directed by the CPY and not by the Communist Party of Bulgaria, linked across the southern borders of Macedonia and Albania with EAM, the resistance movement in Greece directed by the Greek Communist Party. His ambition to set up a Balkan General Staff soon had to be abandoned, as the Greek and Bulgarian communists would have none of it. The new Albanian Communist Party was more amenable, chiefly because until late 1943 it had seemed that communist parties under the Comintern were committed to the principle of self-determination, and that this would apply in Kosovo and western Macedonia if the communist parties came to power as a result of the war.

Tempo visited Albania three times between March and August 1943. During his last visit it began to appear that the CPY's commitment to self-determination was being subordinated to its need to cultivate Serbian national feeling and preserve the territorial integrity of the old Yugoslavia. But by then it had already been agreed that the Albanian National Liberation Army (ANLA)[4] would send two detachments to join the Kosmet forces, which were being headed by Fadil Hoxha,[5] an Albanian who had been appointed by Tito's General Staff to conduct operations in northern Albania and Kosovo, and another detachment to cooperate with the Yugoslav Macedonian command in Dibra and the other Albanian-populated areas of western Macedonia. This latter detachment was put under the charge of Haxhi Lleshi,[6] who was a delegate of the General Staff of the ANLA.

After the dismemberment of Yugoslavia in mid-1941, Kosovo and western Macedonia had been given to Albania. Albanians everywhere could not fail to regard this as other than the rightful correction of a grave injustice to their nation dating from 1912.[7] Their satisfaction at having at last a Greater Albania was diminished by their sense of being a puppet state, first of Italy and then of Germany. But it ensured that the attitude of most Albanians towards the Allies on one side and the Axis on the other remained ambivalent throughout the war. The ambivalence was aggravated by hereditary fear of Serb domination, which was greatest among those who lived nearest to the Serbs, i.e., the Albanians of Kosovo, north Albania and Macedonia. It became more acute in these areas as the war went on and Tito and the CPY became more dominant in Yugoslavia and more favoured by the Allies. The threat of 'Slav communism', as they invariably called it, was magnified by German propaganda and loomed much larger in north Albanian and Kosovar minds than the undesirability of the German occupation. The CPY called the CPA into existence and made it an auxiliary in Kosovo and western Macedonia in the hope of circumventing this difficulty. The stratagem was not very successful.

The British officers who formed the SOE missions or teams in Albania knew nothing of the interplay between the CPY and the CPA, beyond the general fact that the CPY was the CPA's senior partner. They knew nothing of Tempo's interventions and very little about Fadil Hoxha's Kosmet activities. They knew about the creation of Greater Albania by the Italians and Germans but were not informed about the wider and deeper implications of it, probably because these would have been regarded as 'political'. When they encountered Kosovo and Macedonian issues or entered those territories they did so in a state of innocence. What they found there tended to be baffling, confusing and even unintelligible given their lack of background.

When Brigadier 'Trotsky' Davies[8] arrived in Albania in mid-October 1943 to take command of the SOE missions in Albania, he regarded Kosovo and western Macedonia as belonging to his area of responsibility. Peter Kemp quotes him as saying in late October, 'my parish includes not only the old frontiers of Albania, but the new regions incorporated into the country by the Axis, that is the whole of Kosovo, the western fringe of Macedonia from the Vardar valley to Lake Ohrid and a small corner of Montenegro.'[9] This implied a pragmatic, operational acceptance of Italy's and Germany's creation of a Greater Albania at the expense of Yugoslavia. It is difficult to believe that the Foreign Office in London can have known about it, as the FO regarded Yugoslavia as an allied country towards which Britain had obligations, while it was not sure that Albania was a viable country or what would happen to it after the war.

Already in July before Brigadier Davies's arrival, Flight Lieutenant Andy Hands had been sent to the Dibra region to make contact with the Dibra chieftains, and Major Richard Riddell and Captain Anthony Simcox were parachuted to him near Dibra in mid-September to establish the Stables Mission there, while Hands moved to north Albania near the Kosovo border. There is a Dibra district in Albania proper, with Peshkopia as its capital, but Dibra town, the true centre of the Dibra region, lies with a large part of the Dibra area in Yugoslavia. The British officers in 1943 treated the Dibra region as a continuous whole, regarding Dibra town as the main centre and Peshkopia as the secondary one. This coincided with the Albanian view of what the true order should be.

After Italy capitulated in early September 1943, Haxhi Lleshi occupied Dibra town with his force of Albanian partisans, that is to say a unit of the ANLA as had been agreed with Tempo. Haxhi Lleshi and his family came from the Dibra area. In August 1944 I happened to be with him when he visited his home village near Homesh on the western bank of the Drin river. He was lavishly fêted there by the villagers as their most distinguished son; but that was after the Partisan victory. In September and October 1943 he commanded Dibra town, but the countryside and Peshkopia were in the hands of the traditional chieftains. Of these the most prominent was Fiqri Dinë,[10] who had played a leading part in Zog's Albania and who later, in July 1944, became prime minister of the puppet government in Tirana[11] when the Partisan forces from the south began to overrun the north.

Flt. Lt. Andy Hands and, after mid-October, Major Richard Riddell liaised with both Haxhi Lleshi and Fiqri Dinë and tried to persuade them of the importance of collaborating together if the Dibra area was not to be seized by German forces. They shuttled between Dibra town and Peshkopia developing contacts with lesser leading figures on both sides. Their efforts were fruitless. Unknown to them, the chance of cooperation between the National Liberation Movement (LNC) led by Enver Hoxha and the nationalist groupings known as the Balli Kombëtar (BK – republican) and Legaliteti (LEG, Zogist – royalist) had already been lost at a conference at Mukjë[12] in early August. Under the influence of Tempo and the CPY, Enver Hoxha and the CPA had rejected a compromise with the nationalists precisely because the latter demanded that the Albanian war-aim should be to keep the Greater Albania in being after the war.

The situation in Dibra was therefore full of contradictions. Fiqri Dinë and his fellow chieftains were committed to keeping western Macedonia for Albania but did not possess Dibra town and were not prepared to help Haxhi Lleshi and the LNC/ANLA to defend it against German attack. Haxhi Lleshi and the LNC, who did hold Dibra, had probably not yet digested the implications of the Mukjë meeting or appreciated that self-determination for Dibra was no longer likely to be conceded by the CPY; but they had already received an order from Enver Hoxha not to collaborate with the nationalists, although there could be no hope of holding Dibra if the chieftains did not help to hold a line against the Germans in the surrounding countryside. A further complication was added by the fact that some Albanian chieftains were already in league with the Germans out of enmity to the Serbs, enmity to 'Slav communism' and short-term ambition and misjudgements about the way the war was going. Chief among these at the time was Xhem Gostivari, who had become powerful in Macedonia with Italian and German help. Haxhi Lleshi had liaison arrangements with the Macedonian partisans, but it was not clear how these were organised. When Xhem Gostivari was pressing hard against Dibra in October, the Macedonian partisans provided relief by attacking Gostivar, Xhem's home town. There were said to be one or two Macedonian partisan officers with Haxhi Lleshi's staff, but there was no sign of Albanian partisan units being under Macedonian command or vice versa.

At the end of October Major Richard Riddell learned that an attack on Dibra was being prepared by the Germans and Xhem Gostivari together. Haxhi Lleshi claimed that Fiqri Dinë and his colleagues were conniving with Xhem Gostivari. For his part, Fiqri Dinë complained that Haxhi Lleshi and his Partisans were oppressing the people of Dibra and trying to turn them against the chieftains. When Brigadier Davies received this news at his HQ camp at Biza he despatched Major Peter Kemp and Captain Alan Hare to reinforce and support Riddell. These three British officers and Lt. Michael Lis, a Polish officer who had recently been parachuted in and had joined Riddell, had difficult and of course separate conferences with Fiqri Dinë and Haxhi Lleshi, managing to get the former to agree not to attack Dibra and the latter to agree without much conviction on the desirability of a united front.

At that time it was possible to eat well and sleep comfortably in Dibra in a hotel run by an Italian, and there were many Italians at large in the town. Kemp and Hare enjoyed the luxury for only one night and then made the journey back to Biza to report to the Brigadier. By then it was 6 November and it was clear that German offensives were developing on all sides of the central massif of Cermenikë where Enver Hoxha and Brigadier Davies both had their HQs. Major Kemp was told to turn round straight away in order to go to Kosovo to establish himself there. His route took him back to Dibra, from where he planned to make a reconnaissance deeper into Macedonia, to Gostivar and Tetovo in the Vardar valley, before moving further north to Kosovo.

These aspirations were rapidly swept away by events. Xhem Gostivari and his Albanians, stiffened by some German troops, attacked Dibra on 16 November and rapidly overwhelmed Haxhi Lleshi's Partisans. Although Fiqri Dinë denied that he was collaborating with Xhem Gostivari, he sent to Riddell, through Simcox, advance warning of the day and hour of the attack. At the last moment Haxhi Lleshi reluctantly agreed to a proposal by Major Riddell that the British officers should fall back on Peshkopia and rally the chieftains for a flank attack on Xhem Gostivari's forces. But it was already too late, Peshkopia had also come under attack from mixed German and Albanian forces, and Captain Simcox had had to escape northwards into the mountains of the Drin valley. Riddell and Kemp were themselves captured on the way to Peshkopia by the Albanian followers of local chieftains who were collaborating with the Germans against 'Slav communism' or anything or anyone else who might interfere with their patriarchal ways and local despotisms. These 'collaborators' did not want trouble with the Allies, and Riddell and Kemp were soon able to make their way to the house of a more friendly chieftain, Ramadan Kalloshi, who was closer to Fiqri Dinë's circle and had already been one of Riddell's contacts. Thence they were able to retreat further northwards and to rejoin Simcox in the house of Cen Elezi at Sllovë.

Cen Elezi was a leading figure in the Drin valley and indeed in the northern Dibra area. He was the head of the Ndreu family and had numerous sons, brothers, nephews and relations by marriage, giving him useful contacts of every political colour everywhere in north eastern Albania. His brother Esat Ndreu was acting as Haxhi Lleshi's political commissar. One of his nephews, Dali Ndreu, occupied an even higher position in the LNC and ANLA, becoming Enver Hoxha's leading general in 1944. Other members of the family cultivated relations with the authorities in Tirana, the Balli Kombëtar and the Zogists (Legaliteti). Cen himself was prepared to be the Allies' principal friend in north-eastern Albania if only they would choose to turn to him and channel funds and supplies to the 'nationalists' through him. He was not alone in this. There were other important chieftains in the north who regarded themselves as equally or more suitable for such a role. Unfortunately for Albania, none of them ever did more than hold out vague promises of resistance.

When he reached Sllovë, Kemp still had thoughts of exploring western Macedonia. Cen Elezi had connections there and the neighbouring Lita family also claimed to be well connected there, but their coverage was more exclusively nationalist than that of the Ndreus.

The Germans gave no respite. They attacked Sllovë, again with the help of Albanian auxiliaries, and scattered all those who had taken refuge there. This completed their victory in north-eastern Albania. In the space of a few days in mid-November they had destroyed the LNC's hopes of raising the flag of resistance among the Albanians of Macedonia, the British Mission's hopes of including Macedonia in Brigadier Davies's parish, and the CPA's hopes of establishing a grip on northern Albania; and by making an example of the Ndreu family they had warned the nationalist chieftains and their followers of the severe price that would be exacted for any attempts at resistance. Haxhi Lleshi withdrew the remnants of his force westwards across the Drin and eventually rejoined Enver Hoxha's General Staff in the south. Fiqri Dinë went to Tirana and became increasingly committed to collaboration with the Germans against the LNC. Esat Ndreu became the leader of a small remaining LNC *cheta* which had difficulty in surviving through the winter among the hostile 'nationalists' of the Drin valley. Major Riddell and Captain Simcox began a frustrating winter of shifts between houses in the mountains above the Drin as they tried to persuade the various chieftains to declare themselves for resistance. Cen Elezi returned to Tirana and took the rank of Colonel in the service of the quisling government, while his family re-established its client network, at the same time becoming more prudent about helping the British. Major Kemp moved off northwards and, with the help of the Litas, met Muharrem Bajraktar[13] in Luma. Muharrem was a chieftain with national and not only local standing, or at any rate conducted himself as such. He introduced Kemp to the Kryeziu family[14] of Kosovo.

Kemp joined Andy Hands for a time in northern Albania, north of the Drin, and there he came in touch with the Kosmet partisans under Fadil Hoxha. Fadil's political commissar was a certain Mehmet Hoxha, a former Prefect of Dibra district, whom Kemp had met previously under Enver Hoxha's auspices near Tirana and then again with Haxhi Lleshi at Dibra. Fadil was Tito's nominee for the Kosmet task and Mehmet was Enver Hoxha's. Both worked with equal zeal to frustrate Kemp's activity in Kosovo, and more particularly his relationship with the Kryezius. Like western Macedonia, Kosovo was not going to be assimilated to Brigadier Davies's 'parish'.

Brigadier Davies was wounded and captured by the Germans, assisted by Albanian auxiliaries, in early January 1944. At the same time Enver Hoxha and his General Staff had to flee from the Cermenikë massif east of Tirana and make their way to south Albania. They managed to survive the Germans' winter offensives, but any activity in the direction of Dibra and Macedonia was out of the question. Dibra and Macedonia did not feature again in LNC/ANLA activity until late June 1944, by which time the LNC's strength in the south was rapidly increasing and the ANLA, having gathered recruits for several new brigades in the spring, was expanding sufficiently to form a couple of divisions.

Haxhi Lleshi reappeared in the Dibra region as delegate of the ANLA General Staff on 23 June 1944. On 27 June, Faik Shehu, a chieftain from the Peshkopia area who had been supporting Haxhi Lleshi in October and November and had taken refuge along with the British officers at

Cen Elezi's house at the time of the November debacle, announced to Major Riddell that a National Liberation Council for Dibra had been formed a few days earlier. A little later we learned (I had been a member of Riddell's mission since December) that the 1st Division of the ANLA, consisting of the 1st, 4th and 5th Brigades, under the command of Dali Ndreu, had crossed the Shkumbin river into central and northern Albania on 26 June. Esat Ndreu, as leader of the local partisan *cheta*, had been in touch with us only rarely in the winter months but now began to approach us importunately with demands for air-drops of supplies, arms, ammunition, uniforms and boots.

In conformity with Enver Hoxha's strict instructions, none of the LNC/ANLA leaders told us anything about their intentions; but we were soon able to piece together a picture of their somewhat disjointed operations. The fighting was begun by local forces. Aqif Lleshi, a member of Haxhi's family, attacked and burned the house of Hysni Dema, a notorious gendarmerie commander, in south Dibra, while Esat Ndreu and Faik Shehu seized Peshkopia in the north. Two days later, on 8 July 1944, the 1st Partisan Brigade of the ANLA, commanded by Mehmet Shehu,[15] appeared on the scene from the west while the 2nd Macedonian Brigade appeared from the east. German forces from Dibra engaged them but were repulsed. The 2nd Battalion of the 1st Brigade was detached to strike at Peshkopia with Esat Ndreu's cheta but suffered a serious mauling when they attacked the stronghold of a local collaborationist chieftain. This caused local opinion to turn against them. Peshkopia changed hands twice, but the Battalion ran out of supplies and on 13 July retreated with Haxhi Lleshi, Esat and a number of wounded to our mission's mountain base on the flank of Mount Korab, pleading for supplies. Meanwhile the 4th Brigade had arrived to the south of Dibra and took over the attack on the town jointly with Macedonian Partisan forces, while Mehmet Shehu marched north and re-took Peshkopia. By the 15th July he too had run out of ammunition and, like his 2nd Battalion, retreated up the mountain to our camp. By then the 2nd Battalion, with Haxhi Lleshi and Esat Ndreu's cheta, had marched off over the mountain in the direction of Macedonia in order to find a way back to the main ANLA forces near Dibra. The 5th Brigade had joined the 4th Brigade in front of Dibra, but they too were running short of supplies and had to withdraw. This meant that the Germans, who had been reinforced from Struga, could not hit them, but the Partisan offensive was for the moment stalled.

HQ Balkan Air Force[16] at Bari refused to send any air-drops of supplies because of their belief (only temporary) that the Partisans had precipitated civil war; and we had only scanty reserves from three air-drops which we had received in June. Our predicament was highly uncomfortable. The 1st Brigade was the elite formation of the ANLA and had been shaped by Mehmet Shehu into a good, hardened fighting force. The men (and some young women partisans) were almost entirely in rags; almost none of them had boots; many had nothing on their feet at all. They were living on starvation rations, had made forced marches for many days and had been engaged in severe fighting with German troops. And yet we could not obtain supplies for them. We looked after their wounded as best we could without medical resources. We were able to feed a few of them. Mehmet Shehu rapidly decided to march over Mount Korap into Macedonia and return to the Dibra region from the east. Major Riddell decided that we would go with him and we gave our signallers brief messages to radio to Bari explaining what we were doing. At that stage of the war in the Balkans we were under no illusion that western Macedonia was in the Albanian 'parish'. Brigadier Fitzroy Maclean had been in Yugoslavia since September 1943 and his network of officers supporting Tito's National Liberation Movement now extended throughout the country. We pleaded 'force majeure' as our excuse for trespassing.

The march into Macedonia began on 16 July 1944 and was arduous, much of it on precipitous paths in pouring rain. The partisans seemed very much concerned about possible hostile reaction from Albanian villages where they were suspected of being carriers of 'Slav communism'. There were occasional exchanges of fire at long range across deep valleys and ravines. It was forbidden to attract attention by lighting fires. We descended to the Dibra–Gostivar road, climbed to the Bistra Plateau, descended to the Dibra-Kicevo road and climbed again in the direction of Struga and Lake Ochrid. On the way we passed several villages which stood empty and in ruins. These seemed to be Macedonian villages which had been destroyed by Albanians settling accounts with Slav neighbours. The partisans blamed Xhem Gostivari's brigandage, but this was probably too facile an explanation.

On 19 July 1944 we arrived at a large and prosperous-looking Macedonian village and received a warm welcome. The exhausted partisans could at last rest a little and eat. On the 20th we camped in some beautiful high meadows with views of splendid mountains stretching in every direction, and we addressed ourselves to the task of persuading HQ Balkan Air Force at Bari that it would make sense to drop

'Albanian' supplies in Macedonia. Mehmet Shehu, meanwhile, was in touch with the Macedonian HQ of the Yugoslav National Liberation Army. The ANLA 1st Brigade received some supplies from that source. We understood that Tempo was in charge. We were repeatedly reproached by the Partisans for our inability to obtain supply-drops from Bari when, we were told, there was an officer of Brigadier Fitzroy Maclean's Yugoslav operation only four hours' march away who had received seven aircraft loads for the Macedonian forces in the last two days. The delay lasted only seven days, but it was a most uncomfortable time. At last, on 27 and 28 July, we received four drops (perhaps 8 tons in total). There was plenty of ammunition for the Brigade's Italian weapons and a quantity of arms and equipment. Two days later, on 30 July, Mehmet Shehu announced that he was taking his Brigade back to Dibra for an attack on the town jointly with the Macedonian forces on 1 August.

We used the interval to seek out the officer who had been receiving drops for the Macedonian partisans. On the way we had some fine views of Struga and Lake Ochrid. He turned out to be a friend of mine from Cairo, a South African officer of Scottish origin, Captain Donald Macdonald.[17] We soon decided that we did not need to envy him. The partisan war in Yugoslavia and Brigadier Maclean's cooperation with Tito had developed to a point at which outlying missions such as Donald Macdonald's functioned as little more than quartermasters or supply officers funnelling loads of 'matériel' to units whose operations were outside their scope and often outside their knowledge. Donald Macdonald was lonely, bored by lack of action and variety and not living at all comfortably. We suspected that this was how Enver Hoxha would have liked us to be. We were very glad that we were still enjoying a more primitive stage of the national liberation war, in which we could be in touch with front-line action and indulge in a good deal of movement and individual enterprise. Donald Macdonald willingly and helpfully joined us in putting across to Bari the desirability of treating our partisans on a par with his as both were attacking a common target.

By hard marching we managed to rejoin Mehmet Shehu on the hills overlooking Dibra from the east by the morning of 1 August 1944. We were so tired that we slept through the first hours of the fighting. We learned that Tempo had issued an order for the assault and Mehmet Shehu had been put in command of a joint Albanian and Macedonian force, with joint rear and advance HQs. We were told that the Macedonian commander equivalent to Mehmet Shehu was absent at a political conference. The attack on 1 August was launched by two battalions of the Albanian 1st Brigade and one Macedonian battalion. It appeared that a large part of the available force was deployed to cut and block access routes and guard the flanks and rear, presumably because of mistrust of Albanian nationalists in the hinterland who were potentially hostile to partisan purveyors of 'Slav communism' and who might facilitate and assist German attempts to reinforce the town. The three battalions engaged in the battle fought well but could not penetrate the Germans' fortified innerline.

While we had been in Macedonia, and unknown to Mehmet Shehu, the 4th and 5th Brigades of the 1st Division had closed in towards Dibra from the west and north, the 5th Brigade having first secured Peshkopia. Dali Ndreu now ordered Mehmet Shehu and the 1st Brigade to leave the investment of Dibra to the 4th and 5th Brigades, in cooperation with the Macedonians, and to move westwards to the Mati valley to contain and eventually crush Abas Kupi[18] and the Zogists and to begin the build-up of a threat to Tirana. We marched away from Dibra with Mehmet Shehu's column on 2 August. A few days later it was announced that a 2nd Division was being formed, that the two Divisions would now form 1st Corps, that Dali Ndreu was being promoted to command 1 Corps, and that Mehmet Shehu would take over the command of the 1st Division. So by 9 August Mehmet Shehu was back in command of operations against Dibra, with his Divisional HQ at Peshkopia.

Major Victor Smith[19] had arrived shortly before this from south Albania (where he had been with Lt. Col. Alan Palmer's HQ mission at Enver Hoxha's General Staff HQ) to become British Liaison Officer with 1st Division and 1st Corps. Richard Riddell sent me to meet him and I marched back from the Klos area to Peshkopia with Haxhi Lleshi and his partisan escort. It was then that I saw Haxhi Lleshi being fêted in his native Homesh area near the Drin, as recounted above, and also watched him regulating affairs in villages as we passed, preaching severity against inveterate enemies of the LNC and moderation for waverers or opposition rank and file. The battle of Dibra was still swaying to and fro, the Germans having been reinforced and Victor Smith having secured some good supply drops for the 1st Division. The inner ring of fortifications near the barracks in Dibra still proved too much of an obstacle for the Partisans. Victor Smith called on the Balkan Air Force at Bari to intervene, and on 10 and 11 August Beaufighters of the RAF destroyed the barracks with rocket-fire, much to Mehmet Shehu's satisfaction.

This delayed German plans for a counter-attack with support from Xhem Gostivari. When they finally succeeded in breaking out towards Peshkopia they were driven back and the Balkan Air Force struck again. Dibra was finally freed on 30 August 1944.

By then I was back with Major Riddell in the Mati valley, where we received 17 air-drops in August, about 30 tons of supplies. At the end of the month we left the 1st Brigade very well equipped and we moved southwards to Biza, Brigadier Davies's old camp site, to liaise with the new 2nd Division HQ and prepare for moves against Tirana.

I had one more glimpse of Dibra. Bari had authorised Richard Riddell and me to leave Albania when we could contrive to do so. We had with us at Biza Lt. the Hon. Rowland Winn (later Lord St. Oswald) who had broken his leg when parachuting to join us. I went off to Dibra on 20 September to see if the old landing field there could possibly be used by an aircraft from Bari to fly the three of us out. It proved to be unusable. Dibra town was in a sorry state. Food supplies were short; the ruins had not been cleared; the place seemed dead. Esat Ndreu's *cheta* had taken in many recruits from Dibra and had become the 18th Brigade and had moved northwards along the Drin valley supporting the ANLA Brigades which were destined to move into Kosovo in October. It was difficult to make out who was in charge in Dibra town. The town command appeared to be run by Albanians, but they were said to be responsible to the Macedonian General Staff. Aqif Lleshi was said to be recruiting a new Brigade which would come under Macedonian command. There was no difficulty in moving to and fro across the old frontier. There was nothing for a British officer to do there.

The Albanian National Liberation Movement and the Albanian National Liberation Army had played a major role in 'liberating' Dibra town and the surrounding area, but they had not achieved anything beyond Dibra in western Macedonia. For its part, the Macedonian branch of the Yugoslav National Liberation Movement did not seem to have had much success in western Macedonia. It did not feel strong enough to take the major part in the Dibra operation. Xhem Gostivari and his Albanian followers, with material and propaganda support from the Germans, remained a force to be reckoned with to the end. Throughout the war Albanian nationalist, anti-Slav feeling made western Macedonia a sterile region for Tito and Tempo on the one hand and for Enver Hoxha and Haxhi Lleshi on the other. The Yugoslavs were able to ensure that the old frontier stayed where it was and to frustrate the Albanian communists' dreams of self-determination. The ethnic Albanian problem in western

Macedonia stagnated and proved to be in no way easily amenable to manipulation by the Yugoslav and Albanian Communist Parties. The situation has not changed fundamentally in the half century which has elapsed since then. The problem remains unresolved.

Notes

1. The Special Operations Executive, SOE, was a secret organisation set up in London in mid-1940 to coordinate all action, by way of subversion and sabotage, against the enemy overseas. Its offices for the Balkans were in Cairo in 1943, under the wing of GHQ Middle East. They moved to Bari in 1944 and came under the command of HQ, Balkan Air Force under the Supreme Allied Commander, Mediterranean.
2. For a fuller account of the formation of the Albanian Communist Party, see Hibbert , *Albania's National Liberation Struggle'* (Pinter, 1991), pp. 11–22. (A paper-back edition is being published by Zeno, London, in the spring of 1999.)
3. Ibid. pp. 23–6. Tempo's own account of these events can be found in his book *Struggle for the Balkans'*, by Svetozar Vukmanovic (General Tempo) (Merlin Press, 1990).
4. The ANLA was the military arm of the LNC (the Movement of National Liberation). Both of them were controlled by Enver Hoxha and the small, tightly organised, and secretive Albanian Communist Party. In 1943 the main emphasis was on national liberation and not on communist revolution. The General Staff of the ANLA was therefore the body in which most of the top talents of the CPA were to be found at that time. These included Haxhi Lleshi. The ANLA was more commonly known as the Partisans. Delegates of the General Staff were sent into areas where ANLA units were operating to ensure that the Party line was strictly applied by commanders and in areas which became 'liberated'.
5. Fadil Hoxha was a Kosovar, educated in Albania, and an early participant in communist groups in Albania. From 1941 he returned to Kosovo and occupied high positions in Tito's Yugoslavia until the collapse of that country began at the end of the 1980s.
6. Haxhi Lleshi's family was prominent in the Dibra province of Albania. After the war he occupied prominent offices under Enver Hoxha and was for a time President of the country.
7. In 1912, as an outcome of the Balkan wars, Kosovo was allocated to Serbia by the then Great Powers.
8. Brigadier Davies's own account of his mission in Albania is in his book *'Illyrian Venture* (Bodley Head, 1952).
9. See Peter Kemp, *No Colours or Crest* (Cassell, 1958), p. 153.
10. Fiqri Dinë was personally on bad terms with the Lleshi family and was strongly anti-communist and therefore anti-LNC. He had fallen out with King Zog in the 1930s and was republican in sentiment as well as strongly nationalist, which was the hallmark of the Balli Kombëtar or 'National Union' movement.
11. When the Germans occupied Albania after the collapse of Italy they restored the pre-war constitution, but with a Council of Regency instead of a King.

The government was allowed to profess itself neutral, but the Greater Albania carved out of the Albanian areas of dismembered Yugoslavia remained in being. By these manoeuvres the Germans sowed confusion among the 'nationalist' politicians of the old order and identified the communist-led LNC as the enemy. In the end this opened the way for the latter to become the total victors.

12. For the Mukjë conference, see Hibbert, *'Albania's National Liberation Struggle'*, pp. 56 and 57.

13. Muharrem Bajraktar, like Fiqri Dinë, had helped Ahmed Zogu to power in the 1920s but had then been pushed aside. He had a network of contacts in Yugoslavia and more especially in Kosovo and Macedonia and considered himself to be as capable and worthy of assuming power in Albania as anyone else. The Lita family was less ambitious but at the same time more extreme in its anti-communism, and was closer to the old type of border baron in the high country under Mount Korap.

14. The Kryeziu family in Kosovo, like the Ndreu family in the Black Drin valley, had connections in every political direction. Unlike the Ndreu high-landers, and being Kosovars, they had a more open attitude and worldly-wise experience. They held out the hope of a centrist compromise between nationalists and Partisans/communists. This made them very attractive to the British. But in the last stage of the war the victorious Partisans, having toyed with them, destroyed them.

15. Mehmet Shehu was the outstanding military figure on the Partisan/LNC side. He formed and led the 1st Partisan Brigade which was the corps d'élite of the ANLA. It played a key part in the survival of the LNC through the winter 1943/44 and then served as the spearhead of the rapidly growing ANLA in 1944. But Mehmet Shehu was subordinated to Dali Ndreu (nephew of Cen Elezi) in the ANLA and was not co-opted into the Politburo of the Albanian Communist Party until after the war. He then became . Enver Hoxha's hatchet man, the mailed fist around which Hoxha purported to draw a velvet glove. Finally, in 1981, Shehu too was destroyed by Hoxha (Dali Ndreu and other Partisan leaders having been destroyed many years earlier). He was much feared and hated and to this day no one has ventured to rehabilitate him in Albania.

16. HQ Balkan Air Force. See footnote 1. For a full account of the battle of Dibra and British reactions to it, see Hibbert, *Albania's National Liberation Struggle*, chapter 11. For the organisational structure of the British command, see *ibid.*, p. 169. For an account of events from the 'nationalist' point of view, see Julian Amery, *Sons of the Eagle* (Macmillan, 1948) and *Approach March* (Hutchinson, 1973), or David Smiley *Albanian Assignment* (Chatto & Windus, 1984), all three of which concentrate on the civil war aspect of the fighting.

17. Donald Macdonald is still living in Capetown. He has kept in touch with the author ever since the war and with Yugoslav Partisan leaders whom he knew in Macedonia in the war; but he has not made any written record.

18. Abas Kupi was a loyal follower of King Zog and formed and led the Zogist 'Legaliteti' party from 1943 until he was forced to flee from Albania at the end of 1944. He was the chieftain of the Mati district, which was Zog's home district. In 1942 and 1943 he worked with the LNC but left it as it

became more obviously communist-dominated. Amery's *Sons of the Eagle* gives a full account of Kupi's activity. He did not manage to build a movement outside his own area and, being illiterate, could not hope to do so. He was a fine example of an Albanian chieftain in the old style, and was totally destroyed by the Partisan victory.

19. Victor Smith succeeded Lt. Colonel Alan Palmer as head of the British Mission at Enver Hoxha's HQ in September 1944, and he became a member of the British Military Mission in Tirana which maintained relations with Enver Hoxha's government until 1946, shortly before the Corfu Channel incident put an end to diplomatic relations between the UK and Albania for over 40 years. Unfortunately, neither Palmer nor Smith has written about the Partisan experience, although I was able to draw on their memories to some extent when writing my book.

Part IV

International relations of the new state

Chapter **14**

Engineering the foreign policy of a new independent state: the case of Macedonia, 1990–6

Dimitar Mirčev

I

In an already wide range of memoirs, studies and publications on the dissolution and death of Yugoslavia, Macedonia is only occasionally mentioned as an agent and participant in that process. Even in Macedonia itself only one study has been published so far, examining in depth the Macedonian policy and developments in the course of emancipation from the former Yugoslav Federation (Milosavlevski, 1996).

This may seem unusual since, according to the Badinter Arbitration Commission of the EC in its report of 13 January 1992, Macedonia, together with Slovenia, was the first to demand and fulfil all *de jure* and *de facto* conditions for acquisition of sovereignty and independence. In addition, it is still the only ex-Yugoslav republic that has regulated its inter-state relations with all other successors and members of the former federation, including the establishment of diplomatic relations, opening of embassies as well as signing of the basic set of bilateral agreements with all of them.

Why have analysis and observers ignored or avoided Macedonia in discussing the intra-Yugoslav and international aspects of the dispersion of the former federation? Probably because of a variety of reasons which make Macedonia a rather unusual case. It had not taken part in the Yugoslav conflicts of 1991–5 which involved all the other republics; by no action or measure has it contributed to the crisis and dispersion of Yugoslavia; on the contrary it simply dissociated itself from the federation – peacefully, legally and democratically; despite the large proportion of ethnic groups within the population (33 per cent) neither inter-ethnic tensions, nor ethno-centric and ethno-political mobilisation have prevailed in Macedonian politics and the electorate. At the first free parliamentary elections, 1991, Macedonia even appeared to be the only case among former Yugoslav republics where ethno-political groups and parties had not won a majority (Mirčev, 1993).

Furthermore, there are no indications that the difficulties and threats that Macedonia was repeatedly exposed to from its neighbours since independence in 1991 have created animosity, hatred or ethnophobia among the population, at least not sufficient to cause any real dispute or conflict. Many observers have been 'caught' or surprised by this, and most have built their hypotheses on the Yugoslav crisis on the black-white screen of divided or polarised sides; highly developed and backward societies, Christian and Muslim, Catholic and Orthodox, westernised and oriental. Due to its position, Macedonia was considered to be very much on the unfavourable, risky and conflict-producing side of these divisions but it appeared that the hypothesis simply did not apply.

II

Nevertheless, it is true that in the second half of the 1980s, at the outset of the fall of the former federation. Macedonia was not among the front-runners for leaving Yugoslavia, at least its top politicians did not give such signals. On the contrary, Macedonian representatives in the Party and State presidencies at that time were thought to be rather conservative, obedient to the top, dogmatic, and pro-Serbian.[1]

Matched with the fact that Macedonia as a recipient of aid from the federal development funds was not a self-reliant republic, such evidence strengthened its image as a dogmatic, pro-federation and pro-Serbian republic. A leading Slovenian analyst in 1989 wrote of Macedonians that they were not 'mature enough for independent statehood' (Urbančič, 1989).

Outside the country, particularly among the neighbours of Macedonia, two basic premises gave grounds for the belief that Macedonia would not choose the course of independence or leave the federation. First, Macedonia was a land-locked and small country, surrounded by unpleasant neighbours who had claims and aspirations towards it. Secondly, the Macedonian nation was an artificial nation created during the Second World War by Tito and the Communist Party to counter the national interests of the neighbours. Both these points counted either on Macedonia's remaining at any price in the federation or on its emerging as a national state if the communist system disappeared. These issues have been largely discussed and explained in various texts (Troebst, 1992; Glenny, 1992; Pettifer, 1992; Meyer, 1995), but nonetheless they had and still have considerable impact on some neighbours' policies towards Macedonia. Later on, the entire Macedonian strategy would be directed at the practical demonstration of the worthlessness of these premises, even when the backing of the federation had gone.

It is also true that at the onset of the fall of the federation, Macedonia was a republic where not even a modestly elaborated project or programme for dissociation from the Federation or a strategy for acquisition of sovereignty had been developed, despite the fact that the deficiencies and disfunctions of the federal bodies had been felt not only in the dissident groups and intellectual circles. By then in most other republics such platforms had already sketched at least a serious restructuring of the constitutional principles of the federation.[2]

However, this type of evidence creates false assumptions that this or that republic was less or more pro-Yugoslavia, less or more for its own independence. In fact, the dissolution of Yugoslavia was a result of deeper economic and developmental contradictions and discrepancies which socialism, without democracy, without the protection of human rights and without a market economy (Schierup, 1993) could not have resolved. It was equally a result of the legitimacy and power struggle among and inside political elites at both federal and republic level. The privatisation and market reforms initiated by Prime Minister A. Marković 1988–9, as well as the spread of pluralism all over Eastern Europe, radically threatened the long-established reproduction of republic/federal political elites. They could no longer have drawn their legitimacy hierarchically 'from above', from the federal centre. For these reasons they put an end to the Party Presidency, the skeleton of the federation, and turned to a new source of legitimacy; ethnicity and an ethnic state. The turning point was no doubt the 14th Congress of LCY, January 1990.

Nevertheless, the research evidence from the end of the 1980s, including the Yugoslav public opinion surveys and content analysis of the programmes of the newly established political parties, did not indicate that separatist or declining pro-federation attitudes were prevailing in individual republics, nor that these public opinions differed considerably from one republic to another (Bačcvić *et al.*, 1991; Goati *et al.* 1989). This related equally to the Macedonian public and the Macedonian political elite whose position and policies, despite its stronger presence in the dogmatic wing of the federal leadership, were not deviating from the rest of the elites.

III

The events, disputes and the split at the 14th Party Congress had a cathartic effect on the public in Macedonia. They caused an immediate discharge of the party elite, a massive conversion and migration of the membership to the newly established parties and finally a reconsideration of the position of Macedonia in the federation. In this respect media and researchers revealed unfavourable facts unknown or only partly known to the public. For example, that within the period 1947–90, the development gap between Macedonia and the rest of the federation, particularly the developed part, had considerably widened and that in the economic policies of the federation Macedonia's role was as a supplier of cheap food and raw-material (Bogoev, 1993; Reuter, 1993). The bulk of the Macedonian economy was, like a tail, linked and dependent on the Serbian economy. The Macedonians had been far under-represented in the Yugoslav diplomatic service and military top echelons (Mirčev, 1993). The distribution and consumption of federal (Serbian) media, communication and cultural production in Macedonia far exceeded the consumption of native and local production. Historians revealed documents on the suppression and elimination (by the secret services) of non-communist groups and well-known leaders striving for Macedonian independent statehood or union before or after Liberation in 1945.

The nationalistic wave appearing at that time everywhere in Yugoslavia and particularly in Serbia, had much added to the cathartic and transforming pattern of Macedonian political public opinion. A fear of the overall Serbian predominance, whose 'trade-mark' was protection of all-Yugoslav national interests, was given rich ground to grow in. The political pluralisation, denationalisation and privatisation of property which was taking place in all former communist countries, in Macedonia could have undoubtedly led to such a predominance.[3] In addition, the Serbian Orthodox church strengthened its claims over the jurisdiction of the autonomous Macedonian church, while strong Serbian political parties (Drašković, Šešelj, etc.) renamed the Republic into south Serbia or *Vardarska banovina*, a name given by the Serbs after the occupation in 1913. In Serbia there were even some who were crossing off Macedonia from the new maps of 'reconstructed' Yugoslavia.

All in all, the psychological ground had been laid for consideration of the possibilities of dissociation from the federation, although a real strategy for gaining independence and sovereignty was still lacking. In the spring and summer of 1990, four fairly serious political parties were registered and attracted considerable support among the electorate, together with some twenty-four smaller, satellite, local or quasi-political parties. The reformed communist party (Party for Democratic Transformation), PDT launched the slogan 'Macedonia can do it alone'; The Reformist Forces (Liberals), whose platform was 'For another, democratic Yugoslavia'; the VMRO-DPMNE (Democratic Party for Macedonian National Unity) whose electoral programme was 'Yugoslav confederation'; and PDP (the Party for Democratic Prosperity) which did not support the reconstruction of Yugoslavia and claimed that all Albanians should live in one state (Mojanoski, 1996).

At the first parliamentary elections, in November 1990, these four parties together with the minor Socialist Party and several independents or one-seat parties, won the 120 seats in parliament. However, the election outcome was surprisingly undecided regarding the power of the ethno-oriented and civil-oriented parties: 50:50.[4] This balance of power made it very difficult and time-consuming to constitute the parliament, to elect the head of State and to appoint the government, not to speak of making decisions on crucial issues on the functioning of the state and conducting the transition. The parliament was not constituted until 8 January 1991, the President was elected 20 days later, and the government after another two and a half months.[5]

Nevertheless, the parliamentary elections in 1990 produced three results which had far-reaching effects on the early period of Macedonia's independence:

(a) the nationalistic parties did not win a majority in the parliament. This was the first and only such case among the former Yugoslav republics and a rare case among the East European countries at least at the first free elections.[6] Consequently the extremist, hegemonistic and nationalistic components of their platforms have not prevailed or even been put on the political agenda;

(b) an expert government was established which was dependent on consensual support from civil and ethno-oriented parties. It additionally neutralised the political extremism, towards both domestic and foreign policy issues, and had a calming effect on the country as a whole. However the presence and the active role of the ethno-oriented parties in the governmental and parliamentary process had had a corrective and even productive role in the overall developments of the democratic process;

(c) again for the first time in the East European countries in transition, an ethnic minority party was included on an equal footing not only in the government but in all governmental bodies, ministries, agencies, etc. sharing the responsibility in the process of government.

On its first regular session, on 25 January 1991, a month after the referendum on dissociation of Slovenia, the new parliament adopted unanimously the *Declaration on the Sovereignty of the Republic*, a short but strategically important act. By the declaration, the parliament reaffirmed the full sovereignty of the republic and revoked the part of its sovereignty transferred and linked to the federation since 1944.[7] This act still did not mean the independence of the state but stressed the principle that 'Macedonia as a sovereign state autonomously decides on the future relations with the states of the other nations in Yugoslavia' and that if these relations would not be determined democratically or in a way which threatened the sovereignty of the republic, then the Assembly would adopt Constitutional law on the independence and full implementation of the rights of a sovereign state.

IV

In 1991 it was expected that the issues of the new relations in the Federation would settle down. In the absence of the already disintegrated Federal presidency its role was undertaken by the newly elected presidents of all republics who met several times to try to redesign the federal state. In May–June of that year, Izetbegović and Gligorov offered a joint proposal on what could have been described as an 'asymmetrical confederation', the last attempt at serious negotiations. Instead, open conflicts began in Slovenia, Croatia and later in Bosnia-Herzegovina. For Macedonia, staying any longer in the federation would have meant taking part in conflicts which were not their own, and aligning themselves with one side of the conflict would have been to risk losing the sovereignty which had been for centuries a dream of Macedonians. In a referendum in the autumn of the same year a large majority of the electorate voted for independence.[8] That day, 8 September, was later declared the Day of Independence. Immediately after the referendum, the Assembly of the Republic, on 18 September, adopted a Declaration by which a sovereign state was constituted while the legal aspects of independence were completed. Still, the declaration points out the right of the republic to enter into an eventual future union of the sovereign states of Yugoslavia. However, independence had been legally accomplished. The declaration expresses a full loyalty to the principles of the international relations laid down in the documents of the UN, OSCE and the Paris Charter, emphasising also its interest in cooperating peacefully with all countries, developing good neighbourly relations with surrounding countries and fully integrating into all European structures. More specifically it stresses that Macedonia does not have territorial claims, that it recognises and expects respect of the existing borders, and that it has an interest in the position of its minorities in the neighbouring countries but not such that this should interfere in their own policies.

A new constitution was drafted quickly, and after a short but stormy debate was adopted on 17 November 1991. It was a short act which included most of the achievements of modern constitutionality, declared a parliamentary democracy, market economy, and the full range of human rights and civil freedoms, including the rights of national minorities but avoiding any implication for the ethno-organisation of the state.[9] The constitution was previously reviewed and 'approved' by many legal experts of EU, CE and other bodies. At the beginning of December 1991, President Gligorov opened the campaign for the international recognition of Macedonia. He wrote to Heads of States and governments throughout the world. He sent special letters to the EU member states, and a letter to some neighbouring countries, and international organisations, in which he called for both recognition and establishment of diplomatic relations, listing all prerequisites the country fulfilled for independence. The international community was in the letter indirectly warned that failure to recognise Macedonia could have unfavourable effects on peace and stability in that part of the Balkans and even in the wider region.[10]

Meanwhile, the situation in Slovenia, Croatia and Bosnia was gradually worsening. The International Conference on Yugoslavia in the Hague issued several documents and resolutions. On 17 December, the European Council in Brussels adopted a Declaration on Yugoslavia and directions for recognition of new states in Eastern Europe and the Soviet Union.

It became clear that the European Union (Community) would play the main role in the political process in the former Yugoslavia. On 17 December the parliament in Skopje adopted another Declaration on the international recognition of Macedonia, relating formally to the European Union and authorising the president and government to continue activities relating to recognition. A few days later, the Foreign

Ministry delivered to the Badinter Arbitration Commission all the necessary documents for recognition of the Republic. As the constitutional provision on minorities could have caused dilemmas in neighbouring countries the parliament promptly amended the constitution and clarified this issue. Similarly clarification was needed for the provision that the state border could be changed only by parliamentary decision, implying dilemmas on the unilaterality of such an act. On 11 January 1992, the Badinter Commission Report positively assessed the conditions of Slovenia and Macedonia in meeting the EU criteria for recognition and recommended that the Union do so. Having already had some questions from Greece relating to the name of the state, the Badinter Report clearly stated that 'the name of the state does not imply any territorial claims'. The report was published on 15 January. A few hours later, news agencies broadcast that the European Council had decided to recognise Slovenia and Croatia but not Macedonia, which caused a shock and great disappointment in the country.

V

In that moment Macedonia found itself in an extremely difficult foreign and internal position. Disillusion soon replaced the euphoria of the easy and even process of recognition. The public had been deeply convinced that the international community would this time have corrected the unjust and unfair policy towards Macedonia in the course of modern history, and that the state would be given the place that it morally deserved in the community of independent states. The leading political circles which for a year and a half had been contributing so well on both the foreign and domestic stage was also caught by surprise. The nationalistic forces immediately used the non-recognition to press for conflicts and struggle since allegedly 'nowhere was independence won through letters and without struggle and victims'. Macedonia appeared not to have a foreign policy strategy for the long road to independence and to have only modest and insufficient resources for survival in isolation. In January–February 1992, the State energy and food reserves were sufficient only for several months. The foreign currency reserves were not higher than 30 million US dollars, while around 65 per cent of production and trade had been linked to the Serbian economy which was already involved in war. By that time, production in Macedonia fell by almost 50 per cent compared with 1989, while GDP decreased from 1,300 USD per capita to 1,000 USD. Investments were almost stopped. In addition, the Yugoslav army was still located in Macedonia and it was known that, according to the earlier doctrine and risk assessments, the Skopje Army District was one of the best equipped. After Macedonia ceased to send recruits to the Army, it was no longer considered as its own or even a friendly army. The newly established Macedonian army was practically without arms except the poor stocks of the civil and territorial defence. The police force (around 9,000 men) was the only efficient protection force.

In February 1992 the first Greek blockade closed the southern border; in June the same year, the UN declared sanctions and an embargo against Serbia (UN Resolution) which completely closed the northern border. Since railway connections with Bulgaria and Albania did not exist and road traffic was almost inoperative, Macedonia was completely isolated. Strict rationing of basic food supplies and medicaments was introduced, export firms were closing down one by one and the economy suffered greatly. To the public, these facts seemed paradoxical: Macedonia which did not permit the victory of nationalist forces, which did its best to avoid conflict and war and which peacefully, legally and democratically dissociated from Yugoslavia, was *de facto* punished and deprived of normal life.

At the beginning of 1992 the country was not only without a foreign strategy, but it had not even a strategy for survival. However nor had its neighbours a strategy towards Macedonia. Certainly, having specific interests and developed ideologies of 'great nations' in the Balkans (Milosavlevski, 1997; Katardziev, 1997), most of them expected that Macedonia being small, unprotected and self-insufficient would no doubt choose to approach them for assistance, association or even consensual 'Anschluss'. This explains the series of clear tactical measures undertaken by most of the immediate neighbouring countries to speed up Macedonian dependence on them individually, and to meet its demands for assistance. The Bulgarian recognition in January 1992 was followed by complete opening of the border for supplies, petrol transportation, cheap food exports, etc. Albania opened the port of Durres for transport and exports to the West. Serbia (FRY) withdrew the Army from Macedonia comparatively easily, believing that Macedonia itself would soon ask for military protection. Greece counted on the impossibility of survival if the southern transport corridor was cut off.[12] The common denominator of all these expectations was that Macedonia would either be annexed by one neighbour or be divided between or among them, finally solving in such a way the still existing 'Macedonische Frage'. On this basis, a symbolic prerequisite for this appeared: to deny and repudiate the Macedonian ethnicity.

The Macedonian political leadership had to reconsider the whole position and to answer these challenges, quickly taking into account the fact that internal economic, democratic and inter-ethnic stability was essential for any answer, as well as that the answer should be internationally legitimate and acceptable. It also counted on the objective analysis and assessment of the neighbours' disadvantages and Macedonian advantages in foreign and regional issues. Serbia itself was deeply involved in both a war in central Yugoslavia and in pacification of Kosova; opening a third front of conflict would have exceeded its capacity. Albania and Bulgaria were preoccupied with their own domestic, economic and transformative difficulties, while Greece had its own difficulties in the European Community in addition to the regional problems. A positive approach to this oversensitive situation could have been productive by promoting only the principles of peace, non-interference and europeanisation of the Balkans. Macedonia then adopted this approach and tried to apply it in its strategy, trying equally to gain wide international support. Gligorov would a few months later in London describe the approach in the following way:

- immutability of the borders among the republics of former Yugoslavia and guaranteed inter-state borders;
- normalisation of inter-state relations of all countries concerned including recognition and establishment of full diplomatic relations;
- political dialogue and peaceful means of resolving any inter-state issues or disputes;
- full introduction and protection of human rights including ethnic rights as the only prerequisite for peace and democracy within the ethnically mixed Balkans;
- free flow of goods, ideas and people, open borders, good neighbourly relations and full cooperation among all countries in the Balkans which provides compatibility with the processes and policies of European integration.[13]

Two more strategic principles were soon added to this: the principle of *active equi-distance to and with all neighbouring countries*, in the sense of equally good relations and equal political distance from all of them; secondly, not entering into any inter-state, bilateral or multilateral alliances or associations. These two basic objectives were first emphasised in an interview with Gligorov for a Belgrade daily in October 1993[14] referring to the 'new balance in the Balkans'. Keeping in mind the experience of history and that two Balkan wars and many more disputes were caused by the claims towards Macedonia and its division, it was clear that the independent and neutral Republic of Macedonia was a factor in the balance of forces and interests in the Balkans. If in any way it showed particular interest towards one of its neighbours, it would certainly disrupt this balance and would unavoidably cause intervention or interference of the others, including the possibility of new armed conflicts. The equi-distance became a strong instrument of Macedonian foreign policy. As to the new political alignments, the first such proposition came in September 1992 from the Yugoslav prime minister M. Panić to revive the idea of a Balkan confederation instead of the failures in re-establishing former Yugoslavia. This proposition was later followed by a proliferation of ideas for new associations, unions and leagues on a number of grounds.[15] Macedonia in all these ideas saw nothing but new divisions and regional grouping in the Balkans, new isolations and struggles for leadership and predominant positions. For this reason it decisively rejected all such propositions and was even cautious in accepting political initiatives for all kinds of intra-Balkan or regional cooperation (SECI, the Royaumont Initiative, etc.).

In many cases, Macedonia had to explain carefully to its western partners that this stance was a matter of principle and not of refusal to join intra-Balkan cooperation or to introduce regional market, economic, communication or technical and defence systems.

VI

At the beginning of 1992 neither EU nor USA manifested particular concern about the conflicts and disputes in former Yugoslavia. Most of the earlier or parallel cases of federations and states in dispersion had similar disputes which did not develop into wars or sharp conflicts. So seemed the issue of the recognition of Macedonia and Greece's first demand to postpone its recognition. Immediately after the EC meeting recognising the independence of Slovenia and Croatia, G. de Mikelis, on 15 January, stated at a press conference in Rome that the matter was only postponed for a short time to clarify some Greek reservations, but that it would need no more than a few weeks to find a solution. The issue of the name for him was not a real issue, nor had the EU made it a precondition for recognition. On 10 March the EU and USA issued a joint declaration emphasising the need for a positive approach to the demand for recognition of Macedonia. President Bush informed Gligorov of this, expressing at the same time the US sensitivity for the concerns of Greece as a friend and ally of the USA.

Most of the comments in the foreign press and academic institutions assessed in the first half of 1992 that the EU would and could not have kept Macedonia in the waiting room for recognition. Frequently these assessments were grounded on arguments of political morality or on indications that the grey-zone status of Macedonia increasingly contributed to the risk of the ongoing conflict in Bosnia and Croatia spilling over. However, the Greek policy, obviously coordinated or matched with the interests of Serbia, became more determined, more offensive and active in the EU and elsewhere. As a result, at several EC meetings (Brussels, Gimaresh) the decision to recognise Macedonia was being either postponed or made unacceptable for the country. Finally, in Lisbon, on 27 June 1992, the Declaration adopted by the EC was a severe setback for Macedonia's expectations, stating that it would recognise it but only under a name not containing the word 'Macedonia'. The document shocked the republic and gave 'victory' to Greece, as it went furthest in the denial of the country's independence, national identity and international position. The reaction of the public to that document even in Western Europe and the USA was unfavourable, while some observers anticipated immediate intervention from neighbouring countries. This was the peak of the EU compromises with Greece, coinciding with a variety of internal controversies in the Union.

However, soon it became clear that the policy of the EU was leading to a blind-alley, or as some authors put it 'the Greek stance prevented any reasonable EU policy for the South Balkans'. The temperature inside Macedonia dramatically rose as the dissatisfaction with the foreign policy results paralleled a social unrest caused by the economic effects of the UN embargo on Serbia and closing down of the Greek border. The position of Gligorov and the Government was in jeopardy, the social and economic reforms almost blocked.[16]

Most probably the middle of 1992, the period that immediately followed the Lisbon Declaration of the European summit on Macedonia, was a time of penultimate and critical importance both for the international community's approach towards Macedonia and for Macedonia's policy towards recognition. Two policies were put to a critical test. For Gligorov and Macedonia it was felt to be a historical test and great risk. Meanwhile several scenarios had been worked out in the neighbourhood of Macedonia, taking into account the potential consequences of the Lisbon Declaration. The government took the risk of not changing the policy. It was decided in Skopje only to intensify the efforts of the foreign affairs apparatus, of the non-governmental organisations, lobbies, cultural and information circles to explain and promote the Macedonium cause abroad.

VII

This policy began to bring results. Research carried out by *Nova Makedonija* on the basis of content analysis demonstrated that the issue of the recognition of Macedonia in mid-1992 appeared to be one of the top issues of international political public opinion and that the leading world media were mostly supportive of and sympathetic towards Macedonia's position (Ajanovski, 1993). The huge Greek propaganda campaign was not effective and as a rule proved to be counterproductive.

The war in Croatia and the initial conflict in Bosnia had already begun to cause serious anxiety at the possibility of it spilling over into Macedonia. The closing down of the border by Greece, and the UN embargo towards Serbia, considerably worsened the social and economic situation inside the country. Social unrest or even breakdown was realistically expected. The overall pressure on Macedonia caused by the lack of its recognition led to new dangers and it had to be relieved. The dissociation of the European Union from Greek policy and rising Greek nationalism had an impact on three important decisions: to hand over the dispute to the UN, to reconsider and change the rigid stance on the name issue from the Lisbon Declaration and to enable Macedonia to utilise international funds and assistance.

The decisions were embedded in the EU declaration at the summit in Edinburgh on 12 December 1992, on the basis of the report of the EU mediator between Greece and Macedonia, Robin O'Neal, as well as on the advice of the YU-conference coordinators. In addition the EU welcomed the proposal of UN General Secretary to send UNPROFOR troops to Macedonia with a monitoring mandate. Humanitarian assistance from most EU countries largely increased.

A real gain for the Macedonian policy was the fact that a process of recognition and establishment of diplomatic relations on individual bases began. More and more countries declared their recognition, many of them using the constitutional name of the state – Republic of Macedonia.[17]

However, semi-official relations and frequent political contacts had already been established with many more countries, including members of the UNSC. In the middle of 1992, Foreign Ministers De Michelis, Dumas and Hurd spoke of *de facto* recognition of Macedonia, while the USA, after the joint declaration on Macedonia with the EU of

10 March, commenced sending signals of a more autonomous and positive approach to that country. Paradoxically, many Asian, African, developing and non-aligned countries, India among them, ignored the issue of Macedonia, probably due to sympathies for former Yugoslavia, the leader of the non-aligned movement, or perhaps so as not to encourage the fragmentation of national states.

Finally, Russia, on 5 August 1992, officially recognised Macedonia and this was the turning point in strengthening the position of the Republic. Only a few members of the CIS followed Russia. The rest of the Central and Eastern European states hesitated to do so, being either friends or neighbours of Serbia or candidates for EU membership. Nevertheless, the Russian decision meant a lot, demonstrating first of all a more balanced approach to the Balkan crisis, then a reconsideration of their hitherto unreserved support for Serbia and Greece. Indirectly, the assumptions of involving Macedonia in eventual pan-orthodox unions or 'walls' to prevent the penetration of Islamism into Europe became irrelevant. Later on the PR of China recognised Macedonia, like Russia, by the constitutional name and this meant not only a further relaxation of the position of the Republic but also a large channel of support in the UN Security Council.

Despite the large and sophisticated campaign and actions of Greek diplomacy to prevent the international affirmation of Macedonia as well as the influence of the powerful Greek lobbies in the USA, Canada and Australia, (strangely enough, countries with the largest Macedonian communities and emigration) the wall of isolation could not have been sustained.

International organisations, both non-governmental and governmental, began to accept Macedonian membership, many of them, again, under the constitutional name. Some of them, in the field of air-traffic, telecommunications, seismology, meteorology, etc., simply could not have avoided Macedonia, because of technical reasons.

With such a pretext 'die Mazedonische Frage' was internationalised at the end of the year – that is, directed at the global and complex mechanism of the United Nations.

VIII

In January 1993, in accordance with a decision of the Security Council, the first contingent of UNPROFOR troops was deployed in Macedonia as a part of larger UN units in Croatia and Bosnia. The size of the unit was comparatively small, the mandate limited to symbolic monitoring of the north and west border. Nevertheless, the mental effects both on Macedonians and their neighbours were considerable. The fear of intervention, annexation or aggression by any neighbour diminished. Apart from that, the government achieved a larger space for manoeuvre to redirect the modest defence budget to productive economic and social purposes.[18]

In January 1993 the foreign strategy of the Republic was reassessed and finalised. In addition to the already corroborated principles of good relations, positive and active equi-distance with all neighbours, as well as the policy of peace, dialogue and confidence-building measures, the strategy assumed:

(a) obtaining UN membership at whatever price;
(b) settling the dispute with Greece on an equal footing or discussing them as equal partners, not as a member of UN or NATO and non-member of UN, NATO, etc.
(c) membership of the UN should only facilitate and not complicate bilateral relations and understanding between Macedonia and Greece, since the UN offers a variety of instruments for dispute resolution;
(d) full membership of Macedonia in the UN would contribute considerably to the process of peace and stability in the Balkans.

These points made the outline of the Memorandum that Macedonia delivered to the Security Council and to Secretary General B. B. Ghali on 3 February 1993, thus answering the prior Greek memorandum from January of the same year. The memorandum renewed the application for full membership, now followed by the recommendation of EU. The stance of the Greek memorandum was in complete contrast: to prevent the reception of Macedonia in the UN, to show that it would create new dangers and risks for the peace and stability in the Balkans, to make it conditional on 'prior settlement of certain outstanding issues', to utilise as much as possible the fragile position of Macedonia before the reception.

It was the first time in UN history that one country had objected to the reception of another country, to require giving it a new name or to make it conditional for the reception of it. For many legal experts and UN members the case was curious and strange, but the case was created and existed. It was clear it could not have been resolved either by force or by application of mere principles of ethics: it required consultations, talks and negotiations. It was also clear to Macedonia that in the course of negotiations it would not be possible to reach an agreement without some concessions, or by convincing the other side. The position was to be realistic, Slovenia was asked to sponsor the resolution of reception of Macedonia in the UN and she did it successfully and amicably.

After difficult talks and consultations, finally on 7 April 1993, the Security Council by Resolution No. 817 (1993) recommended the General Assembly to accept the application of Macedonia, using a delicate formulation – 'the state which, for the use in the Organization will temporarily be referred to as 'former Yugoslav Republic of Macedonia', until the resolution of the differences on the name of the state...'. The meeting of the Security Council lasted six minutes. Next day the General Assembly unanimously adopted the recommendation and Macedonia became unconditionally the 181st member state of the UN. Both in the preamble of the Resolution adopted and in the statement of the President of the Assembly there were guarantees that the temporary reference of the state does not imply any connection with the Federal Republic of Yugoslavia. The states concerned with the name would continue to talk on overcoming the differences in the interest of peace in the region, accepting the mediation and good services of the co-chairs of the Conference on former Yugoslavia. At the General Assembly session, President Gligorov produced a speech of gratitude and promises, which in the view of some commentators was ranked a landmark in the modern political history of Macedonia. Most actors in the process and procedure felt content with the solution. The temper and reaction in Skopje and Athens varied from full satisfaction to complete disappointment, depending on the government–opposition division. The UN resolution was called 'an act of justice' by Gligorov, and 'a productive compromise' by the *New York Times*, envisaging the road of complete recognition of Macedonia all over the world. Other well-known observers assessed it quite justifiably as a triumph of diplomacy.

The real results of entering the UN have been for Macedonia, and for the peace and stability in the region, undisputably and ultimately important; notably in the fact that the world recognised, accepted and legally verified the independence, sovereignty and legitimacy of the Macedonian state and statehood. By doing so, it set aside all grounds for denials, claims, pretensions and interest confrontations regarding Macedonia.

As a matter of fact, by that act of the UN the political map of Europe was finally and definitely completed. Macedonia was no longer a limbo zone, a protected territory or a political vacuum. As a recognised and neutral country it had the opportunity to influence a new security balance in the region, to stabilise that balance, and to no longer to be a security risk. Its negotiating capacity became much stronger and independent while the process of recognition continued on a *de jure* basis.

Although all 180 member states of the UN by acclamation voted for the membership of Macedonia which meant an act of formal recognition, many of them, asked so by Greece, have been avoiding the establishment of diplomatic relations 'until the successful end of talks with Greece'. The Macedonian flag which had also been disputed by Greece, was not hung on the East River. In May 1993, the efforts of the diplomatic and foreign affairs activity of Macedonia were, because of that, redirected towards three basic priorities: (a) to begin and accomplish negotiations with Greece, now mediated by the Conference on Yugoslavia as well as those directly conducted in the UN in New York under the auspices of Mr C. Vance; (b) to establish an as large as possible network of diplomatic relations, missions and contacts on a bilateral basis; (c) and to enter the basic multilateral institutions and organisations: the UN agencies first of all – UNESCO, UNDP, UNIDO – then FAO, IFAD, etc., then the Council of Europe, OSCE and the NATO Partnership for Peace. A priority goal was also to approach the European and Euro-Atlantic integrative structures.

Parallel with these priorities a battle on the domestic front was in progress – for economic recovery and stable democracy. Membership of the UN made it possible to join the World Bank and IMF, and somewhat later the EBRD as well. The first contingent of fresh capital and credits gave a boost to the performance of some branches of production and exports, while limited exports improved cheap supplies to the domestic markets. In November–December 1994, the first direct presidential and second general elections took place giving a landslide victory to Gligorov and the Union for Macedonia (a weak coalition of social-democrats, liberals and socialists with the participation of the moderate Albanian party, PDP). Although in 1996 the liberals left the government and joined the opposition benches, the system proved to be stable, democratically propulsive and functional as well as receptive to the challenges of the new circumstances. The involvement of the Albanian ethno-polities continued to have an active role and presence in the parliament, government and local administration.

Meanwhile, Macedonia launched a series of campaigns in the UN, in OSCE, in the regional structures – for peace and good-neighbourly relations in the Balkans. Over the whole year 1993 hundreds of state delegations, multilateral groups, peace monitors, and democracy-promoting institutions stayed in the country and most of their reports were favourable, positive and supportive. The impact of these contacts and reports was too weighty to be ignored and finally, in December 1993, the major countries of the EU declared diplomatic relations with the country and immediately after that opened embassies in Skopje, though some of them had even earlier opened representative offices. That wave went on rapidly during the first half of 1994. The ice was broken.

IX

However, much more difficult was the process of entering multilateral organisations and structures. In the EU and OSCE the Greek veto was still in force, while many of the rest were conditioned by diplomatic relations or recognition by the EU. Macedonia experienced, like no other modern state, all the technicalities and negative interdependencies of the international legal and political order.[19]

Despite the fact that full diplomatic relations on a bilateral basis with EU member countries had been set up by the end of 1994, it was no earlier than 30 December 1995 when the Union itself established officially these relations. Meanwhile, apart from Greece (although Macedonia was a full member of the UN), relations with neighbours were not regulated: FR of Yugoslavia (Serbia) refused to normalise relations and to establish any diplomatic links having fully harmonised policies with Greece, and kept open the whole packet of claims (the minority issue, the church issue, the border issue, etc.); Bulgaria, having recognised the state of Macedonia refused to recognise the Macedonian language, while Albania insisted on the name 'Former Yugoslav Republic' implying that Macedonia belonged to Yugoslavia so that the Albanian issue would be resolved in a 'unified way'. All of the neighbours of Macedonia counted on some concessions and profits arising from the dispute and negotiations with Greece.

Realistically, most of the open issues of the foreign position of Macedonia, in its second stage, are connected with and interdependent on the outcome of negotiations with Greece in New York. There, instead of a quick agreement on the issue of the name of the state, the talks developed into long-lasting informative contacts on the overall positions and policies of both states. There was no doubt that a sincere wish of Greece was to overcome the problem, that its prolongation was not even in Greece's interest and that the maintenance of high temperature in relations was indeed detrimental to the peace process in the Balkans. Nevertheless, the limitations and the goals earlier set up were too high, too rigid and too transparent to be simply abandoned or changed. A high level of realism, reconsideration of the position and readiness for compromises was required by both sides.

The methodological but also essential stance of Macedonia was that, first, relations should have been established between the states, then normal contacts, cooperation and confidence-building measures introduced and developed, and last, in such a relaxed climate to try to resolve the real issues. The Greek side still insisted on the change of the name as a condition for approaching the rest of the issues.

The time pressure was acute since a report was expected for the autumn sessions of the Security Council and the General Assembly.

Finally, the Rubicon was crossed in the first days of September 1995, by the indispensable assistance of Mr Vance and his diplomatic-legal services. A draft Interim Accord was prepared, latter qualified by some as 'a pearl of a diplomatic paper'. The governments accepted the paper not without hesitation and difficulties and not without risking a fall. On September the 13th, the Foreign Ministers and the mediator signed the act in New York, followed by a short ceremony and cheer with a glass of obviously dry but bitter champagne.

X

By the Interim Accord Macedonia obliged itself to change the national flag, whose design allegedly reflected the symbols of the antique Macedonian dynasty of Philip II and whose heritage, Greek or Macedonian, was disputed. In fact both nations and states felt no identity with that symbol-design, discovered in 1977 near Salonica; it meant rather a symbolic renouncement of the antique origin of the Macedonian nation. In return, Macedonia got most of its substantial demands; recognition as an independent and sovereign state, establishment of diplomatic relations, confirmation and inviolability of the existing frontier, a packet of confidence-building measures, free entry for Macedonian citizens to Greece, promotion of economic cooperation and trade, cultural exchange, and even refrain of objection from the Greek side to application by or membership in international, regional or multilateral organisations (unless Macedonia applies under a name other than the one referred in UNSC Resolution 817-1993).

The ultimate gain for Macedonia was the fact that interstate relations were fully normalised, that a gate was open for full membership in all international organisations, and that no neighbour or state or organisation thereafter could have grounds to refuse relations with

Macedonia, while the name and the symbol indicating the national character of the statehood remained unchanged. In the text of the Accord, Macedonia did not undertake any obligation to change the name Macedonia. In Article 5 of the Accord, there is only a provision that the parties agree to continue negotations under the auspices of the Secretary General of the United Nations pursuant to Security Council resolution 845 (1993) with a view to reaching agreement on the difference... on the name (Interim Accord, 1995). The negotiations on that issue still go on.

The immediate consequences and effects of the Interim Accord on both states' position were direct and visible, although the popularity of the governments did not increase at all. However, the Accord immediately began to produce results and effects, particularly in the finalisation of the peace process and regulation of multilateral relations in the Balkans. The multilateral confrontations considerably lost their strength. New peace and cooperation initiatives such as SECI, Royaumont, South-East Europe Cooperation, and many other projects, were born.

As a direct result of the agreement and of a parallel foreign campaign, Macedonia was accepted on 13 October 1995 to membership of OSCE in Vienna, to membership of the Council of Europe on 9 November 1995 as well as in the Partnership for Peace on 15 November. Certainly in most of these structures, there have been reports containing suggestions, critical assessments and development proposals for Macedonia, but no political or foreign-political objections have been raised anywhere.

The recognition process was accomplished and came full circle. Being under strong pressure by the effects of the Interim Accord, by the international community as well as by policy changes in Greece, Serbia (FRY) signed in Belgrade on 8 April 1996 the Agreement on regulation of the relations and promotion of the cooperation between the Republic of Macedonia and Federal Republic of Yugoslavia (Agreement, 1996). Again, this act had long-reaching significance for Macedonia, since Serbia was directly involved and represented an interested party to the Bucharest Treaty from 1913 on the partition of Macedonia, and also was the only member of the Former Yugoslav federation to object to the independence of Macedonia. In breaking with the former Serbian–Greek strategy on Macedonia, Serbia went a step further. It not only returned to the conception of national statehood and identity name of Macedonians, but also recognised state continuity and the existence of Macedonia as a state back to 1944. By that act, the story of the battle for independence and sovereignty of Macedonia was almost finished.

XI

In a sketch for an epilogue, it could be assessed that the events that followed in Macedonia and the surrounding region were mainly seeking peace, reconciliation and better mutual relations. The risks of inter-state confrontations considerably decreased although the potential of inter-state conflicts are still relevant and actual (Bosnia and above all Kosovo). Macedonia is nonetheless not on the list of conflict-creating areas or factors and this is why a prime interest of the international community is to protect, strengthen and promote the independent, sovereign, peaceful, stable and prosperous position of Macedonia.

The talks on overcoming the differences with Greece on the name issue still continue, although Macedonia is no longer in a position to have to offer any concessions with regard to its national and state identity. The mechanisms envisaged in the Interim Accord function more than well; the border between the countries is most propulsive and largely open. Over a period of two years, Greece became the third largest economic partner and the most important individual investor in Macedonia.

Businessmen, tourists, passengers and the population from both sides of the border are campaigning for both governments to open contacts and cooperation on as wide a basis as possible. The progress of Macedonia in getting closer and more integrated in the EU and NATO work in the same direction.

A set of problems and unresolved issues with neighbours remain relevant factors for improvement of intra-Balkanic relations: the demarcation of the frontier with Serbia has not been concluded and the northern neighbour still manifests some territorial claims in this respect.

Bulgaria still insists on the illusion that the Macedonian nation and language do not exist but are merely an amorphous state unit. Some circles in Albania still support minority ethno-extremism in Macedonia in a direction of establishing a bi-ethnic state. And in Macedonia itself, nationalistic circles and forces have not been entirely disarmed and calmed down.

Even in these days of the laser and digital technology, the Balkans require a little more time to replace the powder-keg of confrontation with modern patterns of reasoning.

Notes

1. The highest-ranking official, Lazar Mojsov, president of the Yugoslav presidency until 1987, was selected in March 1989 to declare and defend the parliamentary introduction of the emergency state in Kosovo. At that time the chief of the Party Presidency was Milan Pančevski, a rigid advocate of hard-line policy against Slovenian and Croatian reform trends. Even the popular and much younger party leader Vasil Tupurkovski at the XIV party Congress in January 1990 called the Slovenian and Croatian reform-demanding groups an 'unprincipled coalition'. Inside Macedonia itself, the party elite controlled by Tito's favourite and disciple Koliščvski, had been strongly directing the overall dynamics for almost 20 years.

2. In Serbia, the Memorandum of the Academy of Sciences on repositioning the status of Serbs in Yugoslavia was outlined in 1986 and published in the spring of 1989. The Contributions to the Slovenian National Programme came out in Nova Revija–57 in 1987, while the Croatian 'road to independence' was drafted at the secret constituting meeting of 11DZ (The Croatian Democratic Community) in February 1989, on the basis of a report by F. Tudjman.

3. In 1989 a draft-law was prepared in the Federal Assembly for returning land or recompensating the Serbian pre-war colonists in Macedonia. Much of the arable land, forests and other properties before The Second World War in Macedonia had been donated either to them or to the Serbian orthodox church or to the dynasty Karadjordjevič.

4. On one side, the reformed communists (later social democrats) socialists and reformists (later liberals) with a few independents won exactly half of the seats. On the other side the ethno-centric VMRO got 37 seats, PDP, the Albanian ethno-centric party, was on 23, leaving only half of the Assembly to the Macedonian nationalists. Nevertheless, the two ethno-centric parties could not have formed a government as their policies were radically opposed and mutually exclusive.

5. Kiro Gligorov was a candidate of the civil-oriented parties but enjoyed the undisputed respect and reputation of the public; yet a party or coalition government with even a small majority could not have been formed and instead an expert government composed of technicians of different parties and ethnicities was appointed. It lasted a year only, until the ethno-centric parties in the parliament were no longer discredited and some of their representatives had left their benches.

6. In the 1990 elections, ethnically based parties were victorious in all Yugoslav republics with the sole exception of Macedonia. Their respective seats in parliaments was as follows: Macedonia 50 per cent, Slovenia 51.6 per cent, Croatia 58.6 per cent, Serbia 78 per cent, Montenegro 66.4 per cent, Bosnia and Herzegovina 83.8 per cent.

7. The legal formulation was 'The Constitution of Yugoslavia, the federal laws and other federal regulations and by-laws shall be implemented on the territory of Macedonia only if they do not contradict the Constitution of Macedonia, the republican laws and the decisions of the Assembly in carrying out the sovereignty of Macedonia.'

8. The question on the ballots was very carefully formulated – Are you for an independent Macedonian state having the right to associate with the other

Yugoslav nation states? Such a question could not harm anyone in the still existing federal structures nor could it cause intervention in Macedonia, while the doors for further negotiations with the rest of the Yugoslav republics were not closed. Yet the answer was very clear and decisive: 71.9 per cent of the electorate voted, of whom 95.1 per cent voted yes. Many Albanian minority voters did not take part in the referendum since their party policy was not for an independent Macedonia.

9. The preamble, nevertheless, in a couple of lines determines 'the historical fact that Macedonia is constituted as a national state of the Macedonian people in which full equality as citizens and permanent co-existence with the Macedonian people is provided for Albanians, Turks, Vlachs, Romanies and other nationalities living in the Republic...' This provision would later be disputed by the Albanian minority claiming the 'national statehood of both the Macedonian and the Albanian nation', as well as by Serbs complaining that they were not even mentioned in the preamble.

10. Gligorov was in the letter quite polite and receptive to advice on eventual obstacles for the recognition, as 'those obstacles would equally have impact on the peace', and asks for advice how to advance the cooperation after the recognition. In the direction of peace, regional and collective security.

11. A year later, the government report to the UN spoke of 50 million US dollars direct economic damages each month. International humanitarian assistance was mainly coming *ad hoc* and drop by drop.

12. In the first days of January 1992, the first high-level and semi-official contact between the Macedonian and the Greek side was held in Athens. It appeared that the Greek side still did not have any policy and even idea of denial of the name and national identity of Macedonia. It was an informative discussion, with a subtle warning of the Albanian factor and of the possibility of remaining isolated.

13. Address given in the Centre for Political Studies, London, on 15 October 1992.

14. Interview with Gligorov by editors Nikolić and Gjorgović, in *Borba*, Belgrade, 26 October 1992.

15. The former prime minister Mitsotakis revealed later that in 1993, president Milosević offered an idea of confederation to include certainly Macedonia and perhaps Bulgaria and even Cyprus. No matter how unrealistic such an idea could have been, it was undoubtedly grounded on rational elements: easier access to EU and NATO via Greece, pretension of stopping the Islamic penetration to Europe, equal support or sympathy from Moscow and, not the least, 'in-house' resolution of the issues of Kosovo and Macedonia. Similar projects were accorded with Moscow, particularly with the circles around Zirinovski on an orthodox or at least Slavic union covering the eastern Balkans.

16. Two months later the foreign minister D. Maleski resigned. On 12 July, in the capital Skopje, massive protests took place demanding the resignation of Gligorov, in addition to petitions of intellectuals and others asking for more aggressive, radical and non-compromising policies.

17. While in 1992 only 5 countries recognised and established diplomatic relations with Macedonia, in 1993 the number increased to 27, in 1994 to 46, in 1995 to 65.

18. The defence budget of the Republic was comparatively minor and smaller than that of the security forces budget. It was used only for maintenance and training of a small force of infantry. It should be added that Macedonia was the only republic of the former Yugoslav republics that strictly respected the UN resolution of prohibition of arms supplies to those republics.

19. For instance, in 1993 Macedonia was given the international trade and traffic code 'MKD' and it still function well. However, the WTO, on a proposal by Greece, required Macedonia to change that code as a prerequisite for becoming a member of WTO. Without membership of WTO Macedonia cannot apply for membership in CEFTA free trade association and is still on the list of risky countries. Because of that, interest-rates for credits and business or investment insurance are considerably higher, even in countries like Slovenia, which are bilaterally in a common duty free-zone with Macedonia.

References

Agreement... (1996) Law of Ratification of the Agreement on Regulation of the Relations and Promotion of the Cooperation between the Republic of Macedonia and Federal Republic of Yugoslavia. Skopje: *Official Gazette of the Republic of Macedonia*, no. 22, 7 May 1996.

Ajanovski, Georgi (1993) *Priznavanjeto na Makedonija. Izbor* [The Recognition of Macedonia. Selection] (Skopje: Nova Makedonija).

Bačcvić Ljiljana *et al.* (1991) *Jugoslavija na kriznoj prekretnici* [Yugoslavia on a Crisis Crossroad] (Beograd: Institut društvenih nauka).

Bogoev, Ksente (1993) 'A Sketch for a Global Presentation of the Macedonian Economy', *Balkan Forum*, (Skopje) vol. A, no. 2.

Djikov, Stavre (1993) *Makedonija vo komunistiĕkiot triagolnik* [Macedonia in the Communist Triangle] (Skopje: MOBI-ART).

Glenny, Misha (1992) *The Fall of Yugoslavia. The Third Balkan War* (London: Penguin).

Goati, Vladimir *et al.* (1989) *Smisao jugoslovenskog pluralistiĕkog šoka* [The Nature of Yugoslav Pluralistic Shock] (Beograd: Književne novine).

Interim Accord (1995) Law of Ratification of the Interim Accord between the Republic of Macedonia and Republic of Greece. Skopje: *Official Gazette of the Republic of Macedonia*, no. 48, 12 October 1995.

Katardžiev, Ivan (1997) 'Republika Makedonija in njene sosede' [Republic of Macedonia and Her neighbours] *Revija Borce* (Ljubljana), vol. XI. IX, no. 559/560.

Meier, Viktor (1996) *Zakaj je razpadla Jugoslavija* [Why Yugoslavia Dispersed] (Ljubljana: CO LIBRIS).

Milosavlevski, Slavko (1996) *Dveto lica na sobitijata* [Two Faces of the Events] (Skopje: ZUMPRES).

Milosavlevski, Slavko (1997) 'Pogovor z Dobrico Ćosićcm' [Talks with Dobrica Ćosić] *Revija Borce* (Ljubljana), vol. XI. IX, no. 559/560.

Mirčev, Dimitar (1993) 'Ethnocentrism and Strife among Political Elites: The End of Yugoslavia, *Governance*, (Oxford), vol. 6, no. 3.

Mirčev, Dimitar (1997) 'Edificando Nuevas Estructuras Democraticas: El Caso de Macedonia', in *Las Nuevas instituciones politicas de la Europa Oriental* (Carlos Flores Jubcrias, Dir. Madrid/Valencia: CEC-IVEI).

Mojanoski, Cane (1996) *Socijalniot i politički profil na političkite partii vo Makedonija* [The Social and Political Profile of Political Parties in Macedonia] (Skopje: LIBER).

Reuter, Jens (1993) 'Policy and Economy in Macedonia', *Balkan Forum* (Skopje), vol. 1, no. 3.

Schierup, Carl-Ulrih (1993) 'Prelude to the Inferno. Economic Disintegration and the Political Fragmentation of Yugoslavia', *Balkan Forum* (Skopje), vol. 1, no. 3 (June).

Silber, Laura and Allan Little (1996) *Smrt Jugoslavijc* [The Death of Yugoslavia] (Ljubljana: CO-LIBRI).

Spirovski, Jgor and Dimitar Mirčev (1997) 'The Role and Early Experiences of the Macedonian Parliament in the Process of Transition', in *Working Papers on the New Democratic Parliaments. The First Years*, eds D. Lawrence Longley and Drago Zajc (Appleton, Wisconsin: IPSA RC and Lawrence University).

Troebst, Stefan (1993) 'Makedonische Antworten auf die "Makedonische Frage" 1944–1992. Nationalismus, Republiksgründung, Nation Building', *Südosteuropa*, vol. 41, no. 7/8.

Urbančič, Ivan (1989) 'Sedemdeset let Jugoslavije' [Seventy Years of Yugoslavia], *Nova Revija* (Ljubljana), vol. 8, no. 85/86.

Chapter **15**

Greek policy considerations over FYROM independence and recognition

Evangelos Kofos

The changing Balkan scene and its impact on Greek policy options

The collapse of the bipolar system was welcomed in the West as terminating the global confrontation of the Western democracies with the world communist movement headed by the Soviet Union, while ushering in a new era of generous economic and political opportunities, particularly for the big industrial nations. For the United States it offered challenges to put to test visions of shaping a novel world order under the leadership of a single superpower. The European Community/European Union could aspire to a less ambitious but equally challenging role of promoting a new European order to the extremities of the old continent.

In the Balkans, the emerging new societies were fast shedding centralised communist authority, while condemning the quasi 'socialist internationalism and solidarity'. Uncertain about their future course, they appeared to be torn between the pursuit of the 'European dream' and the resurrection of traditional, pre-war – if not nineteenth-century – 'greater nation' visions. In the northern tier of the peninsula, such ideas soon led to open armed clashes of a semi-fratricidal, semi-interethnic nature. In the southern belt of the former communist states – which incidentally bordered along the entire northern frontier of Greece – a chain of potential crisis spots appeared on the political map. In the view of Greek policy-makers at the time, top of the list was the formerly internal Yugoslav problem of Kosovo. With the disintegration of the Yugoslav federation, it showed signs of emerging as a major international question, capable of disrupting the borders of four countries, spilling over into the neighbouring mostly Albanian-inhabited areas of the former Socialist Republic of Macedonia (SRM), and involving in hostilities a wider range of countries in the area. A second problem which could stress Greek–Albanian relations to boiling point, referred to the status and rights of the sizeable Greek minority in the southern part of Albania, long oppressed by the Enver Hoxha regime.[1] Furthermore, on the eastern end of the borderline, in Bulgaria, the large Moslem/Turkish minority, maltreated by the Zhivkov regime, was a cause for much concern to new Bulgarian leaders, sensitive to the prospect of Turkish pressures and interventions, at a time when the country had lost its security umbrella of the Warsaw Pact. Finally, a major issue likely to destabilise the entire region of the Balkans, was the new status and the future course of the SRM. Analysts at the time concocted a multiplicity of scenarios ranging from new federal or confederal arrangements in the regions of ex-Yugoslavia, to independent statehood, and even partition.

Undoubtedly, all these issues, in various forms, existed before the disintegration of the FSR of Yugoslavia and the collapse of the communist rule in Eastern Europe. The former regimes, as well as the fossilised security arrangements which had preserved peace in post-Second World War Europe, had been successful in preventing the eruption of these problems, albeit at a considerable cost for the oppressed peoples and minorities. By 1991, the new conditions and the agonising quest for new leaderships for economic survival, social reconstruction and new security arrangements, brought the Balkans to the brink of chaos. At least, such was the view from Athens at the time.

Of all the members of the EC/EU, Greece, located in the southern periphery of the troubled area, was the only one likely to be implicated, in a direct or indirect way, in such potential crises. Ironically, for Greece, long an outpost of the West at the East–West confrontation line, the withering-away of the Soviet bloc and the breaking-up of the Soviet Union augmented rather than diminished perceptions of insecurity. Its former comfortable and valuable geopolitical position was gradually diminishing, posing serious doubts as to the efficacy of the Cold War period security arrangements of the country. Worldwide, Western loyalties towards ideological friends were fast evaporating, although in the case of Greece, its EC connection was holding strong.[2] In Balkan terms, Greece's membership of the EC/EU and the Western security network, plus its comparatively strong economy and its democratic political system, rendered it a potential element of stability for the entire region rather than an actor for doomsday scenarios. Indeed, this was the role its partners in the EC/EU and in Washington were expecting Athens to assume.[3] In short, compared to its northern neighbours, emerging from half a century of communist rule, Greece held an enviable position – a position, however, won the hard way, being compelled to endure a disastrous three-year civil war (1946–9) in order to stem off the spread of communist rule all the way to the southernmost tip of the Balkan peninsula. It is worth noting that at that time Greece's future partners in the Western European alliances were completing the first stage of their post-war reconstruction, while its neighbours to the north were engaged, by force or choice, in constructing their panacea of socialism-toward-communism societies under the comfortable umbrella of the seemingly all-powerful Soviet Union.

With the dawn of the new decade of the 1990s, despite this privileged position, the future of Greece's insecure eastern flank loomed bleaker. Turkish political elites under the late President Turgut Ozal, with the support of the powerful military establishment, stimulated by developments in the Soviet Union and the Balkan backyard, began to voice views inspired by visions of the Ottoman imperial grandeur. From a Greek perspective, the spectre of an emerging 'Islamic arch' extending to the Balkans, spearheaded by Ankara nationalists, could not augur well for Greek stability; more so, since at that time the voice of Balkan nationalists was becoming stronger in the respective countries.[4] Such concern was particularly vocal among the Greeks of the border regions of Macedonia and Thrace, where memories of the Second World War 'triple occupation' (German–Bulgarian–Italian) and the ensuing Civil War were rekindled.

An odd picture was emerging. In contrast to the euphoria shared by Western countries for the collapse of the Soviet bloc, the apprehensions of junior partner Greece over the gathering of dark clouds over the Balkan region were viewed as insignificant and exaggerated, if not 'unreasonable'.[5]

In terms of short-range implications, such assessments by Greece's partners were not entirely groundless. Not a single one of the emerging new democracies in the north of Greece was capable of posing a direct threat to its security in the near future. In this respect, hardly a Greek would disagree. The predicament of the Greeks, however, centred on the medium- and long-range implications of new developments in the region, which included a probable revival of traditional Balkan nationalisms, the spread of Islamic fundamentalism and the reshaping of the external frontiers of the Balkan states. It is worth recalling that in the early 1990s, serious analysts and journalists in the West were engaged in constructing similar doom scenarios.[6] Significantly, most local actors in the emerging democratic societies were voicing similar opinions.

The fact that the Greeks, despite their comparative advantageous position, appeared to share the apprehensions of their Balkan neighbours rather than the euphoric expectations of their Western European partners, should be traced to their traumatic experiences with, what their politicians had termed, the 'threat from the North'. Twice during the twentieth century, during the First and the Second World Wars, they had seen large parts of their northern regions of Macedonia and Thrace occupied by the armies of a neighbouring country (Bulgaria), acting in concert with and under the umbrella of an outside Big Power (mainly Germany). For a third time, during the Civil War, these same regions ran the risk of being reclaimed by the neighbouring communist countries of Yugoslavia and Bulgaria, supported this time by the Soviet Union.[7] In the light of such experiences, the spectre of a repetition of such 'unholy alliances' in the future by neo-nationalist Balkan regimes acting in concord with nationalist elements of the Turkish establishment in Ankara, was at the core of analyses which shaped Greek perceptions and stirred initiatives during the critical years of 1990–2.

As a flashback, it is worth recalling that in the years just prior to the crisis of the 1990s, Greece had maintained very good relations with Zhivkov's Bulgaria, ironically, the most loyal of the Warsaw Pact partners. That was an almost unique phenomenon in Greek–Bulgarian relations, even if one needed to look for historical precedents all the way back to Byzantine times. Historians are likely to attribute this development to a meticulous process of confidence-building, highlighted, on the one hand, by Zhivkov's positive reaction to Greece's traditional sensitivities over territorial and minority issues, and, on the other, by Karamanlis's and subsequently by A. Papandreou's reciprocal endeavours within the Western alliances in support of Bulgaria, as well as by concessions of economic interest to Bulgaria (port facilities in Thessaloniki, opening up of new border crossings, etc.).[8] Similarly, Greece's relations with Yugoslavia, until the closing years of the 1980s, had been positive for over three decades, despite recurring flare-ups connected with the Macedonian question. By the 1980s, a marked improvement was apparent in Greek–Albanian relations, due mainly to the PASOK government's initiatives to terminate the legal framework of a 'state of war' existing between the two countries since the Second

World War and to remove Albanian suspicions of Greek territorial claims to Northern Epirus/Southern Albania. Of course, the situation of the Greek minority remained an irksome issue, but the climate of bilateral relations had been improved markedly.[9]

Thus, on the eve of the eruption of the Balkan crisis, the omens for Greece in its relations with the Balkan neighbours appeared promising. Even on the multilateral level, Balkan leaders – with the Greeks as keen zealots – were re-initiating the inter-Balkan conferences on a more positive basis, this time even with the participation of hitherto isolated Albania. In such a climate, Greek political leaders of almost all parties shared the view that the traditional 'threat from the north' had finally come to an end.[10] The only sore spot was the rising nationalism of the Slav Macedonians in the SR of Macedonia.

The legacy of the post-war Macedonian controversy

Future historians of Greece's Balkan relations during the post-war decades, with access to diplomatic archives, might be intrigued by the extent of the impact of the 'Macedonian Question' on the formulation of Greece's Balkan policy options. It suffices, here, to observe that the post-Civil War political, military and diplomatic establishment of the country, during both the 1950s and early 1960s, as well as during the military dictatorship (1967–74), had been haunted by the fate of the northern Greek provinces of Thrace and Macedonia in the event of a major armed confrontation. It was this concern that had prompted successive Greek governments to seek during the Cold War the safety of Western security arrangements. The threat perception, however, persisted in certain circles even though the objective elements of the problem had been removed or sufficiently curtailed. More precisely, the alien-oriented segment of the Slavophones of Western Greek Macedonian, initially Bulgarian- and subsequently Slav Macedonian-oriented, had left the country en masse at the end of the German–Bulgarian occupation (1944), the Tito–Cominform feud (1948) and the termination of the Civil War (1949).[11] Thus, there was no population element of any significant numbers left in the country to substantiate minority and/or territorial claims, as was the case during the war decade of the 1940s. Nevertheless, by the early 1970s, the 'Cold War' had given way to the Helsinki Final Act spirit of peaceful coexistence and the contractual obligations of the North American and the European states to uphold the post-war territorial status quo in Europe.

In Greece, preoccupation with the Macedonian issue continued to persist in the collective public mind. For one, it had been associated for too long with the anti-Communist rhetoric which accused the Greek Communist Party (KKE) of national treachery for attempting, at the height of the Civil War, to detach (Greek) Macedonia from the Greek state. Moreover, the re-emergence from Skopje and the Slav Macedonian Diaspora of complaints against the Greek government's policy of non-recognition of a 'Macedonian' minority within its borders, as well as demands for repatriation, were viewed as a coordinated effort to reawaken revanchist and irredentist claims.[12]

Nevertheless, neither of these two issues would have merited much attention by the Greeks were it not for a third element of friction, a lesser known or understood component of the traditional Macedonian controversy. By the 1980s, the Greek public was gradually becoming aware of 'Macedonism', i.e., the nationalist ideology which had succeeded to a considerable degree in mutating into ethnic 'Makedonci' the Slavonic as well as segments of non-Slavonic (Vlachs, Greeks, etc.) inhabitants of the SRM. By the 1980s, this ideology was diverting its activities and projecting its thesis to worldwide audiences, hoping to gain international recognition for the new ethnicity. At the same time, it was claiming as 'Makedonci' all Slav-speakers, or descendants of Slav-speakers of the wider Macedonian region. Such maximalistic claims, however, were challenging the right of those Slav-speaking inhabitants of, or emigrants from, Greek Macedonia and Bulgarian Macedonia (Pirin) to identify themselves as Greek Macedonians and Bulgarian Macedonians, respectively. During earlier stages (1940s to early 1960s), the mutation process had been focusing on the Bulgarian-oriented Slavs of Macedonia, recasting as national 'Macedonian' almost the totality of Bulgarian history and Bulgarian cultural presence in Macedonia through the ages. In subsequent decades (1970s to 1980s), the emphasis shifted to the Diaspora, where the target area comprised the Slav-speaking emigrants, who had left Greek Macedonia, mainly as a result of the Civil War of the 1940s.

Unlike the mutation process in the SRM, in the Diaspora this process needed to overcome the crust of Hellenic heritage shared by Grecophone and most of the Slavophone emigrants. Thus, in faraway countries, such as Canada and Australia, in an environment where personal histories – or perceptions thereof – took precedence over hazy knowledge of the century-old historical past of the 'old countries', educators, clergymen and government propagandists from Skopje began to focus their attention on, and to tamper with, Greek history and heritage. It is interesting to note that against all historical odds, the Slav Macedonians of the Diaspora turned to the saga of Alexander the Great as a vehicle of proselytism. In the process they developed a new brand of 'Macedonism'. Contrary to the official dogma which referred to thirteen centuries of 'Macedonian' existence, they would seek to retrieve the origins of their nation to a further thousand years. Their aim was to foment a linkage with the Ancient Macedonian kingdom, and thus extend the 'imagined' roots of present-day 'Makedonci' to Alexander the Great and his descendants. It was a daring operation which could either be viewed as a belated, romantic nineteenth-century-type construction of a national myth, or be exposed to international ridicule for creating yet another 'salade macedoine', this time of mixed adulterated historical facts and racist theories of blood lineage to glorious 'ancestors'.[13]

The Greeks of the Diaspora, however, were in no mood to humour or to tolerate incursions into the 'sacrosanct' tenets of their identity and heritage. Their strong reaction finally reverberated in Greece, awakening influential segments of the public to what was viewed as a direct challenge not necessarily to their land (Greek Macedonia), but to the Macedonian dimension of their Hellenic heritage.

Greek government policy in the decades since the termination of the Civil War had viewed Yugoslavia as a useful buffer state on the fringes of the Soviet-dominated communist world. Despite frequent irritants from the local government officials, the press and radio of Skopje, Athens had never raised any objections to the constitutional framework of the SFR of Yugoslavia, not even questioning its internal administrative structure of federate republics. Thus, a Greek consulate continued to function in the capital of SRM, Skopje, maintaining normal *de facto* relations with the republican authorities of the republic, although officially it was accredited to the federal government in Belgrade. On the other hand, official Greek policy, supported by all major Greek political parties, rejected the existence of a 'Macedonian' nation. This denial, however, did not mean the negation of the existence of a separate Slavonic people in SRM, but to its Macedonian name; a name which was considered a constituent element of Greek cultural heritage.[14] In this respect, the Greek position differed from that of the Bulgarians, who categorically refused to accept that a 'Macedonian' nation existed or was even constructed. In short, the Bulgarian view perceived the Slav-speaking people in the SRM as 'Bulgarians' or of 'Bulgarian origin'. Contrary to the Greeks, the 'Macedonian' name was of no problem to the Bulgarians, who accepted it as a regional one; indeed, one defining the 'Bulgarians' of the Macedonian region at large.[15]

As a way out of the predicament, Greek official policy – both of the New Democracy Party and of the socialist PASOK – opted for and used the name 'Slav Macedonians' to identify the 'Makedonci' of the SRM and its adherents in the Diaspora. It should be noted that the KKE had adopted this name for the Slav speakers of Macedonia, even prior to the Second World War. Similarly, historians in the SRM have referred repeatedly to 'Macedonian Slavs', when writing on Macedonian history prior to the 1870s, a period, allegedly, prior to 'Macedonian' national emancipation.[16]

By the advent to power, in 1981, of the populist PASOK party, the government of Andreas Papandreou sought to introduce to Greek society and politics its own brand of patriotism. More specifically, it promoted a Greek-centred, xenophobic, Third-World mentality, under the slogan, 'Greece belongs to the Greeks'; a little-veiled attempt to reap easy political dividends by juxtaposing it to Karamanlis's dictum – on the eve of the country's adhesion to the EC – 'Greece belongs to the West'. PASOK's 'patriotic' orientation legitimised nationalism – so harshly manipulated by the dictatorial regime – this time among the leftist segments of the population. Undoubtedly, the recurring crises with Turkey over Cyprus and the Aegean were natural contributors to this shift in public reaction.[17]

Tito's successors in Belgrade had succeeded in curtailing the strong anti-Bulgarian rhetoric of Skopje, so common during the past decades. Instead, Slav Macedonian nationalists were allowed a certain latitude to channel their nationalistic effervescence in the direction of Greece. From the mid-1980s on, Skopje became the harbinger of a major escalation of propaganda against Greece, supported by Slav Macedonian nationalists of the Diaspora. The new irritants from the Slav Macedonian nationalists began to filter into the front pages of newspapers, even of leftist orientation, catching the eye and raising concern among wider circles of the Greek public, politicians and academics.[18] When, however, rhetoric began to take the form of demarches to international bodies for grievances originating back to the Civil War years, an issue of major sensitivity to Greek society as a whole, the reaction in Greece, in official circles, as well as in the media, was strong.

It was in such a climate that the spectre of the dissolution of the Yugoslav federation and the future status of the SRM as an independent Macedonian state on Greece's northern border, began to preoccupy seriously not only Greek policy-makers, but a wider circle of publicists and academics.

Greek concerns over Yugoalav Macedonia's future status

It should be noted that prior to the mid-1980s, with the exception of occasional flare-ups in the press, there was little serious public debate about the various aspects of the Macedonian issue, which was limited to a confined number of academics, journalists and politicians, centred mainly in Thessaloniki.[19] By 1990, however, the picture had changed drastically. New 'experts' of the Macedonian question emerged to take control and monopolise the media – particularly the radio and TV stations in Thessaloniki – to enlighten the public on a rather complicated issue. A number of them chose instead to sensationalise by projecting their own brand of the 'Macedonian question', with an assortment of distorted historical facts and half truths.

Gradually, a unique consensus emerged, linking the traditional bastions of Greek nationalism, such as the strongly anti-Communist part of the Right (which continued to hold the KKE *dosilogos* (accused) for its wartime and Civil War Macedonian policy), the Army, and the Church, with the adherents of the socialist 'patriotic' PASOK and followers of the leftist party 'Synaspismos'. It is true, however, that a significant number of academics did offer their contribution to a sober and scholarly analysis of the issues at hand. Others, however, chose to join the bandwagon of nationalist fundamentalism. Their theories about the Macedonian question and, subsequently, their perception of what Greece's policy should be in the light of current developments in the Balkans, influenced to a considerable degree the formulation and to some degree the conduct of official Greek policy on the issue. In this respect, it is worth reviewing briefly their 'revisionist' theories.

Departing from the generally accepted premise that the Ancient Macedonians constituted part of the Hellenic world and that the territory of the Macedonian Kingdom of King Philip coincides, more or less, with the present Greek province of Macedonia, they coined the slogan '*I Makedonia einai elliniki*' (i.e. 'Macedonia is Greek'). It was a slogan, however, which raised not a few eyebrows in Europe where people had been associating for years the name of Macedonia with the Yugoslav province of the 'Socialist Republic of Macedonia'. Given the utter confusion reigning in Western media at the time of the Yugoslav disintegration, it was no surprise that certain commentators chose to interpret the slogan and the huge public demonstrations that followed in Thessaloniki and other Greek towns, as a nationalist Greek move seeking to profit from the chaotic situation in order to advance territorial claims on the neighbouring Macedonian republic. Certainly, observers with even rudimentary knowledge of Greek and Balkan history and politics could easily detect the misunderstanding over terms. Nevertheless, as the slogan became the 'battle cry' of the Greeks demonstrating all over the world against the recognition of the new state bearing the name of Macedonia, the government in Skopje and its supporters abroad chose to make propaganda capital of an inaccurate slogan to discredit the Greek motives in opposing recognition of FYROM.[20]

The debate over that slogan sheds some further light into the gradual formulation of Greek positions during the critical period of 1991–2. Indeed, those who took the initiative in coining the slogan on the eve of the huge, one-million-strong, public demonstration in Thessaloniki, in February 1992, could hardly imagine that the outside world was more familiar with the Macedonian state of the FSR of Yugoslavia rather than with the ancient Macedonian kingdom and its boundaries of 24 centuries ago. By proposing that slogan they had two things in mind: on the one hand, to straighten the record of the Hellenic connection of Ancient Macedonia, and in so doing they felt that they were rightly defending a people's collective right to its heritage; and, on the other hand, to voice in no uncertain terms their determination that they would not tolerate the re-emergence of wartime irredentist yearnings for the annexation of Greek Macedonia. Such yearnings were gaining much popularity in Skopje and the Slav Macedonian Diaspora. As such, the Greeks sought to make it clear, *urbi et orbi*, that Macedonia (i.e., the Greek province of Macedonia) was an inalienable component of the Greek state.[21] At about that time (1992) the state-controlled Greek Post Office issued a series of stamps portraying Ancient and Byzantine Macedonian cultural treasures marked 'Macedonia was and will always be Greek'.

A side-effect of the popularisation of the misleading slogan and other related literature, was to convey to the Greek public the perception that there is only one 'Macedonia': the Greek Macedonia. The inference was clear. Since no other region in the Balkans, apart from the Greek province of Macedonia, could be associated or identified with the ancient kingdom of Macedonia, it would be historically preposterous for a Slavic country to assume the Macedonian name as the official designation of a new independent state entity. Carrying further this argument, no other people, apart from the Greeks, were entitled to use the Macedonian name either as a cultural-ethnic or a geographic-regional appellation.[22]

The new brand of Greek 'Macedonologues', in ways similar to those of their Slav Macedonian colleagues, soon found themselves trotting along slippery roads, even distorting historical facts in their endeavour to recast Macedonian history to suit political needs. In trying to establish the thesis that lands outside the confines of Greek Macedonia had no historical justification for appropriating the name 'Macedonia' or its derivatives, they suppressed the fact that in modern times, and certainly since the emergence of the Macedonian question in the nineteenth century, it was commonly accepted, even by Greek historians and politicians,[23] that Macedonia, as a geographical region of the Ottoman state, comprised roughly the lands of present-day Greek Macedonia, FYROM and the Pirin district of Bulgaria.

Like a dry forest in August, the logic of the 'one and only Macedonia' argument caught fire in the imagination of an ill-informed Greek public in Greece and the Diaspora. The first victim of this mobilisation was the traditional post-war Greek policy *vis-à-vis* the phenomenon of 'Macedonism'. Even suggestions to use the term 'Slav-Macedonian' or any other compound name – for example, 'Vardar Macedonia' – were viewed as 'national treachery'.[24] The new independent state was christened 'Skopje', in public parlance as well as in official documents, while its people were referred to as 'Skopjans'. Even that central 'Macedonian Question' was purified as 'Skopiano'.

Strong Greek public reaction over these issues were responses to nationalist manifestations across the border in the SRM through 1990–1, i.e. even prior to the declaration of the independence, in September 1991, of the 'Republika na Makedonija'. Indeed, a nationalist fever had infected large segments of the population. As early as October 1989, public demonstrations had been held in Skopje and elsewhere, projecting – for the first time since the 1940s – slogans calling for 'reunification of Macedonia', or 'Solun [Thessaloniki] is ours'. Unimpeded, similar graffiti covered walls in various towns of the Republic. A nationalist party, the VMRO-DPMNE (Internal Macedonian Revolutionary Organisation-Democratic Party of Macedonian National Unity), founded in January 1990, provided further impetus to such nationalist yearnings. Traditionally, VMRO had been known as a terrorist Bulgarian Macedonian organisation. Whereas the new VMRO did not appear to share its predecessor's tactics or its Bulgarian orientation, it had endorsed in its statutes a political platform aiming at the independence and the unification of the three Macedonian regions. Pointedly, it had chosen as the party's symbols the Ancient Macedonian 'Vergina sun' and the medieval Bulgarian lion. While other smaller parties, such as the MAAK (Movement for Pan-Macedonian Action), adopted similar nationalist positions, it was the VMRO which gained first position in popular votes and parliamentary seats during the first multi-party elections held in SRM, late in 1990. During 1991, public statements and irredentist literature, such as calendars, tourist mementos, car stickers, and maps portraying a united Macedonia were fanning the flames of nationalism.[25]

In Greece, despite such irritants, official policy did not change overnight. Throughout 1991, the Greek government of the New Democracy Party, headed by Prime Minister Constantine Mitsotakis, with Andonis Samaras as Foreign Minister, was pursuing the traditional line on Yugoslavia, while coordinating its efforts with the United States and the majority of EC member countries for the survival of the Yugoslav federation or for a new Yugoslav federal version, minus Slovenia and possibly Croatia. When, however, the process for the dissolution of the old structures in Yugoslavia appeared irreversable, Athens shifted its attention to securing international guarantees against changes to the external borders of the Balkan countries.

Sensing that most EC countries were either ignorant of, or indifferent to the intricacies of Balkan issues – with the notable exception of Germany and Italy – the Greek Government turned to Belgrade and Sofia in search of a common approach to the emerging problems in the southern part of the Balkans. The Greeks' major concern was to avoid the outbreak of hostilities, mainly in, or over the territory of the SRM. They found no consensus of views in the two capitals.[26] The Bulgarians accepted developments in Yugoslavia as an unexpected bonanza. Their traditional opponent in the Balkans, the Serbs, had been caught in a whirlpool of their own making which, one way or the other, was bound to wreck their hitherto dominant geopolitical position in the region. More important, however, the Bulgarians sensed that developments in the north would reduce or even terminate Yugoslav/Serb control over the territory of the SRM, a land the Bulgarians had not ceased to view as one of the three 'historic Bulgarian lands' (the other two being Moesia and Thrace). Under the circumstances, they were in no mood to accommodate Belgrade – or, for that matter, the Greeks – in sustaining a structure which would perpetuate Serbian hegemony over the region. Dormant Bulgarian nostalgia for the lands and the people to their west, in terms of a closer relationship with long estranged 'brethren' and the eventual razing of border barriers, was gradually becoming once again vocal, after decades of Zhivkovian nationalist hibernation.[27]

Bulgaria, in the Greeks' view, was still very weak and, for some time to come, unable to influence developments in Macedonia. On the other hand, the international community, particularly the EC member states, were expected to be receptive of Greek sensitivities and interests. That was the period of Maastrich euphoria for 'European solidarity'. As a result, Athens opted for a strong Serbia, capable under Milosevic to run successfully a new federal entity and hold in check Skopje's reawakened irredentism.[28]

Greek assessments and expectations were wrong on all counts. Bulgaria was, indeed, too weak to interfere. But, certainly, it was far from indifferent to Macedonian developments and to Greece's apparent rapprochement with the Serbs on this issue, to the extent that it would not hesitate to sacrifice the climate of good relations that had prevailed with Athens over a quarter of a century. In the case of Milosevic's Serbia, pressing priorities in the north and in Kosovo led to withdrawal of the Yugoslav Army from FYROM, to the painful surprise of the Greeks, who belatedly realised that they were acquiring a new neighbour to their north, free of the tutelage of, and influences from Belgrade.

Diplomatic tug-of-war over the recognition of 'Republika na Makedonija'

A brief presentation of the diplomatic initiatives in connection with the recognition of FYROM is pertinent at this point for a better understanding of the formulation and conduct of Greek policy on the subject.

The declaration on Yugoslavia issued by the EC/EU Foreign Ministers on 17 December 1991 was undoubtedly a turning point for the Macedonian issue. It drew up a framework of prerequisites for the international recognition of the former SRM which, to a considerable degree, met the main points raised by Greece. It specifically asked 'for constitutional and political guarantees ensuring that [the applicant state] has no territorial claims towards a neighbouring Community State [Greece] and that it will conduct no hostile propaganda activities versus a neighbouring Community State, including the use of a denomination which implies territorial claims'.[29] In subsequent weeks, the government in Skopje did introduce certain minor amendments to its Constitution, but it bypassed the core issue of the name of the new state. The Badinter Arbitration Commission rendered an advisory opinion in favour of recognition, but Greece considered the commitments inadequate and the EU concurred, requesting the Portuguese Presidency (Foreign Minister Pineiro) to approach the two sides in order to find a suitable solution to the problem. Pineiro, after consultations with both sides, drew up two draft documents on the basis of the December 1991 declaration. The first dealt with guarantees 'against territorial claims', and the second with further guarantees 'against hostile propaganda'. Orally, Pineiro suggested as a suitable state denomination, the name 'New Macedonia'. The Pineiro mission proved inconclusive. FYROM apparently was responsive to the two first points but remained non-committal on the name, probably awaiting first Greece's response. Greek Foreign Minister Andonis Samaras tentatively accepted the two draft documents, but turned down the name proposal.[30] Prime Minister Mitsotakis reluctantly consented to Samaras' stand when faced by the endorsement of the maximalist line – 'no Macedonia or its derivatives' – by the Council of Party Leaders (with only KKE's Paparriga demurring), held on 13 April, under the chairmanship of President of the Republic C. Karamanlis. Mitsotakis, at this point dismissed Samaras and took over himself the Foreign Minister's portfolio.

Subsequently, despite mounting tensions and fighting in the northern tier of ex-Yugoslavia, the EU, still headed by the Portuguese Presidency, showed its solidarity with Greece in two more instances. In their meeting at Gimaraes, on 2 May 1992, the EU Foreign Ministers declared their readiness to recognise the former SRM as an independent and sovereign state, adding the trailer, *'under a name which could be acceptable to all interested parties'*. Thus, its partners granted Greece a quasi veto on the name.[31] Two months later, while international pressures for recognition were mounting (already the US had compelled the EU to expedite recognition to Bosnia-Herzegovina), the heads of EU states and governments, at their Lisbon meeting of 26–27 June 1992, went even a step further in meeting Greece's requests. While they reiterated their readiness to recognise the new state, this time they added, in no uncertain terms, that they would proceed in this direction *'under a name which will not include the denomination Macedonia'*.[32] That was a phrasing that went beyond the 17 December 1991 declaration, excluding specifically the name *Macedonia*. Much later it was revealed that the Greek Prime Minister had given confidentially his consent that such a denomination would be applicable to international usage.[33]

In the face of these documents, it appears that by mid-1992, Greece, against all odds, had gained most of its points within the councils of the EC/EU. President Gligorov's refusal, however, to abide by the EU's rulings, delayed the recognition of his country for more than a year, but, in the end, he obtained it in a roundabout way, by petitioning the UN for membership status. Indeed, the UN Security Council granted its consent conditional on two important points: First, that the hoisting of the new member's flag, bearing the Ancient Macedonian emblem, the so-called 'Vergina sun' was deferred to a future date; it was an important recognition of Greece's right to protect and defend its cultural patrimony. Second, that the new member state would be admitted under the provisional name of 'the Former Yugoslav Republic of Macedonia' (FYROM), for as long as 'the difference over the name [was] pending'. The SC justified its decision 'in the interest of maintaining peace and good-neighbourly relations in the region', another concession to the Greek argument that the 'constitutional' state denomination of FYROM could affect negatively the promotion of peaceful and good-neighbourly relations among the peoples and the states in the region (Decision 817/7.4.1993).[34]

In subsequent months, the UN, through its mediators Lord Owen and Cyrus Vance and with strong US backing, took over from the EU the burden to bring the two parties to an agreement. By May 1993, it appeared that a solution was within arm's length. A draft treaty, prepared by the mediators after exhaustive consultations with the two government delegations in New York, sought to synthesise the main considerations of both sides. The mediators were hopeful that even their proposed name 'Nova Makedonija' (the old Pineiro proposal in its Slavic version) would be a breakthrough.[35]

It was at that moment that the simmering pressures in Greece – and apparently in FYROM – blew up any chance of a compromise solution to the problem. Instead, the way was paved for a further escalation of the crisis at considerable cost to both sides. For Greece, this cost would be measured in political terms, while for FYROM it would be associated with economic and social burdens for years to come.

More specifically, in the case of Greece, the course of the diplomatic developments, already cited, had weaved a canvas of multiple problems, upsetting and polarising the internal political scene, derailing the country's foreign policy orientations and priorities, and setting in motion new social cleavages inside the country and among the diaspora Greeks.

The thrust of the 'Skopiano' in Greek politics

The first phase: Mitsotakis at the wheel (1991 to October 1993)

It has already been noted that the 'Macedonian question' had sharply divided the Greeks into two camps during the Civil War and, for years, had poisoned the internal political scene. By the latter part of the 1970s, however, all segments of the political spectrum had finally come to terms with the issue, almost to the point of reaching consensus on a number of important points.[36] More important, the two leading parties – 'Nea Dimokratia' and 'PASOK' – which were succeeding each other in government since the fall of the military dictatorship in 1974, despite their polemics on almost every issue, shared similar strategic objectives and agreed even on tactics in the handling of the Macedonian problem. Nevertheless, by 1992, this bipartisan approach appeared to be shelved when Andreas Papandreou, leader of the Opposition at the time, adopted an unbending negative attitude toward any attempt by Prime Minister C. Mitsotakis – heading a two-vote majority government – for a compromise solution on FYROM's name.

At first, PASOK's opposition tactics were overshadowed by internal New Democracy dissensions, presented as a personal Mitsotakis–Samaras duel that ended, as we have seen, in the latter's dismissal.

In the best tradition of the emotive political debate in Greece, the internal crisis descended upon the Greek political scene with the thunder of a summer storm. The point of departure was the interpretation of the 17 December 1991 declaration; a decision which, when announced, had been hailed by all sides as a feat of Greek diplomacy. Given the circumstances and the strong opposition of certain delegations, with Italy at the head, the final unanimous vote on the phrasing of the declaration was, indeed, a success. Its implementation, however, was an entirely different matter. The impression on the Greek public was that the new state would not be recognised as 'Macedonia'. However, while the architect of that decision, Samaras, was reaping the general public recognition, PASOK political strategists undertook to tarnish the impression of a major government achievement. They would accept it as successful provided the declaration signified that not only the name 'Macedonia' but any of its derivatives would be excluded from the denomination of the new state. That apparently excluded also any form of a compound Macedonian name. Certainly, by no stretch of the imagination could the agreed formula be interpreted in this way. Samaras, however, was hardly a politician who would be outsmarted by demagogues. He had no scruples about confirming the maximalist interpretation. The public rejoiced. But in the councils of the EU, the chancelleries of the European capitals and in the international press, the mood in no way corresponded to the prevailing atmosphere in Greece. Indeed, it was evident, particularly to seasoned Greek diplomats, that although the 'maximalist' thesis could be a useful bargaining departure point, it could only provide the stepping stone for a fair compromise solution.[37]

Recently (1995–6), the publication of books, with ample confidential documentation, written by, or through the consent of the political protagonists at the time, offered the Greek public sufficient insight into the political bickering and behind-the-scenes secret bargaining on the handling of the Macedonian issue.[38] On the basis of these revelations, it is safe to conclude that while Foreign Minister Samaras was hard at work presenting to his colleagues in the EU documentation and arguments in favour of the maximalist solution, Prime Minister Mitsotakis had been sounding out his own colleagues, in the same capitals, for a compromise solution on the name. Consequently, it was a matter of time for a major political crisis to explode, first within the ruling New Democracy Party and then on a national scale. When Mitsotakis dismissed Samaras, and reserved also for himself the post of Foreign Minister, instead of promoting his own conciliatory views he proceeded to pursue publicly not his own views for a compromise solution, but the maximalist line of his dismissed Minister; a line, however, which, by that time, had been endorsed by three of the four party leaders represented in parliament and, apparently, by President C. Karamanlis. Mitsotakis's move might be seen as a masterstroke in petty internal politics. It allowed him to outmanoeuvre the internal opposition of the 'maximalists' in his own party and to checkmate the eroding tactics of his arch enemy Andreas Papandreou. As it turned out, however, the real loser in all these confusing developments, as most Greek analysts came to assess years later, was the 'national issue'.

The positive decisions at Gimaraes and Lisbon undoubtedly bear the personal mark of Mitsotakis. Nevertheless, on the basis of subsequent revelations, those decisions were far from constituting a full endorsement of Greece's desiderata on its dispute with Skopje. They aimed primarily at bolstering Mitsotakis's own precarious parliamentary position inside Greece. A conservative and pragmatist politician, Mitsotakis was viewed as a preferable counterpoise to Papandreou, who, on his former performance record in the European councils, was perceived, at best, as an unpredictable leader.

Following Lisbon, Mitsotakis chose to rest for a while on his diplomatic 'laurels'. In doing this, however, he failed to capitalise on the strength of the unanimous support of his peers in the EU in order to negotiate with Skopje a positive compromise solution. Thus, he offered Gligorov a much needed respite during the summer and autumn months of 1992, and allowed him to recuperate from the Lisbon shock, to rally back, and to stand firmly by his own maximalist position. As the situation in the northern ex-republics of Yugoslavia was worsening, the FYROM President could now press more convincingly for immediate recognition of his country as a means of stabilising peace in the region and containing the extension of the fighting to the south. It was a pleasant tune in the ears of Western diplomats.

In fairness, it should be recalled that the EU had, initially, sought to accommodate Greece's sensitivities and concerns by attaching to FYROM's recognition three conditions (EC Foreign Ministers' Council, 17 December 1991). Gradually, however, after a period of confused 'indifference', developments in Croatia and the opening up of a new front of armed confrontation in Bosnia, the European Powers, along with the United States were compelled to be involved actively. In the process of constructing a 'cordon sanitaire' around Serbia, the territory of FYROM became a useful pawn in the unfolding international chess game of Great Power pacifiers vs. Balkan unruly villains. As such, the small landlocked state to the south of the warring zone acquired an ephemeral importance far exceeding its geostrategic value. At that critical moment (first half of 1992), the interests of the European Community began to veer in the opposite direction from Greece's specific pursuits in the Balkans.

Inside Greece, however, Prime Minister Mitsotakis had apparently reached his decision that, at that moment, his first priority was to endeavour to lower the tone of public excitement and to cool off the growing party dissension on account of Samaras's dismissal. To initiate directly or indirectly negotiations with Skopje would expose him to a renewal of public outcry about 'selling out' on the national issue. The new British Presidency accommodated him, as it was in no hurry to carry out the Lisbon mandate.[39]

A year later, Mitsotakis was faced with a similar dilemma; this time, in May 1993, when he was presented by UN mediators Vance and Owen with the compromise version of a draft treaty covering all outstanding questions between Athens and Skopje, including the name issue. Despite the fact that his government – with Michalis Papaconstantinou, an experienced and moderate politician and native of Macedonia, as the new Foreign Minister – had given signs, early in 1993, of departing from the maximalist line, ready to discuss a compound name,[40] Mitsotakis retreated at the last moment. This time, a number of influential MPs of his party, including Miltiadis Evert, presented him with a quasi ultimatum, not to proceed with the signing of the proposed draft. Otherwise, they warned the government would lose its parliamentary majority and would be forced to resign.[41] The Prime Minister succumbed and ordered Papaconstantinou to return to Athens.[42] The Vance–Owen draft treaty, a masterpiece of diplomatic dexterity drafted by two eminent international experts, with the cooperation of the delegations of the two parties – which, however, never met – fell victim to internal politics back in the two capitals. In Greece, the New Democracy leader was offered a breathing space of less than four months. In September, two of his deputies deserted him, causing the fall of the government. The 'Macedonian issue', following Samaras's dismissal, was claiming its second victim. The October elections returned to power a triumphant Papandreou, at the head of the 'patriotic' faction of PASOK.

The second phase: Papandreou at the helm (October 1993–end 1995)

The second phase of the Macedonian imbroglio in Greek politics commenced with the PASOK government strongly condemning its predecessor's handling of the 'Skopiano' as *endotiki* (yielding). Rather ill informed about the mediation procedure in the UN, Prime Minister A. Papandreou hastened to declare, *urbi et orbi*, that Greece would remain firm by its maximalist position on the exclusion of the name 'Macedonia' *and* its derivatives from the neighbouring state's name. Furthermore, he saw little hope in the negotiations under the auspices of the UN, unless Gligorov abandoned his 'intransigent' position and gave assurances to abide by three terms, which in fact had been included in the EC Foreign Ministers declaration of December 1991. In short, the new Greek government was reintroducing, in official documents as well as in public pronouncements, a rather crude performance of dated slogans of an early 1992 vintage.[43]

It was evident that, here again, internal political exigencies – i.e., the discrediting of the entire handling of the issue, 'inherited' by the former government – were assuming top priority. This time, however, the government was no hostage in the hands of a few dissidents in its own party. It had a convenient majority of seats in parliament, a four-year term ahead, and a leader who enjoyed the unequivocal support and respect of the cadres. What went unspoken was PASOK's own responsibility for the malignancy it had inherited. In retrospect, however, PASOK's public denunciations while in Opposition, whenever a compromise solution was in the offing, and its president's position at the Council of Party Leaders in April 1992, do not exonerate either the Party or its leader of the responsibility – or 'honour', to the followers of nationalist orthodoxy – for the course of Greek policy on this issue in the preceding years.[44]

Undoubtedly, Papandreou's initial statements and initiatives as Prime Minister were an unexpected bonanza to Gligorov, who soon began to reap, instead of pressures by foreign governments, the official recognition of his state. True, most of them, including all the EU member states and the United States, extended recognition to the 'Former Yugoslav Republic of Macedonia'. In doing so, they were signalling their support to the 1993 Security Council's decision for the provisional name 'FYROM' and to the UN mandate for mediation.

When the recognition of FYROM by EU countries and the United States became known, the Greek public correctly assessed them as serious setbacks. It failed, however, to throw the blame on the initial, reflex reactions of the new government, finding solace in the traditional scapegoat of 'hostile foreign interests'. Massive new demonstrations broke out in Thessaloniki, Athens and other cities in order to condemn the 'desertion' of Greece by its partners and allies and to reiterate the sensitivity of the Greek people on matters touching upon their historical and cultural heritage. Once again Papandreou proved to be a master of the psychology of the masses, choosing to ride along with the public sentiments, and to place the blame on foreign powers, bypassing his own role in the new twist of events.[45] More serious, and fraught with unforeseen consequences, was his decision to endorse the most extremist recommendation of certain of his advisers – certainly not of the Foreign Ministry[46] – to slam, in February 1994, a total embargo on FYROM, with the exception of food and pharmaceutical goods.

The embargo – euphemistically termed 'counter measures', against Gligorov's 'intransigence' – fitted the strategy of raising the stakes. It ensured the support of an excited and injured public, projected the image of a Prime Minister as an active leader in the service of the national interest and responsive to the sensitivities of the Greek people, and outmanoeuvred the tactics of the new president of the New Democracy Party and leader of the Opposition, Miltiadis Evert, who had veered his party back to the maximalist line on the name issue. Publicly, however, Papandreou appeared confident that his determined position would reactivate the interest of the United States and the European Union in resolving the issue. What, indeed, it succeeded in doing was to raise a world outcry against Greece and to place the country in the unenviable position of a social pariah of Europe; a position reminiscent of the seven-year ostracism during the colonels' regime. It was unfair for the Greeks, who for more than two years were striving to project to the international community their case, not as a vendetta with their new, small and weak independent neighbour, but as legal self-defence in preserving their heritage and ensuring long-term peaceful and good-neighbourly relations within a troubled region. Be that as it may, the embargo era placed its mark on the international perception of Greece's Macedonian policy, as bullish and aggressive.[47]

On the internal front, the Papandreou government focused its efforts on a unique manipulation exercise of Greek public opinion which was adroitly misled by government spokesmen, with a daily dose of nationalistic hyperbole. The government was portrayed as honouring its electoral pledge to defend steadfastly the maximalist position, 'no Macedonia, no derivatives'. Behind the scenes, however, the same government's emissaries were labouring to bypass the name issue while negotiating an agreement more or less in the spirit of the 1993 Vance–Owen draft treaty, ironically a text castigated by PASOK both prior to and after coming to power in 1993.

Papandreou's miscalculation on the impact of the embargo decision on Greece's international standing created much concern inside Greece to the point that influential segments of Greek society began to voice publicly their objections to the policy pursued.

Strong economic and commercial interests, particularly in Northern Greece, suffering losses and losing opportunities in the emerging new markets of the Balkans and Eastern Europe, were becoming restive and critical of new barriers to trade and economic initiatives. Undoubtedly, certain 'embargo busters' did reap rich dividends; but they were no more than an insignificant minority. A 'silent majority' was emerging, pressing discreetly on the government the need for a speedy reappraisal of policy, including the lifting of the embargo.[48] Similarly, serious academics, including historians, were by now able to present more sober analyses of the Macedonian issue, which, in the early stages of the dispute, had been maltreated at the hands of amateurs and ultra-nationalist colleagues.[49] The thrust of their intervention was to rehabilitate the history and to set straight the facts over the Macedonian Question. Criticism now centred on the negative impact of the maximalist aims – and the means adopted in their pursuit – on international public opinion and the relations of Greece with its EU partners.

By now, the Court of the European Communities had rejected the Commission's initial petition for 'temporary measures' against Greece for the embargo decision, and a year later, in the summer of 1995, the Advocate General of the Court accepted in substance Greece's arguments.

The signing of the Interim Accord in September 1995 relieved the European Commission of a rejection of its case against Greece by the Court, although it was asked to pay the costs.[50] Meanwhile, Cyrus Vance had reactivated the UN mediation efforts for a final settlement of the dispute.

The third phase: the New York 'Interim Accord' (September 1995) and its aftermath

Whereas it is true that Cyrus Vance did, indeed, take the initiative in March 1994 for a new round of negotiations with the two parties, this was the result not of the embargo, but of the Greek government's silent consent to take as the basis of the negotiations, without preconditions, a slightly modified version of the 1993 Vance-Owen draft treaty.[51] It took a year and a half before the two parties finally signed in New York in September 1995 an 'Interim Agreement'. It provided for Greece's recognition of FYROM, under the latter's provisional name, and the lifting of the embargo, whereas Skopje consented to replace its flag without the Greek Macedonian emblem, and accepted the interpretation by the treaty of certain clauses of its Constitution which, in Greece's view, were likely to foment irredentist claims, as well as to justify interference in Greek internal affairs, under the pretext of 'caring for the status and rights' of Macedonian minorities in neighbouring countries. Furthermore the two countries endorsed a number of clauses dealing with economic relations and establishing quasi diplomatic relations by opening up in the respective capitals 'Liaison Offices' headed by ambassadors. In fact, both sides had successfully rid themselves of their additional burdens – Greece, the embargo, and FYROM, the flag – which they had added in the course of their four-year-old feud, and proceeded to normalise working neighbouring relations. What was left in abeyance, allegedly to be resolved in a new round of negotiations, was the key issue of the state's name, the real culprit of the dispute. Judging from statements by Greek government officials, including Foreign Minister Karolos Papoulias, that issue was also expected to be resolved soon.[52]

The Interim Accord and its implementation ushered in a new approach both to the dispute over the name and to bilateral relations between the two neighbouring independent states. Few, if any, had noticed, even prior to the conclusion of the agreement, a nuance in the Greek government's public statements, which proclaimed that 'the Greek government will never recognise a state bearing the name *Macedonia* or its derivatives'; a phrasing which had been substituted for the traditional line that 'the new state should not bear the name Macedonia or derivatives of that name'. Those who noticed it could not avoid recalling Papandreou's similar tactics in the early 1980s. Then, while in Opposition, the socialist leader had vowed to remove the US bases from Greece (a popular issue with the leftist masses at the time), but once in power he negotiated a new arrangement and signed an agreement which, in fact, ensured their continued presence on Greek soil. The signing of that agreement with the US government was heralded with the hoisting of banners proclaiming that 'the bases are on the way out' (*'oi vaseis fevgoun'*). In 1995, Papandreou, by now an aged and infirm Prime Minister, continued reassuring the masses that he stood firm by the maximalist line 'no to the name *Macedonia* and its derivatives', while, in the event, the 'Interim Accord' with FYROM had, indeed, divested his country of any plausible leverage for a fair compromise solution on the Macedonian name.

In January 1996, because of the deterioration in his health, Papandreou resigned and was replaced by Kostas Simitis, a modernist, who had not been associated with the so-called 'patriotic' – or 'maximalist' – wing of the party. Nor had his Foreign Minister, Thodoros Pangalos. From the outset, both appeared determined to 'close' the sour problem of the name, by reaching an accommodating compromise with Skopje, on the basis of a compound name, not the best, under the circumstances.[53] They, likewise, proceeded to resolve certain irksome issues with Albania, in order to set in motion a reappraisal of Greece's role as a stablising element in the Balkan sub-region and a link of the European Union with the emerging new democracies.

Their opening to the Albanians – which had been initiated a year earlier by the former Minister of Foreign Affairs Karolos Papoulias – was successful and a cordial relationship appeared in the making. Different, however, was the case with FYROM. While there was a marked improvement in bilateral economic and personal relations (more than half a million FYROM citizens visited Greece, particularly the shores of Macedonia and Thrace, in 1996), the Greeks soon realised that the 'Interim Accord' had left them with no substantial bargaining arguments to put on the table. Moreover, in their pursuit of erecting a new Balkan edifice of cooperation, they were in no mood to turn to confrontational situations in order to exert pressures for a solution.

On his part, Gligorov did not fail to exploit the favourable circumstances. Despite the mandate of the Security Council and the relevant reference in the Interim Accord that the two parties should seek a solution to the name dispute, he temporised with the UN talks, for over three years. During this period, Gligorov made no secret of his belief that the name dispute gradually would be diffused, with no concessions on his part, as the two countries proceeded to strengthen their economic relations and their borders were opened to the free movement of peoples. Finally, in the summer of 1997, FYROM submitted to Cyrus Vance its official position on the name, which was simply the country's constitutional name, 'Republic of Macedonia'.[54] In Greece, even the most ardent supporters of the 'de-Skopianisation' of Greece's policy were beginning to realise that this time the label 'intransigent', so frequently attached to Gligorov by Greek advocates of the tough line, appeared justified. Only this time, the aged politician in Skopje felt he could afford it, at no visible cost.

Meanwhile, the 'hawks' in the ruling PASOK party, responding to Simitis's and Pangalos's attempts to prepare the Greek public for a compromise solution, stepped up their criticism for their alleged 'yielding' attitude. It was a belated reaction addressed to the wrong recipients, as the real 'culprit' was no longer alive.[55]

In retrospect, it appears that a unique opportunity was lost for a lasting settlement of the problem, when, on the eve of the Dayton agreement, in August 1995, the American diplomacy, anxious to bring about the pacification of the warring regions in the north, intervened urgently to mediate the settlement of the Athens–Skopje dispute. Papandreou, however, chose the so-called 'small package' solution – with Gligorov consenting – which evaded the issue of the name, referring the substance of the dispute *ad graecas calendas*. That opportunist approach by the two elder leaders was no doubt due to their concern that a balanced adjudication of the name issue would undoubtedly raise the violent criticism of ardent nationalists, supporters of the maximalist view in both countries and their corresponding 'diasporas'. Such criticism, it was feared, would bring upon their parties the burden of 'political cost'. Furthermore, at the twilight of their political careers and lives, they ran the risk of having their personal ethnarchic image tarnished – so painstakingly weaved over the years in the service of the 'patriotic' causes of their countries. The ramifications, however, of their decision on the long-term relations between the two countries and, indeed, their peoples, were left aside for the judgment of future historians.

General assessments and projections

The handling of the recent phase of the Macedonian question by two PASOK governments and one of the New Democracy party revealed a departure from traditional patterns in Greek foreign policy-making and conduct. Not since the mass demonstrations of the Cypriot anti-colonial struggle of the 1950s had the Greek society and the Greeks of the diaspora exhibited such awareness and involvement on a foreign policy issue, as was the recognition of a new independent state on their northern boundaries. As a result, the formulation of strategic targets as well as the discharge of tactical moves – long a rather exclusive domain around the Prime Minister of an inner circle of cabinet ministers and the diplomatic bureaucracy of the Foreign Ministry – was eroded by the involvement of a wider range of concerned individuals, editors and influential groups. By their sheer numbers, their status in society, their political and economic clout, they acted as lobby groups seeking to press upon the government and the political parties their perceptions of the problem and how to deal with it. On the other hand, the mass demonstrations of a much grander scale than anything registered in Greece, could not be explained only in terms of the concern of the Greek people with their national security. They were rather the collective response of people personally affected by the issues at hand, namely their sense of identity and their perception of heritage.[56] Undoubtedly, their awakened awareness enriched the internal debate and provided the professionals with supportive argumentation. Nevertheless, a limited understanding of the drastically changing European and Balkan political environment, as contrasted with a rather expanded input of Greek history, led these 'lobbies' to adopt and promote 'maximalist' claims. Emotionally charged ('the name is our psyche'), their intervention denied even the most sober politicians any room for manoeuvring, bypassing the counsels of professionals and seasoned publicists.

A kaleidoscopic appraisal of these lobbies reveals that, while the pendulum of Greek politics was at the 'maximalist' end of the curve, it was mainly academics – historians, archaeologists, as well as theologians and intellectuals, but not political or social scientists – who drew up the theoretical framework for the policy to be pursued. Understandably, their perception of the issue at hand focused on the Macedonian Kingdom of antiquity and its *Makedones* rather than on the Socialist Republic of Macedonia and its *Makedonci*. It was a foregone conclusion that the 'archaeologisation' of Greece's foreign policy would become unavoidable; more so, when amateur historians and publicists entered the debate promoting a series of historical theories in retrospect, such as that the region of the SRM had never been part of Macedonia, or that it had acquired its Macedonian name as a result of the Second World War. When the general public endorsed these 'findings', political leaders of all factions joined the bandwagon.

During its first phase (1991–3), political analysts sought to interpret the dichotomy of New Democracy's Macedonian policy in terms of a political duel between the two protagonists at the time, C. Mitsotakis and A. Samaras. There was wide speculation that Samaras was simply exploiting the Macedonian problem in order to reap personal political dividends. This is still the prevailing view. Such motives, however, were not limited to Samaras alone. Indeed, the number of politicians in both the New Democracy and the PASOK parties who fell prey to such temptations was far from negligible. Nevertheless, Mitsotakis and Samaras should be seen as the representatives of two different currents in their party at the turn of the 1990s: the 'conservative' one – as pursued by Constantine Karamanlis in the 1970s – and the 'maximalist', respectively. Their personal ambitions and political priorities aside, their dissenting views on the handling of the Macedonian problem split the party's parliamentarians and perplexed the rank and file of the New Democracy party over the endorsement of the maximalist view. Particularly vulnerable were New Democracy deputies, running for office in electoral precincts in Macedonia and Thrace. Mitsotakis's 'conservative' approach of seeking a moderate compromise solution to the name issue, could expose his followers not only to the nationalist harassment of their local PASOK opponents, but also to the erosion of their electoral clientele by Samaras's newly-formed 'Politiki Anoixi' party.

Samaras was a relative young, ambitious and over-zealous politician, with family connections to Macedonia. He shared the growing anxiety of a segment of the electorate – particularly in the northern provinces of Macedonia, Epirus and Thrace – over the dramatic developments taking shape north of the Greek border. In the volatile climate of resurgent Balkan nationalisms, he perceived threats as well as opportunities for the Greek 'national issues', such as the 'Northern Epirus' and the 'Macedonian'. He felt he had a cause to serve. As a zealot, sensing the approval of the masses on his back, he entered forcefully into the quagmire of Balkan politics, betting on maximalist stakes. He refused, however, to manoeuvre when the odds were clearly against such stakes. Thus, he failed to compromise, even when compromise was clearly not 'treason', but a fair service to the mission he had assigned to himself.

On the other side stood Mitsotakis, an elder, experienced statesman, master of political manoeuvring and hence the logical hand to promote an exodus out of the Macedonian imbroglio through compromise. Although he was aware that at that historical turning point his country's best interests and its European orientation required the further strengthening of its ties with its partners in the European Union, he let himself be drawn into petty Balkan intrigues. In fairness, it should be acknowledged that he sought to cast himself in the role of a Balkan 'honest broker' and earn dividends for himself and his country. By associating, however, too closely with Milosevic, he defeated his own aims and exposed his country to unwarranted criticism in the West, particularly by anti-Serbian lobbies. It is true, however, that the EU governments and the United States offered him some latitude to manoeuvre when he asked their support for a fair hearing of Greece's reservations *vis-à-vis* FYROM's recognition. Nevertheless, the European and American environment, already in a violently anti-Serbian mood, remained suspicious of Mitsotakis's intentions and motivations on the Macedonian issue, to the point of pressuring their respective governments against Greek initiatives at pacification in Bosnia–Croatia, but also on the Macedonian question. In the end, the Greek conservative leader, pressed by the opposition in his own party, chose to temporise. His loss in the October 1993 elections ushered in the second phase of Greek policy toward FYROM recognition (1993–5).

New players entered the Greek political arena; this time with Papandreou and his party in the dominant roles. It was a different terrain. Despite an almost daily dose of official pronouncements reassuring Greek audiences of the new government's steadfast maximalist position, there was a gradual decrease of the patriotic fervour so typical of commentary in the media of the previous two years. At the same time, new voices by a growing number of influential publicists, intellectuals and political analysts challenged the monopoly of maximalist views. On the one hand, the leftist Synaspismos Party had already come out publicly in favour of a compromise solution on the name. Indeed, one of its leading members is credited with publishing, in 1992, in book form a political diatribe with arguments for a compromise approach to the whole issue of recognition, including the acceptance of a compound name. In the end, however, it was Papandreou's brinkmanship in applying the embargo on FYROM that raised havoc and shifted the focus of the debate from the issues of Greece's security and the Greeks' perceptions of identity-heritage, to issues of human rights and regional Balkan security considerations. Thanks to the Greek government's bonanza offering, FYROM propagandists adroitly exploited a pro-'underdog' mentality among Western European and American human rights activists, to augment the ranks of their supporters.[57]

Steadily, political analysts, academics as well as publicists in Greece took over the rostrum from historians and archaeologists. Closer to international political realities and more sensitive to the negative impact of the Macedonian issue on Greece's overall orientations, they sought to assess the issue from the perspective of Greek foreign policy strategic interests as a whole. Their criticism of both the New Democracy and PASOK governments centred on the 'Skopjanisation' of Greek foreign policy to the detriment of other vital Greek priorities. In their view, these priorities should have focused on strengthening Greece's position and stature in the EU, upgrading the Greek role in the economic and social reformation of the Balkan sub-region, and gaining international support to contain Turkish challenges and provocations over Cyprus and the Aegean. Understandably, these proponents of the 'realist' school tended to bypass, if not to ignore altogether, the more abstract aspects of heritage and identity, such as the appropriation of the 'Vergina sun' as a national symbol on FYROM's national flag and the monopolisation of the Macedonian name. Nevertheless, even the 'realists' would not venture to suggest the recognition of FYROM by its current denomination, 'Republic of Macedonia'.[58]

By this time, the internal debate in Greece grew to the point where two trends had become visible, transcending party lines. The Greeks were rediscovering their popular pastime of assigning derogatory labels to opponents. On the one side stood the 'maximalists', or 'ethnocentrists', advocates of the pure 'patriotic' line denying any thought of concessions over the name and symbols. On the other side, were the *endotikoi* ('yielders') and the *evroligourides* ('euro-addicts' or 'euro-zealots') supporters of a compromise approach to the 'Skopiano' issue and the re-orientation of Greece's Balkan policy along the lines and priorities pursued by the EU partners and the United States.

By August 1995, when the international community had finally decided to intervene militarily in Bosnia, the voices of the maximalists in Greece had been substantially weakened, drawn by the active lobbying of advocates of compromise. Despite the fact that both the government PASOK and the major Opposition New Democracy Party appeared to stand by their 'maximalist' views, parliamentarians and rank and file were crossing party lines. It was at that moment that the 'maximalist' Papandreou grasped the opportunity to extricate himself from the problem, giving his consent to the 'Interim Accord'. By deferring the name issue at some future final accord, he tried to convince his audiences that he had honoured his pledge not to recognise the neighbour state by the name Macedonia, whereas in essence he had joined the 'yielders' in indirectly compromising even the use of the temporary name of FYROM. Once again, the 'Papandreou magic' worked miracles, as the announcement of the Interim Accord was received in Greece with almost general relief and little criticism, as Greece's normalisation of relations with its Balkan neighbours opened up the prospect of a rewarding Greek economic 'penetration' into the 'Balkan hinterland'.

It was apparent that the 'Euro-zealots' had gained the upper hand in Greek politics, particularly since in January 1996 Simitis succeeded the ailing Papandreou, who, a few months later, died. Conditions were ripe for the pendulum of Greek Macedonian policy to veer toward the other end. Supporters of the maximalist line came under sharp and unnecessarily harsh attacks as 'chauvinists' or 'ultra-nationalists', even when they donned the more respectable gown of 'patriotism'. They were summarily accused of being the culprits of Greece's recent Macedonian adventure and were publicly ostracised, sometimes from the very media which had offered them, for well over four years, extensive print and electronic coverage.[59] The 'modernists' of PASOK, supported by followers of Synaspismos and New Democracy, set out to delineate and pursue Greece's new 'Balkan Spring' policy of open doors–no walls.

How real was this seemingly 'about face' in Greece's foreign policy which had dominated the country's foreign relations over a period of almost four years and had monopolised the public's attention? The withdrawal of Papandreou from the public scene, a few months after the signing of the Interim Accord, coincided with a new crisis with Turkey over the Imia islets of the Aegean. It turned out to be of long duration. Accordingly, the Macedonian controversy was removed from the dailies' first pages, conveniently deferred to two lonely diplomats in faraway New York, pursuing, as dictated, their quixotic chores for 'gaining time'.

Following the Dayton agreements and the Greek-FYROM Interim Accord, a period of calm appeared to return to the region. This was not least due to Greece's modernist approach to the solution of disputes with its northern neighbours and the advancement of cooperation on bilateral as well as multilateral regional level. The Crete November 1997 first summit meeting of Balkan leaders was a unique example in that direction.

In Macedonian affairs, however, appearances might be misleading. The core of the problem over national identities, historical and cultural perceptions and, indirectly, over claims of 'historical space', projected by Gligorov's insistence on the monopolisation of the Macedonian name, has remained unresolved. In Athens, politicians and diplomats probably felt relieved of the pressing burden which for a long time had hindered their foreign policy initiatives. However, in Thessaloniki, the euphemistically named 'co-capital' of Greece, moods were mixed. On the one hand, there was considerable consensus over the Simitis– Pangalos practical approach to the development of relations with the northern neighbours. On the other hand, there was widespread and growing suspicion among (Greek) Macedonians toward the 'Athenian state' for allegedly conniving to leave the dispute in limbo, thus undermining the cherished elements of their identity.

Once again, the Macedonian issue appeared to be dividing the Greeks, this time along a line of 'Northerners', i.e. Macedonians, Epirotes and Thracians, and 'Athenians'. Not only the Foreign Ministry, but also Athenian-based major mass media, influential political analysts and powerful economic and commercial interests were perceived to favour a long trench-war of inaction toward Skopje over the name issue, which would lead to a *fait accompli*. The resentment of the 'Northerners', however, appeared to be shared by grass-roots segments of the public throughout Greece, as well as by a highly sensitive Diaspora, entrenched in maximalist positions.[60]

On the other side of the frontier, despite the initial euphoria of the first year of the removal of frontier barriers and the commencement of business contacts, officials and public in FYROM came to realise that so long as no compromise over the name was visible, relations with Greece would remain abnormal.[61] As such, the Greek opposition to the replacement of the temporary name FYROM for the 'Republic of Macedonia' in international official usage, stirred nationalist resentment in FYROM. Such reaction was not necessarily the result of differences with the Greeks only. Since its emergence as an independent state, a series of disputes had emerged with the Albanians, the Bulgarians and the Serbs, touching upon nationalist sensitivities. These sensitivities directly addressed the question of the existence of a separate 'Macedonian' national identity. Within the framework of an independent Macedonian state, the new state elite encouraged nationalism as a defence against real or imagined adversaries of Macedonian' nationhood. Despite official diplomatic disclaimers, the doctrine of a united 'greater' Macedonian state was introduced into the school curriculum. It is a doctrine which expands the history of the 'Macedonian' nation not simply to thirteen centuries – i.e. to the descent of the Slavic tribes to the Balkans – as was the national doctrine under the communist regime, but backtracks it to the Ancient Macedonians of Alexander the Great; a rather naïve experiment, but still an additional irritant in the relations between neighbouring peoples sensitive of their identities.[62]

Irrespective of the diplomatic aspects of the completion of the 'Interim Accord' with an agreement on the name dispute, it is safe to conclude that the independent Macedonian state, still in its infancy, radiates in its vicinity a fan of irritants capable of sparking future crises. 'Compromise' is still an ugly word in the Balkans, almost synonymous with treason. Modernist or euro-zealot politicians in both countries face the challenge to educate their respective publics on the true meaning of compromise, namely, that it is 'an adjustment for settlement by arbitration and mutual concessions usually involving a partial surrender of purposes or principles'.[63]

FYROM's declared intention, however, to seek, instead of a compromise, the annulment of the UN Security Council's 1993 decision for a temporary name (FYROM), and its substitution for the constitutional name, 'Republic of Macedonia', might initiate yet another round in the old Macedonian controversy.

Notes

* An earlier version of this essay was presented by the author and discussed in his seminar series on 'Greece and the Balkans' during his term as Visiting Fellow of Hellenic Studies at Brasenose College, Oxford, 1995–6.

1. *'Omonoia' Memorandum to the CSCE Conference on the Human Dimension; Moscow, 10 September–4 October 1991* (Athens, 1991), 12pp.

2. Thanos Veremis, *Greece's Balkan Entanglement* (Athens, ELIAMEP, 1995), p. 72.

3. Yannis Valinakis, *Greece's Security in the Post-Cold War Era* (Ebenhausen, Stiftung Wissenschaft und Politik, April 1994), 128pp. Sotiris Wallden, *Makedoniko kai Valkania 1991–1994. I Adiexodi Poreia tis Ellinikis Politikis* [The Macedonian Question and the Balkans: The Dead-end Course of Greek Policy] (Athens, 1994), p. 14.

4. Leonidas Kyrkos, *To Adiexodo Vima tou Ethnikismou. Skepseis gia to Makedoniko* [The Dead-End Step of Nationalism: Some Thoughts about the Macedonian Issue] (Athens, 1993), pp. 28–9, quoting Ozal's statements. Alexis Alexandris, 'Simerini Valkaniki Politiki tis Tourkias' [Turkey's Present Balkan Policy], in Thanos Veremis (ed.), *Valkania. Apo to Dipolismo sti Nea Epochi* [The Balkans: From Bipolarism to the New Era] (Athens, 1994), pp. 850–63. Also, Christopher Cviic, *Remaking the Balkans* (London, RIIA, 1991).

5. Personal assessment (p.a.).

6. Veremis, *Balkan Entanglement*, p. 61.
7. *Borders, Symbols, Stability* (Athens, The Citizens' Movement, 1993), 13pp. For a historical review of this aspect of the Macedonian problem, Evangelos Kofos, *National and Communism in Macedonia: Civil Conflict, Politics of Mutation, National Identity* (New York, A. Caratzas Publisher, 1993), 336pp.
8. E. Kofos, 'Greece and the Balkans in the '70s and the '80s' (Athens, ELIAMEP, 1991), pp. 12–18. An earlier version appeared in Speros Vryonis (ed), *Greece on the Road to Democracy: From the Junta to PASOK, 1974–1986* (New York, Caratzas Publisher, 1991), pp. 97–122. Nikolaj Todorov, 'Etat actuel des rapports greco-bulgares', *Etudes Balkaniques* no. 3 (1985), pp. 45–6. Kyriakos Kentrotis, 'Voulgaria', in Veremis, *Valkania*, pp. 395–414.
9. Kofos, *ibid.*, pp. 18–25. Chr. Halourides and Stelios Aleifantis, *Diethneis Sheseis kai Valkania* [International Relations and the Balkans] (Athens, 1987), pp. 411–14. George Harvalias, 'Alvania', in Veremis, *Valkania*, pp. 182–205.
10. Kofos, *ibid.*, pp. 25–30. Constantine Svolopoulos, *I Elliniki Politiki sta Valkania, 1974–1981* [The Greek Policy in the Balkans] (Athens, 1987).
11. Kofos, *Nationalism...*, p. 324.
12. 'Statement by the Head of the Greek Delegation, CSCE Conference on the Human Dimension, Copenhagen, June 5–29, 1990', *Yearbook 1990 Southeastern Europe* (Athens, ELIAMEP 1991), pp. 353–60.
13. *Kratka Istorija na Makedonija* [Short History of Macedonia] (Melbourne?, date early 1980s), quoted in E. Kofos, 'National Heritage and National Identity in Nineteenth- and Twentieth-Century Macedonia', *European History Quarterly*, vol. 19 (1989), reprinted in Kofos, *Nationalism...*, p. 336, ft, 64.
14. E. Kofos, 'The Macedonian Question: The Politics of Mutation', *Balkan Studies*, vol. 27, (1986), reprinted in Kofos, *Nationalism...*, p. 300. A year and a half prior to FYROM's declaration of independence, the then PASOK Minister for Macedonia-Thrace, Stelios Papathemelis, in an article in *Kathimerini* (4.3.1990) wrote: 'For Greece, "there is no Macedonian question" in terms of a so-called "Macedonian" minority; there is, however, a "Macedonian question" in so far as Skopje "appropriates our history and traditions and usurps the Greek name of Macedonia". The appropriation of the Macedonian name by a (Slavic) state entity implies territorial claims', reprinted in S. Papathemelis, *Politiki Epikairotita kai Prooptikes* [Current Politics and Future Prospects] (Thessaloniki, Barbounakis, 1990).
15. On Bulgaria's post-war position, see Robert R. King, *Minorities under Communism* (Harvard University Press, 1993), pp. 188–204. Stephen Palmer Jr and Robert King, *Yugoslav Communism and the Macedonian Question* (Archon Books, 1971), pp. 184–98. Stefan Troebst, *Die bulgarisch-jugoslawische Kontroverse um Makedonien, 1967–1982* (Sudost-Institut, Munchen, 1983) 243 pp. E. Kofos, 'The Macedonian Question from the Second World War to the Present Day', in *Modern and Contemporary Macedonia* (ed. I. Koliopoulos and I. Hasiotis), 'Paratiritis'–'Papazisis', 1993, Vol. II, pp. 277–80.
16. Dragan Tashkovski, *The Macedonian Nation* (Skopje, 'Nasha Kniga', 1976), pp. 69–79, passim, Palmer and King, *Yugoslav Communism...*, pp. 199–203. Elizabeth Barker, *Macedonia; Its Place in Balkan Power Politics* (London, RIIA, 1950), p. 10. Duncan Perry, *The Politics of Terror: The Macedonian Liberation Movements, 1893–1903* (Durham, 1988), p. 19.

17. Wallden (*To Makedoniko*) observed that PASOK in Opposition had chosen 'nationalist demagoguery as the central axis of its policy' (p. 31), and that 'the PASOK leadership, in a vulgar way, subdues the [national issues] to its efforts to return to power' (p. 77).

18. Most notable, *Pontiki*, a well-informed political-satirical weekly newspaper, with a left-centre orientation, influential among leftist political and intellectual circles as well as government cadres.

19. Most scholarly works were dealing either with the period of the 'Macedonian Struggle' (1903–8) or with Ancient Macedonia and current archaeological discoveries. It is interesting that the impressive collective volume, *Macedonia, 4000 Years of Greek History and Civilization*, ed. M. Sakellariou (Athens, Ekdotiki Athinon, 1981), 572pp., spared only seven pages for 'The Macedonian Question in our time'. Some publications during this period, dealing with contemporary aspects of the problem, include: The monthly journal *Makedoniki Zoi*, edited by Nikos Mertzos, who is also the author of the book, *Emeis oi Makedones* [We the Macedonians] (Athens, Sideris, 1986), 459 pp. Also, Nikolaos Martis, *The Falsification of the History of Macedonia* (Greek and English editions) (Athens, 1983), 204 pp. Also, Stelios Papathemelis, '*Estin oun Ellas kai I Makedonia*' (speeches by the Minister of Macedonia-Thrace) (Thessaloniki, 1989). ['Macedonia is also Greece'], Basil Gounaris, 'Reassessing Ninety Years of Greek Historiography on the Struggle of Macedonia, 1904–1988', *Journal of Modern Greek Studies*, 14/2 (1996), pp. 237–51.

20. Nikos Mouzelis, 'Ethikismos', *To Vima*, 16 March 1993, reprinted in the author's book, *O Ethnikismos stin Ysteri Anaptyxi* [Nationalism in Later Development], pp. 50, 69.

21. Personal interview with Dimitris Zannas, member of the Macedonian Committee of citizens of Thessaloniki, which organised the mass demonstration of 14 February 1992.

22. Numerous statements at the time by members of the Academy of Athens, university professors, intellectuals, journalists and politicians.

23. N. Mouzelis, among others, criticised this attitude, assessing that the tactics of 'misinformation' and 'disorientation' of the citizens had 'assumed Kafkaesque proportions'. *To Vima*, 10 April 1994.

24. A leading Synaspismos Party member, ventured in late 1992 to suggest as a suitable denomination the 'Macedonian Republic of Vardar'. He was harshly criticised by Opposition leader A. Papandreou as well as leading members of the New Democracy Party. Kyrkos, *To Adiexodo...*, p. 85.

25. Hugh Poulton, *Who are the Macedonians? (Indiana University Press, 1995), pp. 172–5. Xavier Raufer and François Haut, Le chaos balkanique* (Paris, 1922), p. 73. Also, Eirini Lagani, 'The Macedonian Question: Recent Developments', in Koliopoulos and Hasiotis, *Modern and Contemporary Macedonia.* Vol. II, pp. 296–9.

26. For a critical view of Greece's appraisal of Serbia's and Bulgaria's role at the time, see Wallden, *To Makedoniko*, pp. 29–30 and 73–8, quoting his own article in *Avgi* (22.9.1991). On Greek–Bulgarian rapprochement in 1990–1, Cviic, *Remaking the Balkans*, p. 102.

27. Following Zhivkov's fall, the Bulgarian delegation at the Copenhagen CSCE Conference on the Human Dimension referred to two million 'Bulgarians' living in Yugoslav Macedonia. Subsequently, the Bulgarian leaders adopted

the more nuanced term 'of persons of Bulgarian origin'. For Bulgaria's recognition, Lagani, 'Macedonian Question', pp. 302–3.

28. Wallden, *To Makedoniko*, pp. 29–30. Stavros Lygeros, *Anemoi Polemou sta Valkania; Skopje* [Winds of War in the Balkans. Skopje], 3rd edn (Athens, 1992), pp. 69–73. Arnold Sherman, *Perfidy in the Balkans: The rape of Yugoslavia* (Athens, 1993) p. 82.

29. Texts of documents in Yiannis Valinakis and Sotiris Dalis (editors), *To Zitima ton Skopion: Episima Keimena, 1990–1996* [The Skopje Question. Official Documents, 1990–1996] 2nd edition (Athens, ELIAMEP, 1996), pp. 51–2.

30. *Ibid.*, pp. 87–90. Veremis, *Balkan Entanglement*, p. 95 ft. 12, *Eleftherotypia*, 5.7.1993. The minutes of the Pineiro-Samaras talks (1.4.93) in Alexandros Tarkas, *Athina-Skopia: Piso apo tis Kleistes Portes* [Athens-Skopje: Behind Closed Doors] (Athens, 1995), pp. 332–6.

31. Valinakis and Dalis, *To Zitima...*, p. 94.

32. *Ibid.*, pp. 100–2.

33. *Ibid.*, pp. 97–9. Text of Mitsotakis letter initially published in *Epetirida 1993*, ELIAMEP, pp. 343–4.

34. *Ibid.*, pp. 147–8.

35. Details of the New York negotiations in Michalis Papaconstantinou, *To Imerologio enos Politikou. I Emploki ton Skopion* [The Diary of a Politician: The Skopje Entanglement] (Athens, 1994), pp. 243–412.

36. The Secretary General of the KKE Charilaos Florakis stated repeatedly during the 1970s and 1980s that for his Party there was neither a 'Macedonian Question', nor any 'Macedonian' minority in Greece.

37. p.a.

38. Papaconstantinou, *To Imerologio....* Tarkas, *Athina-Skopia...* (reflecting A. Samaras views and documentation). Thodoros Skylakakis, *Sto Onoma tis Makedonias* [In the Name of Macedonia], with a preface by C. Mitsotakis (Athens, Elliniki Evroekdotiki, 1995), p. 332 (reflecting the Prime Minister's views and documentation).

39. p.a.

40. *Memorandum of Greece Concerning the application of FYROM for admission to the UN, New York 25.1.1993* (Athens, ELIAMEP 1993), 10pp.

41. Interview with Miltiadis Evert, President of the Opposition New Democracy party.

42. Papaconstantinou, *To Imerologio...* pp. 405–6.

43. Letter from Foreign Minister Karolos Papoulias to the UN Secretary General Butros Butros-Ghali, 5.11.1993, in Valinakis and Dalis, pp. 175–6.

44. Mouzelis, *O Ethnikismos*, pp. 54–5.

45. *Ibid.*, pp. 44, 46–7, 56.

46. The idea has been attributed in some circles to the Minister for Press and Information, Evangelos Venizelos.

47. Veremis, *Balkan Entanglement*, pp. 90–2. Suzan Woodward, *Balkan Tragedy* (Washington, D. C., The Brookings Institution, 1995), p. 387, was probably right when she observed that the embargo have made the victims more stubborn, and 'interrupted negotiations and quiet moves toward concessions on the part of Macedonia'. Two years later, FYROM's Foreign Minister Hadziski in a press interview to Skopje's weekly *Forum* stated that during the first two or three years over the recognition crisis, the FYROM government examined

the possibility of a compound name, but this idea has been abandoned. Reported in *Eleftherotypia*, 19.1.1998.

48. For a strong criticism of the government's tactics, see a series of articles by Professor Nikos Mouzelis in the influential Sunday newspaper *To Vima* (20 Feb., 6 March, 3 and 10 April 1994), reprinted in *O Ethnikismos*, pp. 53–70. Mouzelis shared the view that the denomination 'Republic of Macedonia' was unacceptable as it fomented irredentism. Contrary to the government's and the Maximalists' position he opted for the denomination Republic of Vardar Macedonia, p. 70. Similarly critical of the 'Skopianis-ation' of Greece's foreign policy during 1991–4 was Professor Theodore Couloumbis in D. Constas and P. Tsakonas (editors), *Elliniki Exoteriki Politiki, Esoterikes kai Diethneis Parametroi* [Greek Foreign Policy. Internal and International Dimensions] (Athens, Institute of International Relations, 1994), pp. 92, 93. On the contrary, Papathemelis – by then Minister of Public Order – was declaring that the Macedonian name, 'either alone or as a compound name', would remain a vehicle of irredentism, *ibid.*, p. 100. Also, Th. Veremis and Th. Couloumbis, *Elliniki Exoteriki Politiki. Prooptikes kai Provlimatismoi* [Greek Foreign Policy. Prospects and Concerns] (Athens, ELIAMEP, 1994), pp. 35–6.

49. Among others: *Modern and Contemporary Macedonia*, Vol. II, pp. 104–37, 246–95. Also, Ioannis Koliopoulos, *Leilasia Fronimaton, Vol. I To Makedoniko Zitima stin Katehomeni Dytiki Makedonia 1941–1944* [Plundering Loyalties. (A) The Macedonian Question in Occupied Western Macedonia] (Thessaloniki, 1994), 284pp. Vol. II *To Makedoniko Zitima stin Periodo tou Emfyliou Polemou (1945–1949) sti Dytiki Makedonia* [B. The Macedonian Question during the Civil War in Western Macedonia] (1995), 351pp. Also, B. Gounaris, I. Michailidis and G. Angelopoulos (editors), *Taftotites sti Makedonia* [Identities in Macedonia] (Athens, Papazisis, 1997), 262pp. Also, Marilena Koppa, *Mia efthrafsti Dimokratia. I PGDM anamesa sto parelthon kai to Mellon* [A Fragile Republic; FYROM Amidst the Past and the Future] (Athens, 1994).

50. Documents on the case 'Commission vs Greece, Case C-120/94' before the Court of Justice of the European Communities, including the final 'Opinion of Advocate General Jacobs delivered on 6 April 1995, in Valinakis and Dalis, pp. 239–360.

51. Privileged information.

52. An analysis supporting the New York agreement, in Christos Rozakis, *Politikes kai Nomikes Diastaseis tis Metavatikis Symfonias tis Neas Yorkis metaxy Elladas kai PGDM*[Political and Legal Dimensions of the Interim Agreement between Greece and FYROM] (Athens, Sideris, 1996) 77pp. (text of agreement annexed).

53. Speaking in Parliament (2.2.1997), Foreign Minister Thodoros Pangalos termed the Interim Accord 'one sided' and revealed that the Simitis government was working toward a compromise. This statement raised havoc among PASOK deputies and offered Opposition deputies a unique opportunity to attack the government's 'yielding' attitude. *Greek Press reports*, 3.2.1997.

54. In a long interview to Skopje State TV, Channel One (22.7.1997), President Gligorov revealed that FYROM had proposed to the UN mediator that his country should be recognised by all by its constitutional name, 'Republic of Macedonia', except for Greece in their bilateral relations. Late in December

1997, Foreign Minister Hadziski announced that his government intended to ask the UN Security Council to admit his country with its constitutional name. *Eleftherotypia*, 31.12.1997.

55. S. Papathemelis, by now just a PASOK MP, better informed on Macedonian affairs than most of his colleagues, appeared to assume the leadership of a group within his own party criticising strongly any attempts toward an agreed solution which would retain, in one way or another, the Macedonian name. Numerous press articles and interviews in 1996–7.

56. For an assessment of the issues of 'security' and 'identity' in Greek policy conduct and behaviour, see S. J. Raphalides, 'Sacred Symbol, Sacred Space: The New Macedonian Issue', and Peter Bratsis, 'The Macedonian Question and the Politics of Identity: Resonance, Reproduction, Real Politik', in *Journal of Modern Hellenism*, no. 11 (Hellenic College Press, Winter 1994), pp. 89–108 and 108–22, respectively.

57. Criticism of the Greek government's policies over the recognition of FYROM and its name, sparked certain Human Rights groups to focus their polemics on the issue of an alleged national 'Macedonian' minority in Greece (Human Rights Watch/Helsinki, *Denying Ethnic Identity: The Macedonians of Greece*, New York, April 1994, 85pp.). Their one-sided and frequently exaggerated reports indicate that the minority issue had been concocted to put additional pressure on the Athens government in order to abandon its maximalist position *vis-à-vis* FYROM. For a critical analysis: Vlasis Vlasidis and Veniamin Karakostanoglou, 'Recycling Propaganda: Remarks on Recent Reports on Greece's "Slav-Macedonian" Minority', *Balkan Studies*, vol. 36/1 (Thessaloniki, 1995), pp. 151–70. Similar was the case of certain American anthropologists, neophytes in the Macedonian issue, who tried to assume the *ex cathedra* role of supreme arbiters for social, political and historical cleavages in the volatile Macedonian terrain. On the rather humourous side, it suffices to observe that one of them, apparently lacking the historical background to comprehend the issues at hand, sought to construct his 'own' revisionist history of Macedonia, by conveniently ignoring, misquoting or even degrading specialist historians of long standing (Loring Danforth, *The Macedonian Conflict, Ethnic Nationalism in a Transnational World*, Princeton University Press, 1995). For an overall assessment of this phenomenon, see Professor Ioannis Koliopoulos's 'Introduction', in the Greek translation (Thessaloniki, 'Paratiritis' 1996, pp. 7–17) of Elizabeth Barker's *Macedonia; Its Place in Balkan Power Politics* (London, RIIA, 1950). Basil Gounaris *et al.* (eds), *Taftotites sti Makedonia* [Identities in Macedonia] (Athens, 'Pa-pazisis'), pp. 27–61.

58. Th. Couloumbis and Sot. Dalis (Introduction and prefaces by M. Papaconstantinou, N. Mouzelis, M. Papayannakis), *I Elliniki Exoteriki Politiki sto Katofli tou 21ou Aiona: Ethnokentrismos i Evrokentrismos* [The Greek Foreign Policy at the Doorstep of the 21st Century: National-or Eurocentrism] (Athens, 'Pa-pazisis', 1997), 212pp.

59. G. Kontoyannis reporting in *Ependytis*, 13.12.1997 that both in the government party and the Opposition parties a new dichotomy is emerging on the national issues between 'endotikoi' or 'synetoi' ('yielders' or 'prudents') and 'patridokapiloi' (patriotic zealots'). On this debate, a strong attack against 'nationalists' by Richardos Someritis in *To Vima*, 28.12.1997.

60. Statements and press conferences by representatives of the World Congress of Pan-Macedonian Associations, presenting their maximalist views on the name issue, *Press Reports*, Thessaloniki, 22–26 July 1997.
61. According to press reports, Greece's insistence in international fora against the use of the name 'FYROM' is an element of frequent frictions between the two sides which, at times, result in unpleasant public demonstrations at sports events. *To Vima*, 21.12.1997 and *Ellinikos Vorras*, 14.12.1997.
62. Evangelos Kofos, *The Vision of 'Greater Macedonia': Remarks on FYROM's New School Texbooks* (Thessaloniki, Museum of the Macedonian Struggle, 1994), 34pp.
63. *Webster's Dictionary*, 1992 edition (Chicago 1992), p. 207.

Chapter 16

Macedonia in the context of present-day Russian foreign policy

Nina Smirnova

The policy of the new Russia with respect to Macedonia is closely connected with Russian Balkan policy as a whole. Since the second half of the nineteenth century the Balkans have been an inseparable part of Russian national interests. At that time the maintenance of security suggested the idea of achieving at least two objectives:

(1) obtaining the Black Sea coast straits or Russian control over them;
(2) the creation of its 'own' group of states on the Balkans united by the community of interests in the Eastern Mediterranean. The Balkan line was central to the European policy of Russia.

Russia resolutely supported the national liberation movement of the Balkan peoples against the Ottoman yoke with a view to founding independent states. The south of Russia with its Black Sea coast turned into a peculiar bridge or link for the strengthening and development of commercial, cultural and spiritual relations with the peoples of the region. It was there where the settlements of the Greek, Bulgarian and Albanian refugees appeared long ago.

After the First World War Soviet Russia – a new socialist state built on the ruins of the empire – was kept out of participation in the peace settlement. Almost all countries of Central and South Eastern Europe joined the anti-Soviet *cordon sanitaire*. The Balkan line ceased to exist as an independent part of Russian foreign policy.

The tendencies to return to the imperial traditions became apparent on the eve and during the first period of the Second World War after the Soviet–German treaties and agreements of 1939. The illusion of the possibility of achieving agreement with Germany and Italy on the recognition of Soviet interests in the Balkans was customary with the Kremlin leaders. The unexpected attack by Nazi Germany put an end to those illusions.

The end of the Second World War brought a new set of contradictions. Ousting its allies from Greece the USA became the undeniable leader in the region and proclaimed the Balkans its zone of security. It was a brazen violation of the national interests of Russia. The Balkans took on the most important role in international relations, as the dividing line between the NATO South flank and the Warsaw bloc passed through the territory of the Balkan states.

But more favourable conditions emerged for the Soviet foreign policy of creating a system of international relations which provided for the sovereignty of every nation, on condition of non-participation in enemy blocks, and it envisaged this being the political solution to the growing problems.

Instead however, the construction of the socialist community was characterised as the dictatorship of 'the elder brother' – the Soviet Union – that in fact reduced national independence of the minor partners to a minimum. The Soviet politico-economical model was enforced, levelling out the historical and national peculiarities.

Driving out Yugoslavia (1948) and Albania (1961) from the socialist community undermined the political and military strategic position of Russia in the Balkans. By the autumn of 1989 only Bulgaria remained a supporter of Soviet policy when the chain reaction process demolished the communist regimes in Eastern Europe. This vitally important tie was finally broken with the collapse of Zhivkov's regime in 1990/91.

In 1991 the Soviet Union broke up. The new Russia could not influence the new alignment on the Balkans. The necessity to establish new relations with 14 neighbouring states, the destiny of Russian citizens outside the Russian borders, and inner political and ethnical conflicts reduced the attention given to Balkan problems.

The disintegration of Yugoslavia took the Russian Foreign Office unawares. The superficial similarity of the processes in the USSR and the SFRY induced the attitude towards the Yugoslavian crisis that became one of the main factors in Russian domestic policy since 1992. The link 'the Russians–the Serbians' determined the guidelines for the foreign policy actions of the Russian Foreign Office that had to respond or react to the decisions of the then Supreme Soviet, that was itself gradually turning into the centre of the opposition to Yeltsin.

Russian policy towards Macedonia depended on the national approach to the Yugoslav crisis as a whole. However, there was no clear idea of what had happened there and no precise concept of Balkan policy in general. Russian diplomacy did not take into consideration the possible reaction of the neighbouring states.

Summing up the first year of Russian foreign policy in December 1992 the last minister of the Foreign Affairs Ministry of the Soviet Union, A. Bessmertnyh, confirmed the spontaneity of its course and the lack of coordination with national security interests. Citing an example he spoke about 'the almost non-existing Macedonian problem which was tackled without any concrete approach to the Balkans in the general'.

Where did Russian foreign policy miscalculate and did it really exist?

It is a well-known fact that after the declaration of independence of Slovenia and Croatia in June 1991 the leaders of the rump Yugoslavia expressed their hopes that Macedonia as well as Bosnia and Herzegovina would remain within its federal structure. However, the referendum that was held in Macedonia in September 1991 polled 70 per cent of the vote on the slogan 'For the sovereign Macedonia with the right of the entry into the union of the sovereign states of Yugoslavia'. The Albanians boycotted the referendum. After the victory in the referendum the supporters of complete independence 'forgot' the second half of the statement and did not mention the idea of a confederation or federation any longer. That made it possible not only for Macedonia to withdraw from Yugoslavia painlessly but for the military detachments of JNA (Yugoslavian People's Army) to leave in April 1992.

The separation of Macedonia from Yugoslavia gave rise to several grave political problems in the Balkans. Russia demonstrated its reluctance to display any initiative, such as the recognition of the sovereignty of the republics that had broken away from Yugoslavia. It took into consideration the necessity to coordinate its efforts with the leading states of CSCE. Proceeding from this, Croatia and Slovenia were recognised as independent states in February 1992. In May 1992 the Minister of Foreign Affairs, A. Kozyrev, stated the principal readiness of Russia to recognise the state independence of the Republic of Macedonia with the reservation that it 'would be done in accordance with other countries'. The Foreign Minister's position aroused severe critisism even in Russia. The opposition accused Yeltsin's administration of 'going a long way down the line to the West', 'following the American waterway', of 'the absence of independence'. In June the

Committee of the Supreme Soviet on international affairs and the Communist newspaper *Pravda* launched a campaign to condemn the foreign policy of the Russian government in connection with the Serbian problem, questioning the support given to the United Nations sanctions in respect of Yugoslavia by the Russian representative.

On the last day of his visit to Sofia (4 August 1992) Yeltsin made the statement that caused a sensation. At the final press conference the Russian President stated that after the talks on Macedonia with Zh. Zhelev he had taken the decision that it was necessary to recognise its independence. The name of the country had to be decided only by the country itself. On 5 August in Skopje, Deputy Foreign Minister V. Churkin, handed in the note on recognition of the Republic of Macedonia as an independent and sovereign state to Minister of Foreign Affairs Denko Maleski. The note was signed by B. Yeltsin on 4 August. Russia was the seventh country after Turkey, Bulgaria, Slovenia, Croatia, the Philippines and Lithuania to recognise Macedonia.

That diplomatic move evoked a tough response in Athens. The representative of the Greek Foreign Affairs Office made a statement that the recognition of independence of Macedonia was qualified as an unfriendly act towards Greece. The Russian Foreign Office dismissed the allegations of the Greek note. Referring to the letter from the Minister of Foreign Affairs of the Russian Federation, A. Kozyrev, to the Prime Minister of Greece, K. Mitsotakis, on the inadmissibility of delaying further the decision on the Macedonian problem, the Russian note insisted on the timely recognition of Macedonia. As for the name of the country and the choice of national symbols that Greece criticised, the decision on these problems depended on the will and choice of the people. 'This does not exclude a coordinated search for the settlement of the problems that could satisfy the neighbouring states,' the note concluded.

Later on, Kozyrev explained why Russia and Bulgaria in particular had had to take the initiative to recognise Macedonia as an independent and territorially integral state. If unrecognised, within several months the country could have fallen easy prey to other states in the region, where rather aggressive forces are in action. He stated that after the elucidation of the point, Greece showed understanding of the decision made by Russia.

Russia did not take any hasty actions having declared the recognition of the independence of Macedonia. The exchange of ambassadors took place only a year later. The commercial and economic ties were put in place gradually. However, these ties remain feeble in spite of the existence of the intergovernmental agreements that are serious declaration of intentions.

Russia is deeply interested in the development of the relationship with Macedonia as well as with any other Balkan country. But the economic instability characteristic of the overwhelming majority of post-communist society prevents it. Moreover, a new formula for political interrelation, under the conditions of the developing market economy, should be found.

Chapter 17

The Balkans and the Mediterranean policy of Russia*

Nina Smirnova and Alla A. Yaskova

The Balkans are a traditional sphere of interest for Russia. This idea is common to almost all trends of Russian public life.

There are different dimensions to these interests. Among them are the geopolitical dimensions. In so far as the Balkans are near to Russian territory, it determines the permanent Russian intention to have friendly relations in this region. The perception of the necessity to maintain constructive and good-neighbourly relations with all Balkan countries increased particularly at the end of the twentieth century. The geopolitical factor influences the Russian line for stability in the Balkans.

The economic dimension includes the appreciation of the Balkan states by Russia as traditional business and commercial partners. The tendency to further develop these relations is a characteristic feature of the last decades. The problems of sea trade routes through the Mediterranean from the Black Sea to South Europe, Asia, Africa, and the Western Hemisphere are also among the economic factors.

Besides, the important events in Russian history should be mentioned. The Balkans occupied an important place in the European policy of nineteenth-century Russia. Its main concern was to safeguard free passage through the Bosphorous Straits to the Mediterranean region. This policy coincided with the movement of Balkan people toward independence.

It was the great Balkan crisis of 1875–8, culminating in war between Russia and Turkey and the Congress of Berlin, that produced Bulgarian autonomy, Romanian and Serbian independence, the partition of

---

* This article was first published in *Russia, the Mediterranean and Black Sea Region* (Moscow, Academy of Sciences, 1996).

Macedonia, Austrian occupation of Bosnia-Hercegovina, and so on. It was the beginning of a process called 'balkanisation'. The frontiers of the new states did not coincide with the ethnic and linguistic areas. The Greeks and the Serbs could not agree on the future of Macedonia, while the Bulgarians claimed it as well. The Serbs and Romanians planned to divide the region which should have become an independent Bulgaria, while the Greeks and the Bulgarians both claimed Thrace. The Berlin Congress assigned to Montenegro substantial areas where the population was Albanian, while the Greeks were claiming the region of Korca and Gjirokastra, which they regarded as 'northern Epirus'. Meanwhile Albanians pretended to be united in one independent state and refused to accept the loss of Kosova – the centre of the national movement not long ago.

The Balkans, because of its geostrategical position, has been an historical crossroad of interests for Eastern and Western powers. Russia supported the new independent states and the key points of her influence were, by turn, Bulgaria, Serbia and Montenegro. However, Russia could not maintain influence there.

From the First World War to the Second World War

During the First World War and the immediate postwar years territorial issues continued to trouble the relations of the Balkan countries, with each other and with their neighbours. The spheres of interests were gradually being redistributed among the winners. Russia and Austria, however, had not inherited traditions of 'their' empires. They found themselves barred from solving the Balkan problems. Thus Greece gravitated towards the Eastern Mediterranean, which was transforming into a reserved British zone. Romania and Yugoslavia inclined towards France, and later integrated into the French alliance system. Albania became the Italian springboard for the offensive to the Balkans. Only Bulgaria remained 'no-man's land', being oppressed with reparations.

The birth of Soviet Russia and successive formation of the USSR brought about a change in the system of international relations in Europe and in the world. The 'capitalist West' and the 'socialist East' – this was the borderline of basic confrontation of the two worlds. Thus belt of small independent 'bourgeois' states (the Balkans included) separated Russia from Europe.

The dissolution of Austro-Hungary brought the liberty of choice to the Slavs who inhabited the territory of former Empire. In autumn of

1918 the Croats declared their independence, but some weeks later the prince-regent of Serbia proclaimed the union of his country with the Croats and Slovenes. A Yugoslav state had become a reality. But the Croats and Slovenes did not obtain assurances of equality from the Serbs. The outline of a future conflict were obvious: the whole foundation of the Yugoslav state rested on an assumption of Serbian supremacy which the other Slav peoples were reluctant to accept. So the settlement that emerged from the Paris Peace Conference added new problems.

Small and middle-sized states, which affirmed themselves as subjects of international politics, became a new factor. Their associations were frequently acquiring qualities of a 'collective great power', as was the case of the Little Entente and the Balkan Entente.

The Balkan Entente became a factor of stability in the region and contributed to the Balkan understanding. But this tendency at times seemed reduced to their common wish to hold Bulgaria and Hungary down. This influenced in a negative way the foreign relations of the inter-war years.

The Soviet policy in Europe in the 1930s (membership of the League of Nations, approach to the French doctrine of collective security, and so on) influenced the decision to change the former negative attitude towards the Balkan Entente. But the European pre-war crisis put an end to this move.

During the Second World War, especially in its final stage, the peoples and governments of all Balkan states expressed their solidarity with the aims of the fight, held by the anti-Hitler coalition. As the liberation movement, in fact, was going through inner polarisation, their orientation points were also gradually changing. Communist and pro-communist politicians were casting glances towards the USSR, and 'bourgeois-democratic' politicians towards Anglo-American allies.

A new knot of contradictions was emerging in the Eastern Mediterranean. After ousting the British rivals from Greece, the USA became absolute leader in the region, and proclaimed it its security zone.

The socialist camp and its dissolution

Political and ideological rivalry of the 'capitalist West' and the 'socialist East' yielded ground to the rivalry between the USA and USSR. From the beginning of the 'cold war' the Balkans adopted the function of the buffer in the bipolar geopolitical structure of the world. Their import-ance increased in view of the fact that over the territory of the penin-sula there was a demarcation line between NATO's southern flank and the Soviet bloc. In this situation Albanian ports in the Adriatic and Ionian Seas (as well as the Adriatic ports of Yugoslavia) could counterbalance the effect of total dominance of NATO 'atlanticists' in the Mediterranean.

Every country of the peninsula had its history of relationship with the 'Big Neighbour', and it was far from always being smooth. The postwar settlement did not abolish national and territorial problems existing between the Balkan states proper; moreover, in some cases they became even more complex. However, instead of a system of relations which could have secured sovereignty of every country, the USSR began the for-mation of a socialist camp by imposing the Soviet model. The dictate of the 'elder brother' reduced the independence of junior partners to a minimum, and denied their historical and national peculiarities.

The attitude of the USSR to the national question in Eastern Europe was typical. In wartime, a change of emphasis in Soviet propaganda is known to have taken place: the slogan of defence of socialist values was replaced by a patriotic appeal to defend the Motherland. At the final stage of the war, when the Soviet Army approached the state fron-tiers and entered the territory of the Balkans, the appeal to strengthen Slavic unity was intensified (an All-Slavs Committee was founded as far back as 1942). At the same time, *Slavyane* ('The Slavs') magazine was started, and its editorial staff consisted of Soviet representatives (Russians, Byelorussians, Ukranians), as well as those of Yugoslav, Bulgarian, Polish, and Czech emigrants.

In September 1945 Stalin formulated the tasks of the said magazine and pointed to how the national question had to be regarded. Thus, according to him, the community of Slav peoples represented a kind of transitory stage to 'a higher form of unity of peoples, a fraternal coop-eration within the framework of a united socialist system'. In other words, the creation of a 'Soviet people' had to become standard for many multinational states of the socialist camp.

In foreign politics the formation of two blocs manifested a transition to confrontation, based primarily on force.

At the final stage of the Second World War it had already become clear that the process of restoring national independence in all Balkan countries was combined with the struggle for social and economic transformation. In place of reactionary dictatorial regimes, chiefly monarchies, parliamentary republics sprang up. And the political platforms of Popular Fronts, which in all countries except Greece came to power, were aimed at a development of democracy, although they were headed by Communist parties. The slogans of fighting for socialism had already been withdrawn from the agenda during the war. Illustrative, in this respect, is the example of G. Dimitrov: from the moment of official dissolution of the Comintern in 1943 till autumn of 1945, his address was: Moscow, the CC of the All-Union Communist party (Bolsheviks). In November 1945 he seemed to abandon the role of spokesman of the socialist idea, returned to Bulgaria and, at a pre-election meeting in Sofia, spoke in favour of unity of all patriotic forces having in view the country's reconstruction; he also offered assurances that Communists did not strive for dictatorship.

The liberation of the Balkans from German troops stimulated reconstruction of economic links, and coordinated actions of the anti-fascist coalition member countries favoured the same trend towards unity. The first pan-Balkan programme of postwar cooperation was suggested by Ismet Inonu, President of the Republic of Turkey. On 1 November 1944, at the opening of a new session of the Great National Assembly, he underlined his wish to promote relations with allied powers – the USSR, Great Britain, France, as well as with Greece and Yugoslavia. At the same time he stated that Turkey was disposed to do everything necessary to eliminate old contradictions between the Balkan peoples and to establish relations of peace and confidence between them. But his words remained only good wishes.

Relations within the 'Big Three' were changing as well as those in the Balkans. It had already become obvious during the preparation stage of the peace treaties with Bulgaria, Romania and Italy, that the great powers intended to defend the interests of their eventual clients, although at that time, the choice in favour of the USSR or the West had not yet been predetermined. During the Paris Peace Conference the constellation of forces became more evident. Territorial problems, and conditions of reparation payments were decided upon in accordance with political expediency, for example, with the Trieste question. E. Kardelj was forced to reproach V. Molotov for betrayal, in connection with the shift in Soviet policy from unconditional support of Yugoslav claims, to agreement in favour of a pro-Italian variant. 'Mister No' answered with silence, but on the party line, the Yugoslav communists were advised to show prudence: 'Your positions are firm, it was said, but Italian communists would be able to gain a majority in forthcoming parliamentary elections, using the claim for Trieste to be transferred to Italy...'.

The unity of the socialist camp, in its formation, was attained by force. But artificially suppressed national problems, suppression of independence, and substitution of state power's democratic principles by a mono-party structure of the Soviet type, all these factors in the end conditioned the crisis of the system.

Any symptom of independence was punished. The 1948 Soviet–Yugoslav conflict was also interpreted by Soviet propaganda as a betrayal of internationalist principles and a triumph of nationalism. The reaction to Tito's position and the subsequent excommunication of Albania were both attempts 'to punish' for the right to adopt independent decisions. In both situations, dictator Stalin and 'democrat' Khrushchev acted in the same manner. The system forced them to make the same decision, i.e. apply force in domestic and foreign policies. As a result, the USSR position in the Balkans was abruptly weakened, and disintegrative processes in the region were strengthened.

The rupture of all relations with Albania in 1961 created grounds for a revival of the Eastern policy of Italy, Germany and France – and China, as a new factor, appeared in Europe. Not only Albania, but Romania and Yugoslavia as well, favoured the Chinese emissaries. A scanty, but very active organisation called 'Union of Friends of New China', was effective in Greece. Inspired by these manifestations of general interest, the Balkan countries began showing more independence towards the two great powers patronising them.

In the late 1970s, 'The Balkans to the Balkan peoples' appeal was revived. Just as it was at the end of the nineteenth century, the beginning of the twentieth century and in inter-wartime, the essence of the appeal consisted in protesting against interference of non-Balkan states into the affairs of the peninsula. The Balkan countries tried to establish multilateral economic and cultural cooperation, but these efforts were blocked by Moscow. The very idea of founding a regional union (albeit only on an economic basis), capable of independently acting in the international sphere, was inadmissible. But the tendency towards regionalisation of international relations and, consequently, of strengthening the independent role of small and middle-sized states, nevertheless, was gaining ground.

The process of inner-Balkan rapprochement reached its peak by the beginning of 1988. Albania took part in the Belgrade meeting of the Balkan states' Foreign Ministers, and priority trends in cooperation were defined. But the revolutionary upheavals of autumn of 1989 stopped the process.

Main trends of the contemporary Balkan situation

An attentive observer of the Balkan situation in the late 1980s and early 1990s will be sure to mention, at least, its two characteristics – the real independence of the Balkan region countries' growth, on the one hand, and their simultaneous 'crawling' into an acute economic and political crisis, aggravation of conflict potential, and spread of nationalism and inter-ethnic contradictions.

Radical changes in the correlation of forces in the Balkans were brought about by the collapse of regimes in Bulgaria, Romania, and Albania and the cessation of bloc confrontation, which for many years had separated the Balkan countries according to their membership in the NATO or the Warsaw Treaty. Traditional ties between the Balkan states and the European powers, as well as their alliances, began to revive and come into existence. After the disintegration of the USSR, they faced the difficult tasks of establishing relations with former Soviet republics, with Russia, the Ukraine and Moldova, in the first place.

At the same time the Balkan countries, to some degree, found themselves involved in the 'instability arc', which appeared on the territory of former Yugoslavia (SFRY) and in southern regions of the former Soviet Union, as a result of acute inter-ethnic conflicts. The influence of pseudopatriotic parties and movements on the domestic and foreign policies of some newly created states became evident in the conditions of deepening economic crisis. Experience shows that nationalist ideas and appeals, induced into mass consciousness, are sufficient in such conditions to provoke bloody conflicts.

At the previous stages, especially in the 1980s, the primary reason for crisis in the economy and politics of the majority of Balkan countries was the command administrative system, which promoted the decay of society, inefficient production, a steady decrease in the standard of living and accelerated technological lag, compared to non-socialist countries, such as Greece and Turkey in the Balkan neighbourhood. Deep contradictions between the ruling leadership and the basic layers of society, full discreditation of regimes, loss of support on behalf of the Soviet Union – all these factors have brought about a situation in which former ruling parties, even those rejuvenated, with a changed name and essence of activity, proved unable to retain power, as was the case in Bulgaria and Albania in the early 1990s. In those countries, however, where the ruling parties, in one or another form, have conserved their positions (for example, in Serbia), they have struck an agreement with ultra-nationalist forces and groups, a fact which in itself created a dangerous situation not only in their countries but in the Balkan region as a whole.

All these circumstances served to reduce multilateral cooperation within the region, which in the second half of the 1980s had revived and following the 1988 meetings of Foreign Ministers and other bodies, representing all Balkan countries, became regular. The increasing political instability made them turn, in the first place, to their home problems and search for ways to prevent conflicts with their immediate neighbours. The balance of forces, however, was radically shaken in summer 1991 after the rupture of former Yugoslavia and open military operations between the republics began.

Ethno-political conflict as a source of tensions

Successive events on the territory of former Yugoslavia demonstrated the depth and complexity of up-to-date ethno-political contradictions in the Balkan region. The present high conflict potential in the sphere of inter-ethnic relations in the Balkans convincingly testifies that after the end of Cold War, nationalism has become the main danger in post-communist regions of Europe.

Heterogeneous national structure in the majority of countries in the Balkan region has been an objective premise to aggravating inter-ethnic contradictions. Greece, Albania and Slovenia might be considered to be relatively homogeneous from this point of view, where national minorities constituted, in the late 1980s, 2 per cent, 4 per cent and 12.1 per cent, respectively. In Bulgaria their share is 20.2 per cent, in Croatia 20 per cent, Macedonia 42 per cent, Montenegro 33.6 per cent, Serbia 34.5 per cent, Romania 19.8 per cent. In Bosnia and Hercegovina national composition is the most complex: in this country there are 1,905,000 Muslims, 1,364,000 Serbs, 752,000 Croats, and 240,000 inhabitants who in the last population census declared themselves as being Yugoslavs, as well as 130,000 representatives of other nationalities.

It has to be added that national minorities dispersed throughout the Balkan peninsula have, as a rule, their ethnic Motherland within its limits, and in a series of cases they inhabit regions bordering their Motherland. In conditions of growing crisis, economic and political confusion, this gives rise to irredentism and separatism, which are based on the hope of receiving patronage and support from abroad.

This, in its turn, is known to lead to complications in inter-state relations, to conflicts and wars.

The sharpest contradictions emerged on these grounds in the geopolitical space of former Yugoslavia (conflict between Serbia and Croatia, as well as military actions on the territory of Bosnia and Hercegovina between the Serbs, Croats and Muslims). In the case of an unfavourable development of events, the Autonomous Region of Kosovo as an integral part of Serbia, inhabited chiefly by ethnic Albanians, as well as the Republic of Macedonia with its numerous groups of Serbian and Albanian population, might become potential seats of conflict. Certain contradictions remain in force in relations between Hungary, on the one hand, Romania, Serbia and Slovakia on the other, connected with the existence of a significant Hungarian minority in these countries. Periodic aggravation of the Balkan situation was produced due to the unresolved problems of ethnic Turks in Greece and Bulgaria, and the same with the Greek minority in Albania and the Albanian minority in Greece. Finally, the Macedonian question, in its different aspects, still has not found a final settlement in the Balkan region.

The above situation does not reflect the whole complexity of national and ethnic problems of the Balkans, which are aggravated by social, political, historical and cultural factors. All of them are profound and have been taking shape over entire historical epochs. However, at the end of the twentieth century these problems acquired new vigour, conditioned by the length and in many cases troublesome transition of the majority of Balkan countries to democracy and co-operation. Under these circumstances, inter-ethnic contradictions and conflicts inevitably gain political sense and turn into ethno-political ones by nature.

There are certain limiting factors in the trend of the Balkan countries' movement towards cooperation with Western Europe. Every Balkan state, be it voluntarily or not, has to correlate its relations with neighbours, within the constraints of European politics, which, in reality, play a positive role in lessening inner confrontation in the region. The Balkans, nevertheless, remains an area which combines Western and Eastern cultural traditions and special characteristics, in spite of all the political changes and integration processes gaining momentum in Europe. This results in a slower transition of the post-communist societies of Bulgaria, Romania and Albania towards democracy and market, as compared with their Central European neighbours. It also determines a more steady character of nationalism in all its manifestations, beginning with traditional barriers of suspicion and mistrust towards neighbours that are difficult to overcome and end in open conflicts with them.

Specific traits of Balkan nationalism were historically determined by the late creation of nation-states in this region. The majority of new states created after the First World War had considerable ethnic minorities which were the source of future inter-ethnic clashes. After the Second World War, nationalism was used by the regimes as an instrument to strengthen their dominance. Trying to profit by emotional and irrational instincts, finding ground in the backward strata of society, nationalism was used as an instrument to resolve various political tasks put forward.

That is why one can state that fundamental political democratisation in the Balkan countries is the most important precondition for preventing national clashes and for crisis management in this unstable region.

A special problem of the Balkan states is the urgent necessity to adopt a harmonious attitude to the two interconnected principles of European security: the defence of national minorities' rights, and stability (inviolability) of state boundaries. According to the Balkan experience this is one of the most complicated and as yet unresolved problems of the present. Of late, pseudopatriotic parties and groupings are raising the issue of some state borders 'correction' more and more openly, and do not exclude the possibility of resolution by force. In the present circumstances it might lead not only to local wars, but to a more serious European conflict. As the Balkan experience shows, the imperial ambitions inherent not only to 'great powers' are now being revived on the basis of rapprochement of pseudopatriotic and former totalitarian structures, might be the most dangerous. The absence of strong democratic opposition, its lack of structure, and its heterogeneity, typical to the present stage of development of societies, make this danger real, especially in the conditions of instability given the unpredictable character of political processes in the Balkan countries.

The inter-state conflicts which are growing in the present situation where agreements on national minorities' rights and legal international forms of their defence are lacking, are difficult to overcome, and this fact has been worrying the political circles of Europe for a long time. Yugoslavia showed special interest in the issue. In 1978, on its initiative, a workshop in the UNO system was created with the aim of drawing up a draft declaration 'On the Rights of National, Ethnic, Religious and Linguistic Minorities'. Due to a series of reasons, the work on the mentioned declaration went on slowly, and the draft passed its second reading only in February of 1991. Nevertheless for the first time in international practice, the notion of 'collective rights' of national minorities was especially actively proposed by Yugoslavia, Hungary and the Ukraine.

As to the CSCE documents, in the Helsinki Final Act the proper term of 'national minority' was mentioned, but with a reservation. These minorities had to be previously recognised as being such by respective governments. In successive CSCE documents, including the Paris Charter for a New Europe, agreements on national minorities were formulated, beginning with individual human rights to be recognised, which in itself could not mean securing such collective rights as that of cultural autonomy, self-management, etc. Not all Balkan states manifest the same approach to the solution of the problem, which may be explained by differences in concrete situations and historical traditions.

Thus, not one of the four post-war Greece constitutions has had even a theoretical recognition of collective rights of national minorities. In Romania certain shifts could be observed on the agenda, minorities were granted the possibility to found political organisations according to ethnicity: nowadays the Democratic Union of Romania's Hungarians is the second largest political party after the FNS. The Albanian constitution recognises the existence of national minorities – Greek, Serbian, Macedonian – and their rights of cultural development are declared. In Bulgarian official papers the term 'national minority' is not mentioned, although the 1991 constitution proclaims basic rights and obligations which proceed from international documents referring to national minorities. As to Turkey, the main criteria in its approach to the issue of national minorities is their religion, and in this connection Turkey shows special interest in the Muslim population of the Balkan countries and is disposed to be spokesman of their interests.

The given data reveal radical differences in the national politics of the Balkan states, which may be an easy source of contradictions and conflicts between them. It is thus obvious that the adoption of national minorities' collective rights as an alternative to the existent and extremely explosive principle of national self-determination up to secession would be an important precondition to a new security system. It is worth mentioning that the above mentioned principle was proclaimed by the Bolsheviks with the intention of destroying the old tsarist empire. In fact it evoked acute contradictions among nations and national groups, especially since the situation concerned a mixed population and uncertain territorial borders. This is the reason why it is worth searching for new forms of ethnic groups' self-determination: for instance, national-cultural autonomy, a large-scale system of self-management in regions populated by national minorities, and so on. In our opinion, in the Balkans it would lead to a gradual appeasement of the contemporary situation, although the road to a stable peace in this region will be extremely long.

The regional forms of mutual cooperation

Having became an important trend for contemporary European development, the regional forms of mutual cooperation in the Black Sea–Mediterranean area are significantly varied now. The erosion of political structures that existed in South Eastern Europe after the Second World War were as a result of the historically important political events of the late 1980s–early 1990s, namely:

- the collapse of respective societies in Central and South East Europe and their slow transition to uncertain and still unstable democracy;
- the disintegration of the Soviet Union, combined with the formation of new independent states;
- the break-up of Yugoslavia, extremely painful, tragic and dangerous for all the Mediterranean and South European area.

Following the collapse of so-called socialist systems the countries of Eastern and South Eastern Europe can be put into three groups. The first one, consisting of Hungary, Poland and the former Czechoslovakia, was the first to begin radical political as well as economic changes. In the second group – Romania, Bulgaria, Albania – political and economic changes occurred slowly and are less radical. The third group of countries consists of the former USSR republics – new independent states. Together with Russia almost all these countries situated in the former Soviet Union European part – the Ukraine, Moldova and Georgia – are closely connected with the Black Sea–Mediterranean area. A special – although sufficiently different – position is taken today by new independent states that are successors of disintegrated Yugoslavia, of which Slovenia, Croatia and Montenegro are not only Balkan, but also Mediterranean (Adriatic) countries. Being an integral part of Mediterranean civilisation these countries have had over centuries stable ties not only with their neighbours but with the wider Mediterranean area as well.

Speaking about the perspectives of cooperation and the possible future integration processes in the region, one can state that any forms of cooperation between the neighbouring countries are always natural and therefore necessary and welcome. The Balkans and the Caucasus were however for centuries known as unstable regions, the regions of conflicts and wars, of separation more than cooperation. Unfortunately we still observe many open or potential 'hot points' on the map of the Black Sea and Mediterranean area which of course do harm to the majority of mutual cooperation attempts.

All the mentioned circumstances have determined a decrease in the Balkan multilateral cooperation which became significantly active in the late 1980s. The balance of forces was radically shaken in the summer of 1991 after the disruption of Yugoslavia and the start of military operations between its former republics.

Taking into consideration that the majority of the Black Sea and Balkan countries have inherited a very specific road of development determined by the former ideological, political and even economic division of the region, one can forecast the unstable situation connected with the process of new nation-states formation, and a series of unresolved national minorities problems combined with the borders' reshaping claims. The best way of preventing the conflict situations could be the mutual cooperation processes of development. That is why the initiative of Black Sea subregional cooperation supported by all the Black Sea and some of the Mediterranean countries in June 1992, when the Bosporus declaration was signed by 11 countries, among them Albania and Greece, has been appreciated by the majority of countries of the region.

This contributed to the emergence of some positive factors which determine future development of subregional cooperation. The geographical frame of cooperation became broader, and now it is possible to forecast the inclusion of some former Yugoslav republics into the process.

Having in view all the existing problems it is necessary to mention a prospective role for some Black Sea–Mediterranean countries: Turkey, which after all was an initiator of Black Sea cooperation, Greece which holds an important place in the region, and Italy, a great Mediterranean–Adriatic country which in the last years became a powerful motor of all the processes of cooperation in South Eastern and East Central Europe.

Being a rapidly developed member of NATO from the early 1980s, Turkey is the main Islamic country in the region. In the sharp religious confrontation in Bosnia or Nagorny Karabach the specific position of Turkey may have both positive and negative political effects on the processes of subregional cooperation. Which of the two influences will get the upper hand will perhaps be shown by the way in which both the above-mentioned conflicts will be resolved. In any case the role of Turkey as an economic motor of subregional cooperation is indisputable.

Greece, a NATO and EU member, has become more and more active in subregional cooperation. Greece represents a very important, if not the most important, bond in Black Sea–Mediterranean cooperation and the subregion's linkage with European structures. Its role not only as an economic but also a traditional ally of the Balkan and Black Sea countries is also indisputable.

The Balkan states seem to be deeply interested in promoting all spheres of mutual regional cooperation. A very good example is shown by Romania, the Black Sea University organiser. The interest of foreign participants to its activity confirms the idea that such institutions can play a beneficial role in imparting knowledge and values for the societies of the area. Bulgaria's geopolitical position determines the permanent interest in the activation of economic life in the region taking into consideration countries' transition to a market economy and integration in European structures. The prospects of Bulgarian–Greek cooperation in the common oil pipeline Burgas–Alexandropolis construction testify to the countries' high interest in regional cooperation development.

Exterior factors of stability and cooperation in the Balkan area

Finally, it is necessary to mention the more significant importance of exterior factors of Balkan security, i.e., the policy of European powers, and the role and place of the Balkan countries in the European, especially Mediterranean, integration process.

In the situation of the contemporary Balkan crisis the Balkan countries – former members of the Warsaw Treaty Organisation (Romania and Bulgaria) – in one form or another, expressed their intention to become members of NATO, motivated by their tendency to a more rapid integration into European structures. In reality, however, it is explained by their wish, mostly of necessity, to have the 'defending umbrella' of the Atlantic alliance. The perspectives of post-communist Balkan states to become associated to the EC seem to be very problematic.

The possibilities exist for the Balkan countries to participate in different subregional groupings and on this basis extend their cooperation in the Black Sea and Mediterranean region. Together with the Central European direction of multilateral cooperation they promise an unexhausted positive potential, which could, in many aspects, promote a solution to the problems accumulated in the region. It has to be taken into consideration that the Balkan, Black Sea and Danubian subregions embrace the same countries: the Balkan six, Russia, the Ukraine, and Georgia, on the one hand, and the mentioned countries plus Hungary, Austria, Italy and Germany, on the other.

Beginning with the 1970s, Germany was a stable and most important trade and economic partner of all the above mentioned states. After the fall of the communist regimes, it was Germany which initiated rapprochement of these countries with the European structures (it must be stressed that provision for their association and subsequent integration into the EU form part of all treaties signed by Germany with the countries of the region). Finally, it was Germany which offered the most humanitarian and financial help.

Having in mind a changed role of the Balkan and Black Sea–Mediterranean area in Europe and in the world, Western countries demonstrate common as well as specific interests in the region. For the USA, they are connected with the situation in the Mediterranean and on the southern NATO flank, with ethnic groups of emigrants from the Balkan countries residing in the USA; for Germany, it is the fact of having a considerable number of *Gastarbeiter*: the Yugoslavs, Turks, etc.

An increasing interest in Balkan affairs is shown by Italy, which not only claims to be a binding link between the EC and the Balkan countries today, but shows a lively interest in settling ethno-political conflicts in the region immediately bordering it.

To be sure, the relations between the European powers and any of the Balkan countries depend heavily on their domestic policy problems.

The national interests both of Russia and the Western countries are objectively based on the same ground of Balkan stability. As for the Balkan countries, stability and peace are absolutely necessary for them, because the Balkan peninsula is the natural area of its states' existence. The national interest of Russia (its foreign policy as well) could not be identical to that of the former Soviet Union, even in the important Balkan region. On the other hand the specific traits of Russia's Balkan policy (as, is the policy of Western countries) are determined by the complexity of the Balkan situation, the fact that the highest incidence of conflicts and wars is not between states but within them. These internal conflicts are least susceptible to external influence and control, which is why the mediation in conflict resolution is extremely difficult here.

The Balkan foreign policy concept of Russia was periodically influenced by internal national-patriotic forces which have been assumed to have an influence on Orthodox Serbia, but as it is clear now, the historical factors play in the Balkans a more and more subordinate role. Recent events and especially the achievement of the Dayton agreements with the active support of US diplomacy show that the factor of 'historical influence' has basically changed. What the majority of Balkan countries need now is stable economic support, especially important for destroyed Bosnia, Croatia and Serbia weakened by sanctions. Russia might be willing, but is nowadays unable to provide a large economic assistance. Germany has a real capability, but is limited by its internal problems and not least by the great number of refugees from the Balkans. As a result the Balkans are now in a vacuum more than ever in its history. Serious international efforts need to be made to stabilise the situation in the Balkans. American influence has really increased, both in the peacekeeping process and in financial support to Bosnia. But it is obvious that the unilateral orientation does not seem to be the best solution for Balkan stability. That is why the Russian administration decided to take part in IFOR action, although it was a difficult decision because of the present financial problems of RF. It is useful to have the possibility of interaction between the NATO and Russian military forces not only in the Balkans, but in a broader Mediterranean area as well.

The Dayton agreements have stopped an acute military conflict, but did not resolve the most difficult regional problems.[1] The majority of Balkan States economies have been pauperised by state system mismanagement, preparation for wars, embargoes, sanctions and so on. The flood of war refugees affects the majority of neighbouring countries. Finally, a number of the above-mentioned inter-ethnic problems are also potentially dangerous: as is known, the attempts (or even discussions) about the possibility of Greater Serbia creation led to the similar discussions in connection with Greater Albania.

Russia foreign policy possibilities in the Balkan–Black Sea–Mediterranean region are limited now not only because of the regional crisis situation, but through the internal political instability and the opposition pressure in Russia as well. Meanwhile the political concept of the present administration assumes Russian participation in all the multilateral peacekeeping actions and the equal approach to all the conflicting parties.

Finally one could add a realistic observation of J. F. Brown, an eminent specialist in Balkan history: 'Try to content problems rather than solve them. Many problems were solved that way.'

Note

1. D. Radovic, 'From Dayton to Paris. Uncertain Outcome', in *Europe* (Belgrade), January–February 1996, p. 8.

Chapter 18

Former Yugoslav Macedonia, the regional setting and European security: towards Balkan stability?

Sophia Clément

Risk assessment at the regional level and the impact on former Yugoslav Macedonia

The correlation between internal conflicts, their regional dimension and the immediate environment is the essential variable to be taken into account in South East Europe. Internally, since its declaration of independence in 1991, the FYR of Macedonia has experienced a polarisation and fragmentation of the political scene, due to political, economic and social transition and to the inter-ethnic relations between Macedonians and Albanians. While some of the political forces favour integration and reform from within, yet allowing inter-ethnic dialogue, political radicalisation may gradually limit the existing room for manoeuvre of the moderate forces in power, especially since the normalisation of relations with neighbouring countries has shifted the focus towards the tense internal inter-ethnic relations as a result of a possible external threat. Macedonians see any move in favour of Albanians as a first step towards secession while the latter claim proportional representation within state institutions as well as the status of a constituent nation. This perception has deeply increased with the eruption of the Kosovo conflict.

First, at the regional level, the changes that have taken place in South Eastern Europe following the end of bipolarity, the dissolution of former Yugoslavia and the Bosnian conflict modified the nature and form of relations and have made South East Europe today one of the continent's most volatile regions. The range and the depth of regional disputes include the fragility of the Bosnian peace process (especially considering the reduction of the foreign peacekeeping troops), the still unresolved Albanian question and the strained relations between Greece and Turkey, all remain major factors of instability.

The evolution of the internal situation in Bosnia reveals a logic of fragmentation and raises questions about the nature of the Dayton Agreement which can be assessed positively, as it allowed the suspension of hostilities and a successful implementation of the military provisions (separation of warring parties, removal of heavy weapons), but the civilian dimension is hardly implemented: the main socio-economic goals were achieved but the return of refugees and displaced persons, the indictment of war criminals, the freedom of the media, the setting up of common institutions as well as the police forces and legal system are still pending. Concrete achievements have only been achieved by external pressure.[2]

South East European stability goes far beyond Bosnia. The FYR of Macedonia's central geographic location in the Balkan peninsula, the interdependence at the regional level, and the presence of a continuum of Albanian-populated areas along its borders are determinants for internal and for regional stability as a whole. In Kosovo, the tense situation between Serbs and Albanians had given way to a *de facto* partition and to the establishment of a parallel administration. While the Serbs favour status quo within the framework of the Federal Republic of Yugoslavia, Kosovo Albanians aim at independence. For the FYR of Macedonia as well as for the other countries of the region, it raises the problem of a wider 'Albanian world' and its weight in the regional balance of power. It also creates a three-sided relationship between Bosnia, Kosovo and the FYR of Macedonia. A renewal of hostilities in Bosnia could destabilise Kosovo, and vice versa, and spread to other parts of Serbia such as Sandjak and Vojvodina, in part populated by Muslims, then to the FYR of Macedonia. Furthermore, even the maintenance of low-intensity conflict in Kosovo will help to hamper inter-ethnic relations in the longer run in the FYR of Macedonia and limit the room for manoeuvre of the reformist and moderate tendency.

Tensions in Kosovo and an eventual spillover of the conflict would present the European Union with new challenges in its immediate periphery. Unfortunately, the international community's overall policy is repeating the same mistakes as in Bosnia. There has been no real preventive policy for Kosovo and the current crisis management reveals the existing divergences among partners. The eruption of the Kosovo crisis, in spite of its negatively assessed internal dynamics and potential spillover in the unstable Balkan area (Bosnia, Albania, FYROM), met with a reduction of foreign military presence. In other words, when the Kosovo crisis erupted, not only was the international foreign presence, especially American, being reduced (SFOR, UNPREDEP), but no international organisation was willing to deploy forces around the crisis area (Albania, FYROM). The increasing instability should have implied an offensive policy and the maintenance of a stronger foreign presence on the ground.

Instability also slowed the transition process already characterised by a lower economic base and weaker civil societies, turning countries from the region into 'slow-track' political crisis which occurred throughout the region during 1996 and 1997. The stabilisation process remains a long-term one due to deep structural economic problems, political instability stemming from the fragility of the internal consensus and the unpopularity of internal reforms. It is further endangered by additional economic, social and political difficulties (migration and refugees, Mafias, arms transfers and other essentially transnational risks) which would affect the rest of the European continent.[3]

During the Yugoslav conflict, the relations of the FYR of Macedonia with Bulgaria, the Federal Republic of Yugoslavia (FRY), Greece and Turkey went through successive phases of tension and calm. Most neighbouring countries were late in recognising the new state, unwilling, for various reasons, to recognise the existence of a Macedonian nation separate from its ethnic (Bulgaria, Greece) or territorial (Serbia) dimension. For the FYR of Macedonia, the intensification of *equidistant* bilateral relations has been aimed at breaking away from the regional isolation of the first hours of independence. Begun in 1995, the normalisation of the FYR of Macedonia's relations with its neighbours, which were strained during the first years of independence, is diminishing the perception of an external threat. The political, economic and military weakness of most neighbouring countries, and their fear of any calling into question the process of integration into international organisations, makes any political offensive improbable. The crisis in Bulgaria, Serbia and Albania has had only an indirect effect on the FYR of Macedonia. Only instability in Bosnia and Kosovo might constitute a serious source of destabilisation. The situation in Kosovo preoccupies the Macedonian authorities. They fear a *rapprochement* between the various segments of the Albanian movement, particularly since the end of the Bosnian conflict, waves of Kosovo Albanian refugees, and potential autonomist claims from Macedonian Albanians. Considering that Kosovo is an internal Serbian matter, they believe the maintenance of stability depends above all on the evolution of the situation in Serbia and Albania. Although divergences remain with Greece on the name issue, with FRY on the border delineation, with Albania on Albanian minority, the central authorities do not perceive any direct external threat as such. For Albania, the fate of Albanians in former Yugoslavia is an integral part of the 'Albanian question' but the Socialist-led Tirana government promotes non-interference in internal affairs and the handling of the Kosovo crisis by the international community through diplomatic means. The attitudes of the Macedonian and the Serbian governments regarding their Albanian minorities is then determinant for regional stability. Finally, neighbouring countries' perceptions and policies towards the FYR of Macedonia and, by extension, towards *regional security* as a whole (regional balance of power, potential territorial changes), should thus be closely followed.

However, South East European countries are being left out of both EU and NATO enlargement processes while they need membership in terms of both 'hard' and 'soft' security (higher threat perceptions, ethnic conflicts, economic crisis, arms transfer). They run the risk of being marginalised from the process of West European integration and the redefinition of a new political and security space in Europe, supposedly aiming at enhancing security at a pan-European level through the creation of inclusive security structures promoting integration. The nature and the form of Western approaches towards enlargement, together with the high expectations of South East European countries, have created a feeling of insecurity among the former and raise the risk of enhancing an opposite evolution towards exclusive security frameworks, to the detriment of certain group of countries.[4] They are preoccupied by the economic, political and security consequences of the European Union's internal reforms and the 'acquis communautaire' on economic links, protection of external borders, especially in the framework of the extension of the Schengen agreement, on the visa regime and free movement of people and minorities, all being perceived as instruments of a future division in Europe. They also fear consequences on bilateral relations between 'ins' and 'outs', as well as the re-emergence of dividing lines on the European continent or even of a 'grey zone' that would be formed by 'buffer states'. Finally, the gap with neighbouring regions such as Central Europe is widening as the former have developed regional cooperation initiatives which have strengthened ties and helped these countries catch up with economic and political criteria of the West.[5]

The consequences of policies adopted by the West, both for South Eastern Europe and for the European security debate, is a second variable of the analysis. Most European countries have feared a conflict that might have triggered secessionist movements throughout South Eastern Europe, as well as an eventual impact on regional autonomist claims in Western Europe. The European Union and the United States have long awaited a redefining coherent and common strategy towards the region. While they support internal democratisation as an element of legitimisation and additional guarantee of the credibility of reforms, undertaken by the Skopje government in the face of nationalist forces, the difficulty in redefining an overall strategy in a changing and unpredictable environment revealed divergences in perceptions regarding the appropriate policies. Such difficulties in adopting common positions and implementing their decisions on the ground weakened their cohesion and credibility and have had repercussions among countries in the region, increasing divisions and instability. The crisis in Albania, the beginnings of democratisation in Serbia, the conflict in Kosovo, inter-ethnic tensions in the FYR of Macedonia and instability in Bosnia are main causes for concern, and the ability of the international, and particularly the European, community to adopt a common attitude remains at stake. In the short term though, the situation in neighbouring countries should not have direct destabilising effects on the FYR of Macedonia. The stabilisation measures adopted by the European Union (reconstruction, a regional approach, conditionality) have been essentially economic rather than political and military. More than ever, and since conflict resolutions would be more cost-effective than a new outburst of conflict, a strong and long-term presence in Bosnia, the core of the Balkan problem, and a more determined policy in Kosovo are required. To be effective, the post-conflict building process in Bosnia and crisis management in Kosovo should be linked to the stabilisation of the overall Balkan region, where conflict areas are deeply interdependent.

Thirdly, in the mid-run, however, the internal situation in the FYR of Macedonia is bound to evolve due to a certain number of factors: the growing demographic gap between the Albanian population and the Macedonian one as well as the cultural and economic marginalisation of the former; the beginning of the 'after-Gligorov era' with no attributed successor yet; the ways and means the international community will use to address the Kosovo conflict and its impact on internal Macedonian affairs.

Evaluation of international action[6]

In the FYR of Macedonia, the international community has promoted measures such as putting in place peacekeeping forces mainly concerned to avoid any spillover of the conflict in South Eastern Europe, and in response to requests by President Gligorov, with the support of the then US President George Bush, for international guarantees of the country's security.[7] The multiplicity and complementarity of preventive measures adopted, together with the coordination that has taken place between the international organisations represented on the ground, make this case, to a certain extent, a textbook example of conflict prevention.

In September 1992, the OSCE sent a 'Spillover Monitoring Mission' whose task was to monitor the border between the FYR of Macedonia and Serbia with a view to preventing any spillover of the conflict in former Yugoslavia.[8] In parallel, in December 1992, the United Nations set up UNPREDEP, its first preventive mission, which also has a dual, civil and military, mandate covering traditional peace-keeping tasks related to the social and political situation, under the responsibility of a special United Nations representative, early warning by means of observation and reporting, and the exercise of good offices, added in March 1994 in order to adapt the mission to the developing internal situation. It also has an additional deterrent function through its military component, which is partly American, whose symbolic task was the first involvement of the US Army on the territory of former Yugoslavia.[9] The crisis in Albania during winter 1996–97 and a possible impact on the FYR of Macedonia have contributed to a renewal of its mandate and the cancellation of a reduction of its strength.[10] But more recently with the Kosovo conflict, in spite of increasing internal tensions, regional instability, and the request of the Macedonian authorities for a continued international presence, the reduction of the peacekeeping forces, and especially of their American component, which acts as a main deterrent force although symbolic, had been decided.

Since 1991, the UN International Conference on former Yugoslavia (Peace Implementation Council), in particular the *ad hoc* working group on ethnic and national communities and minorities, has formulated detailed recommendations on relations between the two communities. NGOs also contribute to inter-community dialogue, the development of teaching in the Albanian language and the democratisation of the media. To begin with the European Union's role was limited, due to disagreement between member countries on the recognition of independence and consequently on the policy adopted by Greece. The EU has since made up for lost time by increasing economic aid in the framework of the PHARE programme and has signed an Association Agreement.

In some ways, certain initiatives taken to stabilise the FYR of Macedonia constitute an example of effective coordination between international organisations and the complementarity of preventive measures. That was thus the case with the succession of those nominated to mediate between Greece and the FYR of Macedonia, by the European Union (Hans van den Broek), the United Nations (Cyrus Vance, and then Lord Owen and Cyrus Vance as EU and UN mediators) and bilaterally by the United States (Matthew Nimetz). It was also the case with the common wish to integrate the latter into the different international institutions (United Nations in April 1993, NATO's Partnership for Peace and the OSCE in 1995, Association Agreement with the EU in 1996), which is both a recognition of the results of the reforms achieved at the internal level and an additional incentive which draws upon the European Union's 'power of attraction' and the desire for membership of international organisations. As such, an Association Agreement with the European Union and economic aid have helped encourage continued internal reform, an asset that could be more systematically and effectively used in future.

However, the tensions between Western partners, like the absence of *a priori* coordination between international organisations in some cases, should be stressed for the benefit of future analyses. The difficulties that the European partners had in adopting a common position in the CFSP framework, on the issue of recognition, and the absence of adequate decision-making mechanisms, initially restricted their ability to act and to use all the CFSP mechanisms, and left in the end the field open to American diplomacy. These divergences also prevented the use of WEU's conflict prevention capability in the framework of its Petersburg tasks, leaving the United Nations and the OSCE to act alone. Finally, interinstitutional coordination reveals a certain 'excessive zeal'. Thus, the composition and mandate of the UNPREDEP show a certain duplication of its tasks and those of the OSCE,[11] which results from unacknowledged competition between the two organisations. Admittedly, this led to cooperation in practice. It also goes without saying that the proliferation of similar measure adopted in parallel, particularly when these are political actions dealing with the immediate causes of a dispute, can only help check tensions in the short term. The absence of a functional sharing of respective tasks may be to the detriment of their rationalisation, in other words the 'broadening' of tasks may be detrimental to their deepening. The concentration of each organisation on the tasks that it is most suited to carrying out must equally be accompanied by a certain functional complementarity, but that does not mean a strict division of labour.

An evaluation of preventive measures is something that has to be undertaken circumspectly. It is difficult, even arbitrary, to value their effectiveness, especially when they are still being applied: is peacekeeping the result of external preventive measures, or of local conditions that have determined the nature and effectiveness of international intervention? In other words, can preventive measures in themselves prevent conflict? Is peace the cause or the consequence, or a combination of both, of (internal) regional factors that are independent of (external) international action? Can the experience of the FYR of Macedonia therefore serve as a model for future preventive missions? An examination of preventive measures reveals both advantages and limitations.

The first positive aspect relates to the international presence. The level and permanence of the international community's support indicate a determination to be involved based on a defined interest. There is a clear definition of UNPREDEP's mandate, and its dual military and civil nature define both its deterrent and its persuasive capability. The *simultaneous* presence of, and close coordination between international organisations allows for a division of labour among the political, economic, social and military fields, despite sometimes inevitable cases of duplication. Lastly, preventive measures were implemented sufficiently far in advance of a potential conflict to allow them to be adapted progressively to the situation on the ground at the bottom end of the scale. The second positive factor in the evaluation of results concerns the internal situation in the FYR of Macedonia. The level of violence was very low. Despite polarisation of the political scene, the mobilisation of certain radical forces does not seem capable of calling into question the established order and the position of the moderates, while at the same time it remains a preoccupation that strengthens the case for permanent international support. As regards timing, the internal situation, in other words the relatively low level of tension, has permitted deployment of the preventive force and its adjustment to developments. Lastly, the agreement of the authorities concerned, which is necessary for any preventive deployment and its maintenance in being, is still unanimous. Thus, to take just a few of the most significant examples, the OSCE and UNPREDEP missions made it possible to check and contain border incidents between Serbia and the FYR of Macedonia in 1992–3 at a time when the border between the two had not yet been clearly demarcated. Internally, they contributed, together with the HCNM, to alleviate inter-ethnic tensions, particularly in August 1993, February 1995 and again in early 1997.

Preventive measures do however have functional limits. To what extent are preventive diplomacy or intervention suited to the nature of new causes of destabilisation, which are very diffuse, and what degree of external involvement is necessary for preventive measures to be credible and therefore effective? For example, to what extent does the presence of UN troops constitute a guarantee against challenges to internal and external security in the event of a spilover of a conflict in Kosovo? Lastly, how might the internal situation develop if the international community withdrew?

The effectiveness of preventive measures therefore depends to a great extent on regional actors' attitudes and political choices. The absence of any military form of intervention on their part, or a deliberate choice of a policy of moderation, whether in order to avoid the negative consequences of destabilisation of the region or because of different policy priorities, is an essential element. This is, for example, the case with the policy of non-violence adopted by the Kosovo Albanians, whereas a change of attitude might upset the whole balance and give rise to doubts concerning the effectiveness of present preventive measures. Furthermore, some preventive measures may in the end turn out to be inappropriate. This could concern UNPREDEP itself, particularly its military mandate (unsuitability given the nature of the threats, lack of means), in the case of a spillover of the conflict,[12] and especially in view of the decreasing American presence, which is considered symbolic. Lastly, economic sanctions against Serbia and Montenegro have aggravated the internal economic crisis, not only in the FRY but also in neighbouring countries, and cost the FYR of Macedonia over two billion dollars.

An evaluation of the various scenarios and appropriate solutions applied to them should also address the intrinsic dynamics of regional problems. The appropriateness or otherwise of the means employed depends on the perception of security in the countries concerned. The Macedonian government would thus want an extension of UNPREDEP's mandate, which would provide a guarantee against an eventual internal destabilisation consequent to the deterioration of inter-ethnic relations, which Skopje considers to be the main threat. It has therefore proposed that part of the SFOR be transferred to the FYR of Macedonia when it is withdrawn from Bosnia, and the setting up in Skopje of a NATO training centre in the framework of Partnership for Peace, in order to guarantee the stability of the Republic.[13] Macedonian Albanians welcome the presence of international forces which they perceive as a safeguard against potentially offensive government policy; but they reject any function of protection aiming at preventing the free circulation of eventual waves of Kosovo Albanian refugees between the FYR of Macedonia and Kosovo. Hence the necessity to avoid any policy that applies different standards to the two communities. As the case of the FYR of Macedonia has no endogenous, immediate risks of armed conflict, and as it faces a process of consolidation of the state implying long-term stabilisation of the situation, long-term measures would be needed.

However, NATO rejected any deployment on the northern border of Albania (in spite of the destabilising risks due to movement of troops and the arms flow), exclusively providing observers for further investigation,[14] and in FYROM. In the latter, the UN remained, until recently, hesitant about an extension of UNPREDEP's mandate and there are still no provisions for an increased international presence, a reinforcement of the military dimension of UNPREDEP's mandate, or increased European visibility. This attitude is all the more preoccupying in view of the destabilisation potential and the fact that a failure to resolve the Kosovo crisis would imply the failure of other preventive and post-conflict building measures undertaken by the international community in the area (Bosnia, FYROM, Albania). A more rational approach at the regional level would maximise the international community's actions and potential.

Conditions for regional stability

The process of 'recasting' South Eastern Europe depends to a great extent on the goodwill of leaders within the region and the ability of countries outside the region, in particular European countries, to form long-term strategies based on a comprehensive approach. In view of internal instability and external uncertainties, the FYR of Macedonia is aware of regional countries' responsibility in dealing with and addressing the problems of the region through their own initiative. Bilaterally, central authorities in Skopje have pursued a policy of equal distance with all neighbours and initiated a process of normalisation of bilateral relations at a regional level. Multilaterally, after initially rejecting regional cooperation frameworks which they believed might hamper integration into Western political and security organisations, they promote regional approaches perceived as a main conflict prevention and problem-solving approach, as well as a means to meet the necessary criteria for EU accession. As far as the role of the international community in conflict prevention is concerned, foreign presence is welcomed. The UN's and the OSCE's roles are assessed as being essential in view of the fragility of the internal situation. It is believed any reduction of UNPREDEP would increase the potential for internal instability and might be interpreted by all actors as an international withdrawal from the region. Furthermore, since the outbreak of the Kosovo conflict, the central authorities clearly welcomed a NATO presence as a guarantee for both internal and external stability. A strong and clear commitment of the international community in the Republic is then expected.

Coherence and coordination of Western policy are necessary conditions for the region's stability and security. The international community should define common positions, as divergences between Western countries have been harmful to crisis management during the Yugoslav conflict. There is thus a need to reaffirm and comply to basic principles such as national sovereignty and territorial integrity for common evaluation and coherent and effective policy implementation.[15] Faced with the Yugoslav crisis, the international organisations ended up pursuing a reactive policy, rather than anticipating events. The 'compartmentalised management' in which each organisation deals with just one aspect of the problem without this amounting to a true division of labour, led to duplication rather than complementarity, thus simply contributing to reducing the scope of ethnic conflicts rather than producing a solution.[16] It is the unity and coherence of the European Union that are at stake, for its credibility will inevitably be eroded if there is a persistent inability to define a common position on strategy and listing priorities in South East Europe. Unfortunately, Western strategy towards the FRY of Macedonia has only been partially defined, except for the United States, albeit implicitly: the nature of their presence in Europe, their role within NATO's crisis preventive and management (Bosnia, the Greek–Turkish dispute, the Middle East). Such a lack of policy is all the more important in view of the Kosovo conflict and the deteriorating internal situation in the Republic. The Macedonian government's commitment to internal reform, the dialogue with the Albanian minority and the predominance of moderate forces on the political scene cannot hide the radicalisation of certain political forces on both sides and the growing tension between the Albanian movement and Macedonian public opinion. Recent economic difficulties (including the failure of the pyramid bank TAT) and growing interethnic tensions suggest that practical support should be given to the efforts made by the ruling coalition. The deepening of reforms begun in order to ensure a fair representation of Albanians within state institutions and guarantee education in the Albanian language should be enforced as immediate, but gradual, measures in order not to exacerbate inter-ethnic tensions (quotas, lessons in Albanian, technical assistance and training), and as a package linking political and economic measures. It could be part of a dual policy, aimed simultaneously at supporting all the moderate forces, who see their room for manoeuvre being reduced, while at the same time keeping up the pressure on the radical forces, whose excesses should be met by a policy of political and economic containment.

In spite of a decreasing external threat due to the normalisation of the country's relations with its neighbours, uncertainty over developments in the region and national consensus may justify a continued international presence, and not withdrawal or too large a reduction in its size. It would leave room for manoeuvre for the moderate forces while allowing them to consolidate. A reduction of UNPREDEP, in particular American troops, does not meet the country's requirement for stability. If it is to be so, it could give way to a greater European visibility through an increasing presence of European forces. The continued presence of multinational UN troops, or even their reinforcement by WEU forces, given the enhancement of WEU's peacekeeping capability after Amsterdam and Erfurt, particularly if there is a gradual reduction of American troops, could be a credible alternative.[17] A strengthening of the Partnership for Peace, and its transformation into a 'PfP-plus' similar to one adapted to Albania, might be considered in parallel, if PfP is to act as a preventive instrument and not simply as an alternative security framework for the countries that are not part of NATO enlargement. In the FYR of Macedonia, no major border incidents have been noticed (only isolated incidents and no movement of refugees from FRY into FYROM). While an outburst of the conflict and full-scale war could lead to a dismemberment of the country because of the ethnic composition of the population (23 per cent Albanians), a sustained low-intensity conflict might destabilise the internal political situation by hampering the inter-ethnic dialogue. The issue being essentially an internal one, NATO's presence is not appropriate. Furthermore, internal public opinion should be taken into consideration. While the Macedonian government has repeatedly asked for an increased NATO presence, this has been strongly rejected by the two main Macedonian Albanian political parties. However, current measures should be reinforced in view of the impact of the Kosovo crisis on the internal political scene and the deterioration of inter-ethnic relations. For example, an extension of UNPREDEP's mandate would be a first step. In the case of an escalation of the conflict, UNPREDEP has not sufficient strength to take on enforcement capabilities, which bears certain risks. A larger force with a stronger military component under UN's mandate should then be considered, with an increased European (or WEU?) presence. It should be accompanied by a reinforced OSCE mission, for increased border monitoring and immediate control of eventual refugee movements (although such measures will not have any influence of eventual conflict). As discussions in spring 1998 indicated, the UN presence might be extended, most probably with the same mandate and level of forces and with minor adaptations. Americans remain a key factor (albeit symbolic) within the protection force. The US have been somehow reluctant to approve an extension, as they wish to reduce the presence of American soldiers in the region in general. Their presence however is essential, at least until Europeans have a more coherent and unified approach to conflict prevent and crisis management in the region. Without a change and adaptation of both mandate and means, Americans will nevertheless remain reluctant to undertake proactive measures.

The question of the Albanians' status within the FYR of Macedonia is part of the process of consolidation of the Macedonian state in the long term, and might stem from a policy of normalisation of inter-ethnic relations in the future. More generally, it raises the question of the civil or ethnic definition of the state. A solution might be found by giving greater importance to the civil definition of the Macedonian State. The Albanians' *de facto* status could be strengthened by making reference to 'a State of Macedonian citizens', instead of a 'nation-state of the Macedonian people', thus granting the Albanian minority equality with the Macedonian population.[18] Although inspired by the French model, this solution could however meet fierce opposition from Macedonian nationalist parties like the VMRO, for whom such a measure that favours Albanians would imply a dilution of Macedonian identity. But the constitutional status of Albanians could also be denuded for any significance in the event of genuine participation and representation in political and economic life, which can only happen in the perspective of membership of a wider regional framework. The EU should re-think its policy regarding South East Europe, particularly concerning the FYR of Macedonia, as it did for Romania and Bulgaria. Without amounting to a prior promise of membership, this measure could form part of a strict long-term conditionality approach. Within such a framework, confidence-building measures such as an increase in the number of Albanian officers in the armed forces, in the PfP framework, or arms control in the OSCE framework, might succeed. An additional foreign military presence might be controversial to the Macedonian Albanians who perceive it as a move directed against them. But a training centre for military personnel within the PfP framework might allow better coordination of civil–military relations, the exchange of personnel and the participation of Albanians. WEU, as a forum for dialogue, could follow an approach close to the EU's to consider a *rapprochement* with the FYR of Macedonia.

Conclusion

The prevention of conflicts in a region as complex and turbulent as South Eastern Europe is becoming an imperative and must be adapted to each case. The tools available for conflict prevention are inadequate to meet all of the threats of the post-Cold War period, which stem more from societal security than from traditional balance of power. The approach needs to be thought out afresh with a view to not only having a wider range of preventive instruments but also to the more effective coordination of all governmental and non-governmental actors that might be involved, in order to avoid any overlap or duplication of effort, which could produce the opposite effect to that desired. One of the essential factors remains without doubt the declared political will of the international community or individual countries to become involved in conflict prevention and promote the effective implementation of decisions taken. In South Eastern Europe, the European Union can mostly *act as a mediator*, primacy in decision-making and action falling to the actors directly concerned. As the perception that compromise can bring about results has to come from the local level, preventive measures will have to be accompanied by strong incentives to comply. It is only once the majority of local actors, both at the governmental level and among the public, perceive that more will be gained by cooperation than by pursuing a conflict, that preventive measures will be able to attain their true objective.

But the EU should also put forward its 'soft security' enforcement capabilities. Integration into European institutions and the regional approach are the two main levers at the disposal of the European Union. It will be difficult to speak of European 'integration' if all of South East Europe has not in one way or another been brought on board. From a regional perspective, integration within Western political and security organisations such as EU, WEU and NATO should remain an open process and perspective. The process of European integration proposed by the European Council at Copenhagen in 1993 and the regional cooperation in the framework of the process of stability and good-neighbourliness initiated at Royaumont in 1995 as a conditionality measure for countries left outside the enlargement process, could otherwise end in failure.[19] In themselves true conflict-prevention measures, they will ultimately be factors of political stability and economic development involving a market of over 150 million people, with direct consequences for the European Union. The interdependence of political and economic problems, and the possible spillover of conflicts, also suggest an overall approach, and this should contribute to the creation of a feeling of a 'security space' within which countries would share responsibility for their common destiny. The importance of borders would be reduced as part of gradual regionalisation, as it would be for Europe as a whole, to which countries in the region would progressively be able to become associated. In the same way, greater freedom of trade at the regional level and increased interdependence would relativise the concept of autonomy. This perception, which is already old, is mentioned from time to time by some of the region's leaders. This implies firstly a series of practical measures: an agreement at the regional level on the inviolability of borders and territorial integrity, which should stimulate the adoption of bilateral and multilateral measures; assertion of the principle on the non-use of force in the settlement of differences; partial demilitarisation, although desirable, appears unlikely to be achieved given the lack of confidence and instability in the region, which tend to produce the opposite effect. If demilitarisation happens, it will be a consequence rather than a prior measure and is thus a long-term goal. Controlling the flow of arms is on the other hand necessary and could lead to practical measures for limiting arm transfers in the region.

The plethora of frameworks proposed by the West, ranging from the Royaumont approach of the EU, NATO's PfP and EAPC, and the American-inspired SECI, mainly lack a coherent and global approach and a defined overall strategy for South East Europe. They lack complementarity and risk duplication, all being loosely defined about the means, the time-scale and the impact on political problems as part of a coherent conflict prevention approach of the region as a whole. The 'regional approach' of the EU was limited to the countries of former Yugoslavia involved in the Bosnian conflict, and extended only recently to neighbouring countries' participation. Furthermore, it essentially deals with economic issues. The prospect of joining European institutions itself constitutes one of the most important conflict-prevention measures. While there can be no systematic membership unless the relevant criteria are met, it does permit the beginning of a dynamic movement by fixing a goal to be attained by the countries concerned that could become a one-way process. There is a need to define the scope and aim of alternative security structures via the establishment of regional frameworks. European security might consider a more inclusive approach to the region, avoiding inward-looking Europe favouring a security vacuum that could lead to further instability, namely a slow reform process and rising ethnic tensions and nationalist tendencies. The reinforcement of the Partnership for Peace could lead to a 'PfP plus' more adapted to the regional needs. While Macedonian authorities had initially opposed any regional framework that might act as a substitute to accession, they now perceive regional cooperation as a way to fill the political and security vacuum in the region, avoid further marginalisation and provide channels for further interaction with Western organisations, in view of future accession.[20] Until now, a link between membership and regional approach has been missing. For example, the FYR of Macedonia, having comparatively the most important per capita income, could see its status within European organisations re-evaluated. The right conditions for successful South Eastern cooperation implies a 'top-down' as well as a 'bottom-up' approach with a clear definition of regionalism and a clear response by Western European states to progressive cooperation in South Eastern Europe, including conditionality measures. The existence, on the one hand, of current security problems which are more political and economic in nature and, on the other hand, of hard security issues such as arms control and crisis management operations which cannot be addressed at the regional level, require some major outside involvement, thus leaving enough room for an entry strategy of the Western political and security organisations. On the other hand, a bottom-up approach could have some leverage on short-term issues as part of a confidence-building process. It is also impossible to achieve any regional stability without the participation of the FRY, Bosnia, Albania.

But any *ad hoc* measures which would not be part of a coherent strategy and would only have been created for the sake of avoiding the essential debate on inclusive security structures, would be perceived as incomplete. In the enlargement process, the FYR of Macedonia represents the 'third group' of countries after Turkey, then Bulgaria and Romania. It does not have any association agreement with the European Union and will probably need more time than the countries belonging to the former group. The case of the FYR of Macedonia is interesting in view of the importance of internal reforms undertaken in the economic sector as well as with minority treatment. The definition of a pre-entry strategy, providing the country's eligibility, could be envisaged. At the military level, the article V of Annex 1-B of the Dayton Agreement concerning the regional approach defines very broadly the establishment of a 'regional equilibrium in the outside former Yugoslavia', and has not taken into account until now countries like the FYR of Macedonia and Albania, mostly affected by arms transfer between the various segments of the Albanian populated areas and particularly prone to destabilisation. A wider participation of former Yugoslav states as well as immediate neighbours would thus be required.

Notes

1. Part of this article draws upon recent works of the author. See Sophia Clément, 'Conflict Prevention in the Balkans: The Case of Kosovo and the FYR of Macedonia', *Chaillot Paper 30*, Institute for Security Studies, Western European Union, Paris, December 1997. See also, 'Balkan Stability: Life After SFOR?;, *Brassey's Defence Yearbook 1998* (Brassey's, London).
2. Sophia Clément, 'Balkan Stability: ...', *ibid*.
3. Reinhardt Rummel, 'Common Foreign and Security Policy and Conflict Prevention', Report, *International Alert*, May 1996. See also Ministry for Foreign Affairs, *Preventing Violent Conflict* (Stockholm, 1997).
4. Sophia Clément, 'L'Europe du Sud-est après les élargissements de l'Union européenne et de l'OTAN', special issue on, The Balkans two years after Dayton, Sophia Clément and Thierry Tardy (eds), *Relations Internationales et Stratégiques* (Institut de Relations Internationales et Stratégiques (IRIS), December 1997).
5. Sophia Clément, 'Emerging Sub-Regional Cooperation in the Balkans', in Andrew Cottey (ed.), *Subregional Cooperation in the New Europe* (Macmillan, London, 1998).
6. This whole section particularly draws upon a previous study of the author. See Sophia Clément, 'Conflict Prevention in the Balkans: The Case of Kosovo and the FYR of Macedonia', *Chaillot Paper 30*, Paris, Institute for Security Studies of the Western European Union, December 1997.
7. The departure of the Yugoslav National Army (JNA), the absence of any significant defence structure at the local level and the embryo character of the national army prompted the request for an international presence. The priority is accorded to internal security, external defence being moreover undertaken by foreign countries and security institutions. See *The Military Balance 1996–1997* (Oxford: OUP for the IISS), p. 93.
8. The OSCE mission has a dual mandate: information acquisition (evaluating the degree of stability and recording facts) and good offices/mediation (promoting dialogue between the different ethnic communities and political actors). The monitoring mission is consequently assisted by the High Commissioner on National Minorities (HCNM), who is responsible for

inter-ethnic relations. Heinz Vetschera, 'Cooperative Security in the OSCE Framework B Confidence-Building Measures, Emergency Mechanisms and CFSP', in Erich Reiter (ed.), *Europas Sicherheitspolitik im Globalen Rahmen* (Frankfurt am Main: Peter Lang, 1997).

9. Iso Rusi, 'Tensions Up and Troops In', *Balkan War Report*, no. 174 (December 1993), p. 86. Bob Furlong, 'Powder Keg of the Balkans', *International Defence Review*, vol. 26, no. 5 (May 1993), p. 366. *Tanjug News Agency*, 16 January 1995.

10. United Nations Security Council S/1997/365, 12 May 1997.

11. W. J. Durch (ed.), 'Introduction', *The Evolution of Peacemaking and Peacekeeping, Case Studies and Comparative Analysis* (New York, St Martin's, 1993), p. 3.

12. Brigitte Sauerwein, 'Can Crisis Be Nipped in the Bud?', *International Defence Review*, vol. 26, no. 5 (May 1993), pp. 355–6.

13. 'Macedonia offers area as training centre for NATO – Skopje daily', *SWB* EE/2948 A/9, 10 June 1997.

14. NATO provided eight teams of experts with seven members each, composed of 50 per cent civilian and military, and not permanent, within a PfP framework.

15. Sophia Clément, 'Conflict Prevention in the Balkans ...', pp. 47–53.

16. Michael E. Brown, 'Introduction' in *The International Dimension of Ethnic Conflict* (MIT Press, Cambridge, Mass.), pp. 10–11.

17. Assembly of Western European Union, report on 'Europe's role in the prevention and management of crisis in the Balkans', Document 1589, 5 November 1997.

18. See also Gabriel Munuera, 'Preventing Armed Conflicts in Europe: Lessons from Recent Experience', *Chaillot Papers* 15/16 (Paris, Institute for Security Studies of the Western European Union, June 1994), p. 4.

19. See the Declaration of the Copenhagen Summit, *Europe*, document no. 1844/45, 24 June 1993, the Memorandum on the Stability Pact in Europe, *Europe*, 1846, 26 June 1997, and the Declaration on the process of stability and good-neighbourliness, Royaumont, 13 December 1995, *PIC*, 14 December 1995.

20. Sophia Clément, 'Emerging Sub-Regional Cooperation in the Balkans'.

Further reading

The literature on the Macedonian Question is vast and complex, and is written in many different languages. Views of ancient Macedonia are dominated by Classicists, whose opinions have proved influential in recent political controversy. The standard volume in English is by N. G. A. Hammond (with G. Griffith and F. Walbank), in three volumes, the *History of Macedonia* (Cambridge, 1979–88). The mainstream modern Greek view available in English is to be found in C. Daskalis, *The Hellenism of the ancient Macedonians* (Thessaloniki, 1981). The current mainstream Skopje view is in *History of the Macedonian People* (Skopje, 1988), the standard FYROM school textbook. See also *Macedonia – Its People and History*, by Stoyan Pribechevich (Pennsylvania, 1982) and *The Socialist Republic of Macedonia*, ed. Apostonski and Polenakovic (Skopje, 1974).

There are many descriptions of Macedonia and its geography, history and politics in the works of ancient historians and geographers such as Strabo, and the territory is frequently mentioned in accounts of the Roman and Byzantine periods. After the Ottoman conquest, geographic Macedonia became part of 'Turkey-in-Europe', and remained so for five hundred years. But during the decline of the Ottoman Empire, the many conflicts that arose in the Balkans over the Macedonian territory produced numerous polemical and historical works. See *History of Macedonia 1354–1833*, by A. Vacalopoulos (Thessaloniki, 1973), and *A Modern History of Macedonia 1830–1912* by K. Vakalopoulos (Thessaloniki, 1988).

In English, a clear general survey of the nineteenth-century origins of the Macedonian Question is *Macedonia – Its Place in Balkan Power Politics*, by Elizabeth Barker (RIIA, London, 1950). See also *The Congress of Berlin and After*, by W. N. Medlicott (London, 1938). The social and economic conditions of Ottoman Macedonia are finely depicted in *Researches in the Highlands of Turkey*, by H. F. Tozer (London, 1869), and other works by Victorian travellers. Standard works on late Ottoman history are *The Greek Struggle in Macedonia 1897–1913*, by Douglas Dakin (Thessaloniki, 1966) and *The Macedonian Question, 1893–1908* by Nadine Lange-Akhund, New York, 1998. For the nineteenth century origins of IMRO, see *For Freedom and Perfection – The Life of Yané Sandanski* by Mercia MacDermott (London, 1988).

Macedonia was widely reported by Victorian and Edwardian war correspondents in the various uprisings against the Ottoman government, culminating in the Balkan wars of 1912–13. *Balkan Cockpit*, by W. H. Crawfurd Price (London, 1914) is excellent. Another seminal work was H. N. Brailsford's *Macedonia – Its Races and Their Future* (London, 1906), see also *The Eastern Question* by J. A. R. Marriot (Oxford, 1951) and *Austro-Hungarian documents relating to the Macedonian Struggle, 1896–1912*, ed. F. R. Bridge, Thessaloniki, 1976. The most authoritative journalistic accounts are by Sir Reginald Rankin and James Bourchier in *The Times*. The former wrote a large book, *Inner History of the Balkan Wars* (London, 1926). Bourchier's important dispatches are collected in *The Times Correspondent Reporting from Sofia* (Sofia, 1978). The best picture of fighting on the Macedonian front in the First World War is in *The Story of the Salonika Army* by G. Ward Price (London, 1918). *Wanderings in Yugoslavia* by Nora Alexander (London, 1936) and Rebecca West's *Black Lamb and Grey Falcon* (London, 1938) are essential reading for the pre-Second World War period of Royalist Yugoslavia. For IMRO pre-Second World War, see *Terror in the Balkans*, by Albert Londres (London, 1935) and J. Swire, *Bulgarian Conspiracy* (London, 1939). See the references provided with E. Kofos's chapter in this volume for further reading on Greek issues. There is much less in English on the inter-war period, but a large literature connected with the re-emergence of the Macedonian Question in the Greek civil war between 1944 and 1949. A useful standard work on the Titoist period in Yugoslavia is *Yugoslav Communism and the Macedonian Question* by Stephen E. Palmer and Robert King (Connecticut, 1971). A good picture of social conditions in 1950s' Yugoslav Macedonia is in *Tito's Yugoslavia*, by Bernard Newman (London, 1953). Also, see *Nationalism and Communism in Macedonia* by E. Kofos (Thessaloniki, 1964) and *Modern and Contemporary Macedonia*, ed. I. Kolispoulos and I. Masiotis (Athens, 1993).

Hugh Poulton's *Who Are the Macedonians?* (London, 1995), and the Minority Rights Group report *The Southern Balkans*, by Poulton and Pettifer, and MRG Greece (London, 1994), provide essential basic information on the post-communist period. See also *Albania – from Anarchy to a Balkan Identity*, by Miranda Vickers and James Pettifer (London, 1997) for information on the Albanian question in Macedonia.

A recent English-language production from FYROM on the key border issues, reflecting the current FYROM government's views is '*The Borders of the Republic of Macedonia*' (2 vols), by Jove Dimitrija Talevski (Bitola, 1998). It also has some very useful maps. See also '*Macedonia –Yesterday and Today*', by Jovan and Mischel Pavlouski (Skopje, 1996), and *Atlas of the Inhabited Places of Aegean Macedonia*, by Todor Simovski (Skopje, 1998). Works in the cultural studies field, and in anthropology, have been important in recent controversies. See *Ourselves and Others: The Development of a Greek Macedonian Cultural Identity since 1912*, edited by P. Mackeridge and E. Yannakakis (Oxford, 1997), and the highly controversial *Fields of Wheat, Hills of Blood – Passages to Nationhood in Greek Macedonia 1870–1990* by Anastasia N. Karakasidou (Chicago, 1997), and *The Macedonian Conflict: Ethnic Nationalism in a transnational world* by Loring Danforth (Princeton, 1995). A pioneering work in this field was G. F. Abbot's *Macedonian Folklore* (London, 1903, and Thessaloniki, 1969).

On the Church, see *Church and State in Yugoslavia since 1945* by Stella Alexander (Cambridge, 1979), *The Macedonian Orthodox Church* by Doné Ilievski (Skopje, 1973), and *Our Holy Orthodoxy: A Short History of the Macedonian Orthodox Church* by Archbishop Mihail (Skopje, 1996). On Islam, see *Islam in the Balkans* by H. T. Norris (London, 1993), and *The Bektashi Order of Dervishes* by J. K. Birge (London, 1994).

A recent reference publication is *Historical Dictionary of the Republic of Macedonia* by Sasha Konechni and Valentina Georgieva (Skopje, 1998) Publications from Bulgaria are available from the International Institute for Macedonia, Pirotska street 5, Sofia 1301, and from the Macedonian Scientific Institute (VMRO-UMS). See *Macedonia: Documents and Material* (Sofia, 1974) and also, *90 Years of Greek ethnic cleansing of Bulgarians in Aegean Macedonia* by Stoyan G. Bojadjiev (Sofia, 1996).

Index